T0223212

Lecture Notes in Computer Science　1431

Edited by G. Goos, J. Hartmanis and J. van Leeuwen

Springer

Berlin
Heidelberg
New York
Barcelona
Budapest
Hong Kong
London
Milan
Paris
Singapore
Tokyo

Hideki Imai   Yuliang Zheng   (Eds.)

Public Key Cryptography

First International Workshop on Practice and
Theory in Public Key Cryptography, PKC'98
Pacifico Yokohama, Japan, February 5-6, 1998
Proceedings

Springer

Series Editors

Gerhard Goos, Karlsruhe University, Germany
Juris Hartmanis, Cornell University, NY, USA
Jan van Leeuwen, Utrecht University, The Netherlands

Volume Editors

Hideki Imai
The University of Tokyo, Institute of Industrial Science
7-22-1, Roppongi, Minato-ku, Tokyo, 106-8558, Japan
E-mail: imai@iis.u-tokyo.ac.jp

Yuliang Zheng
Monash University, School of Computing and Information Technology
McMahons Road, Frankston, Melbourne, VIC 3199, Australia
E-mail: yzheng@fcit.monash.edu.au

Cataloging-in-Publication data applied for

Die Deutsche Bibliothek - CIP-Einheitsaufnahme

Public key cryptography : proceedings / First International
Workshop on Practice and Theory in Public Key Cryptography, PKC
'98, Pacifico Yokohama, Japan, February 1998. Hideki Imai ; Yuliang
Zheng (ed.). - Berlin ; Heidelberg ; New York ; Barcelona ; Budapest
; Hong Kong ; London ; Milan ; Paris ; Santa Clara ; Singapore ;
Tokyo : Springer, 1998
   (Lecture notes in computer science ; Vol. 1431)
   ISBN 3-540-64693-0

CR Subject Classification (1991): E.3, G.2.1, D.4.6, K.6.5, F.2.1-2, C.2, J.1,
E.4

ISSN 0302-9743
ISBN 3-540-64693-0 Springer-Verlag Berlin Heidelberg New York

This work is subject to copyright. All rights are reserved, whether the whole or part of the material is
concerned, specifically the rights of translation, reprinting, re-use of illustrations, recitation, broadcasting,
reproduction on microfilms or in any other way, and storage in data banks. Duplication of this publication
or parts thereof is permitted only under the provisions of the German Copyright Law of September 9, 1965,
in its current version, and permission for use must always be obtained from Springer - Verlag. Violations are
liable for prosecution under the German Copyright Law.

© Springer-Verlag Berlin Heidelberg 1998
Printed in Germany

Typesetting: Camera-ready by author
SPIN 10637613   06/3142 – 5 4 3 2 1 0   Printed on acid-free paper

Preface

The PKC'98 conference, held at Pacifico Yokohama, Japan, 5-6 February, 1998, is the first conference in a new international workshop series dedicated to both practice and theory in public key cryptography.

With the widespread use of public key cryptography in electronic commerce, good practice in applying public key and related supporting technologies, together with prudent assessment and comparison of the technologies, has become more important than ever. The new workshop series provides a unique avenue for both practitioners and theoreticians who are working on public key encryption, digital signature, one-way hashing, and their applications to share their experience and research outcomes.

Exactly 20 years ago, in 1978 Rivest, Shamir, and Adleman published what is now commonly called the RSA cryptosystem (see R. L. Rivest, A. Shamir, and L. Adleman: "A method for obtaining digital signatures and public-key cryptosystems," in *Communications of the ACM*, pp. 120-128, no. 2, vol. 21, 1978.) RSA is the first public key cryptosystem that fulfills both the functions of secure public key encryption and digital signature, and hence arguably the most significant discovery in cryptography. While the mathematical foundation of RSA rests on the intractability of factoring large composite integers, in the same year and the same journal Merkle demonstrated that certain computational puzzles could also be used in constructing public key cryptography (see R. Merkle: "Secure communication over insecure channels," in *Communications of the ACM*, pp. 294-299, no. 4, vol. 21, 1978.) Therefore, it is indeed very timely to hold PKC'98 at a time we are celebrating the 20th anniversary of the discovery of the RSA public key cryptosystem and Merkle's computational puzzles.

The program committee of the conference consisted of Hideki Imai of University of Tokyo, Japan, Arjen Lenstra of Citibank, USA, Tatsuaki Okamoto of NTT, Japan, Jacques Stern of ENS, France, and Yuliang Zheng of Monash University, Australia. Hideki Imai and Yuliang Zheng also served as the co-chairs of the committee. There were in total 30 submissions representing 12 countries and regions, these being Australia, Belgium, France, Germany, Japan, Korea, Singapore, Spain, Taiwan, Tunisia, UK, and USA. From among these submissions 15 were selected for presentation at the conference. In addition, there were 3 invited talks (by Yair Frankel and Moti Yung of CertCo, USA, Jean-Francois Misarsky of France Telecom, and Kiyomichi Araki of Tokyo Institute of Technology, Takakazu Satoh of Saitama University, and Shinji Miura of Sony Corporation, Japan) and a special talk (by Jacques Stern of ENS, France). The last session (Recent Results) of the conference was allocated to short talks on latest research results. There were 6 short talks, 3 of which were selected for inclusion into the final proceedings. Taking this opportunity, we would like to thank all the members of the program committee for putting together such an excellent technical program.

This conference was kindly sponsored by Information-Technology Promotion Agency (IPA) of Japan, Mitsubishi Electric Corporation, and Institute of Industrial Science, the University of Tokyo. It was held in cooperation with the Technical Group on Information Security, the Institute of Electronics, Information, and Communication Engineers (IEICE). We appreciate all these organizations for their generous support and cooperation.

Successfully organizing such a relatively large international conference would not have been possible without the assistance from the secretaries (especially Y. Umemura, M. Morimoto, and Y. Nejime), students, research assistants, and associates from the Imai Laboratory at Institute of Industrial Science.

Our thanks also go to the following colleagues who kindly offered help with chairing sessions at the conference: Kiyomichi Araki (Tokyo Institute of Technology, Japan), Chin-Chen Chang (National Chung Cheng University, Taiwan), Arjen Lenstra (Citibank, USA), Tsutomu Matsumoto (Yokohama National University, Japan), Jean-Francois Misarsky (France Telecom), Eiji Okamoto (JAIST, Japan), Tatsuaki Okamoto (NTT, Japan), Jacques Stern (ENS, France), and Moti Yung (CertCo, USA).

Finally we would like to thank all the people who submitted their papers to the conference (including those whose submissions were not successful), and all the 145 delegates from around the world who attended the conference. Without their support the conference would not have been possible.

March 1998
University of Tokyo, Japan   Hideki Imai
Monash University, Melbourne, Australia   Yuliang Zheng

PKC'98

1998 International Workshop on Practice and Theory in Public Key Cryptography

Pacifico Yokohama, Japan, 5-6 February, 1998

Sponsored by

Information-Technology Promotion Agency (IPA), Japan
Mitsubishi Electric Corporation
Institute of Industrial Science, the University of Tokyo

In cooperation with
The Technical Group on Information Security, the Institute of
Electronics, Information and Communication Engineers (IEICE)

Organizing Committee

Hideki Imai, Co-chair	(University of Tokyo, Japan)
Yuliang Zheng, Co-chair	(Monash University, Australia)
Members of Imai Lab	(University of Tokyo, Japan)

Program Committee

Hideki Imai, Co-chair	(University of Tokyo, Japan)
Arjen Lenstra	(Citibank, USA)
Tatsuaki Okamoto	(NTT, Japan)
Jacques Stern	(ENS, France)
Yuliang Zheng, Co-chair	(Monash University, Australia)

Contents

Invited Talks

Special Talk

Regular Contributions

Recent Results

Distributed Public Key Cryptosystems*

Yair Frankel** and Moti Yung***

Abstract. The cryptographic community has developed many tools to incorporate distributed trust mechanisms into cryptographic primitives and protocols as well as primitives where parties are naturally distributed. Since the fastest growing paradigm in computing is distributed systems and communication networks, the importance of distributed mechanisms has been increasing, and will likely to be pervasive in the future. Here, we review the various distributed mechanisms that have been developed and applied to achieve distributed public key cryptosystem. We focus primarily on the more efficient threshold cryptographic schemes (based on sharing public-key functions) and exemplify (only) some of the issues regarding these systems.

1 Introduction

The initial implementations in the direction of distributed cryptography for sensitive cryptographic services has already happened. They include Clipper's two party control for decryption, and distributed root certification key for Master-Card/VISA's Secure Electronic Transaction (SET) root, using function sharing. It is envisioned that many of the distributed mechanisms will develop into a standard protection mechanism for high assurance systems. Such distributed trust mechanisms provide enhanced security protection against internal collusions as well as external attacks by eliminating the centralized control; forcing the adversary to take more risks (and to pay more) since it must penetrate several systems rather than just one (and in proactive system it is also limited to doing it in a small period of time). In addition, the development of multi-party protocols over the Internet will require distributed cryptographic protocols, since parties are naturally distributed in cyberspace. Here we review some of the general areas of distributed cryptography and pointing at some (but definitely not all) the related literature.

The notion of distributed cryptographic protocols has been central in cryptography for over 15 years. Some protocols have been designed to solve communication problems which are impossible from an information-theoretic perspective, like oblivious-transfer [R], the coin-flipping protocol [Blum] and the millionaire-problem protocol [Y82]. General compiler protocols, on the other hand, have been designed to solve generic problems. These protocols can securely compute any public function on secure inputs. The first such protocols were developed

---

* Invited Paper
** CertCo LLC, New York, New York; e-mail: yfrankel@cs.columbia.edu

*** CertCo LLC, New York, New York; e-mail: moti@certco.com and moti@cs.columbia.edu

by Yao [Y86] and Goldreich, Micali and Wigderson [GMW86], and various developments were made in subsequent works.

Recently there has been a thrust to construct more efficient protocols for specific problems, and in particular, problems involving the distributed application of cryptographic functions (surveyed in [Gw97]). Here, we give a brief discussion of the current development and characterize some of the the various distributed public key cryptosystems. Intuitive and informal definitions which introduce notions are provided in this pre-proceedings. A more complete version will appear in the proceedings.

2 Secure distributed function application

Our focus is in systems in which a secret function is shared amongst a group of servers. In essence, a secure distributed function application protocol shares a secret function $f_k(\cdot)$, where f is public and k is secret, such that only a quorum or more of servers can apply the function $f_k(\cdot)$ on an input m to obtain $f_k(m)$ and smaller subsets can not evaluate the function on input m.

Definition 1. (Secure distributed function application)
Let $f(\cdot, \cdot)$ be a publicly known function. A (t, l)-secure distributed function application system of f provides for the availability of a function $f(k, \cdot) = f_k(\cdot)$ by distributing $f_k(\cdot)$ to the set of l servers such that:

function application: with overwhelming probability for a valid argument m, any quorum of t out of the l servers can compute $f_k(m)$, and

basic security: with overwhelming probability for any valid argument m, before function application less than a quorum of servers have no new information about $f_k(m)$ than $f(\cdot, \cdot)$ alone and, after function application no new information is revealed (by viewing the interactions) about $f_k(\cdot)$ other than $\langle m, f_k(m) \rangle$ to any set of less than t servers and outside observers.

The primary research in secure distributed function application has been to find more efficient systems and to provide additional protection above the basic security requirement.

2.1 Threshold schemes

Threshold schemes are the traditional cryptographic example of how to securely and reliably distribute information. With a (t, l)-threshold scheme a secret value k is shared via shadows $\langle s_1, \ldots, s_l \rangle$ during the *shadow generation phase* such that less than a quorum (i.e, $< t$) of shadows does not reveal the secret value k. During the *secret reconstruction phase* any quorum of shadows may be used to efficiently reconstruct the secret value k. Shamir [Sh] developed a threshold scheme based on Lagrange Interpolation over a finite field. A random polynomial $r(x)$ of degree $t - 1$ (over a finite field) is chosen such that $r(0) = k$ is the secret. Each shareholder $i \in \Gamma$ is assigned a unique public number x_i and a secret share

$s_i = r(x_i)$. Due to Lagrange interpolation, the set Λ of cardinality t determine
$k = \sum_{i \in \Lambda} s_i \cdot z_{i,\Lambda}$ where $z_{i,\Lambda} = \prod_{\substack{v \in \Lambda \\ v \neq i}} (x_i - x_v)^{-1}(0 - x_v)$.

One should note that threshold structures (i.e., any set of t out of l) are not
the only possible access structures that have been investigated. Secret sharing
schemes which are defined similarly allow for a more general access structure
were suggested originally in [BL, ISN]. Much work has been done on many
aspects and variants of this basic primitive (which we omit).

Based on the use of tamper-proof hardware[4], [Sh] proposed a secure function
application scheme. First, the function f is enclosed in the tamper-proof device.
To perform function application, a quorum of shareholders transmit their share
to the device and the device computes the secret key k. The device can perform
function application on function $f_k(\cdot)$ for any input m.

2.2 General compiler protocol

Taking the tamper-proof hardware approach discussed in [Sh] one step further, suggests that instead of using hardware that a protocol could simulate
the use of secure hardware by performing the circuit computation in a blinded
fashion (i.e., users can view the actual computation performed). General compiler protocols provides for the evaluation of a circuit (similarly, function) in
a distributed manner such that each party in the computation learns nothing
more than the output and its own secret components of the functions input.
These protocols securely compute any public function on secure inputs. The first
such protocols were developed by Yao [Y86] and Goldreich, Micali and Wigderson [GMW86], and various developments were made in subsequent works, e.g.,
[GHY87, K, BGW, CCD].

The primary difficulty with general compiler protocols is that such systems
are ordinarily inefficient with respect to communication complexity due to their
general nature of being applicable to any circuit or arithmetic operations [Gr97].
However, they constitute a "plausibility result" for many tasks. Also, many of
the definitional underpinning of the field of distributed cryptographic protocols
has initiated in the general domain of the general compiler protocols. Areas
like cryptographic compilers, information theoretic compilers, characterization of
privacy, graph (network) related procedures, models of adversaries in distributed
cryptographic protocols, lower bounds on resources were all influenced by this
sub-area. (See [F93] for a survey of result till 1993, the area is very active and
we omit many references).

3   Characterization of trust distribution

The notion of public key trust distribution has taken several transformations.
We now discuss various forms of trust distribution though in the sequel our focus
is primarily on threshold cryptography.

---

[4] A tamper-proof device is computational devices in which its state, and memory
  contents are private (tapes model the circuits of the actual device) to even its owner.
  The owner gets only an input/output access to the device.

General compiler protocols, and as we will see shortly with threshold cryptosystem, also satisfy a transparency property.

Definition 2. (Transparency property) A secure function application protocol is transparent if its input specification providing the point of evaluation and output specification providing the functions output is independent of protocols access structure.

Transparency implies that the external environment providing the input/output to the protocol are transparent of the trust mechanism. This, however, is not always necessary (and maybe it is even sometimes undesirable), as we will see next.

3.1 Explicit trust distribution

Explicit trust mechanisms on the other are designed with operations which are meant to be traced or followed explicitly (and not to remain hidden). The idea is that the trail of participants is noticeable in the result of the protocol, a property that may be desirable.

To distribute cryptographic power in cryptographic primitives, [D] noticed that [GMW86] and/or explicit trust distribution are very useful tool. For explicit trust distribution, [D] noticed that a sender can encrypt a message with a randomly generated key and then send each receiver a part of the key which they can then decrypt interactively. This interaction is explicit and may be useful when one needs to know the participants (this creates a "hand-shake"). In other settings (like function sharing, this is undesirable, due to abstraction and modularity). Next we review other explicit trust distribution mechanisms.

Group signatures developed in [CvH] provide for a signature scheme in which only members of a predefined group can sign. Upon verification, the group is not identified except for dispute cases where there is a mechanism to identify who signed. [CP] extended the group signature notion.

Multisignatures are signature schemes in which each of the entities explicitly signs, however, the "final signature" is smaller than the a signature from each entity [O].

Micali's fair cryptosystems [M] initiation is explicit (the user directs its interaction to specific escrow agents).

Let us now deal with threshold cryptography, where hiding structures and implicit trust mechanisms are employed.

4 Threshold cryptography & functions sharing

Functions sharing, also called threshold cryptography, independently introduced by [B88, CH, F89] takes the less general approach, however, efficiency has been greatly reduced. Whereas the communication complexity of the secure function evaluation depends linearly on the actual size of circuit computing the crypto-graphic functions, the communication complexity of function sharing is independent of the circuit size (and is typically a polynomial in the input/output size and the number of participants). This difference (pointed out first in [FY93, DDFY]) is crucial to practitioners as the communication latency cannot compete with increases in processor speeds. This can be captured in the following intuitive definition of the efficient procedure, where we fix everything but change the circuit size in use by the parties for any usage in the protocol.

Definition 3. (Efficient function sharing system/ threshold cryptosystem) Let $f(\cdot, \cdot)$ be a publicly available function (family) and $R_{1,f}, R_{2,f}$ be any two circuits (family of circuits) implementing f. Let $P()$ be a function sharing protocol for the function f.

Let the protocol P instantiated with circuit $R_{i,f}$ (called $P_{R_{i,f}}$) be protocol $P()$ where the parties in the protocol use in their computation and communication circuit $R_{i,f}$ whenever they are required to compute the function's result. We call $P()$ *efficient* if the communication complexity of $P_{R_{1,f}}$ and $P_{R_{2,f}}$ are identical.

For the definition of what constitutes a function sharing protocol given a function family specification, see [DDFY] (where they give the definition but limit it to non-interactive protocols applicable to that work).

Discrete log based threshold cryptosystem One of the first practical threshold cryptosystems developed was based on the El Gamal cryptosystem [E] is now presented as an example of a secure threshold cryptosystem. We first briefly explain the El Gamal cryptosystem.

El Gamal Cryptosystem: Large primes P, Q are chosen such that $Q|(P-1)$. Let g be a generator of a subgroup of order Q in Z_P. The public encryption key is $\langle g, g^k, Q, P \rangle$ for some $k \in_R Z_Q$ and the private decryption key is $\langle k, P \rangle$. To encrypt a message m the ciphertext is $C = \langle C_1 \equiv_P g^r, C_2 \equiv_P mg^{kr} \rangle$ where $r \in_R Z_Q$. The decryption operation is performed as $m \equiv mg^{kr}g^{-kr} \equiv C_2 \cdot C_1^{-k} \bmod P$.

In [DF89], the threshold cryptosystem variant of the El Gamal cryptosystem was developed. The public and private keys are generated by a trusted distributor which then performs the Shamir (t, l)-threshold over the group $GF(Q)$ for secret value k to obtain secret shares $\langle s_1, \ldots, s_l \rangle$. The distributor now provides share s_i to server i.

Upon t of the servers receiving a ciphertext C, server i computes a partial result $\langle i, c_i \equiv_P C_1^{-s_i} \rangle$ to the Combiner server. The Combiner can now compute $m \equiv mg^{kr}g^{-kr} \equiv \prod_{i \in \Lambda} C_2 \cdot (g^r)^{-s_i \cdot z_{i,\Lambda}} \equiv \prod_{i \in \Lambda} C_2 \cdot (g^{r \cdot s_i})^{-1 \cdot z_{i,\Lambda}} \equiv \prod_{i \in \Lambda} C_2 \cdot C_1^{-z_{i,\Lambda}} \bmod P$. The combiner can perform this computation since $(x_i - x_j)$ have inverses in Z_Q when $0 < i, j < Q$. As will be discussed later, different techniques will be necessary since the Combiner is not able to compute such inverses.

A threshold discrete log based signature scheme was developed in [P91b]. For DSA [Kra93, NIST] based systems, [L] was the first to consider the problem and design a mechanism.

Threshold RSA Threshold RSA was originally developed independently by [B88, F89] based on (l, l) secret sharing. Though these schemes can be converted into (t, l) threshold RSA schemes, they grow exponentially for some parameters (e.g., $\frac{l}{2}$ out of l schemes).

Unlike the discrete log based systems, the sharing of the RSA private key is in a group in which the shareholders can not be given inverses or know the order of the group. This has been a major difficulty in developing (t, l)-threshold RSA schemes. [DF91] proposed a heuristically secure (t, l)-shared RSA scheme, and [FD92, DDFY] developed a provable (t, l)-threshold RSA. Recently, efficient and provably secure threshold RSA schemes were introduced in [FGMY, FGMY2].

5 Robustness and resilience

We have so far ignored the aspect of what happens if a server cheats. That is, what happens if a sever does not follow the protocol and it engages in additional computation or communication.

"Resilience" is a property describing the number of allowed compromised and misbehaving servers in a time period, which is a parameter called here t. An optimal t ("optimal resilience") means that the total number of servers is $l \geq 2(t - 1) + 1$. For this t, a majority of arbitrarily misbehaving servers can "control" the computation (even for a stationary adversary).

In general, and when efficiency is ignored, general zero-knowledge proofs [GMR] serve as a major tool for assuring robustness as using the fact that every sentence in NP can be proven [GMW86], parties can prove that based on their state, the open history, and randomness which is hidden but committed to, they take the "correct step". This is again, merely a plausibility result.

Verifiable secret sharing provides one aspect of resilience. First introduced in [CGMA], verifiable secret sharing (VSS) are secret sharing schemes with protection mechanisms are incorporated to prevent the computation of the honest servers from receiving the shares of the valid shared key even when a dishonest dealer or dishonest severs are participating in the reconstruction phase. Efficiently robust threshold RSA were first developed by [FGY] for the general case and [GJKR2] for the safe prime case, whereas, robust threshold DSA was developed in [GJKR1]. The schemes in [FGMY, FGMY2] are robust as well.

6 Proactive Security

The notion of "proactive security" (against a mobile adversary) provides enhanced protection of memories of long-lived cryptographic keys that may be distributed (i.e., protected by "space diffusion"). Proactive security adds protection by "time diffusion" as well. Namely, given a distributed function via threshold cryptography (function sharing) as described above, it adds a periodic refreshing of the contents of the distributed servers' memories. This refreshing is a "t-wise re-randomization" of the local servers' values in a way that preserves the global key, but makes previous contents of any set of less than t out of the l servers "useless". This renders useless the knowledge of the mobile adversary (e.g.,: hackers, viruses, bad administrators, etc.) obtained in the past from compromising less than the allowed t servers, and gives the system a self-securing nature.

The notion of a mobile adversary was first introduced by [OY], they presented the paradigm of re-randomization of state (periodic update of memories), the efficient proactive secret sharing, and the inefficient secure distributed compiler (as a plausibility result). A number of very useful cryptographic mechanisms have been efficiently "proactivized", such as pseudorandom number generation, verifiable secret sharing, and maintaining authenticated links in a network [OY, CH, HJKY, CHH97]. Proactive public-key schemes for keys with publicly known keydomain (essentially, those based on the discrete logarithm problem over groups of known order which are suitable for threshold schemes for discrete log based systems [DF89, GJKR1]) were proactivized first in [HJJKY]. Proactive RSA was first solved in [FGMY] based on [AGY] but it was not optimal resilience. Recently, [FGMY2] developed the first optimal resilience proactive public key cryptosystem. Though it is based on [DF91], it is provably secure. The system can be made non-interactive during the signing phase, if each pair of shareholders jointly share a pseudorandom function [FY98]. [HJJKY, FGMY, FGMY2] extend the notion of *threshold cryptosystems* by incorporating mechanisms to protect against a mobile adversary. In [FMY98a] based on [FGMY] protection against an adaptive adversary, one which is able to decide each of its actions such as which participant to corrupt based on its entire history of the protocol to that point. Proving security of cryptographic protocols against adaptive adversaries is a fundamental problem in cryptography.

7 Secure key generation

Another important step regarding "distributed cryptographic functions" is the (efficient) distributed generation of the function (the key shares). For cryptographic functions based on modular exponentiation over a field (whose inverse is the discrete logarithm which is assumed to be a one-way function), a protocol for the distributed generating keys was known for quite a while [P91b]. However, for the RSA function, which requires the generation of a product of two primes and an inverse of a public exponent, this step was an open problem for many years. Note that Yao's central motivation [Y86] in introducing general compiler protocols that "compute circuits securely in communication" was the issue of distributed generation of RSA keys. Indeed the results of [Y86, GMW86] show the plausibility of this task.

Early in the development of threshold cryptosystems, techniques in the organization's servers could jointly generate the organization's public key was developed by [P91b] for discrete log based systems. A major step forward was recently achieved by Boneh and Franklin [BF] who showed how a set of participants can actually generate an RSA function efficiently (detouring the inefficient compiler, i.e. the communication is independent of the circuit size of the primality test and the multiplication circuits). They developed many important new protocol techniques, and showed that their protocol was secure in the limited model of "trusted but curious" parties. They left open the issue of *robustness*, i.e., generation in the presence of misbehaving (malicious) parties (whereas Boneh-Franklin protocol may be prevented from ever generating a shared RSA key by such behavior) Recently, robust efficient distributed RSA key generation was developed in [FMY98b]

8 Using secure hardware for sharing

In distributed high-security systems, the integration of hardware is expected.

A technique for using tamper proof hardware which has the same communication model as threshold cryptography was developed in [FY96]. Each server is provided with a hardware device with the secret key and, moreover, each device i jointly shares with device j a random element from a pseudorandom function family $\mathrm{PRF}_{i,j} = \mathrm{PRF}_{j,i}$ with another unit. The devices use $\mathrm{PRF}_{i,j}(\alpha)$ to randomize the output to achieve non-interactive threshold cryptosystems for essentially any cryptographic function based on the security of the hardware device and the pseudo-random function.

Similarly, in a function sharing architecture components can use jointly shared $\mathrm{PRF}_{i,j}$ to transform the interactive signing to non-interactive signing (i.e., convert [FGMY2] to non-interactive signing). We have developed a method to perform this which has many system level advantages [FY98].

9 Applications and implementations

There have been several implemented and proposed applications for distributed public key cryptography.

Certification authorities in a public key infrastructure provide the trust mechanism through signature generation to create certificates. Since the whole public key infrastructure is based on the security of the Certification Authority, distributed trust mechanism are often used. The RSA Certificate Issuing System uses a tamper-proof hardware device in which a quorum of shareholders must enter their shares to activate the device. Recently, Mastercard/Visa SET root key certification system was implemented as a 3 out of 5 RSA threshold signature scheme.

Key escrow systems enable a "trusted party" to act as a third party which can decrypt encrypted messages without assistance from the intended receiver. They are useful in law enforcement as well as key recovery when a key is lost or unavailable (i.e., employee on vacation or sick). Micali [M] suggested the use of distributed public key cryptography to implement law enforcement based key escrow through the use of verifiable secret sharing and threshold cryptosystems.

More simple explicit dual control cryptography (a threshold of officers' signatures out of a given set) has also been implemented for security officers in commercial systems.

10 Other distributed tasks and protocols

Many cryptographic protocols are distributed or naturally lead to a distribution of a function (for enhancing its properties). Application protocols like voting, e-cash, anonymity provision, etc. use multiple distributed entities.

An early example how "distributization" of a party in a protocol can help, is in the area of voting/ election [CF85], where [BeYu] considered distributed tallying officials rather than a centralized tallying function.

References

[AGY]   N. Alon, Z. Galil and M. Yung, *Dynamic-Resharing Verifiable Secret Sharing against Mobile Adversary*. 3-d European Symp. on Algorithms (ESA)'95. Lecture Notes in Computer Science Vol. 979, P. Spirakis ed., Springer-Verlag, 1995, pp. 523-537.

[Be]   J. C. Benaloh. *Secret sharing homomorphisms: Keeping shares of a secret secret*. Advances in Cryptology, Proc. of Crypto'86 LNCS 263, 1987, pp. 251–260.

[BL]   J. C. Benaloh and J. Leichter, *Generalized secret sharing and monotone functions*. Advances in Cryptology, Proc. of Crypto'88 LNCS 403, Springer-Verlag, 1990, pp. 27–35.

[BGW]   M. Ben-Or, S. Goldwasser and A. Wigderson, *Completeness theorems for non-cryptographic fault-tolerant distributed computation*, Proceedings of the 20th Annual Symposium on Theory of Computing, ACM, 1988, pp. 1-9.

[B]   R. Blakley, *Safeguarding Cryptographic Keys*, FIPS Con. Proc (v. 48), 1979, pp. 313–317.

[Blum] M. Blum, *Three applications of the oblivious transfer: Part I: Coin flipping by phone; Part II: How to exchange secrets; Part III: How to send certified electronic mail*, Department of EECS, University of California, Berkeley, CA 1981.

[BF]   D. Boneh and M. Franklin, *Efficient Generation of Shared RSA Keys*, Crypto 97 proceedings.

[B88]   C. Boyd, *Digital Multisignatures*, In H. Baker and F. Piper, editors IMA Conference on Cryptography and Coding, Claredon Press, 241–246, , 1986.

[BeYu] J. C. Benaloh and M. Yung, *Distributing the Power of a Government to Enhance the Privacy of Voters*, Proc. of the 5th ACM Symposium on the Principles in Distributed Computing, 1986, pp. 52-62.

[CHH97] R. Canetti S. Halevi, and A. Herzberg, *Maintaining authenticated communication in the Presence of Break-ins*, PODC '97, 15-24, 1997.

[CH]   R. Canetti and A. Herzberg, *Maintaining Security in the Presence of Transient Faults*, Advances in Cryptology – Crypto 94 Proceedings, Lecture Notes in Computer Science Vol. 839, Y. Desmedt ed., Springer-Verlag, 19 94.

[Ch81]   D. Chaum, *Untraceable Electronic Mail, Return Address, and Digital Pseudonym.* CACM, v. 24(2) 1981, pp. 84-88.

[CCD]   D. Chaum, C. Crepeau, and I. Damgard, *Multiparty unconditionally secure protocols*, Proceedings of the 20th Annual Symposium on Theory of Computing, ACM, 1988, pp. 11-19.

[CvH]   D. Chaum and E. Van Heyst, *Group signatures*, Advances in Cryptology – Crypto 91 Proceedings, Lecture Notes in Computer Science Vol. 576, J. Feigenbaum ed., Springer-Verlag, 1991, pp. 470-484.

[CP]   L. Chen and T. Pederson, *New group signatures*, Advances in Cryptology – Eurocrypt 94 Proceedings, Lecture Notes in Computer Science Vol. 950, A. De Santis ed., Springer-Verlag, 1994, pp. 171-181.

[CGMA]   B. Chor, S. Goldwasser, S. Micali and B. Awerbuch, *Verifiable Secret Sharing and Achieving Simultaneous Broadcast*, Proceedings of the 26th Symposium on Foundations of Computer Science, IEEE, 1985, pp. 335-344.

[CF85]   J. Cohen and M. Fischer, *A robust and verifiable cryptographically secure election scheme*, Proc. 26th Annual Symposium on the Foundations of Computer Science, 1985, pp. 372-382.

[CH]   R. Croft and S. Harris, *Public-key cryptography and re-usable secret shared secrets*, In H. Becker and F. Piper, editors, IMA Conference on Cryptography and Coding, 1989, pp. 189-201.

[DDFY]   A. De Santis, Y. Desmedt, Y. Frankel, and M. Yung, *How to Share a Function Securely*, ACM Proceedings of the 26th Annual Symposium on Theory of Computing, ACM, 1994, pp. 522-533.

[D]   Y. Desmedt, *Society and group oriented cryptography: A new concept*, Advances in Cryptology – Crypto 87 Proceedings, Lecture Notes in Computer Science Vol. 293, C. Pomerance ed., Springer-Verlag, 1987, pp. 120-127.

[DF89]   Y. Desmedt and Y. Frankel, *Threshold cryptosystems*, Advances in Cryptology – Crypto 89 Proceedings, Lecture Notes in Computer Science Vol. 435, G. Brassard ed., Springer-Verlag, 1989, pp. 307-315.

[DF91]   Y. Desmedt and Y. Frankel, *Shared Generation of Authenticators and Signatures* Advances in Cryptology – Crypto 91 Proceedings, Lecture Notes in Computer Science Vol. 576, J. Feigenbaum ed., Springer-Verlag, 1991, pp. 457-469.

[DFY92] Y. Desmedt, Y. Frankel and M. Yung, *Multi-receiver / multi-sender network security: efficient authenticated multicast / feedback*, Proceedings of IEEE INFOCOM '92, Vol 3, pages 2045-2054, IEEE, 1992.

[DF94]   Y. Desmedt and Y. Frankel, *Homomorphic zero-knowledge threshold schemes over any finite Abelian group*, SIAM Journal on Discrete Mathematics, 7(4), pages 667-679, November 1994.

[DH]   W. Diffie and M. Hellman, *New Directions in Cryptography* , IEEE Trans. on Information Theory 22 (6), 1976, pp. 644-654.

[E]   T. El Gamal, *A public key cryptosystem and signature scheme based on discrete logarithms*, IEEE Transaction on Information Theory, 31, 1985, pp. 469-472.

[F]   P. Feldman, *A Practical Scheme for Non-Interactive Verifiable Secret Sharing*, Proceedings of the 28th Symposium on Foundations of Computer Science, IEEE, 1987, pp.427-437

[F89]   Y. Frankel, *A practical protocol for large group oriented networks*, In J. J. Quisquater and J. Vandewalle, editor, *Advances in Cryptology, Proc. of*

Eurocrypt '89, (Lecture Notes in Computer Science 773), Springer-Verlarg, pp. 56-61.

[FD92] Y. Frankel and Y. Desmedt, *Distributed reliable threshold multisignatures*, Tech. Report version TR–92–04–02, Dept. of EE & CS, Univ. of Wisconsin-Milwaukee, April 1992. (See also; Y. Frankel, *Non-interactive multiparty cryptography*, Phd. Thesis, UWM, 1992).

[FY95] Y. Frankel and M. Yung, *Cryptanalysis of the immunized LL public key systems*, Advances in Cryptology. Proceedings of Crypto '95 (Lecture Notes in Computer Science 963), pages 285-296. Springer-Verlag, 1995.

[FY96] Y. Frankel and M. Yung, *Protective sharing of any function: Trust Distribution via secure multi-processors*, In J. Pribyl, editor, Pragocrypt '96 (Part I). pages 156-168, CTU Publishing House, 1996.

[FGY] Y. Frankel, P. Gemmell and M. Yung, *Witness Based Cryptographic Program Checking and Robust Function Sharing*. Proceedings of the 28th Annual Symposium on Theory of Computing, ACM, 1996, pp. 499-508.

[FGMY] Y. Frankel, P. Gemmel, P. MacKenzie and M. Yung. *Proactive RSA, Advances in Cryptology – Crypto 97 Proceedings*, Lecture Notes in Computer Science Vol. ??, B. Kaliski ed., Springer-Verlag, 1997.

[FGMY2] Y. Frankel, P. Gemmel, P. MacKenzie and M. Yung. *Optimal Resilience Proactive Public-Key Cryptosystems*, Proceedings of the 38th Symposium on Foundations of Computer Science, IEEE, 1997.

[FMY98a] Y. Frankel, P. MacKenzie and M. Yung, *Coping with Adaptive Adversaries in Threshold/Proactive Public-Key Systems*, Available from authors.

[FMY98b] Y. Frankel, P. MacKenzie and M. Yung, *Robust Efficient Distributed RSA-Key Generation*, Available from authors.

[FY98] Y. Frankel and M. Yung, *Integrating Hardware Into Function Sharing Architectures: "separating, binding and blending"*, Available from the authors.

[FY93] M. Franklin and M. Yung, *Secure and Efficient Off-Line Digital Money*, Proc. of the 20th Int. Col. on Automata, Languages and Programming (ICALP), 1993, LNCS 700, Springer Verlag, pp. 265-276.

[F93] M. Franklin, *Complexity and Security of Distributed Protocols*, Phd Thesis, Columbia University.

[GHY87] Z. Galil, S. Haber and M. Yung, *Cryptographic Computations: Secure Fault Tolerant Protocols in the Public Key Model*, Crypto 87, pp. 135-155.

[GJKR1] R. Gennaro, S. Jarecki, H. Krawczyk, T. Rabin, *Robust Threshold DSS Signatures*, Advances in Cryptology – Eurocrypt 96 Proceedings, Lecture Notes in Computer Science Vol. 1070, U. Maurer ed., Springer-Verlag, 1996, pp. 354-371.

[GJKR2] R. Gennaro, S. Jarecki, H. Krawczyk, T. Rabin, *Robust Threshold RSA*, Advances in Cryptology – Crypto 96 Proceedings, Lecture Notes in Computer Science Vol. 1109, N. Koblitz ed., Springer-Verlag, 1996, pp. 157-172.

[Gr97] O. Goldreich, *On Foundations of Modern Cryptography*, an invited paper, Crypto 97.

[GGM] O. Goldreich S. Goldwasser and S. Micali, *How to Construct Random Functions*, J. of the ACM 33 (1986), pp. 792-807.

[GMW86] O. Goldreich, S. Micali, and A. Wigderson, *Proofs that leak nothing but their validity and methodology of cryptographic protocol design*, Proceedings of the 27th Symposium on Foundations of Computer Science, IEEE, 1986, pp.174-187.

[GMW86] O. Goldreich, S. Micali, and A. Wigderson, *How to play any mental game*, Proceedings of the 28th *Symposium on Foundations of Computer Science*, IEEE, 1987, pp 218–229.

[GMR] S. Goldwasser, S. Micali and C. Rackoff, *The Knowledge Complexity of Interactive Proof-Systems*, Siam J. on Computing, 18(1) (1989), pp. 186-208.

[Gw97] S. Goldwasser, *A New Directions in Cryptography: Twenty something years after*, an invited paper, FOCS 97.

[HJKY] A. Herzberg, S. Jarecki, H. Krawczyk, M. Yung, *Proactive Secret Sharing, or: how to cope with perpetual leakage*, Advances in Cryptology – Crypto 95 Proceedings, Lecture Notes in Computer Science Vol. 963, D. Coppersmith ed., Springer-Verlag, 1995, pp. 339-352.

[HJJKY] A. Herzberg, M. Jakobsson, S. Jarecki, H. Krawczyk, M. Yung, *Proactive Public-Key and Signature Schemes* Proceedings of the Fourth Annual Conference on Computer and Communications Security, ACM, 1996.

[ISN] M. Ito, A. Saito, and T. Nishizeki, *Secret sharing schemes realizing general access structures*, In *Proc. IEEE Global Telecommunications Conf.*, Globecom'87, pp. 99–102, Washington, DC., 1987. IEEE Communications Soc. Press.

[Kra93] D. Kravitz. *Digital signature algorithm*, U.S. Patent #5,231,668, July 27, 1993.

[K] J. Killian, "Use of Randomness in Algorithms and Protocols", ACM Distinguished Disertation, MIT Press, 1990.

[L] S. Langford, Threshold DSS Signature without a Trusted Party, Crypto 95.

[M] S. Micali, *Fair Public-Key Cryptosystems*, Advances in Cryptology – Crypto 92 Proceedings, Lecture Notes in Computer Science Vol. 740, E. Brickell ed., Springer-Verlag, 1992, pp. 113–138.

[NIST] National Institute for Standards and Technology, *Digital Signature Standard (DSS)*, Federal Register, vol 56, no 169, 20 Aug. 1991.

[O] T. Okamoto, *A digital multisignature scheme using bijective public-key cryptosystems*, ACM Transactions on Computer Systems, 6(4), Nov 1988, pp. 432-441.

[OY] R. Ostrovsky and M. Yung, *How to withstand mobile virus attacks*, Proc. of the 10th ACM Symposium on the Principles of Distributed Computing, 1991, pp. 51-61.

[P91a] T. Pederson, *Non-interactive and information theoretic secure verifiable secret sharing*, Advances in Cryptology – Crypto 92 Proceedings, Lecture Notes in Computer Science Vol. 740, E. Brickell ed., Springer-Verlag, 1992, pp. 129-140.

[P91b] T. Pedersen, *A threshold cryptosystem without a trusted party*, Advances in Cryptology – Eurocrypt 91 Proceedings, Lecture Notes in Computer Science Vol. 547, D. Davies ed., Springer-Verlag, 1991, pp. 129-140.

[P91] T. Pedersen, *Non-interactive and information theoretic secure verifiable secret sharing*, Advances in Cryptology – Crypto 91 Proceedings, Lecture Notes in Computer Science Vol. 576, J. Feigenbaum ed., Springer-Verlag, 1991, pp. 129-140.

[R] M. Rabin, *How to exchange secrets by oblivious transfer*, Tech. Memo TR-81, Aiken Computation Laboratory Harvard University, 1981.

[RSA] R. Rivest, A. Shamir and L. Adleman, *A Method for Obtaining Digital Signature and Public Key Cryptosystems*, Comm. of ACM, 21 (1978), pp. 120-126.

[Sh] A. Shamir, *How to share a secret*, Comm. of ACM, 22 (1979), pp. 612-613.

[S92]   G. J. Simmons. *An introduction to shared secret and/or shared control schemes and their application*, In G. J. Simmons, editor, *Contemporary Cryptology*, pp. 441–497. IEEE Press, 1992.

[Y82]   A. Yao, *Protocols for secure computations*, Proceedings of the 23rd Symposium on Foundations of Computer Science, IEEE, 1982, pp. 80-91.

[Y86]   A. Yao, *How to generate and exchange secrets*, Proceedings of the 27th Symposium on Foundations of Computer Science, IEEE, 1986, pp. 162-167.

How (Not) to Design RSA Signature Schemes

Jean-François Misarsky

France Télécom - Branche Développement
Centre National d'Etudes des Télécommunications
42, rue des Coutures, B.P. 6243
14066 Caen Cedex, FRANCE

jeanfrancois.misarsky@cnet.francetelecom.fr

Abstract. The concept of public-key cryptography was invented in 1976 by Diffie and Hellman [DH]. The following year, Rivest, Shamir and Adleman provided an implementation of this idea [RSA]. The RSA signature, like any other signature, is message-dependent and signer-dependent. Thus, the recipient cannot modify the message and the signer cannot deny the validity of his signature. However, several attacks have appeared since. These attacks do not challenge RSA in itself but only the way to design a signature scheme based on it.

1 Introduction

Let (P, S) be a RSA key pair, where P is the public function and S the secret one. The RSA's mathematical properties, the reciprocal property (the fact that $P \circ S = S \circ P = Id$, the identity function) and the multiplicative property (the fact that $S(xy) = S(x)S(y)$) lead to potential weaknesses and have been used to attack RSA signatures. In 1985, Gordon exploited the first property to forge RSA key certificates [Go]. The multiplicative property was first employed by Davida [Da] and expanded by Denning [De].

Two standard ways exist to eliminate these potential weaknesses. One is to hash the message before signing and the other is to add some redundancy to the message to be signed. Attacks are feasible on some signature schemes with message digest, for instance see the Coppersmith attack on a previous version of X.509 Annex D [Co]. PKCS ♯1 [P1] and the signature scheme of Bellare and Rogaway [BR] are designed to avoid various types of attacks. Moreover, the last scheme is provably secure in the Random Oracle model. Attacks exist on some redundancy solutions too. De Jonge and Chaum were the first to apply a multiplicative attack on a scheme which used redundancy [DJC]. Recently, with Marc Girault at Eurocrypt '97 [GM], we extended their results. And, at Crypto '97 [Mi], they were further extended by using LLL algorithm [LLL]. Nevertheless, the International Standard ISO 9796 [ISO], which has been designed to resist many kinds of attacks [GQWLS], remains beyond the reach of all the multiplicative attacks known today. Unfortunately, the signature length is twice the length of the message.

The goal of this paper is to present all the known attacks on RSA signature schemes using either a hash function or redundancy. At first, we present a brief reminder about digital signature and RSA algorithm. Then, we explain the different kinds of attack on RSA digital signatures. More precisely, we explain the attacks on basic RSA signature schemes, RSA signature schemes using a hash function and RSA signature schemes using redundancy. We conclude by reporting all currently known solutions to avoid these attacks and by suggesting different ways of research.

2 Generalities

2.1 Digital Signature

Digital signatures have the same functions for the digital messages that handwritten signatures have for documents on paper (see Fig. 1). Consequently, a digital signature must be *message-dependent* and *signer-dependent*. The first property implies that the signature is *not reusable*. Hence, the signature is not valid for another document or a modified initial document. The signature ensures the *integrity* of the signed document. The second property implies that the signature is *unforgeable*. Nobody, except the signer can sign a document. Hence, the recipient is convinced that the signer deliberately signed the document. The signature ensures the *authenticity* of the signer. Finally, these two properties ensure the *non-repudiation* of the signature. The signer cannot later claim that he didn't sign the message.

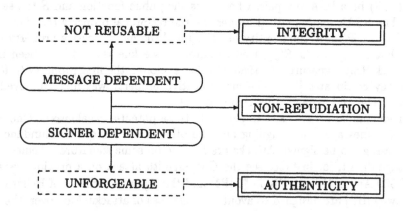

Fig. 1. Properties of digital signature

Although digital signatures are possible with secret-key cryptography, true digital signatures are only possible with public-key cryptography. In 1976, in their famous paper, Diffie and Hellman [DH] described the concept of Public-Key Cryptography. And, the following year, the RSA algorithm [RSA] demonstrated that practical public key algorithms do exist.

2.2 RSA Algorithm

RSA is a public-key cryptosystem invented by Ron Rivest, Adi Shamir and Leonard Adleman in 1977 [RSA]. It is for both encryption and authentication.

RSA Cryptosystem.

- The private key is the couple (n, d).
- The public key is the couple (n, e).
- n is the modulus: the product of two large primes p and q.
- d is the private exponent.
- e is the public exponent.

The private exponent d and the public exponent e are multiplicative inverses mod $\varphi(n) = (p-1)(q-1)$ where φ is the Euler totient function:

$$ed = 1 \ (\text{mod } \varphi(n)) \ . \tag{1}$$

The public key (n, e) is used to encipher or to verify signatures. The private key (n, d) is used to decipher or to sign messages.

Process of Signature.

- To create a digital signature s for a message m or $f(m)$, with f a hash or redundancy function, you use your private key (n, d) to obtain s by exponentiating:
$$s = m^d \ (\text{mod } n) \text{ or } s = f(m)^d \ (\text{mod } n) \ . \tag{2}$$

- To verify a signature s, you use the public key of the signer. You exponentiate and check that the message m or $f(m)$ is recovered:

$$m = s^e \ (\text{mod } n) \text{ or } f(m) = s^e \ (\text{mod } n) \ . \tag{3}$$

3 Attacks on RSA Signatures

An attack on RSA signature was first described by George Davida in 1982 [Da]. His attack was expanded by Dorothy E. Denning [De] in 1984. The next year, Gordon described how to forge RSA Key Certificates [Go] and De Jonge and Chaum published attacks on RSA signature schemes using redundancy [DJC]. The same year, a paper by Desmedt and Odlyzko [DO] described an attack on encryption that can also be applied to signatures, even when a hash function is used. In 1989, Coppersmith discovered an attack on a signature scheme using a hash function [Co]. But, his attack works only with a particular type of hash function. In 1997, we extended the result on signature schemes using redundancy, first at Eurocrypt '97 with Marc Girault [GM], and next at Crypto '97 [Mi].

3.1 Kinds of Attacks

There are three basic kinds of attacks.

Key-only attack The key-only attack is the weakest. In this case, the attacker only knows the public key of the signer.

Known signature attack The attacker also knows different message-signature pairs chosen by the signer.

Chosen message attack The strongest. In this attack, the attacker can obtain the signature of selected messages.

3.2 Levels of Success

There are four levels of success. Starting with the weakest forgery, we have:

The existential forgery The attacker forges a signature but he has no control over the message whose signature he obtains.

The selective forgery The attacker can forge a signature for some chosen messages.

The universal forgery The attacker has not found the private key of the signer but he is able to forge a signature of any message.

Total break It is the strongest level of success. The attacker can compute the secret key.

3.3 RSA's Mathematical Properties

Attacks on RSA signatures use the mathematical properties of RSA, the *reciprocal property* and the *multiplicative property*.

Definition 1. *Let P be the **public function** of RSA cryptosystem.*

$$P(x) = x^e \pmod{n} . \tag{4}$$

Definition 2. *Let S be the **secret function** of RSA cryptosystem.*

$$S(x) = x^d \pmod{n} . \tag{5}$$

Definition 3. *The **reciprocal property** (RP) is the fact that:*

$$P \circ S = S \circ P = Id \text{ the identity function} . \tag{6}$$

Definition 4. *The **multiplicative property** (MP) is the fact that:*

$$\forall x, y \qquad S(xy) = S(x)S(y) . \tag{7}$$

The reciprocal property and the multiplicative property together lead to potential weaknesses, especially when used for signatures. For instance, the reciprocal property can be used to make an existential forgery (see example 1) and the multiplicative property can be used to do a universal forgery (see example 2).

Example 1 (Existential forgery based on a key-only attack using RP).

1. Let s be a random value.
2. Apply the public function P to s:

$$P(s) = s^e \pmod{n} = m \ . \tag{8}$$

3. Then the couple (m, s) is a valid message-signature pair.

Example 2 (Universal forgery based on a chosen message attack using MP).

1. Let m be the message of which you want to forge a signature.
2. Choose two messages x and y such that:

$$xy = m \pmod{n} \ . \tag{9}$$

3. Obtain the signature of x and y.
4. Now, you can easily forge a signature of m:

$$S(m) = S(y)S(x) \pmod{n} \ . \tag{10}$$

A padding could be used to avoid these kinds of attacks because it destroys the algebraic connections between messages. The attack of Davida [Da] on simple RSA signature and the attacks of Gordon [Go] on certificates demonstrate the necessity of using redundancy or a hash-function in a signature scheme.

3.4 Attacks on Basic RSA Signatures

The Davida attack. The attack of Davida [Da] uses the multiplicative property of RSA. His algorithm is designed to break a cryptogram but he explains how to modify it to fake a signature.

1. Let m be the message of which you want to forge a signature.
2. Let $m_1, \ldots, m_t$ be the factors of m.
3. Let $sig = S(m')$ be the signature of a message m'.
4. Suppose that you can obtain $sig_1, \ldots, sig_t$ the signatures of, respectively, $m'.m_1, \ldots, m'.m_t$.
5. Then, you can compute the signature s of the message m:

$$s = \left(\prod_{i=1}^{t} sig_i \right) sig^{-t} \pmod{n} \ . \tag{11}$$

Remark 1. This attack is an improvement on the example 2. The forger hides the different factors of m by multiplying them by m'.

Remark 2. The factorization of m needs not be complete. It is not necessary to factor m into its prime factors.

Remark 3. G. Davida considers that this is a chosen-signature attack. But, as Dorothy E. Denning notes in [De], the term of chosen-message attack is more appropriate because the attacker chooses messages to be signed rather than signatures to be validated.

The Moore attack. In her article [De], Denning describes the algorithm of Judy Moore to obtain the plaintext of a ciphertext. She notes that this algorithm can be used to forge signatures.

1. Let m be the message of which you want to forge a signature s.
2. Let s_1 be a random value.
3. You compute m_1 such that (m_1, s_1) is a valid message-signature pair:

$$m_1 = s_1^e \pmod{n} . \tag{12}$$

4. Obtain the signature of $m_1 m$.

$$s_2 = S(m_1 m) = (m_1 m)^d \pmod{n} . \tag{13}$$

5. Then you compute $s_1^{-1} s_2$ to obtain the signature s of the message m:

$$s = s_1^{-1} s_2 = s_1^{-1} (m_1 m)^d = s_1^{-1} s_1 m^d = m^d \pmod{n} . \tag{14}$$

Remark 4. The first advantage of Moore's algorithm is to require only one signature from the victim.

Remark 5. The second advantage is that the factorization of the message m is unnecessary. It is the attack of Davida with $t = 1$.

The Gordon attack. This attack is an existential forgery of certificates. In his article [Go], Gordon considers that a universal trusted agency directly signs the public key (n_a, e_a) of Alice with his secret function S. Moreover, the public exponent e_a and the public modulo n_a are separately signed:

$$c_1 = S(e_a) \text{ and } c_2 = S(n_a) . \tag{15}$$

A certificate is the set $\{c_1, c_2, e_a, n_a\}$. The attack of Gordon is based on the reciprocal property of RSA and on the possibility of factoring n_a which is obtained by applying the public function P of the agency to a random value c_2.

1. Suppose that the forger wants to forge a valid certificate $\{c_1, c_2, e_a, n_a\}$.
2. The forger arbitrarily chooses c_1 and c_2.
3. He computes e_a and n_a by using the public function P of the trusted agency:

$$e_a = P(c_1) \text{ and } n_a = P(c_2) . \tag{16}$$

4. If n_a cannot be factorized or has repeated prime factors, he returns to the second step. Else (see remark 6), let $p_1, \ldots, p_k$ be the different prime factors:

$$n_a = p_1 p_2 \ldots p_k . \tag{17}$$

5. The forger can easily find the Euler totient T of n_a:

$$T = (p_1 - 1)(p_2 - 1) \ldots (p_k - 1) . \tag{18}$$

6. And by using the Euclid's algorithm, he can try to obtain d_a such that $e_a d_a = 1 \pmod{T}$. He can do this unless $\gcd(e_a, T) \neq 1$. In this case, he returns to the second step to choose another c_1 (but he keeps the same c_2). Else, the set $\{c_1, c_2, e_a, n_a\}$ is a valid certificate and the forger knows d_a such that, by an extension to the Euler-Fermat theorem:

$$x = x^{e_a d_a} \pmod{m} . \tag{19}$$

Remark 6. As n_a is a random number, it will be an unremarkable large integer with a high probability. Consequently, the forger will be able to factorize it.

These weak points are known and different ways exist to prevent these attacks. You can add padding (or redundancy) or you can use hash function. These two methods can be used separately or together. But, attacks also exist on a signature scheme using these solutions.

3.5   Attacks on RSA Signatures Using a Hash Function

The Coppersmith attack. The attack of Coppersmith [Co] applies to a scheme using a particular hash function, whose result is directly submitted to the secret function S. It exploits the multiplicative property of RSA and a weakness of the hash function. With a probability equals to one over 4096, you can find two messages m and m' such that they have related hash values:

$$h(m) = 256 \, h(m') . \tag{20}$$

And the multiplicative property implies that the signatures have also related values:

$$S(h(m)) = S(256) \, S(h(m')) . \tag{21}$$

Hence, if an attacker wants to forge a signature for a message m,

1. He finds three messages m_1, m_2, m_3 such that, respectively, m_1, m_2, and, m_3, m have related hash values:

$$h(m_1) = 256 \, h(m_2) \text{ and } h(m) = 256 \, h(m_3) . \tag{22}$$

2. If he can obtain the signature of m_1, m_2, that is the secret function S applied to the different hash values $h(m_1), h(m_2)$, then he can deduce the value of $S(256)$.
3. And, by obtaining the signature of m_3, $S(h(m_3))$, he can compute the signature of m:

$$S(h(m)) = S(256) S(h(m_3)) = \frac{S(h(m_1))}{S(h(m_2))} S(h(m_3)) . \tag{23}$$

The Desmedt and Odlyzko attack. A variant of the attack of Desmedt and Odlyzko [DO] is possible on signature schemes using a hash function or redundancy. Originally it is an attack on encryption, but it applies equally to signatures when messages to sign are relatively small.

1. At first, you factor the message, whose signature you want to forge, into small primes.
2. Next, you obtain signatures of small primes from appropriate combinations of signatures on other messages whose factors are small.
3. Then, you produce the signature by multiplying the factors' signature.

Remark 7. The probability of success depends on the size of the message, not on the size of the RSA modulus.

Remark 8. You can easily avoid this attack if the message to be signed is as large as the RSA modulus and it is not a multiple of some known values.

3.6 Attacks on RSA Signatures Using Redundancy

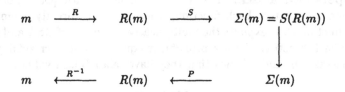

Fig. 2. Insertion of redundancy

Definition 5. *In a signature scheme, a **redundancy function** R is an invertible function applied to the message to obtain a bit pattern suitable for the secret function S.*

Definition 6. *A **modular redundancy** is a value obtained by applying a modular reduction to the message.*

Definition 7. *The **size** of a binary pattern b, denoted by $|\,b\,|$, is the number of bits of b.*

Definition 8. *The **size of redundancy** is the size of the bit pattern to be signed minus the size of the message.*

Signature and verification process when a redundancy function is used (see also Fig. 2):

1. Let m be the message that you want to sign.
2. The invertible redundancy function R is applied to the message m.

3. The secret function S is applied to $R(m)$.
4. Then, $\Sigma(m) = S(R(m))$ is the signature of the message m.
5. The signer only sends $\Sigma(m)$ to the receiver.
6. The latter applies the public function P to $\Sigma(m)$.
7. He verifies that the results complies with the redundancy rule (i.e. that it lies in $\text{Im}(R)$).
8. If it is correct, then he recovers the message m by discarding the redundancy.

The Girault attack. In an unpublished article [Gi], Marc Girault describes how to forge RSA Key Certificates, even when adding redundancy. His forgery works when the public exponent of certification is 3. His forgery makes use of a technique based on Brickell and DeLaurentis algorithm [BDL]. It is a probabilistic algorithm which solves the following problem:

- Given n and Y
- Find X such that:

$$X^3 = Y + \delta \pmod{n} \text{ with } X = O(n) \text{ and } \delta = O(n^{2/3}) \ . \qquad (24)$$

It has been used to break a digital signature scheme of Okamoto and Shiraishi [OS] based on the difficulty of approximate k^{th} roots modulo n. Their algorithm allowed them to break this scheme for exponents 2 and 3.

The attack of Girault is valid when a simple affine function of redundancy is used:

$$R(m) = \omega m + a \text{ with } \begin{cases} \omega \text{ the multiplicative redundancy} \\ a \text{ the additive redundancy} \end{cases} \qquad (25)$$

In certificates that he considers, the additive redundancy is composed of fixed redundancy (a fixed bit pattern) and information (different data such as the identity of the Certification Authority, a period of validity, an algorithm identifier and so on).

For instance, the forgery is possible when the message is on the right or on the left (see Fig 3), and even when the message is in the middle (see Fig 4).

The length of the certificate, that he considers in his paper, is 768 bits. But his attack is possible when the modulo in the certificate is two third of the total length.

To avoid his forgery, he suggested using a one-way hash-function and redundancy. The certificate c for the public key (n_a, e_a) of Alice will be the secret

Message		Information	Redundancy

Information	Redundancy	Message	

Fig. 3. Examples of certificates broken by the attack of Girault

Information	Message	Redundancy

Redundancy	Message	Information

Fig. 4. Examples of certificates broken by the attack of Girault (message in the middle)

function of the certification authority S applied to the information A concatenated with the public exponent e_a, the public modulo n_a and $h(A, e_a, n_a)$ a one-way hash value of A, e_a, n_a:

$$c = S[A, e_a, n_a, h(A, e_a, n_a)] \text{ with } \begin{cases} A \text{ information} \\ e_a \text{ the public exponent of Alice} \\ n_a \text{ the public modulo of Alice} \\ h \text{ a one-way hash-function} \end{cases} \quad (26)$$

When a redundancy function is used, the multiplicative attack is more complicated. The first to show that it was still possible, were De Jonge and Chaum at Crypto '85.

The De Jonge and Chaum attack. De Jonge and Chaum [DJC] exhibit a multiplicative attack when a simple affine function of redundancy, see (25), is used. Their attack is based on the extended Euclidean algorithm.

In a first case, their attack is valid when a is equal to 0 and for any value of ω. It is possible if the size of redundancy is less than one half the size of the RSA modulus n:

$$| \text{ redundancy } | \prec \frac{1}{2} | n | . \quad (27)$$

In a second case, their attack is valid when ω is equal to 1 and any value for a. It is possible if the size of redundancy is less than one third the size of the RSA modulo n (less than one half in particular cases):

$$| \text{ redundancy } | \prec \frac{1}{3} | n | . \quad (28)$$

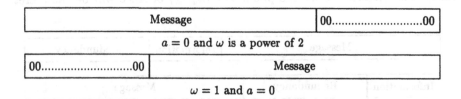

Message	00.............................00

$a = 0$ and ω is a power of 2

00.............................00	Message

$\omega = 1$ and $a = 0$

Fig. 5. Examples of schemes broken by the attack of De Jonge and Chaum

For instance, they can forge a signature if a right-padded redundancy scheme or a left-padded redundancy scheme of signature is used (see Fig. 5). Recently, in a joint work with Marc Girault, we extended these results.

The Girault and Misarsky attack. At Eurocrypt '97, we presented a multiplicative attack [GM] which makes an extensive use of Okamoto-Shiraishi Algorithm [OS]. This algorithm is an extension of the extended Euclidean Algorithm. We have increased the efficiency of multiplicative attacks on a signature scheme with a simple affine function of redundancy, see (25). But, we have also enlarged the domain of the multiplicative attack to schemes with modular redundancy. Now, the attack is possible on a signature scheme using this kind of redundancy:

$$R(m) = \omega_1 m + \omega_2 \varphi(m) + a \qquad (29)$$

$$\text{with} \begin{cases} \omega_1, \omega_2 & \text{the multiplicative redundancies} \\ a & \text{the additive redundancy} \\ m & \text{the message} \\ \varphi(m) & \text{the modular redundancy} \end{cases}$$

When a simple affine function of redundancy is used, $\omega_2 = 0$, our attack is possible for any value of ω_1 and a, when the size of redundancy is less than one half the size of RSA modulo n:

$$|\text{ redundancy }| \prec \frac{1}{2} |n| . \qquad (30)$$

And, our attack is valid on signature schemes with modular redundancy, see (29), when the size of redundancy is less than one half the size of n minus the size of the modular redundancy:

$$|\text{ redundancy }| \prec \frac{1}{2} |n| - |\text{ modular redundancy }| . \qquad (31)$$

For instance, we can forge a signature when the bit pattern that you sign has the form specified on figure 6. In this case, the modular redundancy $\varphi(m)$ is equal to the message m modulo a fixed value m_r, where m_r is called the *redundancy modulus*.

1101...	Message	10...10	$\varphi(m) = m \pmod{m_r}$	01.....011
		$R(m)$: ω_1, ω_2 are powers of 2		
1101...	0...............................0	10...10	0..............................0	01.....011
		Fixed or additive redundancy a		

Fig. 6. Example of scheme broken by the attack of Girault-Misarsky

01	0	00..........001	Message	$\varphi(m)$ (80 bits)	0101

Fig. 7. Binary pattern of ISO/IEC JTC 1/SC 27 Working Draft January 1996

This multiplicative attack has been successfully applied to a part of the project on digital signature schemes giving message recovery ISO/IEC JTC 1/SC 27 [ISO1]. It was a Working Draft, i.e. one of the first stages of the development of International Standards. This project uses a modular redundancy of 80 bits:

$$\varphi(m) = 2(m \ (\text{mod} \ (2^{79} + 1))) \ . \tag{32}$$

The bit patterns signed have (see Fig. 7):

- a fixed redundancy on the left and on the right.
- the message m concatenated with the modular redundancy $\varphi(m)$ in the middle.
- a padding field between the left redundancy and the message.

A modified version of this scheme was also attacked. The modified version used a modular redundancy φ defined by an exclusive OR:

$$\varphi(m) = Mask \oplus 2(m \ (\text{mod} \ (2^{79} + 1))) \ . \tag{33}$$

where the mask is a fixed bit pattern: $Mask = FFF...FF$.

To avoid this kind of attack, the authors of the standardization project have chosen to split the message and the redundancy in different parts [ISO2]. But, their new project has been broken at Crypto '97.

The Misarsky attack. At Crypto '97 [Mi], by using lattices, the multiplicative attack was extended to a redundancy function which has a more complicated form. Now, the message m and the modular redundancy $\varphi(m)$ are split in different parts. Note that, this different parts have not necessarily the same length.

$$R(m) = \sum_{i=1}^{k_1} m_i \omega_i + \sum_{j=1}^{k_2} \varphi(m)_j \omega_{k_1+j} + a \tag{34}$$

with
$$\begin{cases}
\omega_1, \omega_2, \ldots & \text{the different multiplicative redundancies} \\
m_i & \text{the different parts of the message } m \\
\varphi(m)_j & \text{the different parts of the modular redundancy } \varphi(m) \\
k_1 & \text{the number of parts of the message } m \\
k_2 & \text{the number of parts of the modular redundancy } \varphi(m) \\
a & \text{the additive redundancy}
\end{cases}$$

Now, multiplicative attack is possible on signature schemes where the message is split. For instance, when the different multiplicative redundancies ω_1,

| 10111... | m_1 | $\varphi(m)_1$ | ...1001... | $\varphi(m)_j$ | m_i | $\varphi(m)_{j+1}$ | | ...1001... |

$R(m) : \omega_1, \omega_2, \ldots$ are powers of 2

| 10111... | 0...0 | 0...0 | ...1001... | 0...0 | 0...0 | 0...0 | | ...1001... |

a: fixed redundancy (or additive redundancy)

Fig. 8. Example of bit pattern broken by the attack of Misarsky

$\omega_2, \ldots$ are powers of two, the bit-pattern that you sign can have the form of the Fig. 8.

The attack has been successfully applied to an ISO Working Draft [ISO2]. In this new project, the modular redundancy of 80 bits is split in 20 parts of 4 bits. The goal of this project was to simplify ISO 9796 [ISO]. But, we have broken this scheme by using an attack based on the LLL algorithm [LLL].

Moreover, the Crypto's attack could be used to attack other schemes with fixed redundancy. The attack of Crypto is also possible on a scheme using several modular redundancies or on a scheme with a mask. And, you can easily adapt this attack to break a scheme using modular redundancies for different parts of the message.

4 Solutions

Different ways exist to prevent the attacks on RSA signature which we described. You can uses hash function, as recommended in PKCS, ISO or ANSI. Another signature scheme with hash functions is the signature scheme of Bellare and Rogaway [BR], which is provably secure in the Random Oracle model.

You can also use redundancy solutions to prevent the attacks. But, only one standard which uses redundancy is available. It is the International Standard ISO 9796 Part 1 [ISO]. This International Standard has been designed [GQWLS] to resist many kinds of attacks:

- Attacks by shifting or complementing.
- Attacks by natural powers.
- Attacks by natural products.

Moreover, this standard remains beyond the reach of all multiplicative attacks known today. Unfortunately, there is a drawback: the signature length is twice as long as the message.

5 Conclusion

We have shown different attacks on RSA signature schemes. The first attacks we have presented were on simple schemes. The last, the more recent attacks, use a more complicated theory. Now, forgery is possible even when a complex function of redundancy is used. These different attacks allow us to know how not to design a RSA signature schemes.

Different solutions exit to avoid these forgeries, but they use either hash function or a large amount of redundancy. A RSA signature scheme, which resists all known attacks, without the latter inconvenience and without using hash function does not yet exist. Could such a RSA signature scheme be designed ?

The challenge is to design a RSA Signature scheme using redundancy without a hash function and with a shorter redundancy than in ISO 9796 [ISO]. Then, you can hope to obtain a good speed of verification and to reduce the expansion rate. Different means exist to define such a scheme. You can use a modular redundancy, a CRC, splitting and fixed redundancy either independently or combined.

But, at the present time, we do not know of a short signature scheme by which attacks that we have presented could be avoided.

6 Acknowlegements

We would like to thank Hideki Imai and Yuliang Zheng for their invitation at PKC '98. We also thank Marc Girault for his useful comments about the presentation associated with this article and for his help.

References

[BDL]   E. BRICKELL AND J. DELAURENTIS, *An Attack on a Signature Scheme Proposed by Okamoto and Shiraishi*, Proc. of Crypto '85, Lecture Notes in Computer Science, vol. 218, Springer-Verlag, pp. 28.32.

[BR]   M. BELLARE, P. ROGAWAY, *The Exact Security of Digital Signatures - How to Sign with RSA and Rabin*, Advances in Cryptology, Eurocrypt '96, LNCS 1070, 1996.

[Co]   D. COPPERSMITH, *Analysis of ISO/CCITT Document X.509 Annex D*, memorandum, IBM T.J. Watson Research Center, Yorktown Heights, N.Y., 10598, U.S.A., 11th June 1989.

[Da]   G. DAVIDA, *Chosen Signature Cryptanalysis of the RSA (MIT) Public Key Cryptosystem*, Technical Report TR-CS-82-2, Department of Electrical Engineering and Computer Science, University of Wisconsin, Milwaukee, USA, October 1982.

[De]   D. E. DENNING, *Digital Signatures with RSA and other Public-key cryptosystems*, Communications of the ACM 27, 4, April 1984, 388-392.

[DH]   W. DIFFIE, M. HELLMAN, *New Directions in Cryptography*, IEEE Trans. Inform. Theory IT-22, Nov. 1976, 644-654.

[DJC]   W. DE JONGE, D. CHAUM, *Attacks on Some RSA Signatures*, Advances in Cryptology, Crypto '85 proceedings, Lectures Notes In Computer Science, Vol. 218, Springer-Verlag, Berlin, 1986, pp. 18-27.

[DO]   Y. DESMEDT, A.M. ODLYZKO, *A Chosen Text Attack on RSA Cryptosystem and some Discrete Logarithm Schemes*, Advances in Cryptology, Crypto '85 proceedings, Lectures Notes In Computer Science, Vol. 218, Springer-Verlag, Berlin, 1986, pp. 516-522.

[Gi]   M. GIRAULT, *How to Forge RSA Key Certificates (even when adding redundancy)*, unpublished, personal communication.

[Go]   J. A. GORDON, *How to Forge RSA Key Certificates*, Electronics Letters, 25th April 1985, Vol. 21 N. 9.

[GM]   M. GIRAULT, J.F. MISARSKY, *Selective Forgery of RSA Signatures Using Redundancy*, Advances in Cryptology - Eurocrypt '97, Lecture Notes in Computer Science, vol. 1233, Springer-Verlag, pp 495-507.

[GQWLS] L.C. GUILLOU, J.J. QUISQUATER, M. WALKER, P. LANDROCK, C. SHAER, *Precautions taken against various potential attacks in ISO/IEC DIS 9796, Digital signature scheme giving message recovery*, Eurocrypt '90 Proceedings, Lecture Notes in Computer Science, vol. 473, Springer-Verlag, pp 465-473.

[ISO]   ISO/IEC 9796, *Digital Signature Scheme Giving Message Recovery*, December 1991.

[ISO1]   ISO/IEC JTC 1/SC 27, *Digital Signature Schemes Giving Message Recovery; Part 2: Mechanisms using a hash function*, Working Draft, January 1996.

[ISO2]   ISO/IEC 9796-3, *Digital Signature Schemes Giving Message Recovery; Part 3: Mechanisms using a check-function*, Working Draft, December 1996.

[LLL]   A. K. LENSTRA, H. W. LENSTRA, L. LOVÁSZ, *Factoring Polynomials with Rational Coefficients*, Mathematische Annalen, vol. 261, n. 4, 1982, pp. 515-534.

[Mi]   J. F. MISARSKY, *A Multiplicative Attack Using LLL Algorithm on RSA Signatures with Redundancy*, Advances in Cryptology - Crypto '97, Lecture Notes in Computer Science, vol. 1294, Springer-Verlag, pp. 221-234.

[OS]   T. OKAMOTO, A. SHIRAISHI, *A Fast Signature Scheme Based on Quadratic Inequalities*, Proc. of the 1985 Symposium on Security and Privacy, April 1985, Oakland, CA.

[P1]   RSA LABORATORIES, *PKCS #1 : RSA Encryption Standard, Version 1.5*, November 1993.

[RSA]   R.L. RIVEST, A. SHAMIR, L. ADLEMAN, *A Method for Obtaining Digital Signatures and Public-Key Cryptosystems*, MIT Laboratory for Computer Science, Technical Memo LCS!TM82, Cambridge, Massachusetts, 4/4/77. Also Comm. ACM, Vol. 21, N. 2, Feb 1978.

Overview of Elliptic Curve Cryptography

Kiyomichi Araki[1], Takakazu Satoh[2], and Shinji Miura[3]

[1] Dept. Computer Eng., Tokyo Institute of Technology
2-12-1 O-okayama, Meguro, Tokyo, Japan 152-8552
araki@ss.titech.ac.jp
[2] Dept. Mathematics, Saitama University
255 Shimo-ookubo, Urawa, Saitama, Japan 338-8570
tsatoh@rimath.saitama-u.ac.jp
[3] Media Processing Labs., Sony Corporation
6-7-35 Kitashinagawa, Shinagawa-ku, Tokyo, Japan 141-0001
miura@av.crl.sony.co.jp

Abstract. In this article, we look at the elliptic curve cryptography, which is believed to be one of the most promising candidates for the next generation cryptographic tool. The following issues are addressed here;
1. Discrete Logarithm Problem in finite fields
2. Elliptic Curve Discrete Logs
3. Implementation of ECDLP Cryptographic Schemes
4. Attacks on EC Cryptosystems
5. Minimum Requirement for Secure EC Cryptosystems
6. Standardization and Commercialization of EC Cryptosystems
7. Construction of Elliptic Curves

1 Introduction

Since 1985 a lot of attentions have been paid to elliptic curves for cryptographic applications and there is a huge amount of literature on the subject. Koblitz[Kob87] and Miller[Mil86] independently proposed using them for public-key cryptosystem at that time. Although they did not invent a new cryptographic algorithm with elliptic curve over finite fields, they implemented existing public-key algorithms, like Diffie-Hellman, using elliptic curves.

Why are elliptic curves important for cryptographic applications? It is because they provide a *group* structure, which can be used to build cryptographic algorithms, but they don't have certain properties that may facilitate cryptanalysis. For example, there is no good notion of *"smooth"*[t1] with elliptic curves. That is, there is no set of small elements in terms of which a random element has a good chance of being expressed by a simple algorithm. Hence, *index calculus method* does not work for elliptic curves. The reason why the appropriate set of smooth elements cannot be chosen, is described in 3.2.

Elliptic curves over the finite field F_{2^n} are particularly attractive, because the arithmetic processors for underlying field are easy to construct and relatively simple to implement for n in the range of less than 200. They have the potential to provide

---

[t1] Do not confuse this notion with smoothness in algebraic geometry (i.e. non-singularity).

faster public-key cryptosystems with smaller key sizes in comparison with RSA systems. Many public-key algorithms, like Diffie-Hellman, ElGamal, and Schnorr, can be easily implemented in elliptic curves over finite fields.

In 1991 Menezes, Okamoto and Vanstone[MOV93] provided a new cryptanalysis for a set of elliptic curves named by *supersingular*. Their idea is due to the Weil pairing, by which elliptic curve discrete logarithm problems (ECDLP) can be reduced to discrete logarithm problems over some extension field of underlying field. Thus ECDLP over supersingular curves can be solved in *subexponential-time* algorithm.

On the other hand, Smart[Sma97] as well as Satoh and Araki[SA97] announced independently and almost simultaneously another type of cryptanalysis in 1997, which is effective only for *anomalous* elliptic curves. Their algorithm terminates within a *polynomial-time*.

Moreover, it should be noted that a paper of Semaev[Sem98] was published in January 1998, in which a different type of polynomial-time algorithm is described for anomalous curves. The former approach is number-theoretic, whereas the latter one is algebraic-geometrical. See 5.2 for more details.

This review paper is organized as follows. After introducing the discrete logarithm problem and the ElGamal system in Section 2, we describe the reason why the elliptic curve discrete logs are extensively studied in Section 3. In Section 4, the cryptographic systems using ECDLPs are reviewed. Attacking methods on ECDLPs and the minimum requirements are summarized in Section 5. The trends of standardization and commercialization of EC cryptosystems are briefly described in Section 6. Finally a construction method of elliptic curves with a specified number of rational points is provided in Section 7.

2   Discrete Logarithm Problem and the ElGamal System

Originally the discrete logarithm problem has been employed in the Diffie-Hellman (DH) system of key exchange[DH76], and later in the ElGamal system of public-key encryption, together with an accompanying digital signature scheme[ElG85]. Then the discrete logarithm problem in $\mathbf{F}_p$ has been the subject of extensive study, especially in the field of cryptology. We state this problem in the setting of a prime field $\mathbf{F}_p$, as follows;

- For a given set of (p, α, β), where p is prime, $\alpha \in \mathbf{F}_p$ is a primitive element, and $\beta \in \mathbf{F}_p^*$.
- Find the unique integer $a, 0 \leq a \leq p - 2$, such that

$$\alpha^a \equiv \beta \pmod{p}.$$

The discrete logarithm problem in $\mathbf{F}_p$

For surveys of discrete logarithm problem in finite fields, we refer to [Odl85], [McC90] and [Odl94]. Here we note that there is a subexponential time algorithm called index calculus method to solve DLP in finite fields and that in order that DLP in finite fields to be difficult, p should be chosen *carefully*. Even in 1985, [Odl85, p.295] writes: "To protect against sophisticated attacks by opponents capable of building large special purpose machines, n should probably be at least 1500. In fact, to guard against improvement in known algorithms or new methods, it might be safest to use

$n \geq 2000$ or even larger." (Here, n is a bit size of p.) However, there is no known *polynomial-time* algorithm for the discrete logarithm problem in finite fields so far.

On the other hand, modular exponentiation can be efficiently computed by using the fast exponentiation technique, [Coh93, §1.2] or [Knu81, §4.6.3], thus yielding a one-way function without trap door for suitable primes p.

ElGamal has developed a public-key cryptosystem based on the discrete logarithm problem by modifying of DH scheme. In case of DH scheme, only secure key exchange was realized, however. Secure encryption and signature schemes were build with an introduction of one-pad random number, as shown below;

- p : a large prime so that the discrete log problem in $\mathbf{F}_p$ is difficult.
- $\mathcal{P} = \mathbf{F}_p^*$ (Plaintext space)
- $\mathcal{C} = \mathbf{F}_p^* \times \mathbf{F}_p^*$ (Ciphertext space)
- Choose a primitive element $\alpha \in \mathbf{F}_p^*$ and $a \in \mathbf{Z}/(p-1)\mathbf{Z}$.
- Put $\beta = \alpha^a$.
- The values p, α and β are public, and a is secret.
- Define an encryption function, $e_{\alpha,\beta}$ by

$$e_{\alpha,\beta}(x,k) = (\alpha^k \bmod p, x\beta^k \bmod p)$$

where $x \in \mathcal{P}$ and $k \in \mathbf{Z}/(p-1)\mathbf{Z}$ is chosen randomly and secretly.
- A decryption function d_a is defined by

$$d_a(c_1, c_2) = c_2 c_1^{-a} \bmod p$$

for $(c_1, c_2) \in \mathcal{C}$.
- $d_a(e_{\alpha,\beta}(x,k)) = x$ provided β is defined as above.

ElGamal public-key cryptosystem in $\mathbf{F}_p^*$

- As in the ElGamal public-key cryptosystem, p, α and β are selected, computed and publicized, but a is kept secret.
- $S = \mathbf{F}_p^* \times \mathbf{Z}/(p-1)\mathbf{Z}$ (Signature space)
- $\mathcal{M} = \mathbf{Z}/(p-1)\mathbf{Z}$ (Message space)
- Choose a random number, k such that k is relatively prime to $p-1$.
- Solve for y in the following equation,

$$x = a\alpha^k + ky \bmod p - 1$$

where $x \in \mathcal{M}$.
- Define a signing function s_a by

$$s_a(x,k) = (\alpha^k \bmod p, y)$$

where y is a solution to the above equation.
- A verifying function $v_{\alpha,\beta}(x, s_1, s_2)$ is defined by

$$v_{\alpha,\beta}(x, s_1, s_2) = \beta^{s_1} s_1^{s_2} - \alpha^x \bmod p$$

for $(x, s_1, s_2) \in \mathcal{M} \times S$.
- Apparently for a legitimate signing $v_{\alpha,\beta}(x, s_a(x,k)) = 0$.

ElGamal signature in $\mathbf{F}_p^*$

In this scheme, the masked random number α^k via the discrete logarithm problem should be sent simultaneously with the message and the signature for each data transmission, yielding a message expansion factor of about two. Thus, one of features of the conventional secret-key scheme still remains in the ElGamal system.

Suppose the hardness of discrete logarithm problems is true, anyone whoever does not know the secret exponent a, cannot restore the plaintexts. Similarly, anyone other than the legitimate signer cannot make a proper digital signature for which a value of the verifying function vanishes.[2]

3 Why Elliptic Curve Discrete Logs ?

Before the advent of MOV reduction, the best discrete logarithm attacks applied to elliptic curves were general methods applicable in any group, having running time $O(\sqrt{k})$ in a group order k. To avoid a Pohlig-Hellman attack[PH78], elliptic curves should be chosen such that the order of the relevant group has a large prime divisor. The order of the group in question can be determined via a polynomial time algorithm due to Schoof[Schf85][3] ; alternatively, subclasses of elliptic curves are known whose group orders can be easily determined, thus avoiding the need to use Schoof's algorithm. The above-mentioned "square root" attacks are very weak[Odl85, §8], and the apparent absence of stronger general attacks has resulted in the belief that elliptic curve cryptosystems with relatively short keylengths may offer greater security than alternative cryptosystems with larger keylengths. In other words, suppose it were true that the best elliptic curve logarithm attack on a particular curve having an elliptic curve of order about 2^{150} was one of running time precisely $\sqrt{k}$ operations; then extracting elliptic discrete logarithms would take more than 10^{22} operations. Shorter keylengths bring about simpler arithmetic processors, and smaller bandwidth and memory requirements.

3.1 Definitions and Basic of Elliptic Curve

In this section we define the elliptic curve and introduce some notions which are used later. There are many books on this subject, e.g. [Sil86], [Cas91], [Kob95], and [Men93]. In what follows, p stands for a prime and q is a power of p. Let K be a field, $\overline{K}$ its algebraic closure.[4]

Elliptic Curves: Let $a_i \in K$ for $i = 1, 2, 3, 4, 6$. Let E be a cubic curve defined by

$$Y^2 + a_1 XY + a_3 Y = X^3 + a_2 X^2 + a_4 X + a_6$$

---

[2] Strictly speaking, the equivalence between the security of ElGamal system and the hardness of DLP has not yet demonstrated. Obviously if DLP is easily solved, then all the ElGamal systems will be broken, but the converse is not yet proved. For example, a forger wants to seek solutions of s_1 and s_2 to the equation $\beta^{s_1} s_1^{s_2} = \alpha^x$ for a given set of (β, α, x). Both s_1 and s_2 can be varied, therefore it is more likely to find easily these solutions than the DLP solution.

[3] In its first appearance, Schoof's algorithm seems impractical. However its improved versions, Schoof-Elkies-Atkin algorithm and isogeny cycles (see [Mor95], [CM94]), run much faster.

[4] For example, $\overline{\mathbf{R}} = \mathbf{C}$ and $\overline{\mathbf{F}_q} = \bigcup_{n=1}^{\infty} \mathbf{F}_{q^n}$.

over K, that is,

$$E = \{(x, y) \in \overline{K}^2 : y^2 + a_1 xy + a_3 y = x^3 + a_2 x^2 + a_4 x + a_6\} \cup \{\mathcal{O}\}$$

where $\mathcal{O}$ is a special point, called the *point at infinity*. If the discriminant Δ of E, which is a certain polynomial of a_i, is not zero, we call E an *elliptic curve defined over K*.[t5] In case of $\text{char}(K) \neq 2, 3$,[t6] we may assume $a_1 = a_2 = a_3 = 0$ without loss of generality and in this case Δ is given by a simple formula $4a_4^3 + 27a_6^2$.[t7]

Rational Points: Let L be an algebraic extension of K.[t8] If the both coordinates of $P \in E$ lie in L or $P = \mathcal{O}$, we say P is L-rational. The set of L-rational points of E is denoted by $E(L)$.

Addition Formula over Elliptic Curves: An elliptic curve E can be equipped with an Abelian group structure by the following addition on E[t9]:
Suppose $P = (x_1, y_1)$ and $Q = (x_2, y_2)$ are points on E other than $\mathcal{O}$. If $x_1 = x_2$ and $y_1 + y_2 + a_1 x_2 + a_3 = 0$, then $P + Q = \mathcal{O}$; otherwise $P + Q = (x_3, y_3)$, where

$$x_3 = \lambda^2 + a_1 \lambda - a_2 - x_1 - x_2,$$

$$y_3 = -(\lambda + a_1)x_3 - \nu - a_3,$$

and

$$\lambda = \begin{cases} \dfrac{y_2 - y_1}{x_2 - x_1} & \text{if } P \neq Q, \\[2mm] \dfrac{3x_1^2 + 2a_2 x_1 + a_4 - a_1 y_1}{2y_1 + a_1 x_1 + a_3} & \text{if } P = Q, \end{cases}$$

$$\nu = \begin{cases} \dfrac{y_1 x_2 - y_2 x_1}{x_2 - x_1} & \text{if } P \neq Q, \\[2mm] \dfrac{-x_1^3 + a_4 x_1 + 2a_6 - a_3 y_1}{2y_1 + a_1 x_1 + a_3} & \text{if } P = Q. \end{cases}$$

Finally, we define

$$P + \mathcal{O} = \mathcal{O} + P = P$$

for all $P \in E$. Then E together with this addition forms an Abelian group whose identity is $\mathcal{O}$.[t10] The inverse of $(x, y) \in E$ is simply $(x, -y - a_1 x - a_3)$. Since this addition is defined by rational expressions with coefficients in K, $E(L)$ is a subgroup of E.

[t5] We frequently abbreviate "E defined over K" as "E/K".

[t6] Here $\text{char}(K)$ denotes the characteristic of K, that is, the least positive integer n such that $\sum_{i=1}^{n} 1 = 0$ in K, and if there is no such n, we define $\text{char}(K) = 0$. Example: $\text{char}(\mathbf{F}_{p^m}) = p$ for all $m \geq 1$, and $\text{char}(\mathbf{Q}) = 0$.

[t7] However, for cryptographic application, the case $K = \mathbf{F}_{2^n}$ is also important.

[t8] For example, if $K = \mathbf{F}_q$, either $L = \overline{K}$ or $L = \mathbf{F}_{q^n}$ with $n \geq 1$.

[t9] We notice that all arithmetic operations in the elliptic curve addition are evaluated in $\overline{K}$ (or in K if both P and Q are K-rational).

[t10] See e.g. [Sil86, Chap. III.2], [Cas91, Chap. 7] or [Ful69, Chap.5, Prop.4].

Torsion-Points: Let $P \in E$. We denote

$$\overbrace{P + P + \cdots + P}^{n \text{ times}}$$

by nP. The point P is called a n-torsion point of E if $nP = \mathcal{O}$. The set of n-torsion points is denoted by $E[n]$, which is a subgroup of E.

3.2 Robustness to Index Calculus Method – Effect of Non-zero Genus

The algebraic geometric notion "genus of a curve" may be introduced in many ways. Intuitively, it is a restricting condition on rational functions over a curve. Let C be a curve over a field K, and consider the following problem.

For any given $A_1, A_2, \ldots, A_m \in C$ and $n_1, n_2, \ldots, n_m \in \mathbf{Z}$ satisfying $\sum_{i=1}^m n_i = 0$, is there a rational function f on C whose order of zero at A_i is n_i for all $i = 1, \ldots, m$ and $f(x) \neq 0$ for $x \neq A_1, \ldots, A_m$?

For $C = \mathbf{P}^1(K) = K \cup \{\infty\}$, the answer is always affirmative.[11] It is convenient to introduce the notion of a *divisor* in considering this problem. A divisor D on curve C is a function $D : C \to \mathbf{Z}$ such that $D(P) = 0$ for all but finitely many $P \in C$. We denote the $\mathbf{Z}$-valued function taking a value 1 at A, and 0 at anywhere else by $[A]$.[12] With this notation, the function taking values $n_1, \ldots, n_m$ at $A_1, \ldots, A_m$, respectively, and 0 at other points is $\sum_{i=1}^m n_i[A_i]$.[13] The set of all divisors on C is denoted by $\mathrm{div}(C)$. On the other hand, the rational function f on C determines a divisor $\mathrm{div}(f)$ on C by $(\mathrm{div}(f))(P) = \mathrm{ord}_P(f)$.[14] For elliptic curves (i.e. curves with genus 1), the above problem is negative. In order that a rational function satisfying above condition exists, one more additional restriction $\sum_{i=1}^m n_i A_i = \mathcal{O}$ must be satisfied ([Sil86, Corollary III.3.5]). Especially, there is no rational function on an elliptic curve which has a simple pole at only one point. We say a divisor d is *principal* if there exists a rational function f on C satisfying $d = \mathrm{div}(f)$. It is a consequence of the Riemann-Roch theorem[15] that the higher the genus is, the more restrictions there are on rational functions. The following theorem is known as the Mordell-Weil theorem: Let A be an Abelian variety (e.g. elliptic curves and Jacobian of algebraic curves etc.) defined over a finite extension k of $\mathbf{Q}$. Then, the group of k-rational points of A is finitely generated.[16] What does this theorem imply? Index

---

[11] For example, assume none of A_i is ∞. Then, $f(x) = \prod_{i=1}^m (x - A_i)^{n_i}$ is a desired one.

[12] Instead of $[A]$, some authors use (A), which is context sensitive. Let P and Q be points on an elliptic curve. What does $2(P + Q)$ mean?

[13] Do not confuse $\mathbf{Z}$-valued function on C with K-valued function on C. Several authors introduce divisors as *formal sums* on C. Contrary to its name "formal", they are neither imaginary nor virtual objects as is described as above. See e.g. [Ful69, Chap.2, Sect.11] for details. After sums and integer multiplication on divisors are rigorously defined, one can forget what divisors really are.

[14] Here $\mathrm{ord}_P(f)$ is the order of zeros of f at P. As usual, a zero of negative order n is interpreted as the pole of order $-n$. For example, if $f(x) = x^5/(x-1)^2$, then $\mathrm{div}(f) = 5[0] - 2[1] - 3[\infty]$.

[15] For proofs, see e.g. [Ful69], [Har77]. For introductory explanation and usage of Riemann-Roch theorem, see e.g. [LG88].

[16] Mordell proved this theorem for curves in 1922. Later, Weil proved general case in 1928.

calculus method requires a large number of free generators. Hence, index calculus method does not apply to elliptic curves. This is an idea of Miller[Mil86] where more detailed discussion is given.[17] See also [Kob87, Sect. 7] which observes nonsmooth cyclic subgroups.

4   Implementation of Cryptographic Schemes Based on ECDLP

The notion of a one-way function is central to public-key cryptography, and one-way functions are a fundamental building block for most of the cryptographic protocols including key-exchange, digital signature, and public-key cryptosystem. Here we begin by showing the conditions to be satisfied by a one-way function based on the DLP in any finite Abelian group G (or, its cyclic subgroup H).

Let G be a finite Abelian group. We denote its group operation additively. Choose and fix $g \in G$ and put $H := \langle g \rangle$. Let n be the order of H. We have the canonical group isomorphism

$$f : \mathbf{Z}/n\mathbf{Z} \to H,$$

which is defined by $f(a) := ag = \overbrace{g + \cdots + g}^{a^\dagger \text{ times}} \in H$, where $a^\dagger$ is any non-negative integer satisfying $a^\dagger \bmod n = a$. Only the following two conditions are necessary for our purpose.

(1) The f is evaluated easily by using PC, that is, there is an algorithm requiring only small computational time and storage area, whose amount is bounded by polynomial order of $\log n$.

(2) The computation of inverse f^{-1} of f is virtually impossible even if one uses a supercomputer. For large n, there is no algorithm to compute f^{-1} with moderate amount (polynomial order of $\log n$) of time and space complexity

The condition (1) implies that we can compute group operation of H easily. As to the condition (2), more precise statement is:

(2′) It is intractable to compute $f(ab)$ by using only the values $f(a)$ and $f(b)$, where $a, b \in \mathbf{Z}/n\mathbf{Z}$.

The common attack to the key-exchange system, digital signature system, public key cryptosystem based on the general discrete log problem is to find an algorithm to compute f^{-1} quickly. Once such an algorithm is revealed for a particular G (or H), all the cryptographic systems based on the DLP in G are broken and therefore useless. This is a ultimate object of attackers and forgers. Hence, if we find a group G which satisfies the above conditions, we can construct idealistic key-exchange system, digital signature system, and public key cryptosystem. However, no such G has been discovered so far. Historically, the multiplicative group $\mathbf{F}_q^*$ of the finite field ($q = p^k$)

---

[17] Mordell conjectured that if C is a curve with genus $g \geq 2$, then the number of k-rational point on C is finite. This "Mordell conjecture" is proved by Faltings[Fal83]. Nevertheless, Adleman et. al.[ADH94] gives an index calculus method of the Jacobians of hyperelliptic curves with large genus. Hence more detailed analysis on Miller's idea is desired.

and the group $(\mathbf{Z}/n\mathbf{Z})^*$ of invertible elements of $\mathbf{Z}/n\mathbf{Z}$ are considered as candidates of G satisfying the conditions (1) and (2). We notice that additive groups $\mathbf{F}_q$ and $\mathbf{Z}/n\mathbf{Z}$ do not satisfy the condition (2). Indeed, for these groups, we can compute f^{-1} as easy as f using modular arithmetics. Next, the group $E(\mathbf{F}_q)$ of $\mathbf{F}_q$ rational points of an elliptic curve E defined over $\mathbf{F}_q$ is considered for a candidate of G. We call the DLP over $G = E(\mathbf{F}_q)$ ECDLP.

Known attacks, such as

- Silver-Pohlig-Hellman method [Sha71], [PH78], [Pol78]
- Index calculus method[18] [Adl79], [Cop84], [Gor92]

to key-exchange system, digital signature system, public key cryptosystem based on generic DLP attempt to find easier algorithm to compute f^{-1}. As was stated in Sect. 3.2, the reason why we think $G = E(\mathbf{F}_q)$ is superior to $G = \mathbf{F}_q^*$ or $G = (\mathbf{Z}/n\mathbf{Z})^*$ is that we cannot apply index calculus method to $E(\mathbf{F}_q)$.

Anyway, we emphasize again only the following two points are required to the isomorphism $f : \mathbf{Z}/n\mathbf{Z} \to H$:

- There exists an algorithm to compute f quickly.
- It is plausible that computing f^{-1} is intractable.

In the following sections, we review on some key-exchange system, digital signature system, and public key cryptosystem based on the generic DLP. However, as to digital signature system, we observe one based on ECDLP. We fix the finite Abelian group G, its cyclic subgroup H, and group isomorphism $f : \mathbf{Z}/n\mathbf{Z} \to H$ satisfying (1) and (2)

4.1 Key Exchange

Diffie-Hellman key exchange.[DH76]
This is an algorithm to share a key $k \in H$ between user A and user B

- [set up] $f : \mathbf{Z}/n\mathbf{Z} \to H$, $x \in \mathbf{Z}/n\mathbf{Z}$, $y = f(x) \in H$.
  ≪secret key≫ $x \in \mathbf{Z}/n\mathbf{Z}$. ≪public key≫ $y = f(x) \in H$.
  Let $x_A \in \mathbf{Z}/n\mathbf{Z}$ be the secret key and $y_A = f(x_A)$ be the public key of user A. Similarly let $x_B \in \mathbf{Z}/n\mathbf{Z}$ be the secret key and $y_B = f(x_B)$ be the public key of user B.
- [common key generation] User A computes $k_{AB} = x_A y_B = x_A f(x_B) = f(x_A x_B)$. User B computes $k_{BA} = x_B y_A = x_B f(x_A) = f(x_B x_A)$.
  Hence user A and B share a common key, $k_{AB} = k_{BA} \in H$.

Diffie-Hellman key exchange

4.2 Digital Signature

In this section, let p be a sufficiently large prime, E an elliptic curve over $\mathbf{F}_p$ and put $G = E(\mathbf{F}_p)$. We choose $g \in E(\mathbf{F}_p)$ such that the order of g is a large prime

---

[18] Kraitchick[Kra22, Chap.5, §§14-16] already invented the index calculus method for prime fields. However, it lacks running time analysis.

q. Let m be a message to be signed and m' be a size of m, i.e. $m \in \mathbf{Z}/m'\mathbf{Z}$. Let $h : \mathbf{F}_p \times (\mathbf{Z}/m'\mathbf{Z}) \to \mathbf{F}_q$ be a hash function. We define a mapping of $I_q^p : \mathbf{F}_p \to \mathbf{F}_q$ by $I_q^p(a) = (A \bmod q)$ where A is the least non-negative integer such that $A \bmod p = a$. The above settings are publicized. We denote by $x(r)$ the x-coordinate of $r \in E - \{\mathcal{O}\}$.

EC ElGamal signature[ElG85]

- [set up] ≪secret key≫ $t \in \mathbf{F}_q$. ≪public key≫ $v = tg \in E(\mathbf{F}_p)$.
- [signature generation]
  (i) Choose a random number $k \in \mathbf{F}_q^*$. Compute $r_1 = kg \in E(\mathbf{F}_p)$. If $x(r_1) = 0$, go to the beginning of this step and choose a random number again.
  (ii) Put $s = k^{-1}(h(x(r_1), m) + I_q^p(x(r_1))t)$ (in $\mathbf{F}_q$). If $s = 0$, then go to step (i) and try again with another random number.
  (iii) (Note at this point, $x(r_1) \in \mathbf{F}_p^*$ and $s \in \mathbf{F}_q^*$.) The signature of m is $(r_1, s) \in E(\mathbf{F}_p) \times \mathbf{F}_q^*$.
- [signature verification] $sr_1 = h(x(r_1), m)g + I_q^p(x(r_1))v$

EC ElGamal signature

EC Schnorr signature[Schn91]

- [set up] ≪secret key≫ $t \in \mathbf{F}_q$. ≪public key≫ $v = -tg \in E(\mathbf{F}_p)$.
- [signature generation]
  (i) Choose a random number $s \in \mathbf{F}_q^*$. Put $e = h(x(sg), m) \in \mathbf{F}_q$. If $e = 0$, then go to the beginning of this step and choose a random number again.
  (ii) Put $w = s + te$ (in $\mathbf{F}_q$). If $w = 0$, then go to step (i) and try again with another random number.
  (iii) (Note at this point, $e \in \mathbf{F}_q^*$ and $w \in \mathbf{F}_q^*$.) The signature of m is $(e, w) \in \mathbf{F}_q^* \times \mathbf{F}_q^*$.
- [signature verification] $e = h(x(wg + ev), m)$.

EC Schnorr signature

EC DSA[NIST91], [NIST92]

In this case, the hashing function is $h : \mathbf{F}_q \times (\mathbf{Z}/m'\mathbf{Z}) \to \mathbf{F}_q$.

- [set up] ≪secret key≫ $t \in \mathbf{F}_q$. ≪public key≫ $v = tg \in E(\mathbf{F}_p)$.
- [signature generation]
  (i) Choose a random number $k \in \mathbf{F}_q^*$. Compute $r_1 = kg \in E(\mathbf{F}_p)$. If $x(r_1) = 0$, go to the beginning of this step and choose a random number again.
  (ii) Put $r_1' = I_q^p(x(r_1))$ and $s = k^{-1}(h(r_1', m) + r_1't)$ (in $\mathbf{F}_q$). If $s = 0$, then go to step (i) and try again with another random number.
  (iii) (Note at this point, $x(r_1) \in \mathbf{F}_p^*$ and $s \in \mathbf{F}_q^*$.) The signature of m is $(r_1', s) \in \mathbf{F}_q^* \times \mathbf{F}_q^*$.
- [signature verification] $r_1' = I_q^p(x((h(r_1', m)/s)g + (r_1'/s)v))$

EC DSA

4.3 Public Key Cryptosystem

ElGamal type cryptosystem[ElG85]

- [set up] group isomorphism $f : \mathbf{Z}/n\mathbf{Z} \to H$, $t \in \mathbf{Z}/n\mathbf{Z}$, $v = f(t) \in H$.
  《secret key》 $t \in \mathbf{Z}/n\mathbf{Z}$. 《public key》 $v = f(t) \in H$.
- [encryption] $M \in H$: plain text, $r \in \mathbf{Z}/n\mathbf{Z}$: random number, $c_1 = f(r) \in H$, $c_2 = rv + M = f(rt) + M \in H$. $(c_1, c_2) \in H \times H$: ciphertext
- [decryption] $M = c_2 - tc_1 \in H$.

ElGamal type cryptosystem

For simplicity, we assumed the plain text M is an element of H. In general, a plain text is represented as an element of $\mathbf{Z}/m'\mathbf{Z}$ with some positive integer $m'(m' \leq n)$. Therefore, we still need to construct an injective map $h : \mathbf{Z}/m'\mathbf{Z} \to H$ such that both $h : \mathbf{Z}/m'\mathbf{Z} \to H$ and $h^{-1} : \mathrm{Im}(h) \to \mathbf{Z}/m'\mathbf{Z}$ are easy to compute.

However, in case of $G = E(\mathbf{F}_q)$, Menezes-Vanstone[MV90, Sect. 5] proposed the cryptosystem without mapping a plain text $m \in \mathbf{F}_q$ to an element M of H as follows:

- [set up] group isomorphism $f : \mathbf{Z}/n\mathbf{Z} \to H$, $t \in \mathbf{Z}/n\mathbf{Z}$, $v = f(t) \in H$.
  《secret key》 $t \in \mathbf{Z}/n\mathbf{Z}$. 《public key》 $v = f(t) \in H$.
- [encryption] $m \in \mathbf{F}_q$: plain text, $r \in \mathbf{Z}/n\mathbf{Z}$: random number such that $x(rv) \neq 0$. $c_1 = f(r) \in H$. $c_2 = mx(rv) \in \mathbf{F}_q$. $(c_1, c_2) \in H \times \mathbf{F}_q$: ciphertext
- [decryption] $m = c_2/x(tc_1) \in \mathbf{F}_q$.

Menezes-Vanstone type cryptosystem

5 Attacks on EC Cryptosystems

The integrity of ECDLP cryptographic tools would be widely accepted, however, there exist two exceptional families of elliptic curves, i.e., supersingular and anomalous curves and for each case powerful cryptanalysis method has been invented. But both classes of elliptic curves may be easily avoided in practice.

These attacks reduce ECDLP to that in another group whose DLP is easy. Let G_1 and G_2 be groups, $\alpha \in G_1$, and $\beta \in \langle \alpha \rangle$.[19] Assume we have an injective group homomorphism $\rho : G_1 \to G_2$, and DLP in G_2 is solvable. Let h be the order of α. Since ρ is a group homomorphism, $\rho(\beta) \in \langle \rho(\alpha) \rangle$ and by the assumption, we obtain $m \in \mathbf{Z}/h\mathbf{Z}$[20] satisfying $\rho(\beta) = \rho(\alpha)^m = \rho(\alpha^m)$. This implies $\beta = \alpha^m$ because ρ is injective. Thus DLP in G_1 is solved. So all we have to do is to find G_2 whose DLP is solvable and to construct ρ which is easy to compute.

5.1 Supersingular Case – MOV Reduction

Menezes, Okamoto, and Vanstone[MOV93] have made the first significant contribution to the elliptic curve discrete logarithm problem. For certain classes of curve over

---

[19] The symbol $\langle \ \rangle$ stands for "the group generated by".

[20] The order of $\rho(\alpha)$ is exactly h by the injectivity of ρ.

fields $\mathbf{F}_q$, they show how to reduce the elliptic curve logarithm problem in a curve E over $\mathbf{F}_q$ to the discrete logarithm problem in an extension field $\mathbf{F}_{q^k}$ of $\mathbf{F}_q$. This technique is known as the Weil pairing that establishes an isomorphism between $\langle P \rangle$ and the subgroup of nth roots of unity in $\mathbf{F}_{q^k}$, where n denotes the order of P and is assumed to be relatively prime to p. A. Weil introduced the pairing on Abelian variety, which appears in [Wei48, (b), §XI]. For an elliptic curve E, it sets up

$$e_n : E[n] \times E[n] \to \overline{\mathbf{F}_q}^*.$$

(Recall that $E[n]$ is the group of n-torsion points. See Sect. 3.1.) For the MOV reduction, the following properties are crucial:[121]

1. Bilinearity : For all $P_1, P_2, P_3 \in E[n], e_n(P_1 + P_2, P_3) = e_n(P_1, P_3)e_n(P_2, P_3)$, and $e_n(P_1, P_2 + P_3) = e_n(P_1, P_2)e_n(P_1, P_3)$.
2. Alternation : For all $P_1, P_2 \in E[n], e_n(P_1, P_2) = e_n(P_2, P_1)^{-1}$.
3. Nondegeracy : If $e_n(P_1, P_2) = 1$ for all $P_2 \in E[n]$, then $P_1 = \mathcal{O}$.
4. Galois compatibility : If $E[n] \subset E(\mathbf{F}_{q^k})$, then $e_n(P_1, P_2) \in \mathbf{F}_{q^k}$, for all $P_1, P_2 \in E[n]$.[122]

Take (the minimum) $k \geq 1$ satisfying $E[n] \subset E(\mathbf{F}_{q^k})$. The bilinearity implies that for each $Q \in E[n]$, the map $\rho_Q : E[n] \to \mathbf{F}_{q^k}$ defined by $\rho_Q(P) = e_n(P, Q)$ is a group homomorphism. Note the value of ρ_Q lie in $\mathbf{F}_{q^k}$ by the Galois compatibility which is crucial for running time analysis. By the nondegeracy, for randomly selected Q, the probability of ρ_Q being injective is positive. Hence, sooner or later, we obtain injective ρ_Q. Evaluation of Weil pairing only requires probabilistic polynomial time by using algorithm due to Miller.[123]

It seems to be rare to obtain small k if curve is randomly selected. Indeed such a curve with prime order is very rare by [BK96, Theorem 2]. Thus the reduction procedure takes impractical time for the most of curves. However, for *supersingular* elliptic curves, k is small and the reduction needs probabilistic polynomial time, yielding a probabilistic sub-exponential-time elliptic curve logarithm algorithm. Here, an elliptic curve $E/\mathbf{F}_q$ is defined to be supersingular $t_{E,q} \equiv 0 \bmod p$ where $t_{E,q} := q + 1 - \sharp E(\mathbf{F}_q)$. This condition implies much more than its first look. In order that an elliptic curve $E/\mathbf{F}_q$ satisfying $t_{E,q} \equiv 0 \bmod p$ exists, it is necessary and sufficient that $t_{E,q}^2 = 0, q, 2q, 3q,$ or $4q$[Wat69, Theorem 4.1].[124] By the structure theorem on rational points of supersingular elliptic curves[Schf87, Lem. 4.8] one can prove a minimum value of k becomes to be 2, 3, 4, 6, and 1 for $t_{E,q}^2 = 0, q, 2q, 3q,$ and $4q$, respectively. See [MOV93, Table 1] for complete classification.

Remark 1. Semaev[Sem96] also describes an algorithm computing the Weil pairing and reduction of ECDLP to finite field DLP. Although [Sem96] does not state results corresponding to classification of supersingular curves and estimate of running time

---

[121] For the definition of Weil pairing on Elliptic curves, some other properties and the proofs, see [Sil86, III.8].

[122] Usually, this is written as $e_n(P_1, P_2)^\sigma = e_n(P_1^\sigma, P_2^\sigma)$ for all $\sigma \in \mathrm{Gal}(\overline{\mathbf{F}}_q/\mathbf{F}_q)$. But the above (somewhat weaker) statement is enough and convenient for our purpose.

[123] According to [MOV93], Miller's paper on this algorithm is unpublished. However, [MOV93, Appendix A] gives explicit description. See also [Sil86, Exercise 3.16].

[124] See also [Hon69], [Wat69, Chap. 2 and the last paragraph of §4.2].

explicitly ([MOV93, Table 1 and the proof of Th. 11]), [Sem96, p.70, ll.−9 ∼ −8] reads as follows: "Note that this result was obtained in 1990 and the method used can be applied to any Abelian manifold over a finite field."

Remark 2. Using Tate pairing, [FR94] reduces a discrete log problem in projective nonsingular curves of arbitrary genus to that in a finite field.[125]

5.2 Anomalous Case – Algebraic-Geometrical Approach and Number Theoretic Approach

Let p be a prime and q a power of p. The elliptic curve $E/\mathbf{F}_q$ is called to be *anomalous* if $E(\mathbf{F}_q)$ contains a p-torsion point other than $\mathcal{O}$, or equivalently the trace of q-th Frobenious map is congruent to 1 mod p.[126] To make situation clear, we provisionally call $E(\mathbf{F}_q)$ *purely anomalous* if $\sharp E(\mathbf{F}_q) = q$.[127] Under our definition, anomaly is a concept on a curve, whereas pure anomaly is another concept on a group of rational points. Hence pure anomaly depends on a field which determines rationality of points. We can solve p-part of discrete log problem for $E(\mathbf{F}_q)$ in *polynomial time*. There are two polynomial time algorithms to solve the p-part of an anomalous elliptic curve: algebraic geometrical approach by Semaev[Sem98] discovered in 1995, which is extended to a curve with arbitrary genus by Rück[Rüc97] and number theoretic approach by Smart[Sma97] and Satoh-Araki[SA97].

Especially, if $E(\mathbf{F}_q)$ is purely anomalous, we can solve the discrete log problem for $E(\mathbf{F}_q)$ completely. However, anomalous curves over $\mathbf{F}_{2^n}$ admit fast scalar multiplication algorithm[Kob92]. Since above algorithms produce nothing on p-primary part for $q > p$, the strength of carefully chosen anomalous curves over $\mathbf{F}_q$ with $q > p$ is still open.

The Rück's algorithm specialized to genus one runs as follows;[128] Let K be a field of characteristic $p > 0$ and $\overline{K}$ its algebraic closure. There is no non-trivial K-valued logarithm on K^*. However, for a *function* f on E, we can form $\Lambda(f) := \frac{df}{f}$. Note

$$\Lambda(fg) = \frac{d(fg)}{fg} = \frac{g\,df + f\,dg}{fg} = \Lambda(f) + \Lambda(g),$$

and hence $\Lambda(f^n) = n\Lambda(f)$. So, Λ behaves like a logarithmic differential even though there is no logarithm. As we have noted in 3.2, $\sum n_i[A_i] \in \operatorname{div}(E)$ is principal if and only if $\sum n_i = 0$ in $\mathbf{Z}$ and $\sum n_i A_i = \mathcal{O}$ in E. Therefore, if $A \in E[p]$, then there exists $f_A \in \overline{K}(E)$ satisfying

$$p([A] - [\mathcal{O}]) = \operatorname{div}(f_A).$$

---

[125] For hyperelliptic curve cryptosystems, which is out of scope of this survey, see e.g. Chap.6, §6 and Appendix[MWZ98] of [Kob98].

[126] The notion of anomalous curve is introduced by [Maz72] in slightly different context. Let $E/\mathbf{Q}$ be an elliptic curve and p a prime. Then Mazur called p an anomalous prime for E if E has a good reduction at p and the trace of the p-th Frobenious map is 1.

[127] Note for $E(\mathbf{F}_p)$ with $p \geq 7$, being purely anomalous and anomalous are equivalent since $|\sharp(E(\mathbf{F}_p)) - p - 1| \leq 2\sqrt{p}$.

[128] Semaev's algorithm is essentially the same as genus one case of Rück's algorithm. However, the latter runs faster than the former.

Although the function f_A is determined up to constant, $\Lambda(f_A)$ is well defined by A. The first key to Semaev-Rück algorithm is the following fact: the differential of a constant (or a fixed point) collapses to zero. However, the "logarithmic differential" $\Lambda(f_A)$ associated to A is nontrivial. The second key is that

$$\Lambda(f_{A+B}) = \Lambda(f_A) + \Lambda(f_B)$$

for $A, B \in E[p]$. Moreover, $A \to \Lambda(f_A)$ is a group isomorphism by [Sem98, Lemma 2], or more generally by [Ser58, Prop. 10]. Hence, $B = nA$ implies $\Lambda(f_B) = n\Lambda(f_A)$ and we obtain n. In practice, we need not treat functions on E. Let $c(f)$ be a constant term of the Laurent expansion of f around $\mathcal{O}$ (with respect to a fixed local parameter, say $t := -x/y$).[129] We can compute $c(\Lambda(f_A))$ directly with $O(\log p)$ arithmetic operations in $\overline{K}$.[130] Then, clearly $n = c(\Lambda(f_B))/c(\Lambda(f_A))$.

So far, we did not use anomaly of E. Now assume $K = \mathbf{F}_p$ and $E/\mathbf{F}_p$ is an anomalous elliptic curve. Then all p-torsion points of E are $\mathbf{F}_p$ rational. We need only arithmetic operations in $\mathbf{F}_p$ to compute $c(\Lambda(f_A))$ for $A \in E[p] = E(\mathbf{F}_p)$.

On the other hand, the method of Smart/Satoh-Araki is number theoretic. The differentiation of the number is clearly zero. But we have the differential-like operator studied by Eisenstein in 1850. Let p be a prime and a an integer prime to p. We call

$$L_p(a) := \frac{a^{p-1} - 1}{p} \bmod p \in \mathbf{F}_p$$

the *Fermat quotient* of a with base p.[131] Then,

$$L_p(ab) = L_p(a) + L_p(b)$$
$$L_p(a + p) = L_p(a) - a^{-1}$$

where a^{-1} is the inverse element of a in $\mathbf{F}_p$. Observe that L_p induces $\mathbf{F}_p$-valued logarithm defined over $(\mathbf{Z}/p^2\mathbf{Z})^*$. Lerch[Ler05] generalized the Fermat quotient in case of not necessarily prime base case. Ihara[Iha92] reformulated the Fermat quotient in view of modern number theory and arithmetic algebraic geometry. The method of Smart/Satoh-Araki is construction of an elliptic curve version of the Fermat quotient.[132] So, we call this algorithm "the Fermat quotient attack".

Its tool is the p-adic number field $\mathbf{Q}_p$. To define $\mathbf{Q}_p$ or the ring of p-adic integers

---

[129] If f is regular at $\mathcal{O}$ (i.e. the denominator of f is not zero at $\mathcal{O}$), then $c(f)$ is independent of choice of a local parameter.

[130] The explicit procedure runs as follows. We define a binary operation $\oplus$ on $G := E \times \overline{\mathbf{F}_q}$ by $(A, a) \oplus (B, b) = (A + B, a + b + \delta(A, B))$. Here $\delta(A, B)$ is a slope of the line passing through A and B (as usual, the tangent line at A if $A = B$) except for $A = -B$ in which case we put $\delta(A, B) = 0$. It is not so difficult to verify that G is an Abelian group under $\oplus$. Especially $\oplus$ is associative. Then $c(\Lambda(f_A))$ is given by the second component of $(A, 0) \oplus \cdots \oplus (A, 0)$ (p times). Since $\oplus$ is associative, at most $2\log_2 p$ times compuation of $\oplus$ is necessary.

[131] Note $\frac{a^{p-1}-1}{p}$ is always an integer due to Fermat's little theorem. After computing $\frac{a^{p-1}-1}{p}$ in characteristic zero, we take $\bmod p$ to obtain $L_p(a)$. Note also, it is enough to compute $a^{p-1} \bmod p^2$ to obtain $L_p(a)$.

[132] See [OU98b] on relation to a certain ID-based cryptosystem. There is an another application[OU98a] of the (ordinal) Fermat quotient to a new cryptosystem due to Okamoto and Uchiyama.

Z_p rigorously needs rather long description.[133] Here we note the following facts: They have good property under the "limit". The "unit disk" of Q_p is just Z_p. There is the reduction map $\bmod p : Z_p \to F_p$, which is a ring homomorphism. In other words, Q_p and Z_p have nice properties for both analysis and algebra.

Let $\tilde{E}$ be an anomalous elliptic curve defined over F_p for simplicity and E its lifting to characteristic zero.[134] Then, anomalous elliptic curve analogue of a^{p-1} is pA for $A \in E$. We fix a lifting $u : \tilde{E}(F_p) \to E(Q_p)$. Regarding E as a curve over Q_p, E has an logarithm $\log_E$, called Formal logarithm, by nature (see [Sil86, Chap.IV]). However, $\log_E$ converges only on a certain neighborhood $\mathcal{N}$ of $\mathcal{O}$. By the anomaly of $\tilde{E}$, it follows that the map λ_E defined by

$$\lambda_E : \tilde{E}(F_p) \xrightarrow{u} E(Q_p) \xrightarrow{\times p} \mathcal{N} \xrightarrow{\log_E} pZ_p \xrightarrow{\bmod p^2} pZ_p/p^2Z_p \cong F_p$$

is a group homomorphism. Moreover, λ_E is independent of choice of u (but depends on E). For $p \geq 7$, we have only to compute everything in Z/p^2Z to evaluate λ_E.[135] If it is a non-zero map, it must be an isomorphism. Thus, we can solve discrete log problem for $\tilde{E}(F_p)$. Otherwise, we construct another lift E' of $\tilde{E}$ (using coefficients of E) so that $\lambda_{E'}$ is an isomorphism[SA97, Th. 3.7].

5.3 Minimum Requirement for Secure EC Cryptosystems

As far as the authors know, the sufficient condition for elliptic curve cryptosystem to be secure is not known yet. However, as we have seen, there are some necessary conditions. Let E/F_q (q: a power of a prime p) be an elliptic curve and $A \in E(F_q)$ be a base point of elliptic curve cryptosystem. Then E and A should, at least, satisfy the following:

- The order h of A should be divisible by a large prime other than p.[136] At least, $E(F_q)$ must not be purely anomalous.[137]
- Let $p_1, \ldots, p_N$ be primes dividing h which is ether small or equal to p. Write $h = h' \prod_{i=1}^{N} p_i^{e_i}$ where h' is prime to any of p_i. There should be no injective

---

[133] See [Ser73], [Cas91], or any other text on modern number theory. Note Z_p is *not* Z/pZ. The symbol Z_p is reserved for the ring of p-adic integers in the number theory.

[134] More specifically, for $\tilde{E} : Y^2 = X^3 + \tilde{a}_4 X + \tilde{a}_6$, take any integer a_i satisfying $a_i \bmod p = \tilde{a}_i$. Then, define E by $E : Y^2 = X^3 + a_4 X + a_6$.

[135] The explicit algorithm runs as follows. Let (X_1, Y_1) be a lift of $A = (x, y) \in \tilde{E}(F_p)$ to $E(Z/p^2Z)$. For example, take $\xi, \eta \in Z$ satisfying $\xi \bmod p = x$ and $\eta \bmod p = y$. Put $X_1 = \xi \bmod p^2$ and $Y_1 = (\eta + pw) \bmod p^2$ where $2\eta w = \frac{X_1^3 + a_4 X_1 + a_6 - \eta^2}{p} \bmod p$. Compute $(X_{p-1}, Y_{p-1}) = (p-1)(X_1, Y_1)$ on $E(Z/p^2Z)$, which requires at most $2\log_2 p$ additions on the curve. Then

$$\lambda_E(A) = \begin{cases} \left(\frac{X_{p-1} - X_1}{p} \bmod p\right)(Y_{p-1} - Y_1 \bmod p)^{-1} & \text{if } X_{p-1} \neq X_1 \bmod p^2, \\ 0 & \text{otherwise.} \end{cases}$$

See [SA97, Cor. 3.6] for proof.

[136] This simultaneously avoids [Sha71], [Pol78], [PH78] and attacks described in 5.2.

[137] Both Semaev-Rück method and Fermat quotient attack were actually implemented by Mr. N. Takeshita at Araki Lab. Tokyo Inst. Tech. Their running time on Pentium-Pro with 200MHz clock, are as follows.

homomorphism $\rho : E[h'] \to \mathbf{F}_{q^k}^*$ with small k. At least, E should not be super-singular.

6 Standardization and Commercialization of EC Cryptosystems

Although the IEEE is an academic institution in U.S.A., it is also engaging in the standardizations in the fields of electrical, electronics, communication and computer technologies, and there are a lot of working groups for the standardizations. Among them, P1363 is dealing with standardization for public-key cryptography, and the IEEE P1363 Standard is currently under development, with the first version expected to be ready for balloting in 1998. An addendum to the standard (known as P1363a) has also currently revised, in which it is pointed out that two families of elliptic curves (the *supersingular* and the *anomalous*) should be excluded in the standardization for EC parameter generation and verification, because they have less security.[IEEE98]

As approved at the November 1996 meeting, the discrete logarithm problem in the group of points on an elliptic curve over a finite field (EC) was selected as a cryptographic function in the first version of IEEE P1363 standard. For the EC family, the standard will mirror the DL family; the only significant difference is the change in the underlying group.

Several ECDLP cryptographic tools have already been commercially available, which are offered by several companies, e.g., NTT, Matsushita (both in Japan), Certicom (in Canada) and Siemens (in German). They are implemented in a form of software and IC chip.

7 Construction of Elliptic Curves with a Specified Number of Rational Points

To obtain elliptic curves satisfying conditions mentioned in 5.3, two methods are known.

- Search a suitable r for which $E(\mathbf{F}_{q^r})$ has a desired property by Weil conjecture[138] where E is defined over $\mathbf{F}_q$ with small q: [BS91].
- Construct $E/\mathbf{F}_p$ satisfying $\#E(\mathbf{F}_p) = n$ for given n: [Mor91], [LZ94].

Bit size of p	100	150	200	400
Running time of Fermat quotient attack(sec.)	0.81	2.30	4.72	21.9
Running time of Rück algorithm with $g = 1$(sec.)	0.68	1.75	3.52	14.37

[138] Referencing this as "Weil conjecture" is just conventional. We note, as far as curves are concerned, this was already *proved* by [Wei48] before Weil presented conjectures in [Wei49]. Let V be a nonsingular complete algebraic variety of dimension n defined over $\mathbf{F}_q$. (Elliptic curves are examples for $n = 1$.) Define congruence zeta function Z_V by

$$Z_V(u) = \exp\left(\sum_{m=1}^{\infty} \frac{\#V(\mathbf{F}_{q^m})}{m} u^m \right).$$

Weil conjectured the following series of properties of $Z_V(u)$. Rationality: $Z_V(u)$ is a rational function of u. Functional equation: $Z_V((q^n u)^{-1}) = \pm q^{n\chi/2} u^{\chi} Z_V(u)$, with some

Here we review the latter method. Let $p > 5$ be a prime and $E/\mathbf{F}_p$ an elliptic curve. We call $f : E \to E$ is an *endomorphism* of E if f is a rational map and a group homomorphism. The set of such maps forms a not necessarily commutative ring $\mathrm{End}(E)$ with multiplication by composition of maps. By Hasse's inequality,

$$|\#E(\mathbf{F}_p) - p - 1| \leq 2\sqrt{p}.$$

Conversely, for a given integer N satisfying $|N - p - 1| \leq 2\sqrt{p}$, Morain[Mor91] constructed an algorithm to produce an elliptic curve E over $\mathbf{F}_p$ satisfying $\#(E(\mathbf{F}_p)) = p + 1 + N$. We limit ourselves to the case $N \neq 0$, i.e. E is non-supersingular. Then, $\mathrm{End}(E)$ is an order of an imaginary quadratic field[Sil86, Theorem V.3.1]. Hence, there exist a negative square free integer d and positive integer f such that

$$\mathrm{End}(E) = \mathbf{Z} + f\omega_d\mathbf{Z} \quad \text{where} \quad \omega_d = \begin{cases} \frac{1+\sqrt{d}}{2} & (d \equiv 1 \bmod 4), \\ \sqrt{d} & (d \equiv 2, 3 \bmod 4). \end{cases}$$

In $\mathrm{End}(E)$, the p-th Frobenious map φ satisfies

$$\varphi^2 - N\varphi + p = 0.$$

Write $N^2 - 4p = s^2 t$ where t is squarefree and put

$$s' = \begin{cases} s & (d \equiv 1 \bmod 4), \\ s/2 & (d \equiv 2, 3 \bmod 4). \end{cases}$$

Since $\varphi \in \mathrm{End}(E)$, we see $t = d$ and s' is a multiple of f. Conversely, assume $E/\mathbf{F}_p$ is an elliptic curve such that $\mathrm{End}(E) = \mathbf{Z} + f\omega_d\mathbf{Z}$ and that $N^2 - 4p = s^2 d$ with $f|s'$.

$\chi \in \mathbf{Z}$. Riemann Hypothesis on V: there exists polynomials $P_0(u), \ldots, P_{2n}(u)$ (depending on V) of u with integer coefficients such that $Z_V(u) = \prod_{i=0}^{2n} P_i(u)^{(-1)^{i+1}}$ and that absolute values of roots of $P_i(u) = 0$ are $q^{-i/2}$. Degree of P_i: If V is a reduction of algebraic variety V^* in characteristic zero, $\deg P_i$ is i-th Betti number of V^* (which is an integer concerning geometric shape of V^*).

Let us observe consequence of these conjectures for an elliptic curve $E/\mathbf{F}_q$. The rationality of $Z_V(u)$ implies that one can compute $\#E(\mathbf{F}_{q^m})$ recursively from the finitely many numbers $\#E(\mathbf{F}_q), \ldots, \#E(\mathbf{F}_{q^M})$. It is known that the first Betti number of (lift of) an algebraic curve is two times of its genus. Then, functional equation implies only $\#E(\mathbf{F}_q)$ is enough to compute $\#E(\mathbf{F}_{q^m})$ for all $m \geq 1$. The Riemann Hypothesis gives bounds of the numbers of rational points, which is nothing but Hasse's inequality[Has36] (cf. [Sil86, Theorem V.1.1]): $|\#E(\mathbf{F}_q) - q - 1| \leq 2\sqrt{q}$.

Today, Weil conjectures are completely proved. First, Dwork[Dwo60] proved the rationality of $Z_V(u)$. Grothendieck and M.Artin[Gro77] made the theory of "étale cohomology" and settled all these conjectures except for the Riemann Hypothesis on V, which is very deep. Finally Deligne[Del74], [Del80] completed the proof of the Riemann Hypothesis on V. For outline of proof, see e.g. [Kat76] or [Tho77]. Note, many texts state that congruence zeta functions are first studied by E.Artin[Art24]. This history is incorrect. It is Kornblum(1890–1914)[Kor19] that studied congruence zeta functions first. His name appears in [Art24] four times but the title of Kornblum's paper is not mentioned at all. (The second author would like to thank Prof. Nobushige Kurokawa at Dept. Math., Tokyo Inst. Technology for informing him of [Kor19].)

For simplicity, we consider the case $d \neq -1, -3$.[139] Under this restriction, $\hat{\varphi}\varphi = p$ guarantees $\text{Tr}(\varphi) = \pm N$ where $\hat{\varphi}$ is the dual isogeny of φ (see [Sil86, Theorem III.6.1]).[140] If $\text{Tr}(\varphi) = -N$, then $\sharp E(\mathbf{F}_p) = N + p + 1$. Otherwise, twist[141] E' of E satisfies $\sharp E'(\mathbf{F}_p) = N + p + 1$. Therefore, the problem is reduced to the construction of an elliptic curve E such that $\text{End}(E) = \mathbf{Z} + f\omega_d\mathbf{Z}$.[142] Using complex analytic theory of elliptic curves, we can construct an elliptic curve $E_0/\mathbf{C}$ whose endomorphism ring is $\mathbf{Z} + f\omega_d\mathbf{Z}$. By [Deu41] (cf. [Lan87, Theorem 13.12(ii)]),[143] the endomorphism ring of the reduction $\bmod p$ of E_0 is also $\mathbf{Z} + f\omega_d\mathbf{Z}$. In practice we can construct an elliptic curve isomorphic to the reduction $\bmod p$ of E_0 without constructing E_0, which is enough for our purpose. The j-invariant of E_0 is an algebraic integer[Sil94, Theorem II.6.1]. We first compute the minimal polynomial H of j-invariant of E_0 by the algorithm [AM93], [Coh93, Chap. 7]. Let a be one of roots of $H(x) \equiv 0 \bmod p$.[144] The elliptic curve $E/\mathbf{F}_p$ defined by

$$E : \begin{cases} Y^2 = X^3 - 1 & (a = 0), \\ Y^2 = X^3 - X & (a = 1728), \\ Y^2 = X^3 - 3cX + 2c & (\text{otherwise, where } c = a/(a - 1728)) \end{cases}$$

has j-invariant a[145] and $\text{End}(E) = \mathbf{Z} + f\omega_d\mathbf{Z}$. If $\sharp E(\mathbf{F}_p) = p + 1 + N$, we are done. Otherwise, we construct its twist E', which must have a desired property.

References

[Adl79] L. M. Adleman: A subexponential algorithm for the discrete logarithm problem with applications to cryptography, Proc. of FOCS, pp.56-60(1979)

---

[139] For $d = -1, -3$, the unit group of $\mathbf{Z} + \omega_d\mathbf{Z}$ is not $\{\pm 1\}$ and additional consideration is necessary.

[140] The expression $N^2 - 4p = s^2 d$ implies

$$p = \begin{cases} \left(\frac{N-s}{2} + s\omega_d\right)\left(\frac{N+s}{2} - s\omega_d\right) & d \equiv 1 \bmod 4, \\ \left(\frac{N}{2} + \frac{s}{2}\omega_d\right)\left(\frac{N}{2} - \frac{s}{2}\omega_d\right) & d \equiv 2, 3 \bmod 4. \end{cases}$$

i.e., p splits to a product of two principal prime ideals of $\text{End}(E)$, while $\hat{\varphi}\varphi = p$. By $\varphi \notin \mathbf{Z}$ (in $\text{End}(E)$, cf. [Iha67, Prop. 4']) and the uniqueness of prime ideal decomposition, $\text{Tr}(\varphi) = \pm N$. See also [Cas66, p. 242, Footnote §].

[141] Mathematically, twist $E'/\mathbf{F}_p$ of $E/\mathbf{F}_p$ is any elliptic curve over $\mathbf{F}_p$ which is isomorphic to E over $\overline{\mathbf{F}}_p$. (So, E is clearly one of twist of E.) However, in elliptic curve cryptography, it is usually implicit that E' is not isomorphic to E over $\mathbf{F}_p$. For the curve $E : Y^2 = X^3 + AX + B$ with $A, B \neq 0$, twist of E (non-isomorphic to E over $\mathbf{F}_p$) is unique up to $\mathbf{F}_p$-isomorphism, and given by $E' : Y^2 = X^3 + D^2AX + D^3B$, where $D \in \mathbf{F}_p^*$ is any non-square.

[142] To reduce computational time, we may always take $f = 1$. However, the authors do not know whether such a specific curve has a special vulnerability or not.

[143] Since $|N| \leq 2\sqrt{p}$, we see f is not divisible by p.

[144] Note all the roots of $H(x) \equiv 0 \bmod p$ belong to $\mathbf{F}_p$ ([Lan87, Theorem 14.1]). Hence they are obtained by the factorization algorithm for a polynomial over a finite field [Ber70], [CZ81] (cf. [Coh93, Chap. 3.4]).

[145] Actually, the cases $a = 0$ or 1728 do not happen since we assumed $d \neq -1, -3$.

[ADH94] L. M. Adleman, J. DeMarrais, M.-D. Huang: A subexponential algorithm for discrete logarithms over the rational subgroup of the Jacobians of large genus hyperelliptic curves over finite fields, in Algorithmic number theory (Ithaca, NY, 1994), Lecture Notes in Comput. Sci., 877(1994), 28–40, Springer: Berlin.

[AM93] A.O.L. Atkin, F. Morain: Elliptic curves and primality proving, Math. Comp. 61(1993), 29–68.

[Art24] E. Artin: Quadratische Körper im Gebiet der höheren Kongruenzen, Math. Z., 19(1924) 153–246.

[BK96] R. Balasubramanian, N. Koblitz: The improbability that an elliptic curve has subexponential discrete log problem under the Menezes-Okamoto-Vanstone algorithm, preprint (1996), to appear in J. Cryptology.

[Ber70] E. Berlekamp: Factoring polynomials over large finite fields, Math. Comp. 24(1970), 713–735.

[BS91] T. Beth, F. Schaefer: Non supersingular elliptic curves for public key cryptosystems, Proc. EUROCRYPT'91, Lect. Notes in Comput. Sci. vol.547(1991), 316–327.

[Cas66] J.W.S. Cassels: Diophantine equations with special reference to elliptic curves, J. London Math. Soc, 41(1966) 193–291. Corrigenda: ibid, 42(1967) 183.

[Cas91] J.W.S. Cassels: Lectures on elliptic curves, London Math. Soc. student texts vol.24(1991), Cambridge UP: Cambridge.

[CM94] J.-M. Couveignes, F. Morain: Schoof's algorithm and isogeny cycles, in Algorithmic number theory (Ithaca, NY, 1994), Lecture Notes in Comput. Sci., 877(1994), 43–58, Springer: Berlin.

[Coh93] H. Cohen: A course in computational algebraic number theory, GTM vol.138(1993) Springer: Berlin.

[Cop84] D. Coppersmith: Fast evalution of logarithms in fields of characteristics two, IEEE Trans. Info. Theory, IT-30(1984), 587–594

[CZ81] D. Cantor, H. Zassenhaus: A new algorithm for factoring polynomials over finite fields, Math. Comp. 36(1981), 587–592.

[Del74] P. Deligne: La conjecture de Weil, I. Publ. IHES, 43(1974) 273–307.

[Del80] P. Deligne: La conjecture de Weil, II. Publ. IHES, 52(1980) 137–252.

[Deu41] M. Deuring: Die Typen der Multiplikatorenringe elliptischer Funktionenkörper, Abh. Math. Sem. Hamburg, 14(1941) 197–272

[DH76] D.E.Diffie and M.Hellman: New directions in cryptography, IEEE Trans. Info. Theory, IT-22(1976), 644–654

[Dwo60] B. Dwork: On the rationality of the zeta-function of an algebraic variety. Amer. J. Math., 82(1960) 631–648.

[ElG85] T. El Gamal: A public key cryptosystem and a signature scheme based on discrete logarithms, IEEE Trans. Info. Theory, IT-31(1985), 469–472

[Fal83] G. Faltings: Endlichkeitssätze für Abelsche Varietäten über Zahlkörpern, Invent. Math., 73(1983), 349–366.

[FR94] G. Frey, H.-G. Rück: A remark concerning m-divisibility and the discrete logarithm in the divisor class group of curves. Math. Comp. 62(1994) 865–874.

[Ful69] W. Fulton: Algebraic curves (1969), Benjamin: Menlo Park.

[Gor92] D. M. Gordon: Designing and detecting trapdoors for discrete log cryptosystems, Proc. of CRYPTO'92, LNCS 740(1992), pp. 66–75.

[Gro77] A. Grothendieck: Cohomologie l-adique et fonctions L (SGA5), Lect. Notes in Math. vol. 589, Springer-Verlag: Berlin. (1977)

[Har77] R. Hartshorne: Algebraic geometry, GTM vol.52(1977), Springer-Verlag: Berlin.

[Has36] H. Hasse: Zur Theorie der abstrakten elliptischen Funktionenkörper, III, J. Reine Angew. Math., 175(1936), 193–208.

[Hon69] T. Honda: Isogeny classes of abelian varieties over finite fields, J. Math. Soc. Japan, 20(1968), 83–95.

[IEEE98] IEEE P1363 Annex A/Editorial Contribution: Standard Specifications For Public Key Cryptography, available at http://grouper.ieee.org/groups/1363/

[Iha67] Y. Ihara: Hecke polynomials as congruence ζ functions in elliptic modular case, Ann. Math. 85(1967), 267–295.

[Iha92] Y. Ihara: On Fermat quotients and "the differential of numbers", in: Algebraic analysis and number theory Koukyuuroku vol.810(1992), 324–341, RIMS, Kyoto Univ: Kyoto, (in Japanese).

[Kat76] N. Katz: An overview of Deligne's proof of the Riemann hypothesis for varieties over finite fields, Proc. Symp. Pure Math. 28(1976) 275–305.

[Knu81] D.E. Knuth: The art of computer programming. Vol.2 Seminumerical algorithms, 2nd ed. Addison wesley:Reading, Mass., 1981.

[Kob87] N. Koblitz: Elliptic curve cryptosystems, Math. Comp.48,(1987) 203–209

[Kob92] N. Koblitz: CM-curves with good cryptographic properties, in Advances in cryptology—CRYPTO '91 (Santa Barbara, CA, 1991), 279–287, Lecture Notes in Comput. Sci., vol.576(1992) Springer-Verlag:Berlin.

[Kob95] N. Koblitz: A course in number theory and cryptography(Second edition). Graduate Texts in Mathematics, vol.114(1994). Springer-Verlag:Berlin.

[Kob98] N. Koblitz: Algebraic aspects of cryptography. Algorithms and Compuation in Math. vol.3(1998)

[Kor19] H. Kornblum: Über die Primfunktionen in einer arithmetischen Progression. Math. Z., 5(1919) 100–111.

[Kra22] M. Kraitchik: Théorie des nombres, vol.1 Gauthier-Villars: Paris, 1922

[Lan87] S. Lang: Elliptic functions (2nd ed.), GTM vol.112(1987), Springer-Verlag:Berlin.

[Ler05] A. M. Lerch: Zur Theorie des Fermatschen Quotienten $\frac{a^{p-1}-1}{p} = q(a)$, Math. Ann., 60(1905), 471–490.

[LG88] J.H. van Lint, G. van der Geer: Introduction to coding theory and algebraic geometry, DMV seminar vol.12(1988), Birkhäuser: Basel.

[LZ94] G.-J. Lay, H. G. Zimmer: Constructing elliptic curves with given group order over large finite fields, in Algorithmic number theory (Ithaca, NY, 1994), Lecture Notes in Comput. Sci., 877(1994), 250–263, Springer: Berlin.

[Maz72] B. Mazur: Rational points of Abelian varieties with values in towers of number fields, Invent. Math., 18(1972), 183–266.

[McC90] K. S. McCurley: The discrete logarithm problem, in Cryptology and computational number theory, (Boulder, CO, 1989), Proc. Sympos. Appl. Math. vol.42(1990), 49–74, AMS:Providence, R.I.

[Men93] A. Menezes: Elliptic curve public key cryptosystems. Kluwer academic publ.:Boston, 1993

[Mil86] V. S. Miller: Use of elliptic curves in cryptography, in Advances in cryptology-CRYPTO '85 (Santa Barbara, Calif., 1985), Lecture Notes in Comput. Sci. vol. 218(1986), 417–426, Springer: Berlin.

[Mor91] F. Morain: Building cyclic elliptic curves modulo large primes, in Advances in cryptology—EUROCRYPT '91 (Brighton, 1991), 328–336, Lecture Notes in Comput. Sci., vol. 547(1991), Springer: Berlin.

[Mor95] F. Morain: Calcul du nombre de points sur une curbe elliptique dans un corps fini: aspects algorithmieques, J. Théorie des Nombres de Bordeaux, 7(1995), 255–282.

[MOV93] A.J. Menezes, T. Okamoto and S.A. Vanstone: Reducing elliptic curve logarithms to logarithms in a finite field, The 23rd Annual ACM Symposium on Theory of Computing, New Orleans, LA, May 1991, and also IEEE Trans. Info. Theory, IT-39(1993), 1639–1646.

[MV90] A. Menezes, S. Vanstone: The implementation of elliptic curve cryptosystems, Proc. of AUSCRYPT 90, Lect. Notes in Comput. Science, vol.453(1990), 2-13, Springer: Berlin.

[MWZ98] A. Menezes, Y. Wu, R. Zucchertato: Hyperelliptic curves, appendix to Koblitz: Algebraic aspects of cryptography, Springer: Berlin.

[NIST91] National Institute for Standards and Technology: Specifications for a digital signature standard. Federal information processing standard publication 186(1991).

[NIST92] National Institute for Standards and Technology: The digital signature standard, Comm. of the ACM, 35(1992), No.7, pp. 36–40.

[Odl85] A.M. Odlyzko: Discrete logarithm and their cryptographic significance, in Advances in cryptology — EUROCRYPT '84, Lect. Notes in Comput. Sci. vol.209(1985), pp. 224–314

[Odl94] A.M. Odlyzko: Discrete logarithms and smooth polynomials, in Finite fields: Theory, applications, and algorithms, Contemp. Math. vol.168(1994), 269–278.

[OU98a] T. Okamoto, S. Uchiyama: A new public-key cryptosystem as secure as factoring, to appear in EUROCRYPT'98.

[OU98b] T. Okamoto, S. Uchiyama: Security of an identity-based cryptosystem and the related reductions, to appear in EUROCRYPT'98.

[PH78] S.C. Pohlig and M.E. Hellman: An improved algorithm for computing logarithm over $GF(p)$ and its cryptographic significance, IEEE Trans. Info. Theory, IT-24(1978), 106–110.

[Pol78] J. Pollard: Monte Carlo methods for index compuation ((mod p)), Math. Comp., 32(1978), 918–924.

[Rüc97] H. G. Rück: On the Discrete Logarithm in the Divisor Class Group of Curves, preprint, (1997).

[SA97] T. Satoh, K. Araki: Fermat quotients and the polynomial time discrete log algorithm for anomalous elliptic curves, (1997), preprint, to appear in Commentarii Math. Univ. St. Pauli. [Japanese exposition in: Proc. of algebraic number theory and its related topics, Koukyuuroku vol.1026(1998), .pp. 139–150, RIMS Kyoto Univ.:Kyoto.]

[Schf85] R. Schoof: Elliptic curves over finite fields and the computation of square roots (mod p), Math. Comp., 44(1985), 483–494.

[Schf87] R. Schoof: Nonsingular plane cubic curves over finite fields, J. Comb. Theory, A46(1987), 183–211.

[Schn91] C. P. Schnorr: Efficient signature generation by smart cards, J. Cryptology, 4(1991), 161–174.

[Sem96] I. A. Semaev: On computing logarithms on elliptic curves. (Russian) Diskret. Mat. 8(1996) 65–71. English translation in Discrete Math. Appl. 6(1996), 69–76.

[Sem98] I. A. Semaev: Evaluation of discrete logarithms in a group of p-torsion points of an elliptic curves in characteristic p, Math. Comp., 67(1998), 353–356.

[Ser58] J.-P. Serre: Sur la topologie des variétés algébriques en caractéristique p. Symposium internacional de topología algbraica, 1958, 24-53, Universidad Nacional Autónoma de México and UNESCO: Mexico City

[Ser73] J.-P. Serre: A course in arithmetic, GTM vol.7(1973), Springer: Berlin.

[Sha71] D. Shanks: Class number, a theory of factorization, and genera, in 1969 Number Theory Institute, Proc. Symp. Pure. Math. vol.20(1971), 415–440 AMS:Providence, R.I.

[Sil86] J. H. Silverman: The arithmetic of elliptic curves, GTM vol.106(1986), Springer-Verlag:Berlin. (2nd printing: 1992)

[Sil94] J. H. Silverman: The advanced arithmetic of elliptic curves, GTM vol.151(1994), Springer-Verlag:Berlin.

[Sma97] N. P. Smart: The discrete logarithm problem on elliptic curves of trace one, (1997), preprint, to appear in J. Cryptology.

[Tho77] A. D. Thomas: Zeta-functions: an introduction to algebraic geometry. Research notes in Math. Vol.12(1977), Pitman: London.

[Wat69] W.C. Waterhouse: Abelian varieties over finite fields, Ann. sci. Éc. Norm. Sup., 4^{e}série, 2(1969), 521–586.

[Wei48] A. Weil: (a) Sur les courbes algébriques et les variétés qui s'en déduisent, (b) Variétés abéliennes et courbes algébriques, Actualités Sci. Ind., Hermann:Paris 1948. [The collected second edition of (a) and (b): Courbes algébriques et variétés abéliennes, ibid, 1971.]

[Wei49] A. Weil: Numbers of solutions of equations in finite fields, Bull. Amer. Math. Soc. 55(1949), 497-508.

Lattices and Cryptography: An Overview

Jacques Stern
Jacques.Stern@ens.fr

Ecole Normale Supieure
Laboratoire d'informatique
45, rue d'Ulm
75230 Paris Cedex 05

Abstract. We briefly discuss the history of lattices and cryptography during the last fifteen years.

A lattice is a discrete subgroup of $\mathbf{R}^n$ or equivalently the set L

$$\lambda_1 b_1 + \cdots + \lambda_p b_p$$

of all integral linear combination of a given set of independant n-dimensional vectors $b_1, \cdots, b_p$. The sequnece $(b_1, \cdots, b_p)$ is said to be a basis of L and p is its dimension.

From the mathematical point of view, the history of lattice reduction goes back to the theory of quadratic forms developed by Lagrange, Gauss, Hermite, Korkine-Zolotareff and others (see [Lag73, Gau01, Her50, KZ73]) and to Minkowski's geometry of numbers ([Min10]).

With the advent of algorithmic number theory, the subject had a revival around 1980. Two basic problems have emerged: the shortest vector problem (SVP) and the closest vector problem (CVP). SVP refers to the question of computing the lattice vector with minimum non-zero euclidean length while CVP addresses the non-homogeneous analog of finding a lattice element minimizing the distance to a given vector. It has been known for some time that CVP is NP-complete [Boa81] and Ajtai has recently proved that SVP is NP-hard for polynomial random reductions [Ajt97].

The celebrated LLL algorithm computes a so-called *reduced basis* of a lattice and provides a partial answer to SVP since it runs in polynomial time and approximates the shortest vector within a factor of $2^{n/2}$. Actually, a reduction algorithm of the same flavor had already been included in Lenstra's work on integer programming (cf. [Len83], circulated around 1979) and the lattice reduction algorithm reached a final form in the paper [LLL82] of Lenstra, Lenstra and Lovász, from which the name *LLL algorithm* comes. Further refinements of the LLL algorithm were proposed by Schnorr ([Sch87, Sch88]), who has improved the above factor into $(1 + \epsilon)^n$. Babai [Bab86] gave an algorithm that approximates the closest vector by a factor of $(3/\sqrt{2})^n$. The existence of polynomial bounds is completely open: CVP is hard to approximate within a factor $2^{(\log n)^{0.99}}$ as shown in [ABSS97] but a result of Goldreich and Goldwasser [GG] suggests that it is hopeless to try to extend this inapproximability result to $\sqrt{n}$.

The relevance of lattice reduction algorithms to cryptography was immediately understood: in April 1982, Shamir ([Sha82]) found a polynomial time algorithm breaking the Merkle-Hellman public key cryptosystem ([MH78]) based on the knapsack problem, that had been basically the unique alternative to RSA. Shamir used Lenstra's integer programming algorithm but, the same year, Adleman ([Adl83]) extended Shamir's work by treating the cryptographic problem as a lattice problem rather than a linear programming problem. Further improvements of these methods were obtained by Brickell ([Bri84, Bri85]), by Lagarias and Odlyzko ([LO85]), and, more recently by Coster, La Macchia, Odlyzko, Schnorr and the authors ([CJL+92]).

Lattice reduction has also been applied successfully in various other cryptographic contexts: against a version of Blum's protocol for exchanging secrets ([FHK+88]), against truncated linear congruential generators ([FHK+88, Ste87]), for guessing ℓ-th root modulo an integer n ([VGT88]), against cryptosystems based on rational numbers ([ST90]) or modular knapsacks ([JS91, CJS91]), and, more recently, against RSA with exponent 3 ([Cop96]), against RSA signatures with redundancy ([GM97, Mis97] and also in order to attack a new cryptosystem proposed by Hoffstein, Pipher and Silverman under the name NTRU (see [CS97]).

Recently, in a beautiful paper, Ajtai [Ajt96] discovered a fascinating connection between the worst-case complexity and the average-case complexity of some well-known lattice problems. More precisely, he established a reduction from the problem of finding the shortest non zero element u of a lattice provided that it is "unique" (*i.e.* that it is polynomially shorter than any other element of the lattice which is not linearly related) to the problem of approximating SVP for randomly chosen instances of a specific class of lattices. This reduction was improved in [CN97]. Later, Ajtai and Dwork [AD97] proposed a cryptosystem based on Ajtai's theorem. Actually, they introduced three such systems which we will describe as AD1, AD2 and AD3 and showed that the third was provably secure under the assumption that the "unique" shortest vector problem considered above is difficult. The same year, Goldreich, Goldwasser and Halevy [GGH97] proposed another cryptosystem based on lattices.

Again, from a theoretical point of view, the achievement in the Ajtai-Dwork paper is a masterpiece. However, its practical significance is unclear. At the "rump" session of CRYPTO'97, Phong Nguyen, Victor Shoup and the author reported on initial experiments on the cryptosystem AD1: their conclusion was that, in order to be secure, practical implementations of AD1 would require lattices of very high dimension. This would lead to a totally impractical system requiring a message of more than one megabyte to simply exchange a DES key. At the same rump session, Claus Schnorr and his students announced that they had broken many instances of the acheme proposed by Goldreich, Goldwasser and Halevy. Later, my student Phong Nguyen could break even larger instances.

Does this mean that lattice cryptosystems cannot be practically viable. Extensive experiments have to be carried but there is some theoretical indication that it might well be the case. Together with Phong Nguyen [NS], we have established a converse to the Ajtai-Dwork security result by reducing the question of distinguishing encryptions of one from encryptions of zero to approximating CVP or SVP (recall that AD encrypts bits). In a way, it becomes possible to reverse the basic paradigm of the AD cryptosystem "If lattice problems are difficult, then AD is difficult" into the following "If lattice problems are easy, then AD is insecure". It remains to understand which of the two paradigms is the right one.

References

[ABSS97] S. Arora, L. Babai, J. Stern, and Z. Sweedyk. The hardness of approximate optima in lattices, codes, and systems of linear equations. *Journal of Computer and System Sciences*, 54(2):317–331, 1997.

[AD97]   M. Ajtai and C. Dwork. A public-key cryptosystem with worst-case/average-case equivalence. In *Proc. 29th ACM Symposium on Theory of Computing*, pages 284–293, 1997.

[Adl83]   L. M. Adleman. On breaking generalized knapsack public key cryptosystems. In *Proc. 15th ACM Symposium on Theory of Computing*, pages 402–412, 1983.

[Ajt96]   M. Ajtai. Generating hard instances of lattice problems. In *Proc. 28th ACM Symposium on Theory of Computing*, pages 99–108, 1996.

[Ajt97]   M. Ajtai. The shortest vector problem in L_2 is NP-hard for randomized reductions. Unpublished manuscript, May 1997.

[Bab86]   L. Babai. On Lovász lattice reduction and the nearest lattice point problem. *Combinatorica*, 6:1–13, 1986.

[Boa81]   P. van Emde Boas. Another NP-complete problem and the complexity of computing short vectors in a lattice. Technical report, Mathematische Instituut, University of Amsterdam, 1981. Report 81-04.

[Bri84]   E. F. Brickell. Solving low density knapsacks. In D. C. Chaum, editor, *Proceedings of CRYPTO 83*, pages 25–37. Plenum Press, New York, 1984.

[Bri85]   E. F. Brickell. Breaking iterated knapsacks. In G. R. Blakley and D. C. Chaum, editors, *Proceedings CRYPTO 84*, pages 342–358. Springer, 1985. Lecture Notes in Computer Science No. 196.

[CJL+92] M. J. Coster, A. Joux, B. A. LaMacchia, A. Odlyzko, C.-P. Schnorr, and J. Stern. Improved low-density subset sum algorithms. *Computational Complexity*, 2:11–28, 1992.

[CJS91]   Y. M. Chee, A. Joux, and J. Stern. The cryptanalysis of a new public-key cryptosystem based on modular knapsacks. In J. Feigenbaum, editor, *Advances in Cryptology: Proceedings of Crypto'91*, volume 576 of *LNCS*, pages 204–212. Springer-Verlag, 1991.

[CN97]   J.-Y. Cai and A. P. Nerurkar. An improved worst-case to average-case connection for lattice problems. In *Proc. 38th IEEE Conference on Foundations of Computer Science*, pages 468–477, 1997.

[Cop96]   D. Coppersmith. Finding a small root of a univariate modular equation. In U. Maurer, editor, *Proceedings of EUROCRYPT 96*, pages 155–165. Springer, 1996. Lecture Notes in Computer Science No. 1070.

[CS97]   D. Coppersmith and A. Shamir. Lattice attacks on NTRU. In W. Fumy, editor, *Proceedings of EUROCRYPT 97*, pages 52–61. Springer, 1997. Lecture Notes in Computer Science No. 1233.

[FHK+88] A. M. Frieze, J. Hastad, R. Kannan, J. C. Lagarias, and A. Shamir. Reconstructing truncated integer variables satisfying linear congruences. *SIAM J. Computing*, 17(2):262–280, April 1988.

[Gau01] C.F. Gauss. Disquisitiones arithmeticae. Leipzig, 1801.

[GG] O. Goldreich and S. Goldwasser. On the limits of non-approximability of lattice problems. Preprint. Revision of ECCC Report TR97-031, Oct 16, 1997. Can be found at http://www.eccc.uni-trier.de/eccc/.

[GGH97] O. Goldreich, S. Goldwasser, and S. Halevy. Public-key cryptography from lattice reduction problems. In *Proc. CRYPTO'97*, volume 1294 of *LNCS*, pages 112–131, 1997.

[GM97] M. Girault and J.-F. Misarsky. Selective forgeries of RSA signatures using redundancy. In W. Fumy, editor, *Proceedings of EUROCRYPT 97*, volume 1233 of *Lecture Notes in Computer Science*, pages 495–507. Springer-Verlag, 1997.

[Her50] C. Hermite. Extraits de lettres de M. Hermite à M. Jacobi sur différents objets de la théorie des nombres, deuxième lettre. *J. Reine Angew. Math*, 40:279–290, 1850.

[JS91] A. Joux and J. Stern. Cryptanalysis of another knapsack cryptosystem. In *Advances in Cryptology: Proceedings of AsiaCrypt'91*, volume 739 of *Lecture Notes in Computer Science*, pages 470–476. Springer-Verlag, 1991.

[KZ73] A. Korkine and G. Zolotarev. Sur les formes quadratiques. *Math. Ann.*, 6:336–389, 1873.

[Lag73] L. Lagrange. *Recherches d'arithmétique*, pages 265–312. Nouv. Mém. Acad., Berlin, 1773.

[Len83] H. W. Lenstra. Integer programming with a fixed number of variables. *Math. Oper. Res.*, 8:538–548, 1983.

[LLL82] A. K. Lenstra, H. W. Lenstra, Jr., and L. Lovász. Factoring polynomials with rational coefficients. *Methematische Ann.*, 261:513–534, 1982.

[LO85] J. C. Lagarias and A. M. Odlyzko. Solving low-density subset sum problems. *J. ACM*, 32:229–246, 1985. Preliminary version in Proc. 24th IEEE Foundations Computer Science Symposium, 1–10, 1983.

[MH78] R. Merkle and M. Hellman. Hiding information and signatures in trapdoor knapsacks. *IEEE Trans. Inform. Theory*, IT-24:525–530, September 1978.

[Min10] H. Minkowski. *Geometrie der Zahlen*. Teubner, Leipzig, 1910.

[Mis97] J.-F. Misarsky. A multiplicative attack using LLL algorithm on RSA signatures with redundancy. In B. J. Kaliski, editor, *Proceedings CRYPTO 97*, volume 1294 of *Lecture Notes in Computer Science*, pages 221–234. Springer-Verlag, 1997.

[NS] P. Nguyen and J. Stern. A converse to the Ajtai-Dwork security result and its cryptographic implications. submitted.

[Sch87] C.-P. Schnorr. A hierarchy of polynomial time lattice basis reduction algorithms. *Theoretical Computer Science*, 53:201–224, 1987.

[Sch88] C.-P. Schnorr. A more efficient algorithm for lattice basis reduction. *J. Algorithms*, 9:47–62, 1988.

[Sha82] A. Shamir. A polynomial-time algorithm for breaking the basic Merkle-Hellman cryptosystem. In *Proceedings of the 23rd IEEE Symposium on Foundations of Computer Science*, pages 145–152. IEEE, 1982.

[ST90] J. Stern and P. Toffin. Cryptanalysis of a public-key cryptosystem based on approximations by rational numbers. In *Advances in Cryptology: Pro-*

ceedings of Eurocrypt'90, volume 473 of *Lecture Notes in Comp Sci*, pages 313–317. Springer-Verlag, 1990.

[Ste87]   J. Stern. Secret linear congruential generators are not cryptographically secure. In *Proceedings of the 28th IEEE Symposium on Foundations of Computer Science*, pages 421–426. IEEE, 1987.

[VGT88]   B. Vallée, M. Girault, and P. Toffin. How to gues ℓ-th root modulo n by reducing lattice bases. In *proceedings of AAECC-6*, volume 357 of *Lecture Notes in Computer Science*, pages 427–442. Springer-Verlag, 1988.

A Signcryption Scheme with Signature Directly Verifiable by Public Key

Feng Bao and Robert H. Deng

Institute of Systems Science
National University of Singapore
Kent Ridge, Singapore 119597
Email: {baofeng, deng}@iss.nus.sg

Abstract. Signcryption, first proposed by Zheng [4, 5], is a cryptographic primitive which combines both the functions of digital signature and public key encryption in a logical single step, and with a computational cost siginficantly lower than that needed by the traditional signature-then-encryption approach. In Zheng's scheme, the signature verification can be done either by the recipient directly (using his private key) or by engaging a zero-knowledge interative protocol with a third party, without disclosing recipient's private key. In this note, we modify Zheng's scheme so that the recipient's private key is no longer needed in signature verification. The computational cost of the modified scheme is higher than that of Zheng's scheme but lower than that of the signature-then-encryption approach.

1   Introduction

To guarantee unforgibility, integrity and confidentiality of communications, the traditional method is to digitally sign a message then followed by public key encryption. Signcryption, first proposed by Zheng [4], is a new cryptographic primitive which simultaneously fulfills both the functions of signature and encryption in a single logical step, and with a computational cost significantly lower than that required by the traditional signature-then-encryption approach. Two types of signcryption schemes were studied in [4], one based on the ElGamal type of public key cryptosystems and the other on RSA. In this note, we only consider signcryption schemes based on the ElGamal type of public key cryptosystems.

In the signature-then-encryption approach using DSA for signature and the ElGamal public key cryptosysem for encryption, a total of 6 exponential computations are required: one for signature generation, two for encryption, one for decryption, and two for signature verification. Zheng's signcryption scheme needs only a total of 3 exponential computations: one for signcrypting and two for unsigncrypting.

In the traditional signature-then-encryption approach, the message and the sender's signature are obtained after the decryption by using the recipient's private key. The signature is then verified using only the sender's public key. Hence, the validity of the signature can be checked by anyone who has knowledge of the sender's public key. In the signcryption scheme of [4], the unsigncryption (decryption and signature verification) needs the recipient's private key; therefore, only the recipient can verify the signature. As pointed out in [5], the constraint of using the recipient's private key in unsigncryption is acceptable for certain applications where the recipient need not pass the signature to others for verification; however, Zheng's singcryption schemes can not be used in applications where a signature need to be validated by a third party only using the public key as in usual signature scheme. To overcome this problem, some methods are given in [5] by introducing an independent judge. That is done by proving the equality of discrete logarithms. However, [2] points out that the confidentiality is lost in this case.

In this note, we modify Zheng's signcryption scheme such that verification of a signature no longer needs the recipient's private key. Hence, the modified scheme functions in exactly the same manner as that of the signature-then-encryption approach. However, the modified scheme is not as efficient as Zheng's original scheme. Nevertheless, the modified scheme is still more computational efficient than the signature-then-encryption approach.

2 Zheng's Scheme

Task: Alice has a message m to send to Bob. Alice signcrypts m so that the effect is similar to signature-then-encryption.

Public Parameters

- p: a large prime.
- q: a large prime factor of $p - 1$.
- g: an element of $\mathbf{Z}_p^*$ of order q.
- $hash$: a one-way hash function.
- KH: a keyed one-way hash function.
- (E, D): the encryption and decryption algorithms of a symmetric key cipher.

Alice's keys

- x_a: Alice's private key, $x_a \in \mathbf{Z}_q^*$.
- y_a: Alice's public key, $y_a = g^{x_a} \bmod p$.

Bob's keys

- x_b: Bob's private key, $x_b \in \mathbf{Z}_q^*$.
- y_b: Bob's public key, $y_b = g^{x_b} \bmod p$.

Signcrypting:

Alice randomly chooses $x \in_R \mathbf{Z}_q^*$, then sets
$(k_1, k_2) = hash(y_b^x \bmod p)$
$c = E_{k_1}(m)$
$r = KH_{k_2}(m)$

$$s = x/(r + x_a) \bmod q$$

Alice sends (c, r, s) to Bob.

Unsigncrypting:

Bob computes
$(k_1, k_2) = hash((y_a g^r)^{s x_b} \bmod p)$
$m = D_{k_1}(c)$ to recover the plaintext message,
and then checks whether $KH_{k_2}(m) = r$ for signature verification.

In [4], two singcryption schemes were given, called SDSS1 and SDSS2. Here we only describe the case for SDSS1. The case for SDSS2 is similar. In Zheng's **unsigncrypting** process, it is straightforward to see that x_b is involved for signature verification.

3 The Modified Singcryption Scheme

Using the same set of notations as in the last section for public parameters, Alice's key and Bob's keys, the modified scheme is described as follows:

Signcrypting:

Alice randomly chooses $x \in_R \mathbf{Z}_q^*$, then sets
$k_1 = hash(y_b^x \bmod p)$,
$k_2 = hash(g^x \bmod p)$
$c = E_{k_1}(m)$
$r = KH_{k_2}(m)$
$s = x/(r + x_a) \bmod q$.

Alice sends (c, r, s) to Bob.

Unsigncrypting:

Bob computes
$t_1 = (y_a g^r)^s \bmod p$
$t_2 = t_1^{x_b} \bmod p$
$k_1 = hash(t_2)$
$k_2 = hash(t_1)$
$m = D_{k_1}(c)$ to obtain the plaintext message,
then checks whether $KH_{k_2}(m) = r$ for signature verification.

Later when necessary, Bob may forward (m, r, s) to others, who can be convinced that it came originally from Alice by verifying

$$k = hash((y_a g^r)^s \bmod p) \text{ and } r = KH_k(m)$$

Actually, we can use $hash$ to replace the keyed hash function KH. In that case, the modified scheme can be written as follows:

Modified Scheme

Signcrypting:

Alice randomly chooses $x \in_R Z_q^*$, then sets
$$t_1 = g^x \bmod p$$
$$t_2 = y_b^x \bmod p$$
$$c = E_{hash(t_2)}(m)$$
$$r = hash(m, t_1)$$
$$s = x/(r + x_a) \bmod q$$

Alice sends (c, r, s) to Bob.

Unsigncrypting:

Bob computes
$$t_1 = (y_a g^r)^s \bmod p$$
$$t_2 = t_1^{x_b} \bmod p$$
$$m = D_{hash(t_2)}(c),$$
then checks whether $r = hash(m, t_1)$.

Bob may pass (m, r, s) to others, who can be convinced that it indeed came from Alice by verifying
$$r = hash(m, (y_a g^r)^s)$$

4   Discussion

Discussion on Computation Cost

In the comparison of computation costs, we assume that the exponential computation is the most time consuming while the computation time for *hash* and (E, D) can be ignored. Under this assumption, the modified scheme requires a total of 5 exponential computations instead of 6 as in the traditional signature-then-encryption method. At the same time, it achieves exactly the same effect as in signature-then-encryption. That is, after receiving (c, r, s), Bob first obtains the plaintext message m using his private key. Now Bob has Alice's signature (m, r, s). This signature can be verified by anyone using only Alice's public key.

Discussion on Security

The security of the modified scheme is the same as that of the original scheme.

1. Unforgeability – it is computationally infeasible for an adaptive attacker to masquerade in creating a signcrypted text.

2. Non-repudiation – it is computationally feasible for a third party to settle a dispute between Alice and Bob in an event where Alice denies that she is the originator of a signcrypted text.

Both the unforgeability and non-repudiation are based on the assumption that it is computationally infeasible to forge (m, r, s)(without knowing x_a) such that

$r = hash(m, (y_a g^r)^s)$, which is the security basis for SDSS1. It should be noted that the same assumption is made in the Schnorr signature scheme [3].

3. Confidentiality — It is computationally infeasible for an adaptive attacker to gain any information on the contents of a signcrypted text. Here, as in any public key cryptosystems, we assume that $|m|$ is large enough to resist brute force attack from $r = hash(m, (y_a g^r)^s)$.

References

1. T. ElGamal, "A public key cryptosystem and a signature scheme based on discrete logarithms", IEEE Transactions on Information Theory, IT-31(4):469-472, 1985.
2. H. Petersen and M. Michels, "Cryptanalysis and improvement of signcryption schemes", to appear in IEE Computers and Digital Techniques, 1998.
3. C. P. Schnorr, "Efficient identification and signature for smart cards", Advances in Cryptology - CRYPTO'89, LNCS 435, Springer-Verlag, pp. 239-251.
4. Y. Zheng, "Digital signcryption or how to achieve cost (signature and encryption) ¡¡ cost(signature) + cost(encryption)", In Advances in Cryptology - CRYPTO'97, LNCS 1294, Springer-Verlag, pp. 165-179, 1997.
5. Y. Zheng, "Signcryption and its application in efficient public key solutions", Pre-Proceedings of Information Security Workshop(ISW'97), pp. 201-218, to be published in LNCS by Springer-Verlag.

Guaranteed Correct Sharing of Integer Factorization with Off-Line Shareholders

Wenbo Mao

Hewlett-Packard Laboratories
Filton Road
Stoke Gifford
Bristol BS12 6QZ
United Kingdom
wm@hplb.hpl.hp.com

Abstract. A fair public-key cryptosystem consists of multi-party protocols in which a plural number of participants (shareholders) are involved in receiving and verifying distributed shares. It will be desirable if multi-party protocols can be streamlined into two-party ones without lowering the quality of fairness: secret is still shared among many (more than two) parties. In this paper we propose a scheme that distributes secret shares of the factorization of an integer to multi-parties without their participation in the protocols for share distribution and verification. A single verifier suffices to verify the correctness of the shares using the public keys of the off-line shareholders. Due to the universal verifiability, a guaranteed correctness of secret sharing is achieved without relying on the honesty of the verifier.

1 Introduction

A number of fair cryptosystems have been proposed (e.g., [1, 11, 12, 13, 15], a good reference is in [5]). Here, fairness essentially means to share a secret among a plural number of participants called shareholders. This can be achieved via verifiable secret sharing (VSS, e.g., [1, 13, 15]) in which a dealer distributes structured messages called shares to the shareholders via confidential channels. Each of the shareholders must verify the correctness of the share received in order to be sure that whenever needed they can correctly reconstruct the secret via distributed computing.

VSS schemes are multi-party protocols which require the shareholders stay on-line to receive and verify messages. This is so even for non-interactive VSS schemes such as Pedersen's [16]. Moreover, because each shareholder verifies data in private, these schemes require the shareholders honest. Considering possible presence of dishonest shareholder(s), the previous VSS protocols resort to what we call "front-end (t, n)-threshold secret sharing" ([16, 22]), in which the secret is distributed in such a way that it can be correctly re-constructed if t ($< n$) out of n shareholders are honest. The multi-party protocols for threshold secret sharing are very inefficient, and give the user little freedom to choose shareholders they trust (since the shareholders must pre-negotiate some system parameters, e.g., (t, n), in order to correctly run protocols). Some schemes even resort to broadcasting channels which are impractical to realize. Still, they do not offer absolute guarantee on correctness in secret sharing.

In this paper we propose a publicly verifiable secret sharing scheme for establishing correct sharing of the factorization of an integer. The integer factorization problem forms an important class of cryptosystems and protocols such as RSA [20], Rabin [21], Fiat-Shamir [8] and Guillou-Quisquater [19]. The public verifiability means that the secret sharing need not use a plural number of on-line participating verifiers. A single verifier will suffice for the verification job, and because the verification will only use public data such as the public keys of the un-participating shareholders, the verifier can be anybody and the verification can be repeated. Thus, the new scheme not only streamlines multi-party protocols into two-party ones, but also achieves a guaranteed correctness in secret sharing.

1.1 Outline of the Paper

In the next subsection we review the previous integer factorization based fair public-key cryptosystems. In Section 2 we introduce cryptographic primitives that will be used in our technique. In Section 3 we present a new integer factorization based fair cryptosystem. Finally, we conclude the work in Section 4.

1.2 Previous Work on Integer Factorization Based Fair Cryptosystems

Micali [13] and Okamoto [15] have proposed two fair public-key cryptosystems based on the integer factorization problem.

Micali's scheme is based on the following number theoretic facts: (i) there exists efficient protocols for showing probabilistic evidence that a composite number N is the product of two primes [9, 13]; (ii) for such a number, a quadratic residue in Z_N^* has distinct square roots with opposite Jacobi symbols, and such a pair of square roots provide an efficient algorithm to factor N; and (iii) the product of several quadratic residues is itself a quadratic residue with the Jacobi symbol as the product of those of the individuals.

Using these facts, the factorization of an integer N (e.g., an RSA modulus) can be fairly shared as follows. The user generates a quadratic residue modulo N which is the product of several other quadratic residues; sends a square root with Jacobi symbol -1 of the product to a key-management center (KMC); sends a square root with Jacobi symbol 1 of each individual quadratic residue to a respective shareholder; each of the latter verifies that the value received has the correct Jacobi symbol. Thus, when all of the shareholders disclose the square roots received, N can be factored because two square roots of the same quadratic residue with opposite Jacobi symbols are now available. Obviously, the scheme is a multi-party protocol and requires each shareholder to stay on-line and honestly check the correctness of the square root received.

Okamoto's schemes (there are three of them) are based on combining bit-commitment protocols used in his electronic cash scheme [14] and Pedersen's non-interactive threshold verifiable secret sharing (VSS) [16]. So the schemes require on-line availability of multi shareholders. In two of the three schemes, the shareholders must also prepare for some session parameters for each instance of secret sharing, which are are functions of the integer that the user wants to establish as part of the public key. These parameters have to be agreed through real-time negotiations among the shareholders.

2 Cryptographic Primitives

In this section we introduce cryptographic primitives that will be used in our technique.

2.1 Notation and System Setup

Let Z denote the ring of integers. For positive integer p, let Z_p denote the ring of integers modulo p and Z_p^* denote the multiplicative group modulo p. For S being a set, $a \in_R S$ means choosing a from S at random according to the uniform distribution. For integers a, b, we write $a|b$ if a divides b and $a \nmid b$ if otherwise. Let $|a|$ denote the bit length of a, and $abs(a)$, the absolute value of a. Finally, we assume a collision resistant hash function $\mathcal{H} : \{0,1\}^* \to \{0,1\}^l$ ($l \approx 160$).

Throughout the paper we will use two public cyclic groups constructed as follows. Let r be a large prime such that $q = 2r + 1$ and $p = kq + 1$ are also prime where k is an even number. Number theoretic research [10] has shown that it is not difficult to find such primes. Let $h \in Z_q^*$, $g \in Z_p^*$ be elements of order r and q, respectively, and set $H = \langle h \rangle$, $G = \langle g \rangle$ with multiplication as the respective group operations. With these settings the following two congruences hold

$$h^r = 1(\bmod q) \quad \text{and} \quad g^q = 1(\bmod p). \tag{1}$$

We assume that it is difficult to compute discrete logarithms in Z_q^* and Z_p^* to the bases h and g, respectively.

The system will also setup a fixed element $f \in G$ such that nobody knows $\log_g(f)$. Such an element can be chosen by a trusted center who sets f using a secure pseudo-random number generator which is seeded by g, and publishes this relationship between the two quantities.

2.2 Cryptosystem

Encryption will use the ElGamal cryptosystems [7]. Let $x \in Z_r$ be the private key of someone other than the verifier and

$$y = h^x \bmod q \tag{2}$$

be the matching public key. To encrypt a message $M \in Z_q$ under the public key y, the sender (Alice) chooses a session key $k \in_R Z_r$, and calculates the following pair

$$(h^k, y^{-k}M)(\bmod q). \tag{3}$$

The ciphertext pair (A, B) can be decrypted using the private key x as follows

$$M = A^x B \bmod q. \tag{4}$$

Using well-known techniques for building robust threshold cryptosystems [6, 16, 17], the ElGamal cryptosystem can be setup as a robust threshold one. Encryption using such a cryptosystem is exactly the same as that in normal ElGamal. Decryption will be via distributed computing in a threshold manner among a set of principals who share a private decryption key matching the public key y. However, there will be no need to re-construct the shared private key in order to perform decryption. In fact, the private key has never been, and will never be constructed. Section 2.3 of [4] provides a succinct description on how to setup such a threshold ElGamal cryptosystem.

2.3 Verifiable Encryption of Discrete Log

The scheme, due to Stadler [24], will make use of double exponentiation. By double exponentiation to bases g and h we mean the following organization of the quantities $z \in Z_r$, $h \in Z_q^*$ and $g \in Z_p^*$:

$$g^{h^z \bmod q} \bmod p. \tag{5}$$

With the double exponentiation structure, we will be able to prove the following structured knowledge statement. For public quantities A, h, y, U, g,

$$\exists k : A = h^k (\bmod q) \wedge U = g^{y^k (\bmod q)}(\bmod p). \tag{6}$$

Assuming with this statement proven, given value $V \in G$, and a pair of ElGamal ciphertext (A, B), one can be convinced that (A, B) encrypts $\log_g(V)$ under the public key y if $U^B = V(\bmod p)$.

Using a cryptographicly secure hash function, the following procedure provides a non-interactive proof of the structure (6). For $i = 1, \cdots, l$, A prover (Alice) chooses $u_i \in_R Z_r$ and calculates

$$t_{hi} = h^{u_i} \bmod q, \quad t_{gi} = g^{(y^{u_i} \bmod q)} \bmod p. \tag{7}$$

Then she computes the following ℓ-tuples

$$R = (R_1, R_2, \cdots, R_\ell) = (u_1 - kC_1, u_2 - kC_2, \cdots, u_\ell - kC_\ell) (\bmod r) \tag{8}$$

where C_i is the i-th bit of

$$C = \mathcal{H}(A, h, y, U, g, t_{h1}, t_{g1}, \cdots, t_{h\ell}, t_{g\ell}). \tag{9}$$

The non-interactive proof consists of pair (R, C). A verifier (Bob) verifies by computing (for $i = 1, \cdots, \ell$)

$$t_{hi} = h^{R_i} A^{C_i} \bmod q, \tag{10}$$

$$t_{gi} = (g^{(1-C_i)} U^{C_i})(y^{R_i}) \bmod p \tag{11}$$

and checking whether the equation (9) holds.

3   Sharing the Factorization of an Integer

In this section we assume that

$$Y = h^X \bmod q \tag{12}$$

is a public key where its discrete logarithm X has been fairly shared among a number of shareholders as in the case of the robust cryptosystem described in Section 2.2. We will specify protocols that let a user use this public key to verifiably encrypt the factorization of an integer.

We begin with introducing two observations.

The first observation can be described as follows. Let

$$(A_1 = h^{k_1}, \quad B_1 = Y^{-k_1} n_1) \pmod{q}, \tag{13}$$

and

$$(A_2 = h^{k_2}, \quad B_2 = Y^{-k_2} n_2) \pmod{q} \tag{14}$$

be two pairs of ciphertext encrypting numbers n_1 and n_2 respectively under the public key Y. Multiplying A_1 to A_2, and B_1 to B_2, we get

$$(A_3 = h^{k_1+k_2}, \quad B_3 = Y^{-(k_1+k_2)} n_1 n_2) \pmod{q}. \tag{15}$$

The sender can disclose $n_1 n_2 \pmod{q}$ by revealing $k_1 + k_2 \pmod{r}$ since

$$n_1 n_2 = Y^{k_1+k_2} B_1 B_2 \pmod{q}. \tag{16}$$

The value $n_1 n_2 \pmod{q}$ opened from (16) will not reveal any useful information about n_1 or n_2 since arbitrarily setting $n_1 \leq q$, there exists an $n_2 \leq q$ with $n_1 n_2 \pmod{q}$ meeting the left-hand side of (16).

If we have a method to decide the bit-lengths of the messages encrypted in (13) and (14), then under certain conditions we can decide whether the quantities encrypted will precisely divide the value opened. The needed conditions form our second observation which are stated in the following lemma.

Lemma Let $n_1 n_2 = n \pmod{q}$ and $|n| + 2 < |q|$. If $|n_1| + |n_2| \leq |n| + 1$ then $n_1 | n$ and $n_2 | n$.

Proof Suppose to the contrary (without loss of generality) $n_1 \nmid n$. Then $n_1 n_2 = n + kq$ for some integer $k \neq 0$. Noting $0 < n < q$, so

$$|n_1| + |n_2| \geq |n_1 n_2| = |n + kq| \geq |q| - 1 > |n| + 1, \tag{17}$$

contradicting the condition $|n_1| + |n_2| \leq |n| + 1$.   □

3.1 The Proposed Scheme

We are now ready to present our secret factorization distribution scheme. Again, let Alice be the prover (user) and Bob be the verifier, who, for instance, can be a key certification authority.

Protocol P Verifiable Encryption of Integer Factorization.
Task In this protocol Alice shall encrypt two prime numbers P and Q and discloses $N = PQ$ to Bob. Bob shall verify the correctness of the encryption under an agreed public key.
Data preparation by Alice Generates two primes P, Q, $abs(|P| - |Q|) < C$, and C is a pre-specified small constant; in practice, $C \leq 20$). Computes $V_1 = g^P \pmod{p}$, $V_2 = g^Q \pmod{p}$, and $N = PQ$. Encrypts P in A_1, B_1, and Q in A_2, B_2 as follows:

$$(A_1 = h^{K_1}, \quad B_1 = Y^{-K_1}P) \pmod{q}, \tag{18}$$

$$(A_2 = h^{K_2}, \quad B_2 = Y^{-K_2}Q) \pmod{q} \tag{19}$$

where $K_1, K_2 \in_R Z_r$, and Y is the agreed public key in (12). She also prepares bit-commitment values. We will postpone the description of the bit-commitment procedure to Section 3.2.

The protocol steps are as follows.

1. Alice sends to Bob: A_1, B_1, V_1, A_2, B_2, V_2, $(K_1 + K_2)(\bmod r)$ and N.
2. Bob verifies that

$$(h^{K_1+K_2} = A_1 A_2, \quad N = Y^{K_1+K_2} B_1 B_2) \pmod{q}. \tag{20}$$

3. Alice shows to Bob evidence that N consists of only two distinct primes. We assume that Alice has constructed N to be a Blum integer [2]. Then there exists interactive or non-interactive protocols for showing such evidence [9, 13]. (We will discuss some special structure of N in Section 3.3.)
4. Alice proves to Bob that (A_1, B_1) encrypts $\log_g(V_1)$, and (A_2, B_2) encrypts $\log_g(V_1)$, and the encryptions are under the agreed public key Y. This uses the non-interactive prove technique described in Section 2.3.
5. Alice shows to Bob $|P|$ and $|Q|$ using a sub-protocol to be described in the next subsection. He verifies that

$$|P| + |Q| \leq |N| + 1 \tag{21}$$

and

$$abs(|P| - |Q|) < C. \tag{22}$$

6. Bob accepts the proof if every checking in the above passes, or else rejects. Terminate.

Upon successful termination of a run, Bob will certify N as Alice's public key and archive the $A_1, B_1, V_1, A_2, B_2, V_2$ for possible future recovery of P and Q.

We point out that if Protocol P and that for proof of N's two-prime-product structure are run in non-interaction. The cryptographicly strong hash functions used in the proofs act as publicly trustworthy challengers. In these cases, the verification procedures conducted by Bob are universally verifiable (by any third party). Collusion between Alice and Bob is computationally infeasible.

3.2 Proof of Bit-Lengths $|P|$ and $|Q|$

We now provide details for Alice to show $|P|$ and $|Q|$ which has been missing from Step 5 of Protocol P. Describing the case of $|P|$ suffices.

Let $m = |P| - 1$ and

$$P = a_0 2^0 + a_1 2^1 + \cdots + a_m 2^m \quad \text{for } a_i \in \{0, 1\} \text{ and } i = 0, 1, \cdots, m \quad (23)$$

be the binary presentation of P. Alice chooses $u_0, u_1, \cdots, u_m \in_R Z_q$. She computes

$$u = u_0 2^0 + u_1 2^1 + \cdots + u_m 2^m \mod q \quad (24)$$

and

$$E_i = E(a_i, u_i) = g^{a_i} f^{u_i} \mod p, \quad \text{for } i = 0, 1, \cdots, m. \quad (25)$$

The computations in (25) follow a bit-commitment scheme [18], where f is the fixed element in G chosen as in Section 2.1. The prover commits herself to a_i (called *committal*) which is hidden under u_i. It can be proved that (i) the commitment $E(a_i, u_i)$ reveals no useful information about the committal a_i, and (ii) the prover cannot commit to two $a_i' \neq a_i$ using the same E_i unless she can find $\log_g(f)$. We shall see more about this in a moment.

Alice shall send E_i and u to Bob. The verification step for Bob is as follows. He checks whether

$$V_1 f^u \stackrel{?}{=} \prod_{i=0}^m E_i^{2^i} \mod p. \quad (26)$$

Then for each E_i $(i = 0, 1, \cdots, m)$, Alice and Bob shall run a sub-protocol (Bit) to prove one-bit-length of the committal a_i. Protocol Bit shows either $E_i = g f^{u_i}$ or $E_i = f^{u_i}$ without revealing which one is the case. This protocol is obtained by applying the transformation of [3] on the Schnorr identification protocol [23] on the instance $(E_i, E_i/g)$, with a 1-out-of-2 threshold scheme to show that the prover knows the discrete logarithm of either inputs without revealing which is the case. It has many useful applications (see e.g., [1, 4]).

Protocol Bit

Common input: $E, f, g \in G$

Prover's input: $z \in Z_q$

To prove either $E = f^z$ or $E = gf^z$

Prover (Alice)   Verifier (Bob)

$E = f^z$	$E = gf^z$
$w, r_1, c_1 \in_R Z_q$	$w, r_2, c_2 \in_R Z_q$
$a = f^w$	$a = f^{r_2} E^{-c_2}$
$b = f^{r_1}(E/g)^{-c_1}$	$b = f^w$
(above computing in mod p)	

$\xrightarrow{\quad a, b \quad}$

$c \in_R Z_q$

$\xleftarrow{\quad c \quad}$

$E = f^z$	$E = gf^z$
$c_2 = c - c_1$	$c_1 = c - c_2$
$r_2 = w + zc_2$	$r_1 = w + zc_1$
(above computing in mod q)	

$\xrightarrow{\quad r_1, r_2, c_1, c_2 \quad}$

$$c \overset{?}{=} c_1 + c_2 \pmod{q}$$
$$f^{r_1} \overset{?}{=} b(E/g)^{c_1} \pmod{p}$$
$$f^{r_2} \overset{?}{=} aE^{c_2} \pmod{p}$$

Bob will accept $|P| = m + 1$ if the result of running Protocol Bit is accepted for each E_i ($i = 0, 1, \cdots, m$). We reason about the security of the bit-commitment scheme below.

Firstly, if P and u are indeed the numbers that Alice has constructed in (23) and (24), then indeed

$$\prod_{i=0}^{m} E_i^{2^i} = g^{a_0 2^0 + a_1 2^1 + \cdots + a_m 2^m} f^{u_0 2^0 + u_1 2^1 + \cdots + u_m 2^m} = V_1 f^u \pmod{p}. \quad (27)$$

On the other hand from (25) and (27) we note that

$$V_1 f^u \pmod{p} = E(P, u). \quad (28)$$

So if Alice is able to find a $P' \neq P \pmod{q}$ such that $E(P, u) = E(P', u')$, then it has to be $u' \neq u \pmod{q}$ and

$$\log_g(f) = \frac{P - P'}{u' - u} \mod q. \quad (29)$$

This means that Alice knows $\log_g(f)$, contradicting the assumption that this value is known to nobody. Therefore, P in (23) and u in (24) give the only way for Alice to demonstrate $V_1 f^u = E(P, u) \pmod{p}$.

We recall that the bit-commitment $E_i = E(a_i, u_i)$ protects the confidentiality of the bit information a_i. Therefore Bob gets no knowledge about P from E_i (for $i = 0, 1, \cdots, m$), but $|P|$.

Finally we point out that following the technique of [23], the three-move protocol (Bit) can easily be turned into non-interactive by using a hash function to generate the challenge as in the standard method for parallelizing an interactive proof. A non-interactive proof is universally verifiable.

3.3 Key Recovery

The factorization of N can be recovered if the shareholders decrypt (A_1, B_1) and (A_2, B_2) via distributed computing. The protocol that proves two-prime-product structure of N is up to showing that $N = R^t S^u$ for some odd positive integers t, u and distinct primes R, S [9]. So it remains to complete to factor N down to the primes R and S in order to compute the trapdoor information. Below we show that it is easy to complete the factorization.

Without loss of generality, we can assume that Peggy has constructed P (and Q) such that each of them consists of both R and S, maybe powers of them. Then $gcd(P, Q)$ will return either (i) R^i, or (ii) S^j, or (iii) $R^k S^\ell$ for some positive integers i, j, k and ℓ. For the first two cases, binary search for R from R^i in the case (i) for each fixed i takes at most $\log_2(P)$ steps and there are only at most $\log_2(P)$ many $i > 1$ to search. In reality, i should be sufficiently small or else R will be too small for the resulting modulus N to be secure. Analogously for the case (ii) we can efficiently search S out of S^j. In the sequel, whenever we meet a single prime or a power of it, we will regard the job has been done.

Now we consider the case (iii): $gcd(P, Q) = R^k S^\ell$ for $k, \ell > 1$. Let $a := P/gcd(P, Q)$ and $b := Q/gcd(P, Q)$. Then a and b are co-prime, and they cannot both be 1 because $P \neq Q$ or else N is a square and this is impossible since s and t are odd. Thus we will have, by symmetry (without loss of generality), further two sub-cases. The first one is that a is a single prime or a power of it, and we have done. The second sub-case is that a is a composite and $b = 1$. Then obviously we will have $P = aQ$. Noting the bit-length condition (22), $abs(|P| - |Q|) < C$, we will have

$$|a| = (|Q| + |a|) - |Q| \leq abs(|P| - |Q|) + 1 < C + 1.$$

So a will have a length less than $C + 1$ bits. Here C is a small constant, typically between 1 and 20. It is trivially easy to factor a into primes.

Thus, no matter how Peggy has constructed $N = PQ$, key recovery will always return two distinct primes.

3.4 Performance

We now provide analyses on the performance of the scheme.

The scheme consists of three components which are computation intensive. They are the three proof of knowledge steps regarding the factorization of $N = P * Q$: (i) verifiable encryption of P and Q; (ii) proof of the bit lengths of P and Q; and (iii) proof of the Blum integer structure of N.

The complexity of (i) can be measured as follows. Let the hash function $\mathcal{H}$ output 160 bits. When verifiably encrypting a number, for each bit of the hash function output, both prover and verifier should compute 3 exponentiations. Thus for P and Q, they shall each compute $2 * 3 * 160 = 960$ exponentiations. The size of data transmitted is bounded by $2 * 160 * |p|$ bits.

The complexity of (ii) is proportional to the bit length of N. From Protocol Bit we can see that for each bit of N, both prover and verifier shall compute 4 exponentiations. Also 7 numbers of length $|q|$ will be exchanged between them. Therefore, the total number of exponentiations to be computed is $4 * |N|$ by each of the parties, and they exchange $7 * |N| * |q|$ bits. Similar to the case of (i), the proof can be parallelized using a hash function.

Finally, the complexity of (iii). Protocols for proof of the Blum integer structure of N ([9, 13]) require a prover to send roughly 100 integers modulo N to a verifier for a simple procedural checking, and are very efficient. These proofs are also nun-interactive, and universally verifiable.

From the analyses we conclude that the scheme may be considered to have an acceptable performance for sharing of long-term keys, while is not very practical for session keys.

4 Conclusion

We have presented a fair public-key cryptosystem that uses two-party protocols to distribute the factorization of an integer to multi-shareholders without their participation in receiving and verifying the shares. To the author's knowledge the proposed scheme is the first factorization-based fair cryptosystem that uses un-participating shareholders. Because the share distribution can be universally verifiable, the correctness of secret sharing is guaranteed. Further research in improving the performance will be desirable.

Acknowledgments Discussions with Kenneth Paterson and Dipankar Gupta of HP Labs., Bristol improved a few technical details. Colin Boyd of Queens University of Technology, Brisbane provided useful comments on a later draft of the paper.

References

1. M. Bellare and S. Goldwasser. Verifiable partial key escrow. In Proceedings of *4th ACM Conference on Computer and Communications Security*. Zurich, April 1997.
2. M. Blum. Coin flipping by telephone: a protocol for solving impossible problems. In Proceedings of *24th IEEE Computer Conference (CompCon)*, pages 133–137. 1982.
3. R. Cramer, I. Damgård and B. Schoenmakers. Proofs of partial knowledge and simplified design of witness hiding protocols. In *Advances in Cryptology — Proceedings of CRYPTO'94 (LNCS 839)*, pages 174–187. Springer-Verlag, 1994.
4. R. Cramer, R. Gennaro and B. Schoenmakers. A secure and optimally efficient multi-authority election scheme. In *Advances in Cryptology — Proceedings of EUROCRYPT'97 (LNCS 1233)*, pages 103–118. Springer-Verlag, 1997.

5. D. Denning and D. Branstad. A taxonomy for key escrow encryption systems. *Communications of the ACM.* 39,3 March 1996, pages 34–40.

6. Y. Desmedt and Y. Frankel. Threshold cryptosystems. In *Advances in Cryptology — Proceedings of CRYPTO'89 (LNCS 435)*, pages 307–315. Springer-Verlag, 1990.

7. T. ElGamal. A public-key cryptosystem and a signature scheme based on discrete logarithms. *IEEE Transactions on Information Theory,* IT-31(4):469–472, July 1985.

8. A. Fiat and A. Shamir. How to prove yourself: Practical solution to identification and signature problems. In *Advances in Cryptology — Proceedings of CRYPTO'86 (LNCS 263)*, pages 186–194. Springer-Verlag, 1987.

9. J. van de Graaf and R. Peralta. A simple and secure way to show the validity of your public key. In *Advances in Cryptology — Proceedings of CRYPTO'87 (LNCS 293)*, pages 128–134. Springer-Verlag, 1988.

10. J.A. Gordon. Strong primes are easy to find. In *Advances in Cryptology — Proceedings of EUROCRYPT'84 (LNCS 209)*, pages 216–223. Springer-Verlag, 1985.

11. J. Kilian and T. Leighton. Fair cryptosystems, revisited. A Rigorous approach to key-escrow. In *Advances in Cryptology — Proceedings of CRYPTO'95 (LNCS 963)*, pages 208–221. Springer-Verlag, 1995.

12. A.K. Lenstra, P. Winkler and Y. Yacobi. A key escrow system with warrant bounds. In *Advances in Cryptology — Proceedings of CRYPTO'95 (LNCS 963)*, pages 197–207. Springer-Verlag, 1995.

13. S. Micali. Fair public key cryptosystems. In *Advances in Cryptology — Proceedings of CRYPTO'92 (LNCS 740)*, pages 113–138. Springer-Verlag, 1993.

14. T. Okamoto. An efficient divisible electronic cash scheme. In *Advances in Cryptology — Proceedings of CRYPTO'91 (LNCS 963)*, pages 438–451. Springer-Verlag, 1995.

15. T. Okamoto. Threshold key-recovery system for RSA. In Proceedings of *1997 Security Protocols Workshop.* Paris. April, 1997.

16. T. Pedersen. Distributed provers with applications to undeniable signatures. In *Advances in Cryptology — Proceedings of EUROCRYPT'91 (LNCS 547)*, pages 221–242. Springer-Verlag, 1991.

17. T. Pedersen. A threshold cryptosystem without a trusted party. In *Advances in Cryptology — Proceedings of EUROCRYPT'91 (LNCS 547)*, pages 522–526. Springer-Verlag, 1991.

18. T. Pedersen. Non-interactive and information-theoretic secure verifiable secret sharing. In *Advances in Cryptology — Proceedings of CRYPTO'91 (LNCS 576)*, pages 129–140. Springer-Verlag, 1992.

19. L.C. Guillou and J.-J. Quisquater. A practical zero-knowledge protocol fitted to security microprocessor minimizing both transmission and memory. In *Advances in Cryptology — Proceedings of EUROCRYPT'88 (LNCS 330)*, pages 123–128. Springer-Verlag, 1988.

20. R.L. Rivest, A. Shamir and L.M. Adleman. A method for obtaining digital signatures and public-key cryptosystems. *Communications of the ACM* v.21, n.2, 1978, pages 120–126.

21. M.O. Rabin. Digital signatures and public-key functions as intractable as factorization. MIT Laboratory for Computer Science, Technical Report, MIT/LCS/TR-212. 1979.

22. A. Shamir. How to share a secret. *Communications of the ACM* 22, 1979, pages 612–613.

23. C.P. Schnorr. Efficient signature generation for smart cards. *Journal of Cryptology*, 4(3):161–174, 1991.
24. M. Stadler. Publicly Verifiable Secret Sharing. In *Advances in Cryptology — Proceedings of EUROCRYPT'96 (LNCS 1070)*, pages 190–199. Springer-Verlag, 1996.

Lower Bounds on Term-Based Divisible Cash Systems

Tatsuaki Okamoto[†]   Moti Yung[‡]

[†] NTT Laboratories
1-1 Hikarinooka, Yokosuka-shi, Kanagawa-ken, 239 Japan
Email: okamoto@sucaba.isl.ntt.co.jp
Phone: +81-468-59-2511,   Fax: +81-468-59-3858

[‡] CertCo
55 Broad St. (22 fl.), New York, NY 10004, USA
Email: moti@certco.com, moti@cs.columbia.edu
Phone: +1-212-709-8972,   Fax: +1-212-709-6754

Abstract. Electronic cash is one of the most important applications of public-key cryptosystems. This paper gives lower bounds for data size and computational complexity of divisible electronic cash based on the Chaum-Fiat-Naor (CFN) paradigm, with respect to the precision of divisibility, N, which is (the total coin value)/(minimum divisible denomination). Achieving computational lower bounds in the most general model of computations are extremely hard task. We therefore concentrate on a concrete model of computation where the computational unit (like a trapdoor one way function application) is atomic, and where some structure of the coin and its splits is assumed. All previous upper bounds in this area are within this general model. We show that the lower bound for computational complexity of generating a (divided) coin is $\log_2 N \cdot Comp(term)$, and the lower bound for coin size is $\log_2 N \cdot |term| + \log_2 N$, where $Comp(term)$ is a computational complexity unit such as that of one modular exponentiation, and $|term|$ is a unit size of a coin such as the size of a modulus. (Such a unit is called a term.) These bounds are optimal, since they are of the same order as the upper bounds in the previously proposed divisible cash systems.

1   Introduction

Recently electronic cash has been attracting the attention of many people, and various cash systems have been proposed. In the light of privacy and off-line/online of payment procedures, the Chaum-Fiat-Naor's approach (CFN paradigm) [2] seems to be promising and many electronic cash schemes based on the CFN paradigm have been proposed [1, 2, 3, 4, 6, 7, 8, 9, 10, 11, 12, 14].

In the CFN paradigm, consumers withdraw "electronic coins" from a bank, and later spend these coins at a shop in an "off-line" manner. Here, off-line refers to the property that communication with a bank or authorized center is unnecessary during the payment protocol. If a customer spends a coin twice, the customer's identity is revealed by the bank. Otherwise, the customer's privacy is guaranteed. That is, electronic coins are anonymous (i.e., untraceable), unless a customer spends a coin twice. Therefore, a cash system based on the CFN paradigm satisfies the two properties of "untraceability" and "off-line use" at the same time.

A "divisible" coin worth some amount of money, say $x, is a coin that can be spent many times as long as the sum total of all the transactions does not exceed $x. This property, divisibility, is very useful and convenient for a customer. If a coin is not divisible, the customer must withdraw a coin whenever he spends it, or withdraw many coins of various values and store them in his electronic wallet (e.g., smart card). Therefore, in practice, divisibility is a very important requirement for electronic cash systems.

So far, several "divisible" electronic cash systems based on the CFN paradigm have been presented [3, 6, 10, 12, 11]. For a divisible cash system, it is very important to evaluate the data size and computational complexity with respect to the the precision of divisibility, N, which is (the total coin value)/(minimum divisible denomination). However, no result on the lower bounds for the data size and computational complexity of the divisible cash systems has been reported.

This paper, for the first time, shows the lower bounds, with respect to the precision of divisibility, N, for

- the size of data transferred from a customer to a shop during payment (shortly, "coin size"),
- the computational complexity of generating payment data for a customer (shortly, "computational complexity of a coin").

Note that achieving computational lower bounds in the most general model of computations are extremely hard task. We therefore concentrate on a concrete model of computation where the computational unit (like a one way function application) is atomic, and where some structure of the coin and its splits is assumed. All previous upper bounds in this area are within this general model.

Our main results are:

Main result 1 (Theorem 12)

$$Comp(c^{(w)}) \geq \log_2 N \cdot Comp(term),$$

where N is the precision of divisibility, $Comp(c^{(w)})$ is the computational complexity of generating a (divided) coin (worth $w), and $Comp(term)$ is a computational complexity unit such as that of one modular exponentiation.

Main result 2 (Theorem 12)

$$|c^{(w)}| + |e| + |w| \geq \log_2 N \cdot |term| + \log_2 N,$$

where $|c^{(w)}| + |e| + |w|$ is the size of a coin (worth $w), and $|term|$ is a unit size of a coin such as the size of a modulus.

These lower bounds are general within the generic model and their derivation takes advantage of the strict requirement of divisible cash: of disjoint spending of splits and detection of double spending within a split. In addition, these bounds are optimal, since they are of the same order as the upper bounds in the previously proposed divisible cash systems.

This paper is organized as follows: Section 2 shows our model of a divisible cash system, including some assumptions, Section 3 introduces the problems on the lower bounds for divisible coins, and Section 4 gives these lower bounds.

2 Divisible cash system model based on the CFN paradigm

This section briefly describes a generic model of "divisible" cash systems based on the CFN paradigm. This model is generic in the sense that it works for a large class of divisible electronic cash systems.

Let bank B have a secret key, s_B, with corresponding public key p_B. A signature with secret key s_B is worth a fixed amount (say, $N). This signature scheme must have the property that it is possible to make blind signatures.

A divisible electronic cash system can now be constructed as follows:

[Protocol:]

Withdrawal

1. Customer U constructs message m_U with special form, which is related to a secret, s_U, of U, and proves that m_U is constructed correctly without revealing m_U to bank B.
2. The bank makes a blind signature on m_U and withdraws \$ N from U's account.
3. U recovers the signature, $\sigma(m_U)$, on m_U.

Payment

1. U sends m_U and $\sigma(m_U)$ to shop V. U also sends a divided coin value, \$w ($w \leq N$).
2. V verifies that $\sigma(m_U)$ is a valid signature on m_U, chooses a random challenge, e, and sends it to U.
3. U sends back an answer, $c^{(w)}$. [1]
4. V verifies that $c^{(w)}$ is correct as a \$w coin.

Note: Hereafter, coins, $c^{(w)}$, $c^{(w')}$, ..., mean coins divided from the same coin, $(m_U, \sigma(m_U))$.

---

[1] Hereafter, we often call $c^{(w)}$ a (divided) "coin" shortly. More correctly, the total history, $(m_U, \sigma(m_U), w, e, c^{(w)})$, of the payment procedure should be called a (divided) coin with value \$w. However, only $c^{(w)}$ has the essential information regarding the value, so $c^{(w)}$ is often referred to as a coin.

[Procedures and coin structures:]

Structure of a coin Each coin consists of a part (part 1), whose size is constant, and a part (part 2), whose size is variable with respect to the precision of divisibility, N. Part 1 is $(m_U, \sigma(m_U))$, and part 2 is $(c^{(w)}, e, w)$, in which $(c^{(w)}, e)$ consists of several (or one) unit terms. Here, we call the unit term, simply *term*.

We say that a divisible coin scheme has "r layers", if and only if r values of coins are terms (say term coins), and the other coins are combinations of term coins. In other words, the term coins worth the r values can be identified independently, and the other coins are identified by a combination of term coins. Hence, the size of the term coins is the term size, and the sizes of the other coins than the term coins are the total sum of the term sizes.

The size of a term, n, is determined by the underlying problem to construct a trick for B to compute s_U from c_i and c_j. Let $|term|$ be the minimum size of a term. For example, if the factoring problem is used, then n should be more than a constant multiple of a composite size (e.g., when the composite size is 1024 bits, $|term| \geq 1024k$, k: constant).

A computational complexity unit is also defined. The complexity of computing a term is at least the computational complexity unit. The unit is the complexity of computing a primitive unit (trapdoor) one-way function, which is used several (or one) times to obtain a term. Let $Comp(term)$ be the minimum complexity of computing a term, and $Comp(unit)$ be the complexity of computing a primitive unit one-way function. Then, $Comp(term) \geq Comp(unit)$. For example, the RSA (or Rabin) (or inverse) function, (i.e., $x^e \bmod n$ or $x^{1/e} \bmod n$), regarding the factoring problem, and modular exponentiation function (i.e., $g^x \bmod p$) regarding the discrete logarithm problem. ($Comp(unit) = Comp(RSA_{(e,n)})$, or $Comp(unit) = Comp(DL_{(p,g)})$.)

Overspending prevention In order to prevent overspending, the system must be constructed such that if U spends more than $\$N$ by sending multiple coins $c^{(w)}$, $c^{(w')}$, ..., in the payment procedure, then bank B can computes U's secret, s_U. However, if U spends less than or equals to $\$N$, then bank B cannot find U's secret, s_U.

Here, to make s_U become an evidence of the overspending, some additional property is required. For example, in the withdrawal protocol, B obtains $F(s_U)$, and registers it as U's identity, where F is a one-way function, and U proves to B that $F(s_U)$ is constructed correctly without revealing s_U (and m_U). If U does not overspend, it is hard for B to calculate s_U given $F(s_U)$. However, B can get s_U, if U overspends, so s_U is the evidence that U has overspent. Another way to make s_U evidence is to make s_U include U's signature. For more details, see [1, 2, 6, 10, 11, 14].

Revealing rule regarding coin structure If B can compute s_U from c_i and c_j, then s_U is computed from a term in c_i and term in c_j. If B can compute s_U from several coins, c_1, c_2, ...,c_k, then there always exist a pair of coins, c_i and c_j ($i, j \in \{1, 2, \ldots, k\}$) such that B can compute s_U from c_i and c_j. If B can compute s_U from c_i and c_j, and can compute s_U from c_j and c_k, then B can compute s_U from c_i and c_k.

We believe that this model is very general under the Chaum-Fiat-Naor paradigm, and it seems to be hard to find a different model.

3 Problems

In this paper, we raise the following problems regarding the lower bound for divisible coins.

- Find the lower bound for data size of divided coins (the size of data transferred from a customer to a shop during payment), $|c^{(w)}| + |m_U| + |\sigma(m_U)| + |w| + |e|$ with respect to the precision of divisibility, N. Since $|m_U|$ and $|\sigma(m_U)|$ are fixed with respect to N, the lower bound with respect to N is determined by $|c^{(w)}| + |w| + |e|$. Here, $|c^{(w)}| + |w| + |e|$ means

$$\max\{|c^{(w)}| + |w| + |e| \mid w \leq N\}.$$

(Note that to obtain the lower bound of $|c^{(w)}| + |e|$ is the main problem here, since the lower bound of $|w|$ is trivially $\log_2 N$.)
- Find the lower bound for computational complexity of computing a divided coin (the computational complexity of generating payment data for a customer), $Comp(c^{(w)}) + Comp(m_U) + Comp(\sigma(m_U))$ with respect to the precision of divisibility, N. Here, $Comp(x)$ means the computational complexity of U's generating x, and $Comp(c^{(w)})$ means

$$\max\{Comp(c^{(w)}) \mid w \leq N\}.$$

Similarly, since $Comp(m_U) + Comp(\sigma(m_U))$ is fixed with respect to N and $Comp(w)$ and $Comp(e)$ are negligible, to find the lower bound of $Comp(c^{(w)})$ with respect to N is the main problem here.

4 Lower Bounds

4.1 Structure of divisible coins

In this subsection, we will clarify the structure of divisible coins using the property of the above-mentioned model, especially the overspending prevention rule. For example, from the rule, if a divided coin, c^*, is spent, the relationship of c^* with other possible coins, c_i, can be specified by checking whether (c^*, c_i) reveals s_U or not. In addition, if spending coins c_1 and c_2 gives the exactly same effect to other coins as spending c_0, then we can introduce the equivalence relationship between (c_1, c_2) and c_0. Our main results will be obtained by using such structural properties of divisible coins.

Definition 1. [**Revealing:** $(c_1, c_2) \rightarrow s_U, \quad Val(c^{(w)})$]
Let c_1 and c_2 be coins. Let $(c_1, c_2) \rightarrow s_U$, if and only if B can compute s_U from c_1 and c_2. (Similarly $(c_1, c_2) \nrightarrow s_U$, if and only if B cannot compute s_U from c_1 and c_2.[2])

Let $Val(c)$ denote the value of coin c. (e.g., $Val(c^{(w)}) = w$.)

Definition 2. [**Covering:** $c_1 \rightarrow c_2$]
Let c_1, c_2 and c_3 be coins. We denote $c_1 \rightarrow c_2$ if and only if

$$Val(c_1) \geq Val(c_2),$$

and there exists no c_3 such that

$$(c_1, c_2) \rightarrow s_U, \quad (c_2, c_3) \rightarrow s_U, \quad (c_1, c_3) \nrightarrow s_U.$$

Note:
We can instead say that $c_1 \rightarrow c_2$ if and only if

$$Val(c_1) \geq Val(c_2),$$

and for any c_3 such that

$$(c_1, c_2) \rightarrow s_U, \quad (c_2, c_3) \rightarrow s_U,$$

the following holds:

$$(c_1, c_3) \rightarrow s_U.$$

Definition 3. [**Equivalence:** $c_0 \sim (c_1, \ldots, c_k)$]
Let $c_0, c_1, \ldots, c_k$ be coins. Then, we say c_0 is equivalent to $(c_1, \ldots, c_k)$, and denote $c_0 \sim (c_1, \ldots, c_k)$, (or $(c_1, \ldots, c_k) \sim c_0$), if and only if

$$c_0 \rightarrow c_i \quad (i = 1, \ldots, k),$$

$$Val(c_0) = Val(c_1) + \cdots Val(c_k),$$

for any pair of (c_i, c_j) $(i, j \in \{1, \ldots, k\})$,

$$(c_i, c_j) \nrightarrow s_U.$$

Definition 4. [**Disjoint**]
For two sets of coins, $C_1 = (c_1, \ldots, c_k)$, and $C_2 = (c'_1, \ldots, c'_l)$, we say C_1 and C_2 are disjoint if and only if for any pair of coins $c_i \in C_1$ and $c'_j \in C_2$,

$$(c_i, c'_j) \nrightarrow s_U.$$

Let $Val(C_1)$ be $Val(c_1) + \cdots Val(c_k)$.

---

[2] In our model, "cannot compute" means "intractable to compute" for any poly time bounded machine.

Note: When $c_0 \sim (c_1,\ldots,c_k)$, a trivial example of c_0 consists of $(c_1,\ldots,c_k)$. Then, a set of coins, $(c_1,\ldots,c_k)$, is identical to a coin, c_0.

Definition 5. [Composition of disjoint coin sets]
Let $C_1 = (c_1,\ldots,c_k)$ and $C_2 = (c'_1,\ldots,c'_l)$ be disjoint sets of coins. Let $c_0 \sim (c_1,\ldots,c_k)$, and $c'_0 \sim (c'_1,\ldots,c'_l)$. We then denote

$$(c_0, c'_0) \sim (c_1,\ldots,c_k, c'_1,\ldots,c'_l).$$

Let C_1 and C_2 be disjoint sets of coins, and C_3 and C_4 be disjoint sets of coins. If $C_1 \sim C_3$ and $C_2 \sim C_4$, then we say

$$(C_1, C_3) \sim (C_2, C_4).$$

Lemma 6. *Let c_1, c_2 and c_3 be coins, and $c_1 \to c_2$ and $c_2 \to c_3$. Then $c_1 \to c_3$.*

Proof. ¿From the definition, $Val(c_1) \geq Val(c_2)$, and $Val(c_2) \geq Val(c_3)$. Hence, $Val(c_1) \geq Val(c_3)$.
In addition, there exist no c_4, c_5 such that

$$(c_1, c_2) \to s_U, \quad (c_2, c_4) \to s_U, \quad (c_1, c_4) \not\to s_U,$$

$$(c_2, c_3) \to s_U, \quad (c_3, c_5) \to s_U, \quad (c_2, c_5) \not\to s_U.$$

By setting $c_4 = c_3$, we can obtain that

$$(c_1, c_3) \to s_U.$$

We then suppose there exists c_6 such that

$$(c_3, c_6) \to s_U, \quad (c_1, c_6) \not\to s_U.$$

Then

$$(c_2, c_6) \to s_U,$$

since there exists no c_6 such that

$$(c_3, c_6) \to s_U, \quad (c_2, c_6) \not\to s_U.$$

That is, there exists c_6 such that

$$(c_2, c_6) \to s_U, \quad (c_1, c_6) \not\to s_U.$$

This contradicts the assumption. Thus, there exists no c_6 such that

$$(c_3, c_6) \to s_U, \quad (c_1, c_6) \not\to s_U.$$

Lemma 7. *Let C_1, C_2 and C_3 be sets of coins, and $C_1 \sim C_2$ and $C_2 \sim C_3$. Then $C_1 \sim C_3$.*

Proof. First, we prove it when C_1 is a single coin, c_1, and for any coin $c_{2,i} \in C_2$, there exists $(c_{3,i_1} \ldots, c_{3,i_j}, \ldots) \in C_3$ such that $c_{2,i} \sim (c_{3,i_1} \ldots, c_{3,i_j}, \ldots)$.

If $c_1 \sim C_2$ and $C_2 \sim C_3$, then from Lemma 6 clearly $c_i \rightarrow c_{3,i_j}$ for all (i, j). Therefore, $c_1 \sim C_3$.

Next we prove it when C_2 is a single coin, c_2, and

$$c_2 \sim C_1 = (c_{1,1}, c_{1,2}), \quad c_2 \sim C_3 = (c_{3,1}, c_{3,2}).$$

If there exist $c_2 \rightarrow c_{1,1}$ and $c_2 \rightarrow c_{3,1}$, then there exist three disjoint coins, c', c'' and c''', such that $c_2 \rightarrow c'$, $c_2 \rightarrow c''$, $c_2 \rightarrow c'''$,

$$c_{1,1} \sim (c', c''), \quad c_{1,2} \sim (c', c''').$$

(c', c'' and c''' can be empty.)

Therefore, there are four disjoint coin sets, $c_{(1)}, c_{(2)}, c_{(3)}, c_{(4)}$, such that

$$c_{1,1} \sim (c_{(1)}, c_{(2)}), \quad c_{1,2} \sim (c_{(3)}, c_{(4)}),$$
$$c_{3,1} \sim (c_{(1)}, c_{(3)}), \quad c_{3,2} \sim (c_{(2)}, c_{(4)}),$$

since $c_{1,1}$ and $c_{1,2}$ are disjoint, ($c_{3,1}$ and $c_{3,2}$ are disjoint and $Val(c_{1,1}) + Val(c_{1,2}) = Val(c_{3,1}) + Val(c_{3,2})$.

Hence,

$$C_1 = (c_{1,1}, c_{1,2}) \sim (c_{(1)}, c_{(2)}, c_{(3)}, c_{(4)}) \sim C_3 = (c_{3,1}, c_{3,2}).$$

Using the above mentioned results, we can prove it when C_1, C_2 and C_3 are general.

Lemma 8. *Let $\$N$ be the face value of a coin. Let s and t be integers such that $st = N$. Then there are t equivalence classes of $\$s$ (divided) coins with respect to $\sim$.*

Proof. Let c_i $(i = 1, 2, \ldots)$ be $\$s$ (divided) coins. There are at least one set of t $\$s$ coins (say $c_1, \ldots, c_t$) such that, for any pair of c_i and c_j $(i, j \in \{1, 2, \ldots, t\})$,

$$c_i \not\sim c_j.$$

(Otherwise, a customer cannot divide a $\$N$ coin into t $\$s$ coins.)

If there exists a $\$s$ (divided) coin, c^* $(c^* \notin \{c_1, \ldots, c_t\})$, and c_i $(i \in \{1, 2, \ldots, t\})$, such that $c^* \not\sim c_i$, then for all $i = 1, 2, \ldots, t$, $c^* \not\sim c_i$. Therefore a customer can use $(t + 1)$ $\$s$ coins without revealing s_U. This is a contradiction. Hence, for any $\$s$ (divided) coin, c^* $(c^* \notin \{c_1, \ldots, c_t\})$, there exists c_i $(i \in \{1, 2, \ldots, t\})$ such that $c^* \sim c_i$. Thus, there are t equivalence classes of $\$s$ (divided) coins.

Lemma 9. *Let N be the face value of coin c. Let c_1 be a coin (divided from c). Then there exists a coin, c_2, (divided from c) such that,*

$$Val(c_1) + Val(c_2) = N,$$

and for any coin c_3 with $c_1 \rightarrow c_3$,

$$(c_2, c_3) \not\rightarrow s_U.$$

Then, we call c_2 the complement of c_1 wrt N.

Proof. Assume that for any coin, c_2, with $Val(c_1) + Val(c_2) = N$, there exists c_3 such that $c_1 \to c_3$ and $(c_2, c_3) \to s_U$.

Then, from the definition of $\to$, for any c_2,

$$(c_1, c_2) \to s_U.$$

On the other hand, there must exist c_2 such that

$$Val(c_1) + Val(c_2) = N \quad \text{and} \quad (c_1, c_2) \nrightarrow s_U,$$

since otherwise customer U cannot spend $\$Val(c_2)$ (i.e., $\$N$ totally) after U spends $\$Val(c_1)$ by using coin c_1.

Thus, contradiction occurs: $(c_1, c_2) \to s_U$, and $(c_1, c_2) \nrightarrow s_U$ occurs at the same time.

Note:

This lemma guarantees that, a coin, c_1, determines a set of coins, $c_3, c_4, \ldots$, such that they are covered by c_1 (i.e., $c_1 \to c_3$, $c_1 \to c_4$, $\ldots$,) and a disjoint one from the coin, c_2, worth the remaining value (i.e., $\$(N - Val(c_1))$).

Lemma 10. *Let c_2 be the complement of c_1. Then, for any set of disjoint coins, $C_1 = (c_{11}, \ldots, c_{1i}, \ldots,) \sim c_1$, and for any set of disjoint coins, $C_2 = (c_{21}, \ldots, c_{2j}, \ldots,) \sim c_2$, $Val(C_1) + Val(C_2) = N$, and for any coin c_3 with $c_{1i} \to c_3$ ($i \in \{1, \ldots, \}$), for any coin c_{2j} ($j \in \{1, \ldots, \}$),*

$$(c_{2j}, c_3) \nrightarrow s_U.$$

Proof. This proof is similarly obtained from the proof of Lemma 9.

Note:

This lemma says that a set of disjoint coins, $C_1 = (c_{11}, \ldots, c_{1j}, \ldots,) \sim c_1$, implies all possible divisible payment with the same effect to the afterward payment as payment by coin c_1. That is, definition $\sim$ characterizes two ways of payment that have the same effect to the afterward payment.

Lemma 11. *Let the number of layers of a divisible coin system based on our model be r, and $v_1, v_2, \ldots, v_r$ be the values of term coins ($v_1 < v_2 < \cdots < v_r$). Then, v_i divides v_{i+1} for $i = 1, \ldots, r - 1$.*

Proof. Assume that for $i \in \{1, \ldots, r - 1\}$ v_i does not divide v_{i+1}. Let $k = \lfloor v_{i+1}/v_i \rfloor$. Let c_0 be a term coin worth v_{i+1}. Then there exist $(c_1, \ldots, c_k)$ such that c_0 covers $c_1, \ldots, c_k$, which are term coins worth v_i (i.e., $c_0 \to (c_1, \ldots, c_k)$) from a variation of Lemma 8.

Since $Val(c_0) > Val(c_1) + \cdots + Val(c_k)$, c_0 must cover c^* (i.e., $c_0 \to c^*$) which is worth $Val(c_0) - (Val(c_1) + \cdots + Val(c_k))$ and is covered by another term coin worth v_i (say c_{k+1}) (i.e., $c_{k+1} \to c^*$).

Since c_0 does not cover c_{k+1} (i.e., $c_0 \not\to c_{k+1}$) and c_{k+1} covers c^* (i.e., $c_{k+1} \to c^*$), $(c^*, c_0) \not\to s_U$, from Lemmas 9 and 10.

This contracts the fact that c_0 must cover c^*. Thus for any $i \in \{1, \ldots, r-1\}$, v_i divides v_{i+1}.

4.2 Lower bounds for computational complexity and coin size

This subsection shows our main results, the lower bounds for computational complexity in computing a divided coin and coin size.

Theorem 12. *Let N be the precision of divisibility (e.g., $\$N$ is the face value of a coin, and the minimum divisible denomination is $\$1$).*

$$Comp(c^{(w)}) \geq \log_2 N \cdot Comp(term),$$

$$|c^{(w)}| + |e| + |w| \geq \log_2 N \cdot |term| + \log_2 N.$$

Proof. Without loss of generality, we assume that $\$N$ is the face value of a coin, and the minimum divisible denomination is $\$1$.

Let the number of layers of a divisible coin system be r, and $v_1 (= 1)$, v_2, $\ldots, v_r (= N)$ be the values of term coins ($1 = v_1 < v_2 < \cdots < v_r = N$). Let $m_i = v_{i+1}/v_i$ ($i \in \{1, \ldots, r-1\}$), where m_i is always an integer (≥ 2) from Lemma 11. Then $N = m_1 m_2 \cdots m_{r-1}$.

Clearly the maximum number of terms included in a coin is $(m_1 - 1) + (m_2 - 1) + \cdots + (m_{r-1} - 1)$, where the coin with the maximum number of terms consists of $(m_1 - 1)$ terms worth v_1, $(m_2 - 1)$ terms worth v_2, $\cdots$, and $(m_{r-1} - 1)$ terms worth v_{r-1}.

Since $(m_i - 1) \geq \log_2 m_i$ (as $m_i \geq 2$),

$$(m_1 - 1) + (m_2 - 1) + \cdots + (m_{r-1} - 1) \geq \sum_{i=1}^{r-1} \log_2 m_i = \log_2 N.$$

Therefore, the lower bound of the number of terms included in a coin is $\log_2 N$. The lower bounds of the coin size and computational complexity are obtained immediately from this result as follows:

$$Comp(c^{(w)}) \geq \log_2 N \cdot Comp(term),$$

$$|c^{(w)}| + |e| \geq \log_2 N \cdot |term|.$$

5 Conclusion

This paper has given lower bounds for data size and computational complexity of divisible cash with respect to the precision of divisibility, N. The results assumed the Chaum-Fiat-Naor (CFN) paradigm and a concrete model of representation and computation that all implementations of the paradigm follow.

We have shown that the lower bound for computational complexity of generating a (divided) coin is $\log_2 N \cdot Comp(term)$, and that the lower bound for coin size is $\log_2 N \cdot |term| + \log_2 N$.

References

1. Brands, S., "Untraceable Off-line Cash in Wallet with Observers", Proceedings of Crypto 93, LNCS 773, Springer-Verlag, pp.302–318 (1994).
2. Chaum, D., Fiat, A., and Naor, M., "Untraceable Electronic Cash," Proceedings of Crypto 88, LNCS 403, Springer-Verlag, pp.319-327 (1990).
3. D'amingo, S. and Di Crescenzo, G., "Methodology for Digital Money based on General Cryptographic Tools", Proceedings of Eurocrypt 94, LNCS 950, Springer-Verlag, pp.156-170 (1995).
4. De Santis, A. and Persiano, G., "Communication Efficient Zero-Knowledge Proofs of Knowledge (with Applications to Electronic Cash)" Proceedings of STACS 92, pp.449-460 (1992).
5. Even, S., Goldreich, O. and Yacobi, Y., "Electronic Wallet", Proceedings of Crypto 83, Plenum Press ,pp.383-386 (1984).
6. Eng, T. and Okamoto, T. "Single-Term Divisible Coins," Proceedings of Eurocrypt 94, LNCS 950, Springer-Verlag, pp.306-319 (1995).
7. Ferguson, N., "Single Term Off-line Coins", Proceedings of Eurocrypt 93, LNCS 765, Springer-Verlag, pp.318–328 (1994).
8. Franklin, M. and Yung, M., "Secure and Efficient Off-Line Digital Money", Proceedings of ICALP 93, pp. 449-460 (1993).
9. Hayes, B., "Anonymous One-Time Signatures and Flexible Untraceable Electronic Cash," Proceedings of Auscrypt 90, LNCS 453, Springer-Verlag, pp.294-305 (1990).
10. Okamoto, T., and Ohta, K., "Universal Electronic Cash", Proceedings of Crypto 91, LNCS 576, Springer-Verlag, pp.324-337 (1992).
11. Okamoto, T., "An Efficient Divisible Electronic Cash Scheme", Proceedings of Crypto 95, LNCS 963, Springer-Verlag, pp.438-451 (1995).
12. Pailles, J.C., "New Protocols for Electronic Money", Proceedings of Auscrypt 92, LNCS 718, Springer-Verlag, pp.263–274 (1993).
13. Vaudenay, S., "One-Time Identification with Low Memory," Proceedings of Eurocodes 92 (1992).
14. Yacobi, Y., "Efficient electronic money", Proceedings of Asiacrypt 94, LNCS 917, Springer-Verlag, pp.153-163 (1994).

Certifying Trust

Ilari Lehti[1], Pekka Nikander[1]

Helsinki University of Technology, Department of Computer Science,
FI-02015 TKK, Espoo, Finland
{ilari.lehti, pekka.nikander}@hut.fi

Abstract. A basic function of all signatures, digital or not, is to express trust and authority, explicit or implied. This is especially the case with digital signatures used in certificates. In this paper, we study the trust relationships expressed by the certificates used in X.509, PGP and SPKI. Especially, we present and revise the idea of a certificate loop, or a loop of certificates from the verifying party to the communicating peer, requesting access or acceptance. We also show how that kind of certificate loops can be used to explicitly express security policy decisions. In the end of the paper, we briefly describe our own SPKI implementation that is specially tailored towards policy management. The implementation is based on Java and build using Design Patterns. It functions as a separate process, providing security services to the local kernel and applications.

1   Introduction

"Hallo!" said Pooh, in case there was anything outside.

"Hallo!" said Whatever-it-was.

"Oh!" said Pooh. "Hallo!"

"Hallo!"

"Oh, there you are!" said Pooh. "Hallo!"

"Hallo!" said the Strange Animal, wondering how long this was going on.

Pooh was just going to say "Hallo!" for the fourth time when he thought that he wouldn't, so he said, "Who is it?" instead.

"Me," said a voice.

"Oh!" said Pooh.

In the above quote from [10], we have an access control situation. Pooh, who is in control of the door, finds out that something wants to get in. An exchange of messages follows. The participants seem to lack a proper communication protocol and the messages remain pretty meaningless. At the end, an attempt of identification is made, but without proper credentials. Pooh, were he not a bear of no brain, should conclude that the voice has no authority to enter.

We are going to illuminate the ideas of authority delegation and certificate loops. We mainly focus on the IETF proposal called Simple Public Key Infrastructure (SPKI) [14] and on our implementation of a Policy Manager based on that proposal. Our system allows trust and authority to be explicitly represented in the form of certificates.

Suppose Pooh would use such a system. After deciding of a door-opening policy, he could have issued credentials to trusted persons, perhaps even allowing them to further delegate this authority. Then the Strange Animal could push a set of credentials under the door and Pooh, after checking their authenticity, could have let the stranger in. In the following subsections, we will explain these terms in the context of networked entities.

1.1 Trust Models

Trust is a belief that an entity behaves in a certain way. Trust to a machinery is usually a belief that it works as specified. Trust to a person means that even if someone has the possibility to harm us, we believe he/she chooses not to. The trust requirements of a system form the system's trust model. All computer systems, protocols and security frameworks have trust requirements, i.e. they have trust relationships that the user needs to share. We may need to have some kind of trust to the implementor of a software which source code is not public, trust to the person with whom we communicate on a network, trust to the computer hardware that it provides us with correct computation results, and so on. The trust relationships that we are interested in here are those between us and some other networked entities. Those other entities may be fellow human beings or machines providing some service.

It is of equal importance to analyze the trust requirements of a protocol or a framework as it is to analyze the soundness of the technical methods that it uses to achieve security. Trust requirements may be analyzed in several ways. We may consider one generic notion of trust and find the entities that we need to trust. The next alternative would be to classify different types of trust and define the ways we need to trust each entity [16]. Yet another refinement might be to define a degree of trust needed towards the other entities [3]. The ways to categorize and analyze trust may be called trust modeling, but with a trust model we mean the set of trust relationships of a system.

As an example for analyzing trust, a bank may tell me that the most appropriate way to protect the data traffic between my workstation and their server is to use a cryptosystem where they provide me a good-quality keypair. (This is among the most reasonable security-related offers that banks seem to provide.) Not only need I trust this bank's capability to make good keys, I also need to trust the bank completely, because they have the key that is supposed to be secret and identifies the service user as me. Many people are willing to accept that, it is a bank after all. But the truth is that this trust extends to every employee of the bank that has access to those keys. Why would I want to take such a risk, if it is possible for me to create my own key, not known to anyone else? Of course, creating my own keys requires me to have enough trust in my own key generation software and hardware.

1.2 Security Policies

Closely related to the concept of trust is the concept of policy. A security policy is a manifestation of laws, rules and practices that regulate how sensitive information and other resources are managed, protected and distributed. Every entity may be seen to function under its own policy rules. In many cases today, these rules are very informal, probably even unwritten. The policy of an entity or part of it is often derived according to some hierarchy, e.g. next level in a corporate hierarchy.

Security policies can be meaningful not only as an internal code of function, but as a published document which defines some security-related practices. This could be important information when some outsider is trying to decide whether an organization can be trusted in some respect. This is one situation where it is of use to define the policy in a systematic manner, e.g. to have a formal policy model.

Another and a more important reason to have a formally specified policy is that a lot of the policy information should be directly accessible by the workstations and their software. Having a policy control enforced in software rather than relying on the users to follow some memorized rules is essential if the policy is meant to be followed. A lot of policy rules are already present in the operating systems, protocols, applications and their configuration files. A central policy storage and a policy supervising software would make these and other policy settings easier to maintain and analyze.

1.3 Digital Certificates

A certificate is a signed statement about the properties of some entity. In a digital certificate the signature is a number computed from the certificate data and the key of the issuer. If a certificate states something about the issuer, it is called a self-signed certificate or an auto-certificate.

Traditionally, the job of a certificate has been to bind a public key to the name of the keyholder. This is called an identity certificate. It typically has at least the following fields: the name of the issuer, the name of the subject, the associated key, the expiration date, a serial number and a signature that authenticates the rest of the certificate.

Not all applications benefit much from a name binding. Therefore certificates can also make a more specific statement, for example, that some entity is authorized to get a certain service. This would be called an authorization certificate. In addition to the fields in an identity certificate, more detailed validity fields are often needed. The "associated key" -field is replaced by the authorization definition field. The issuer and the subject are typically not defined with names but with keys.

In all certificate systems, but especially in identity certificates, it is important to choose a proper name space. The naming should be unique in the sense that no two principals have the same name, though one principal may have several names. Names should be permanent, if the principal so decides, so no enforced name changes should occur. In the authorization certificate naming schemes, the name binding may be early or late binding. Late means that when authority is bound to some name, the name need not yet be bound to a key, but this can be done afterwards.

Certificates and trust relationships are very closely connected. The meaning of a certificate is to make a reliable statement concerning some trust relationship. Certificates often form chains where the trust propagates transitively from an entity to another. In the case of an identity certificate, this is trust to some name binding. Authorization certificates often delegate some property or right of the issuer to the subject. It is also desirable that the system allows to limit the delegated authority in the middle of a path.

1.4 Certificate Loops

The idea of certificate loops is a central one in analyzing trust. The source of trust is almost always the checking party itself. For example, if a user wants to authenticate that a networked server is, actually, providing the service the user wants to use, the certificates used for this check must be trusted by the user. Specifically, the first certificate in a certificate chain must be trusted, implicitly or explicitly. Similarly, when the server wants to check the user's access rights, the certificates used to authenticate the user must be trusted by the server. Again, the server must be configured to trust the certificates in the chain.

Thus, a chain of certificates, typically implicitly starting at the verifying party and ending at the party claiming authority, forms an open arc. This arc is closed into loop by the online authentication protocol where the claimant proves possession of its private key to the verifying party. Such a loop is called a certificate loop. In Section 4.1, we return to this issue in more detail.

1.5   Outline of This Paper

In the next section we will discuss the currently most popular certification systems and compare the different certification approaches. In section 3 we are going to take a closer look to the SPKI and some of the new ideas behind it. Section 4 shows our view of certificate loops and presents parts of our implementation. In section 5, we will discuss the possible future directions of Internet security. The last section sums up our key ideas.

2   Expressing Trust With Certificates

In this section we describe some concrete certificate infrastructure proposals and compare them with respect to trust. These systems divide into two main categories: those certifying identity and those certifying a specific authorization. In addition to that, the systems have important distinctions in their initial trust requirements and trust hierarchy.

2.1   Certifying Identity

We did briefly mention the name binding function of an identity certificate. More generally, with a binding we mean some important relationship or connection between two or more aspects of a system. In the case of certification, such aspects include the person, the person's name, the cryptographic key, or the remote operation about to be performed. We would wish all the relevant connections to be strong bindings instead of weak ones.

Fig. 1 shows the bindings of an identity certification system used for access control. The certificate chain does the binding of a key to a name. Name is authorized to perform some operation according to an access control list (ACL), stored in the service provider's private storage. When the service is used, a key challenge between the participants binds a key to the operation to be performed. These three bindings can be made strong with appropriate cryptographic mechanisms.

The strength of a binding is here seen to come from the mathematics of cryptography. In reality the strength depends on the trust relationships involved and is always subjective. We could draw the private key and the public key separately. This would bring one more step to the 'loop'. The binding between these two keys is the strongest binding of all.

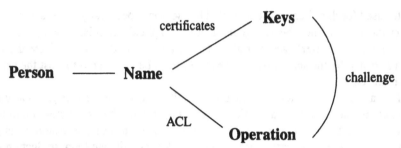

Fig. 1. Identification certificate bindings

But, the person-name binding is subject to some vulnerability. It is rarely taken into serious consideration at all, but usually assumed to be common knowledge. The larger the name space, the less likely that anyone would know the name of a specific individual. Alice might suspect that her old friend Bob Smith has a name in the global directory service, but there are so many people named Bob Smith in the world that it is unlikely Alice would know which of the thousands of Bob Smiths was in fact her old friend [14]. In a few special cases where you know what to look for, this binding can intuitively be considered strong, but it's never strong in the sense of cryptographic strength.

It can be argued that identity-based certificates create an artificial layer of indirection between the information that is certified (which answers the question "who is the holder of this public key?") and the question that a secure application must answer ("can we trust this public key for this purpose?") [4]. Currently each application has to re-implement the mapping of names to actions that they are trusted to perform.

Of the existing identity certifying systems around, two have been taken into quite a common usage. PGP [11] has been a success since its introduction. X.509 [15], while not taking an actual flying start, has lately gained some popularity despite the lack of any working global scale X.500 directory service.

PGP. In the PGP system, a user generates a key pair that is associated with his or her unique ID. Keys are stored in key records. A key record contains an ID, a public or a private key, and a timestamp of when the key pair was created. Public keys are stored on public key rings and private keys on secret key rings. Each user must store and manage a pair of key rings. [4]

If user A has a copy of user B's public key record that she is confident of having not been tampered with since B generated it, A can sign this copy and send it back to B, who can give this 'certified' key-record to other users, such as user C. A thus acts as an introducer of B to C. Each user must tell the PGP system which individuals are trusted as introducers. Moreover, a user may specify the degree of trust in each introducer. [4]

X.509. As in PGP, X.509 certificates are signed records that associate users' IDs with their cryptographic keys. Even if they also contain the names of the signature schemes used to create them and the time interval in which they are valid, their basic purpose is still the binding of users to keys.

However, X.509 differs sharply from PGP in its level of centralization of authority. While anyone may sign public-key records and act as an introducer in PGP, the X.509 framework postulates that everyone will obtain certificates from an official CA. When user A creates a key pair, she has it and the rest of the information certified by one of more CAs and registers the resulting certificates with an official directory service. When A later wants to communicate securely with B, the directory service must create a certification path from A to B. The X.509 framework rests on the assumption that CAs are organized into a global "certifying authority tree" and that all users within a "community of interest" have keys that have been signed by CAs with a common ancestor in this global tree. [4]

The latest version, called X.509 v3, has a mechanism called certificate extensions. Using these extensions it is technically possible, even if not convenient, to use X.509 certificates for authorization purposes. Neither the specifications [12] nor the current usage of the system gives any support for such a practice, though.

Name spaces. As identity certification means binding a name to a key, the first concern is the choice of a name space. PGP really has no name space, which means that the name space is flat and any names can be used. It is common practice to use a name of the form (Full Name, EmailAddress).

X.509 uses hierarchical naming based on the X.500 directory service, which is considered to be realized so that independent organizations and their subdepartments would take care of naming their employees uniquely. X.500 has not come to pass and given the speed with which the Internet adopts or rejects ideas, it is likely that X.500 will never be adopted [7]. Organization-based naming scheme also has the undesirable property that if one changes a job, one's name will change at the same occasion.

One of the main obstacles for a wide acceptance of a global distributed directory service like X.509 is that most companies do not want to reveal the details of their internal organization, personnel etc. to their competitors. This would be the same as making the company's internal telephone directory public and, furthermore, distributing it in an electronic form ready for duplication and automatic processing [8]. A controlled and secure directory service would be possible to create, but apparently there is currently no large market demand for it.

Trust models. The PGP users can trust anyone they want; all users are equal. This kind of freedom will cause a "web of trust" to be created between the users. In addition to trusting a certain key as valid, it is possible to define the degree of trust to a person as an introducer. Each individual creates, certifies and distributes their own keys. PGP rejects the concept of official certifying authorities being more trustworthy than the guy/girl next door.

One of the problems in the X.509 trust hierarchy is that it has a centralized trusted entity as a root that everyone with their differing needs should be able to trust. The system also implies everyone's trust to all the nodes of the certifying tree. In X.509, the authorization decisions are separate from the certification of identity even though all CAs must be trusted with respect to all authorizations.

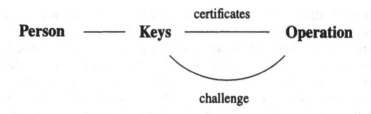

Fig. 2. Authorization certificate bindings

The strong part of X.509 is that the protocol for finding someone's public key is well defined, as long as the assumed hierarchy exists. The non-hierarchical approaches leave something to be desired in this respect.

An interesting effort to combine the hierarchical trust model and the web of trust was made in the ICE-TEL project [5]. The ICE-TEL calls its trust model as a *web of hierarchies* -model. It is based on security domains, which can be as small as single-user domains. A security domain encapsulates a collection of objects that all abide by the rules defined in the domain's security policy. Then each domain can freely choose what other domains to trust. This has the advantage that there is no single trusted root of the hierarchy. ICE-TEL claims to handle authorizations as well, but is essentially an identity-based system that relies quite strongly on the use of Certification Authorities.

2.2 Certifying Authorization

The bindings of an authorization certificate system are shown in Fig. 2. The certificate chain binds a key to an operation. A key challenge also operates between an operation and a key, thus closing the certification loop. These two bindings are based on cryptography and can be made strong. Again, we have chosen to draw the two keys together for clarity. Drawing them separately would just lengthen the certificate loop by one step.

The person-key binding is different from the person-name binding in the case of identity certification. By definition, the keyholder of a key has sole possession of the private key. Therefore, either this private key or the corresponding public key can be used as an identifier (a name) of the keyholder. For any public key cryptosystem to work, it is essential that a principal will keep its private key to itself. If the principal does not keep the private key protected (if the private key gets out to others to use) then it is not possible to know what entity is using that key and no certificates will be able to restore the resulting broken security.

So, the person is the only one having access to the private key and the key has enough entropy so that nobody has the same key. Common names are not automatically unique even if we add company information or other such constructs. So, the identifying key is bound tightly to the person that controls it and all bindings are strong.

The problem with the person-key binding is that from the service provider's point of view it looks like an undefined binding. The provider does not know who has control over the key. However, neither is this question essential in the most usual applications, nor can the traditional identity certification always answer this question. For the cases where the real physical identity of a keyholder needs to be known, [6] discusses different possibilities how to bind persons to keys without certification authorities. [14] proposes so-called process server certificates, issued by commercial enterprises, to aid in handling the extreme cases.

The feature of not having to bind keys to names is especially convenient in systems that include anonymity as a security requirement [4], [7]. It is easy for a user to create new keys for such applications, while creating an authorized false identity is (hopefully) not possible.

The most important authorization certification proposals are SDSI [13], SPKI and PolicyMaker [4]. In section 3, we will have a more detailed discussion about SPKI.

Trust models. Authorization-based systems are very general and flexible. They have no pre-defined trust hierarchy, but any user can define who to trust, which will lead to a PGP-like web of trust. In authorization certificates, the type of trust is always defined as well. The non-hierarchical approach contains fewer initial trust requirements to start with. It allows for single organizations to build their own web of policies and certificate servers inside the organization. After this it is possible to extend the trust to related organizations that you do your business with. It is immediately possible to start writing certificates for others to have when using your resources or to request certificates which allow the use of other services. Furthermore, you do not have to trust a particular CA if you do not want to, and you can choose to trust only some properties of a certain CA. Having the possibility to choose who to trust and in what respects allows for a great flexibility. It is also important that delegated authority can be limited in the middle of an authorization path.

PolicyMaker is even more flexible than SPKI/SDSI. This can be seen either as a positive or a negative thing. All the mechanisms and conventions that are present in an SPKI-like system must be separately constructed in PolicyMaker filters every time they are needed. Filter complexity may make the system vulnerable to denial of service attacks.

A recommendation for certificates to bind keys to a certain task instead of certificates binding keys to a person can be seen in 'the explicitness principle', stated in [1], for example. It says that in order to make cryptography robust, everything (assumptions, goals, messages, etc.) should be stated as specifically as possible. It is more specific to define an operation for a key than to bind the key to a person.

3 Simple Public Key Certificate

The SPKI is intended to provide mechanisms to support security in a wide range of Internet applications, including Internet security protocols, encrypted electronic mail and WWW documents, payment protocols, and any other application which will require the use of public key certificates and the ability to access them. It is intended that the Simple Public Key Infrastructure will support a range of trust models. [14]

3.1 Principals and Naming

The SPKI principals are keys. Delegations are made to a key, not to the keyholder. However, long keys are inconvenient for a mere human to handle. Using names instead of keys is necessary at least in the user interfaces. Names in the certificates also allow late binding, which means that one can attach some properties to a name and later define or change the name-key binding. Names can also serve the purpose of a certain role. Therefore it is useful to also have other names than keys. SDSI abandoned the idea of a global name space and introduced linked local name spaces. SPKI uses this same naming scheme, where everyone can attach names to keys and every name is relative to some principal. The names can be chained so that speaking about Alice's Mother consists of a name Alice in my name space and a name Mother in Alice's name space.

Names need not always refer to single users, but they can refer to a set of users as well. If an issuer makes a name-key binding while another similar binding to the same name is still valid, these two certificates do not conflict but define a group with at least two members. It is, of course, possible to revoke the earlier one, if the intention is to change the binding to a new. In fact, because SPKI certificates always increase the subject's properties, we will never have to deal with a situation where two certificates would conflict.

An SPKI certificate is closer to a "capability" as defined by [9] than to an identity certificate. There is the difference that in a traditional capability system the capability itself is a secret ticket, the possession of which grants some authority. An SPKI certificate identifies the specific key to which it grants authority. Therefore the mere ability to read (or copy) the certificate grants no authority. The certificate itself does not need to be as tightly controlled. [14]

From the certificate usage point of view, the involved principals are called the prover and the verifier. It is the responsibility of the prover to present the needed certificates. Based on these, the verifier determines whether access is granted.

3.2 Certificate Format

The current SPKI proposal uses S-expressions, a recursive syntax for representing octet-strings and lists. An S-expression can be either an octet-string or a parenthesized list of zero or more simpler S-expressions.

The core of the syntax is called a sequence. It is an ordered collection of certificates, signatures, public keys and opcodes taken together by the prover. A signature refers to the immediately preceding non-signature object. Opcodes are operating instructions, or hints, to the sequence verifier. They may, for example, say that the previous item is to be hashed and saved because there is known to be a hash-reference to it in some subsequent object.

The fields of an SPKI certificate are: *version, cert-display, issuer, issuer location, subject, subject location, delegation, tag, validity,* and *comment.* All of these, except issuer, subject and tag, are optional fields.

Version is the version number of the format. Cert-display is a display hint for the entire certificate. Issuer is a normal SPKI principal, i.e. a key or a hash of key. The location-fields define a place where to find additional information about that principal.

For example, the issuer location may help the prover to track down previous certificates in the chain. Delegation is a true/false -type field defining whether the authority can be delegated further. Comment-field allows the issuer to attach human readable comments. Validity defines the conditions which must be fulfilled for the certificate to be valid. It is possible to define a time range of the validity and a detailed description of the chosen validation method.

The most complex fields are the subject and the tag. The subject can be either a key, a hash of key, a keyholder, an SDSI name, an object or a threshold subject. A keyholder subject refers to the flesh and blood (or iron and silicon) holder of the referenced key instead of to the principal (the key). A threshold subject defines N subjects, K of which are needed to get the authority. The tag contains the exact definition of the delegated authority.

3.3   5-tuple Reduction

Five of the certificate fields have relevance for security enforcement purposes: issuer, subject, delegation, authority (tag) and validity. These security-relevant fields can be represented by a "5-tuple":

(I,S,D,A,V)

In the basic case, a pair of 5-tuples can be reduced as follows [14]:

(I1,S1,D1,A1,V1) + (I2,S2,D2,A2,V2)

becoming

(I1,S2,D2,A,V)

if S1=I2 (meaning that they are the same public key)
and (D1 = TRUE)
and A = intersection(A1,A2)
and V = intersection(V1,V2)

The validity intersections are trivial. The authority intersections are defined by the tag algebra. The user does not have to specify an intersection algorithm for his tags, but one does have to write the used tags in such a way that the standard intersection algorithm gives the desired behavior [14].

By reduction, some chains of authorization statements will be reduced to the form:

(Self, X, D, A, V)

where "Self" represents the entity doing the verification. Any authorization chain not reducing to a 5-tuple with Self as an issuer is not relevant to decisions by Self.

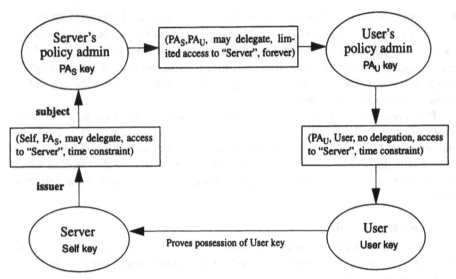

Fig. 3. Basic authorization certificate loop

4   Implementation

We have created a prototype of an SPKI based policy manager. The prototype is written in Java, using the Design Pattern structures [8] in order to promote software re-use and build on best known practices. The purpose of the implementation is to facilitate real life tests with policy based certificates and management.

Before going to the details, we take a look at a typical certificate usage and then introduce some of the architectural elements involved.

4.1   Typical Transaction

So far we have talked about certificates and certificate chains. When a service is used, it must be known that the contacting user really is the entity that is authorized by the given chain. At this point, if not before, the user proves the possession of the identifying key to the verifier. This action closes the authorization chain so that every useful chain can be seen as a loop.

Fig. 3 shows a basic authorization loop implemented with SPKI certificates. The three certificates are possibly created long before they are used. The server has delegated the permission to access the service to its policy administrator. In this certificate, the delegate-property is set to true so that the policy admin may make further delegations. The permission propagates through the policy administrators and their certificates to the service user.

To be complete, this example needs also another loop. Fig. 4 shows the corresponding service identification loop. This is used by the user to authenticate the identity of the service provider, and it may even be completed before the service is used for the first time. This loop does not have to travel the same path as the authorization loop. The middle nodes need necessarily not be official Certification Authorities (CAs) as perhaps suggested by the graph, but the assurance of the server identity and services may sometimes be gained via less official paths.

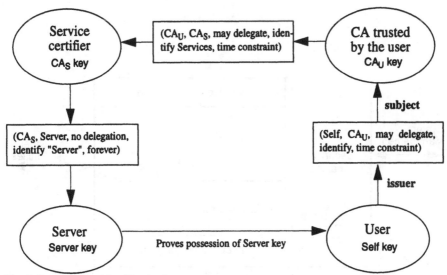

Fig. 4. Basic service identification loop

When the actual service usage takes place, the user provides the authorization certificates to the server. Some systems have proposed a central repository from where the server makes a search. SPKI could use such a storage. However, in the case of authorization certificates, the central repository can be seen as a privacy threat unless it is somehow protected against general searches.

In addition to the server and the user, there may be other participants in the certificate usage process. Some other entity may reduce part of the chain and issue a Certificate Reduction Certificate (CRC), which the server may use as part of the final reduction. One reason for using CRCs may be that the full chain contains certificate formats which the server does not understand. The server may also make its own CRCs for performance reasons, so that it need not make the same reduction several times.

4.2 Design Patterns

Design patterns are simple and elegant solutions to specific problems in object-oriented software design. [8] describes a set of such patterns to start with. These pattern descriptions can widen our design vocabulary in an important way. Instead of describing the designs on the level of algorithms, data structures and classes, we can catch different aspects of the larger behavior with a single word. The benefits of using a pattern are greatly amplified at the stage of documentation or when discussing the design with another person who is familiar with patterns. [8] classifies patterns for three different purposes: creational, structural and behavioral patterns.

4.3 Policy Manager Implementation

Our prototype consists of a main module and a number of protocol adapters. The latter ones interface the policy manager to various security protocols such as IPSEC and ISAKMP. We plan to add support for additional security protocols later on.

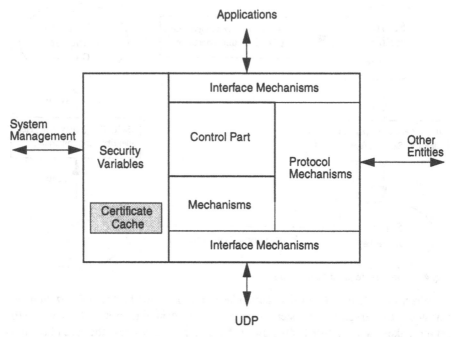

Fig. 5. The structure and connections of Policy Manager

The basic structure of the Policy Manager is shown in Fig. 5. It has a control part, which is the main thread waiting for some tasks to appear to the task queue. The interface mechanisms are called adapters and each of them is implemented as a separate thread. The primary task queue is filled by the three different adapters: the applications adapter, the ISAKMP-adapter and the IPSEC-adapter. The exact usage and output of the Policy Manager depends on the interface created by the specific adapter.

The certificate handling subsection of the main module reads in chains of SPKI certificates, reduces them on demand, and participates on ISAKMP based authentication protocols. The result is a highly configurable ISAKMP security association policy that allows the properties of the created associations to be set up according to the restrictions and limitations expressed with the certificates.

In addition to handling certificate data, the system makes access control decisions, maintains secure network connections and stores policy information. It may also help other protocols and applications in their security-related tasks.

The function of maintaining network connections consists of establishing secure connections to other workstations, accepting connection requests and storing connection information. This may have to be done for the purposes of several different protocols. A secure connection between the parties is usually a prerequisite for any other communication, e.g. requesting a service. The protocols can also have other questions or mappings for the Policy Manager to resolve.

The service provider may use another trusted policy server, which may assist it in access control decisions. There may, for example, be one such a trusted server in an organization. Even if the service provider has all the needed information concerning the

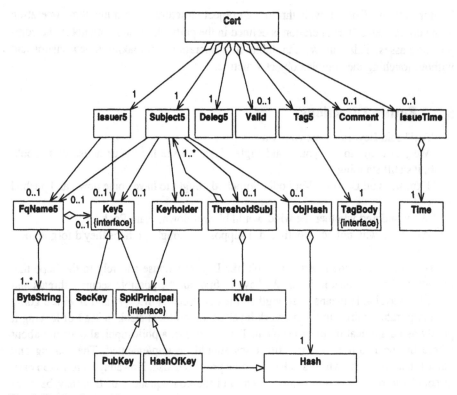

Fig. 6. Fields of a certificate

requested resource, it may have to ask for help in understanding all components of the request. Besides answering access control requests, the Policy Manager may need to create such requests or to parse and store other credential information. One of the resources to control is the policy database that it maintains: who can read or change what policies?

4.4 SPKI Implementation

We have designed an internal format for certificates. This format can hold the certificate information from several different transfer formats, for example PGP, X.509 and SPKI. This generic format is largely based on the SPKI structure and can therefore also contain and reduce certificate sequences. Certificate data can be stored to a certificate cache, which is a part of the trusted security variables of the system.

The data of a single certificate is stored in a tree-like class structure, part of which is shown in Fig. 6. The structure is implemented according to the Composite pattern, which is a way to represent part-whole hierarchies in a tree structure. It enables clients to treat all objects in the composite tree uniformly. All of the classes in the structure are either composites or byte strings. Composites contain other composites and byte strings.

Arriving certificate data is first stored in an instance of a class specific to that format. The conversions between specific formats and generic format are done using the

Visitor pattern. Visitor travels through an object structure performing some operation to the components. The operation is defined in the particular visitor and not in the component classes. This way we can define new operations by making a new visitor and without touching the complex object structure.

5   Future Directions

"Ah!" said Eeyore. "Lost your way?"

"We just came to see you," said Piglet. "And to see how your house was. Look, Pooh, it's still standing!"

"I know," said Eeyore. "Very odd. Somebody ought to have come down and pushed it over."

"We wondered whether the wind would blow it down," said Pooh.

"Ah, that's why nobody's bothered, I suppose. I thought perhaps they'd forgotten."

We do not want the Internet to look like Eeyore's house and rely to the hope that nobody bothers to push it down. We have to find out the possible security threats and use all the available means to strengthen the construct. IPSEC [2] and IPv6 are going to incorporate security to the network layer of the protocol stack instead of leaving it purely as an application layer problem. This is not just a philosophical question about where the peer-to-peer security functions should be implemented. The routing and other functions of the whole stack need to be protected also. Nowadays it is all too easy to spoof the routing or the name system and the consequences of this may be catastrophic.

We are going to have a cryptographic key infrastructure of some kind. In addition to this, we will need means by which entities are authorized to do something. Whether this functionality will be combined with the key infrastructure, like in the case of SPKI, or primarily be done with separate private Access Control List -like constructs, is still an open question. It is practically impossible to predict what the Internet Security Infrastructure will be like in ten years.

6   Conclusions

Digital certificates can be interpreted as expressions of trust. From this viewpoint, certifying user identity is pretty meaningless. Winnie the Pooh doesn't benefit much from the information that his new friend's name is Tiger according to Piglet, however true and trusted this piece of information was. In addition to that, Piglet must tell him how trustworthy Tiger is (or, alternatively, how trustworthy tigers are in general).

Thus, in order to successfully express trust — and thereby security policy constraints — we have to add semantic meaning to the certificates. SPKI, and its cousins SDSI and PolicyMaker are initial steps on this path. The idea behind SPKI is still very immature. Its possibilities and restrictions have not been explored in depth. The current drafts are very much in the state of development. In spite of these facts, the concept looks very promising. We hope that the results of the IETF working group will get enough publicity so that the critical mass of knowledge on these intricate subjects will be reached.

The name of the person is an essential fact in access control only if we happen to use a mechanism that binds the access rights to this name. This is almost never necessary. By binding the rights straight to the key, we get a simpler, more tailor-made system that has additional benefits, such as anonymity. Unless we want to hurry our journey towards the Orwellian society of no protection of intimacy, this is very important.

References

1. Anderson, R., Needham, R.: Robustness principles for public key protocols, In Proceeings of Crypto'95, 1995.
2. Atkinson, R.: Security Architecture for Internet Protocol, RFC 1825, Naval Research Laboratory, 1995.
3. Beth, T., Borcherding, M., Klein, B.: Valuation of Trust in Open Networks, University of Karlsruhe, 1994.
4. Blaze, M., Feigenbaum, J., Lacy, J.: Decentralized Trust Management, In Proceedings of the IEEE Conference on Security and Privacy, 1996.
5. Chadwick, D., Young, A.: Merging and Extending the PGP and PEM Trust Models - The ICE-TEL Trust Model, IEEE Network Magazine, May/June, 1997.
6. Ellison, C.: Establishing Identity Without Certification Authorities, In Proceedings of the USENIX Security Symposium, 1996.
7. Ellison, C.: Generalized Certificates, http://www.clark.net/pub/cme/html/cert.html.
8. Gamma, E., Helm, R., Johnson, R., Vlissides, J.: Design Patterns – Elements of Reusable Object-Oriented Software, Addison-Wesley, 1995.
9. Karila, A.: Open Systems Security - an Architectural Framework, dissertation, Helsinki University of Technology, 1991.
10. Landau, C.: Security in a Secure Capability-Based System, Operating Systems Review, pp. 2-4, October 1989.
11. Milne, A. A.: Winnie-the-Pooh, The House at Pooh Corner, Methuen Children's Books, 1928.
12. Zimmermann, P.: The Official PGP Users Guide, MIT Press, 1995.
13. Housley, R., Ford, W., Polk, W., Solo, D.: Internet Public Key Infrastructure, Part I: X.509 Certificate and CRL Profile, draft-ietf-pkix-ipki-part1-05.txt, 1997.
14. Rivest, R., Lampson, B.: SDSI - A Simple Distributed Security Infrastructure, 1996.
15. Ellison, C., Frantz, B., Lampson, B., Rivest, R., Thomas, B., Ylonen, T.: Simple Public Key Certificate, Internet Draft, draft-ietf-spki-cert-structure-02.txt, 1997.
16. International Telegraph and Telephone Consultative Committee (CCITT): Recommendation X.509, The Directory - Authentication Framework, CCITT Blue Book, Vol VIII.8, pp. 48-81, 1988.
17. Yahalom, R., Klein, B., Beth, T.: Trust Relationships in Secure Systems - A Distributed Authentication Perspective, In Proceedings of the IEEE Conference on Research in Security and Privacy, 1993.

On the Security of Server-Aided RSA Protocols

Johannes Merkle* and Ralph Werchner

Universität Frankfurt, 60054 Frankfurt, Germany
email: merkle@cs.uni-frankfurt.de

Abstract. In this paper we investigate the security of the server-aided RSA protocols RSA-S1 and RSA-S1M proposed by Matsumoto, Kato and Imai ([MKI89]) and Matsumoto, Imai, Laih and Yen ([MILY93]), respectively. In these protocols a smart card calculates an RSA signature with the aid of an untrusted powerful server. We focus on *generic attacks*, that is, passive attacks that do not exploit any special properties of the encoding of the group elements. Generic algorithms have been introduced by Nechaev ([Nec94]) and Shoup ([Sho97]). We prove lower bounds for the complexity of generic attacks on these two protocols and show that the bounds are sharp by describing attacks that almost match our lower bounds. To the best of our knowledge these are the first security proofs for efficient server-aided RSA protocols.

Keywords: server-aided secret computation, RSA, signature, generic algorithms

1   Introduction

In this paper, we investigate the security of server-aided secret computations of RSA signatures. Consider the following scenario: Let $n = pq$ be an RSA modulus, $\phi(n) = (p-1)(q-1)$ and d, e be a pair of private/public exponents. A smart card stores n and d, and signs a message x by computing $y = x^d \bmod n$. This takes $O(\log n)$ multiplications modulo n, which is a heavy task for the card. The solution proposed by Matsumoto, Kato and Imai in [MKI89] is server-aided secret computation (SASC). In their protocol RSA-S1, the main part of the computation is done by a more powerful server.

The RSA-S1 Protocol.

Initialization step. The card chooses an integer vector $d = (d_1, \ldots, d_m) \in \mathbf{Z}^m$ and a vector $f = (f_1, \ldots, f_m) \in \{0,1\}^m$ with Hamming weight k so that $d = \sum_{i=1}^m f_i d_i \bmod \phi(n)$.

1. The card sends x, n and d to the server.
2. The server returns $z_i = x^{d_i} \bmod n$ for $i = 1, \ldots, m$.
3. The card computes the signature y as $y = \prod_{i=1}^m z_i^{f_i} \bmod n$.

* Supported by DFG under grant DFG Leibniz Programm Schn 143/5-1

In the sequel, Matsumoto, Imai, Laih, and Yen proposed a two-phase version of this protocol, called RSA-S1M ([MILY93]).

There exist two kinds of attacks against such protocols: classical searching ones are called *passive attacks*; specific ones, where the server returns false values to get some information from the card are called *active attacks*. In [LL95] Lim and Lee showed, how active attacks can be avoided efficiently. In this paper, we focus on passive attacks on RSA-S1 and RSA-S1M. We do not consider attacks on RSA. We assume that the modulus n has been chosen properly and that RSA is secure. The attacks considered in this paper only use the information given by the server-aided RSA protocol. In the case of RSA-S1, this is n, d, x, y.

An example for this kind of attacks is the attack of Pfitzmann and Waidner ([PW93]), which presently is the best known attack on RSA-S1. We present a variant of this attack, which uses ideas of van Oorschot and Wiener ([vOW96]).

From the definition of the protocol, we have $x^d = \prod_{f_i=1} z_i \bmod n$. Let m, k be even. For all possible $(f_1, \ldots, f_{\frac{m}{2}})$ with Hamming weight $k/2$, the attacker computes

$$\prod_{i \le m/2} x^{d_i f_i} \bmod n$$

and sorts them. Subsequently, for all $(f_{\frac{m}{2}+1}, \ldots, f_m)$ with Hamming weight $k/2$, it computes

$$y \left(\prod_{i > m/2} x^{d_i f_i} \right)^{-1} \bmod n$$

and sorts them as well. It is easy to see that if $(f_1, \ldots, f_{\frac{m}{2}})$ has Hamming weight $k/2$, then there is a collision, which reveals d (at least $d \bmod \text{ord}(x)$). This holds with probability at least $\rho := \binom{m/2}{k/2}^2 / \binom{m}{k}$.

We consider a computation model that generalizes this kind of attack. Since these attacks do not exploit any special properties of the encoding of the elements of Z_n, we call them *generic attacks*. This model covers all known passive attacks on RSA-S1 or RSA-S1M. Generic algorithms have been introduced by Nechaev ([Nec94]) and Shoup ([Sho97]). Both authors proved lower bounds for the complexity of generic algorithms for the discrete log and related problems.

We prove an average case lower bound of $\Omega(N^{1/2})$ for generic attacks against RSA-S1. Here, N is the size of the space that the card selects its secret from (in the case of RSA-S1, we have $N = \binom{m}{k}$). This bound is matched by the attack described. In addition, we prove a lower bound of $\Omega(N^{3/4})$ for *meet-in-the-middle attacks* against RSA-S1M. A meet-in-the-middle attack is a particular kind of generic attack, which still covers all known passive attacks against RSA-S1 and RSA-S1M. This bound is tight up to a small constant factor. To the best of our knowledge, these are the first security proofs for efficient server-aided RSA protocols.

For the discrete log problem, generic algorithms are particularly well suited for certain subgroups G of $\mathbf{Z}_p^*$ with prime p. For instance, the running time of the generic algorithm of Shanks is $\sqrt{|G|}$, whereas more sophisticated, but non-generic algorithms (i.e. the index calculus method ([Sti95, pp 171])) have a running time that depends on p. Thus, if $p \gg |G|$ the best generic algorithms are most efficient. In server-aided RSA protocols the situation is similar. Here, the secret key is known to be an element of a small subset of $\mathbf{Z}^*_{\phi(n)}$. The running time of algorithms that exploit special properties or representations of the group (i.e. the number field sieve ([LLMP90])) have a running time that depends on n. If n is a secure RSA modulus, these methods are less efficient in breaking RSA-S1 than the attack described. This gives evidence that the generic model is appropriate for investigating the security of server-aided RSA protocols.

The structure of the paper is as follows: In Sect. 2 we define SASC protocols and generic attacks. In Sects. 3 and 4 we review the protocols considered and investigate their security. Finally, in Sect. 5 we give some concrete examples of our bounds.

2   Model of Computation

2.1   Server Aided Secret Computation

Since we consider several protocols, we need to briefly define a general model of server-aided computation.

Let n be a product of two large primes p and q. Furthermore, let the security parameters of the protocol be fixed. In order to compute RSA signatures using the help of a server, the client generates a triple (I_s, I_p, d), using a fixed randomized algorithm with input p, q. Then d is the secret key of the client, I_s and I_p are called the secret resp. the public information. (In the case of RSA-S1, we have $I_s = f$ and $I_p = d$). When the client wants to sign a message $x \in \mathbf{Z}^*_n$, he contacts a server, and they carry out the specified interactive protocol. In this protocol, the behavior of the client depends on p, q, x, I_s, and I_p, whereas the behavior of the server depends on n, x, I_p only. At the end of the protocol the client computes the RSA signature y using the information obtained from the server and his secret information generated in the preprocessing. If both parties follow the protocol the result is correct, i.e. $y = x^d \bmod n$.

2.2   Generic Attacks

In [Nec94], Nechaev proves lower bounds for the complexity of the discrete log problem in a cyclic group G. He considers algorithms that access the group elements only via group operations – i.e. multiplications and divisions – and equality tests. This model is closely related to that introduced by Shoup ([Sho97]). Shoup considers algorithms that may perform arbitrary computations, but get their inputs encoded by a random encoding function. Both authors prove a lower bound of $\Omega(\sqrt{p})$ for the discrete log problem, where p is the greatest prime divisor of $\mathrm{ord}(G)$.

Shoup calls these algorithms generic. Generic algorithms can be seen as black box algorithms, i.e. algorithms that do not depend on the representation of the group G. This model has also been used for showing the non-equivalence of the

Diffie-Hellmann and the discete log problem ([MW]), for the analysis of pseudo-random generators for cyclic groups ([MS]) and for proving the hardness of RSA and discrete log bits ([Sch]). Different black box models have been analyzed by Boneh and Lipton in [BL96], and Babai and Szemerédi in [BS84]. We adapt Nechaev's model to prove lower bounds for the server-aided RSA protocols.

Definition 1. *A generic attack against the server-aided RSA protocol is a deterministic algorithm, which for random d, x, I_s, I_p takes as input x, y with $y = x^d \bmod n$. It is required*

to output a $d' \in \mathbf{Z}$ with $x^{d'} = x^d \bmod n$. The computation of the algorithm is done in the following way.

In the νth step of the computation, the algorithm computes an element $F_\nu := y^{a_\nu} x^{b_\nu} \bmod n$, where the exponents a_ν, b_ν depend only but arbitrarily on ν, the set $CO_{\nu-1} := \{(i, j) \mid F_i = F_j, 1 \le i < j < \nu\}$ of previous collisions, and the public parameters n, I_p. Analogously, when the algorithm terminates after t steps, its output d' may depend only but arbitrarily on t, CO_t, n and I_p.

We measure the complexity as follows. Depending on x and I_p, let $t(x, I_p)$ be the number of computed group elements of the algorithm and $\rho(x, I_p)$ its success probability over randomly chosen I_s. Then, the complexity of the algorithm is defined as the expectation of t/ρ, where the expectation is taken over randomly chosen x and I_p.

Note that generic algorithms do not need to be probabilistic. They are non-uniform, and we can always fix the optimal coin tosses making the algorithm deterministic.

Except for the elements of $\mathbf{Z}_n^*$, the algorithm may perform arbitrary computations (e.g. on I_p) at zero costs. The complexity of a generic attack depends only on the number of steps (i.e. the number of computed elements F_ν) and the success probability. Furthermore, the effort for computing the sets CO_ν does not contribute to the complexity. Sorting and equality testing can be done for free.

In practice, an adversary can not take advantage of equations $x^\alpha = y^\beta \bmod n$, unless β divides α. The most obvious way to avoid this problem, is to look for equations with $\beta = 1$, like in the attacks of Pfitzmann and Waidner ([PW93]) or Lim and Lee ([LL95]). We formalize this type of attack.

Definition 2. *We call a generic attack a* meet-in-the-middle attack *if all elements F_ν computed have the form x^{b_ν} or yx^{b_ν}, i.e. $a_\nu \in \{0, 1\}$.*

All known passive attacks against RSA-S1 and RSA-S1M are meet-in-the-middle attacks. For instance, consider the attack on RSA-S1 described in Sect.1. The algorithm computes two sets of group elements of the form $yx^{b_i} \bmod n$ and $x^{b'_i} \bmod n$, respectively, where the exponents b_i and b'_i only depend on the public parameters d. The output is computed using the indices i, j where collisions $yx^{b_i} = x^{b'_i} \bmod n$ have been found and the public parameter d. The exhaustive search is also a meet-in-the-middle attack.

3   RSA-S1

Consider the RSA-S1 protocol described in Sect. 1. In RSA-S1 we have $I_s = f$ and $I_p = d$. For the sake of clarity, we demand that the Hamming weight of the secret vector f is fixed. (Our results hold for more general variants as well, see Remark 1). Then the client has to perform k multiplications modulo n and has a storage of $m \log n + m$ bits.

3.1   The Security of RSA-S1

We show that the attack described in Sect. 1 is nearly optimal. Since sorting can be done for free in the model of generic attacks, the complexity of this attack is $2\binom{m}{k}\binom{m/2}{k/2}^{-1}$.

For a vector $v \in \{0,1\}^m$ let $\mathrm{w}(v)$ denote the Hamming weight of v. In the analysis we assume that d, f, d are chosen in the following way. First d is drawn uniformly from $\mathbf{Z}_{\phi(n)}$. Then f is chosen uniformly from the set $S := \{f \in \{0,1\}^m \mid \mathrm{w}(f) = k, \gcd(\sum_{i=1}^m f_i d_i, \phi(n)) = 1\}$ and finally d is set to $d(f) := \sum f_i d_i \bmod \phi(n)$. Furthermore we assume that $r := (p-1)/2$ and $s := (q-1)/2$ are distinct primes and that $r, s \gg \binom{m}{k}^2 \gg 1$.

The main result of result of this section is the following.

Theorem 1. *Every generic attack against RSA-S1 has at least complexity* $\frac{1}{2}\binom{m}{k}^{1/2}$

Proof. Let $\mathcal{A}$ be a generic attack that (depending on x and d) performs t steps and has success probability ρ (over a randomly chosen $f \in S$). We call (d, x) a good choice if $d(f) \neq d(f') \bmod r$ holds for all $f \neq f' \in S$ and r divides the order of x.

We break the proof into three steps. In the first step we provide a lower bound for t/ρ assuming that (d, x) is a good choice. The second step will show that the probability that (d, x) is not a good pair is negligible. Finally, we show how the theorem follows from the first two steps.

We first show that

$$t/\rho > \sqrt{2|S|} \tag{1}$$

if (d, x) is a good choice.

Fix a good choice (d, x). For $\nu = 1, \ldots, t$ let $F_\nu = y^{a_\nu} x^{b_\nu} \bmod n$ be the element computed in step ν. We may assume that all (a_ν, b_ν) are distinct. The exponents (a_ν, b_ν) only depend on the set $\mathcal{CO}_\nu = \{(i,j) \mid F_i = F_j, 1 \leq i < j < \nu\}$. For $i < j \leq t$, consider the case $\mathcal{CO}_j = \{(i,j)\}$. Since x and d are fixed the exponents $(a_i, b_i), (a_j, b_j)$ are constant. On the other hand, since r divides the order of x, a collision $F_i = F_j$ implies $d(f) = (b_i - b_j)/(a_j - a_i) \bmod r$. For a good choice (d, x), this holds only for one $f \in S$. Hence, $\mathcal{CO}_j = \{(i,j)\}$ holds with probability at most $1/|S|$. Summing over all $i < j \leq t$, we obtain that $\mathcal{CO}_t \neq \emptyset$ (i.e. that there are coinciding F_ν's) holds with probability at most $\binom{t}{2}/|S|$.

On the other hand, the output d' of $\mathcal{A}$ is constant if $\mathcal{CO}_t = \emptyset$. Since d is a good choice this output d' is correct (i.e. $d' = d(f)$) for at most one $f \in S$. Hence, the probability that $\mathcal{CO}_t = \emptyset$ and $\mathcal{A}$ is successful is at most $1/|S|$. Adding the probabilities yields $t^2 > 2\rho|S|$ showing (1).

Now we show that the probability that (d, x) is not a good choice is at most $P_g := \left(\binom{m}{k}^2 + 1 \right) / r$. For fixed $f \neq f' \in S$, the probability (over random d) that $d(f) = d(f') \bmod r$ is at most $1/r$. Hence, the probability that there are $f \neq f' \in S$ with $d(f) = d(f') \bmod r$ is bounded by $\binom{m}{k}^2 / r$. Furthermore, the probability that r does not divide the order of x is at most $1/r$.

We complete our proof by showing that the complexity of $\mathcal{A}$ is at least $\sqrt{2\binom{m}{k}} (\frac{1}{2} - 2P_g)$. The theorem then follows from $P_g \ll 1$.

Depending on x and d, let Ψ be $|S|$ if (d, x) is a good choice, and set $\Psi = 0$ otherwise. Since $|S| \leq \binom{m}{k}$ we have $\mathbf{E}(\Psi) > \mathbf{E}(|S|) - P_g\binom{m}{k}$, where $\mathbf{E}$ denotes the expectation taken over random d and x. Using standard arguments, we can estimate $\mathbf{E}(|S|) \geq \frac{\phi(\phi(n))}{\phi(n)} \binom{m}{k}$. Since $r = (p-1)/2$ and $s = (q-1)/2$ are primes this is $\frac{2(r-1)(s-1)}{4rs} \binom{m}{k}$. Using $r, s \gg 1/P_g$, we can bound this by $(\frac{1}{2} - P_g)\binom{m}{k}$. Thus, we get $\mathbf{E}(\Psi) > (\frac{1}{2} - 2P_g)\binom{m}{k}$.

On the other hand, (1) gives $t/\rho > \sqrt{2}\binom{m}{k}^{-1/2} \Psi$ for all (d, x) (for $\Psi = 0$ this is trivial). Taking expectations on both sides, we obtain the desired bound $\mathbf{E}(t/\rho) > \sqrt{2\binom{m}{k}} (\frac{1}{2} - 2P_g)$. $\qquad\square$

Remark 1. Theorem 1 holds for the non-binary RSA-S1 as well, where the f_i are ℓ-bit integers. In this case, the client performs $k + \ell - 1$ multiplications for each signature. A generalization of the meet-in-the-middle attack described has complexity $2\binom{m\ell}{k}\binom{m\ell/2}{k/2}^{-1}$, and we get a lower bound of $\frac{1}{2}\binom{m\ell}{k}^{1/2}$. In addition, Theorem 1 holds if f are chosen from the set of vectors with Hamming weight *at most* k. There the number of possible choices of f is $N = \sum_{i=1}^{k} \binom{m\ell}{i}$, and we obtain a lower bound for generic attacks of $\frac{1}{2}N^{1/2}$.

Our proof also works if $(p-1)/2$ and $(q-1)/2$ are not prime, but have large prime factors r and s, respectively. In this case, we get a lower bound of $\frac{\phi(\phi(n))}{\phi(n)} \binom{m}{k}^{1/2}$ for the complexity of generic attacks against RSA-S1.

4 RSA-S1M

To counter the attack of Pfitzmann and Waidner, in [MILY93], Matsumoto, Imai, Laih, and Yen proposed a 2-round server-aided RSA computation protocol called RSA-S1M.

4.1 The Protocol

Again, let n be a product of two large primes p and q, so that $r := (p-1)/2$ and $s := (q-1)/2$ are primes. The client wants to sign a message x with his secret key d.

Initialization step. The client chooses an integer vector $d \in \mathbf{Z}^m$ and two vectors $f, g \in \{0,1\}^m$ with Hamming weight k, so that $d = f \cdot g \bmod \phi(n)$, where f, g are defined as $f = \sum_{i=1}^m f_i d_i$ and $g = \sum_{j=1}^m g_j \bar{d}_j$ with $\bar{d}_j = d_j(j + 3m)$.

Preprocessing The client picks an $h \in \mathbf{Z}_n$ and computes $u = h^{-g} \bmod n$.

1. The client sends x, n and d to the server.
2. The server returns $z_i = x^{d_i} \bmod n$ for $i = 1, \ldots, m$.
3. The client computes and sends to the server $z = h \cdot \prod_{f_i=1} z_i = h \cdot x^f \bmod n$.
4. The server returns $v_j = z^{\bar{d}_j} \bmod n$ for $j = 1, \ldots, m$.
5. The client computes the signature y as $y = u \cdot \prod_{g_j=1} v_j = u \cdot z^g \bmod n$.

To avoid multi-round attacks, the client must pick a new h for each execution of the protocol. Since h and u are independent from the message x, and u is never revealed, the computation of u can be sped up using precomputation.

Our protocol differs from the original RSA-S1M ([MILY93]). We insist on a fixed Hamming weight k of f, whereas in [MILY93] f is chosen with a Hamming weight up to k, and in the second round, we let the server use the $\bar{d}_j = d_j(j+3m)$ as exponents instead the d_j. This modifications have technical reasons and do not substantially affect the efficiency of the protocol.

In this protocol, the secret information I_s is f, g and the public information I_p is x, d and z. Since h is a random number, z does not reveal information about d to the server. Thus, we disregard z in the following.

4.2 The Best Known Attack Against RSA-S1M

In [LL95] Lim and Lee show that the ideas of [PW93] are applicable to RSA-S1M as well. They give a meet-in-the-middle attack with complexity $O\left(N^{3/4}\right)$, where $N := \binom{m}{k}^2$ is the number of possible pairs (f, g). We give a variation of this attack, which is slightly more efficient and uses ideas of [vOW96].

Let m and k be even. From the definition of the protocol, we have

$$x^d = \prod_j x^{f g_j \bar{d}_j} \bmod n \ .$$

With probability $\rho := \binom{m/2}{k/2}^2 / \binom{m}{k}$ it holds that $(g_1, \ldots, g_{\frac{m}{2}})$ has Hamming weight $k/2$. For all $f_1, \ldots, f_m$ with Hamming weight k, and for all possible tuples $(g_1, \ldots, g_{\frac{m}{2}})$ with Hamming weight $k/2$, it computes $f = \sum f_i d_i$ and the values

$$\prod_{j \leq m/2} x^{f g_j \bar{d}_j} \bmod n$$

and sorts them. Subsequently, for all $(g_{\frac{m}{2}+1}, \ldots, g_m)$ with Hamming weight $k/2$, it computes the values

$$y \left(\prod_{j > m/2} x^{f g_j \bar{d}_j} \right)^{-1} \bmod n$$

and sorts them as well. It is easy to see that, if $(g_1, \ldots, g_{\frac{m}{2}})$ has Hamming weight $k/2$, then there is a collision which reveals d.

This attack can be written as a generic attack and has complexity

$$2 \binom{m}{k} \binom{m/2}{k/2} / \rho = 2 \binom{m}{k}^2 / \binom{m/2}{k/2} .$$

4.3 The Complexity of Meet-in-the-Middle Attacks

In this section, we will show that best known attack against RSA-S1M is almost optimal for a meet-in-the-middle-attack. We assume that d, f, g, d are chosen in the following way. For fixed d, set $d(f, g) := \sum_{i,j=1}^{m} f_i\, g_j\, d_i\, \bar{d}_j \bmod \phi(n)$ and

$$S := \{(f, g) \mid f, g \in \{0,1\}^m,\ \mathrm{w}(f), \mathrm{w}(g) = k,\ \gcd(d(f, g), \phi(n)) = 1\} .$$

First d is drawn uniformly from $\mathbf{Z}_{\phi(n)}^m$. Then (f, g) is chosen uniformly from S and finally, d is set to $d(f, g)$. Furthermore, we assume $N > 2^{92}$ and $N^6 \ll rs$.

The main result of this section is the following.

Theorem 2. *Every meet-in-the-middle attack against RSA-S1M has at least complexity $2^{-7} N^{3/4}$.*

We briefly sketch how Theorem 2 is proven. The details are given in the sequel. First, we show how for almost all (d, x) a generic attack $\mathcal{A}$ that performs t steps defines a graph G with t vertices. In Lemma 1, we show that the number of edges gives an upper bound for the success probability of $\mathcal{A}$. Exploiting the structure of the set S, we obtain a lower bound for the number of edges in G. This is done in Lemma 2. Finally, the proof of Theorem 2 combines the results of the Lemmas.

Definition 3. *We call (d, x) a good choice if $d(f, g) \neq d(f', g') \bmod rs$ for all $(f, g) \neq (f', g') \in S$ and rs divides the order of x.*

Let (d, x) be a good choice and $\mathcal{A}$ be a meet-in-the-middle attack which performs t steps and has success probability ρ, taken over randomly chosen $(f, g) \in S$. Then the element $F_\nu = y^{a'_\nu} x^{b'_\nu} \bmod n$ computed in step ν only depends on the set $\mathcal{CO}_{\nu-1}$. For $\nu = 1, \ldots, t$ let (a_ν, b_ν) be the exponents that $\mathcal{A}$ chooses when $\mathcal{CO}_{\nu-1} = \emptyset$. Note that $(a_1, b_1), \ldots, (a_t, b_t)$ are constant. We may assume that $(a_\nu, b_\nu) \neq (a_\mu, b_\mu)$ for all $\nu \neq \mu$. Furthermore, since $\mathcal{A}$ is a meet-in-the-middle attack we have $a_\nu \in \{0, 1\}$ for $\nu = 1, \ldots, t$.

The construction of the graph. We define a graph $G = (V, E)$ as follows: For every $1 \leq i \leq t$, set a vertex $u_i \in V$. For $i < j$, set an edge $(u_i, u_j) \in E$, if $a_i \neq a_j$ and there is a pair $(f, g) \in S$, so that i is minimal with $y^{a_i} x^{b_i} = y^{a_j} x^{b_j} \bmod n$ and $y = x^{d(f,g)} \bmod n$. This condition means that $\mathcal{CO}_j = \{(i, j)\}$ if $d = d(f, g)$ and implies $b_i - b_j = (a_j - a_i) d(f, g) \bmod rs$. We label (u_i, u_j) by (f, g). Since (d, x) is a good choice this pair (f, g) is unique, i.e. each edge has only one label. If a pair (f, g) occurs more than once as a label in E we remove all but one of these edges. We also remove all vertices with degree 0.

Note that since $\mathcal{A}$ is a meet-in-the-middle attack G is bipartite. Also note that $|V| = t$.

The following lemma reveals the connection between the number of edges in E and the success probability of the attack.

Lemma 1. *The pair (d, x) is a good choice with probability at least $1 - (4N^2 + r + s)/rs$. In this case,*

$$\rho \leq (|E| + 1)/|S| . \tag{2}$$

Proof. Let (d, x) be a good choice. Consider the corresponding graph $G = (V, E)$. Each edge is labeled by one pair (f, g) and each pair occurs only once as a label. Let $(f, g) \in S$ be chosen at random. Then the probability that there is an edge that is labeled by (f, g) is $|E|/|S|$.

If there is no edge labeled by (f, g) then all F_ν are distinct and we find $CO_t = \emptyset$. (This follows immediately from the construction of the graph.) In this case, $\mathcal{A}$ outputs a fixed d'. Since $d(f, g) \neq d(f', g') \bmod rs$ holds for $(f, g) \neq (f', g') \in S$, this output is correct for at most one $(f, g) \in S$. Thus, the probability (over randomly chosen $(f, g) \in S$) that (f, g) is not a label and $\mathcal{A}$ succeeds is at most $1/|S|$. Adding the probabilities yields (2).

We now bound the probability that (d, x) is not a good choice. Since $\mathbf{Z}_{rs} \simeq \mathbf{Z}_r \times \mathbf{Z}_s$, the equality

$$d(f, g) = d(f', g') \bmod rs \tag{3}$$

is equivalent to equality $\bmod\ r$ and $\bmod\ s$. Thus, for fixed $f, g, f', g' \in \{0, 1\}^m$, (3) corresponds to quadratic equations over $\mathbf{Z}_r$ and $\mathbf{Z}_s$. If $(f, g) \neq (f', g')$ these equations are nontrivial, and since r and s are primes the probability (over randomly chosen d) for (3) holding is at most $(2/r)(2/s)$. Hence, the probability that (3) holds for any $f, g, f', g' \in \{0, 1\}^m$ with Hamming weight k and $(f, g) \neq (f', g')$ is bounded by $4N^2/rs$. On the other hand, the probability that rs does not divide the order of x is at most $1/r + 1/s$. $\square$

Exploiting the nonexistence of certain cycles in G, we obtain a bound for its number of edges. The proof is given in the appendix.

Lemma 2. *With probability at least $1 - 8N^6/rs$ (over randomly chosen x and d) it holds that*

$$|V| > 2^{-4.75}|E|N^{-1/4} . \tag{4}$$

We are now able to prove Theorem 2.

Proof of Theorem 2. Define a random variable Ψ as follows. Depending on x and d, let Ψ be $|S|$ if (2) and (4) hold, and set $\Psi = 0$ otherwise. From Lemma 1 and Lemma 2, we see that $\Psi = 0$ holds with probability at most $\delta := (8N^6 + 4N^2 + r + s)/rs$. Since $|S| \leq N$ we can estimate

$$\mathbf{E}(\Psi) \geq \mathbf{E}(|S|) - \delta N .$$

Using standard arguments, we can estimate $\mathbf{E}(|S|) \geq \binom{m}{k}(\binom{m}{k} - 1)\left(\frac{\phi(\phi(n))}{\phi(n)}\right)^2$, where the expectation is taken over a randomly chosen d. Since $r = (p-1)/2$ and $s = (q-1)/2$ are primes and $\binom{m}{k}$ is large this is $(\frac{1}{4} - \epsilon)N$ for a small $\epsilon > 0$. Hence, we obtain

$$\mathbf{E}(\Psi) \geq (\frac{1}{4} - \epsilon - \delta)N .$$

On the other hand, if (2) and (4) hold we have $t > 2^{-4.75}(\rho\Psi - 1)N^{-1/4}$. Since N is large this implies

$$t/\rho \geq 2^{-4.8}\Psi N^{-1/4} .$$

If (2) and (4) do not hold we have $\Psi = 0$ and this estimation is trivial. Taking expectations on both sides, we obtain a lower bound for the complexity of $\mathcal{A}$ of $2^{-4.8}(\frac{1}{4} - \epsilon - \delta)N^{3/4}$. Since ϵ and δ are small the theorem now follows. $\qquad\square$

5 Conclusions

The following examples show the sharpness of our results. We compare our lower bounds GEN and MM for the complexity of generic and meet-in-the-middle attacks, respectively, with the upper bound ATT which is the (generic) complexity of the attacks described. Since sorting M elements can be done in $M \log M$ steps, the time complexity of these attacks is ATT log ATT.

RSA-S1			
m	k	ATT	GEN
160	40	$2^{65.4}$	$2^{62.0}$
184	36	$2^{66.1}$	$2^{62.7}$

RSA-S1M			
m	k	ATT	MM
50	20	$2^{70.2}$	$2^{61.1}$
60	15	$2^{70.4}$	$2^{61.4}$

These examples show that the bounds of Theorem 1 and Theorem 2 are quite sharp. The gap between the upper and lower bound for the RSA-S1M protocol is basically the constant 2^{-7} in Theorem 2. This constant arises from technical details. We believe that there are no meet-in-the-middle attacks, which have complexity less than 2^7MM.

5.1 Generalizations

The non-binary protocols (there the f_i and g_i are ℓ-bit integers) are more efficient. Here, the client has to perform $k + \ell - 2$ resp. $2(k+\ell) - 1$ multiplications. To achieve the same bounds as above, one can replace m by m/ℓ. Only the MM bound does not apply in this case because Theorem 2 can not be proved for non-binary RSA-S1M, for very technical reasons. However, we feel that RSA-S1M is not less secure in the non-binary case.

It is also possible to prove a lower bound for the complexity of *constant generic attacks* against RSA-S1M, that is generic attacks, where the exponents a_ν of the computed elements F_ν are arbitrary but independent from $d_1, \ldots, d_m$. We obtain a lower bound of $\Omega(N^{2/3})$ for constant generic attacks. Since this bound is not tight and all known efficient generic attacks against RSA-S1M are meet-in-the-middle attacks, we do not give any details.

5.2 Other Protocols

In RSA-S2, RSA-S2M, and the protocol of Béguin and Quisquater ([BQ95]), the decomposition of the secret is done mod p and mod q, separately. Our ideas can be applied only to one of these decompositions and hence, we obtain the lower bounds $\Omega(N^{3/8})$ for RSA-S2M and $\Omega(N^{1/4})$ for RSA-S2 and the protocol of Béguin and Quisquater. In [BQ95], an attack is given, whose generic complexity matches this bound. Its real time complexity is $O(N^{1/4} \log^2 N)$.

6 Acknowledgments

We would like to thank Claus-Peter Schnorr for drawing our attention to the model of Nechaev and Mats Näslund for his helpful comments.

A Proof of Lemma 2

The main property of G we will exploit, is the non-existence of certain cycles. We will then prove a variant of the well known general result that graphs with v vertices not containing cycles of length $L \le 2\kappa$ have $O(v^{1+1/\kappa})$ edges ([Bol78]). The results of non-existence of certain cycles are obtained using the following Lemmas.

By definition of the graph, each vertex $v \in V$ is associated with a pair of exponents $(a(v), b(v))$. Since $\mathcal{A}$ is a meet-in-the-middle attack, $a(v) \in \{0, 1\}$ holds for all $v \in V$. Obviously, $G = (V_1, V_2, E)$ is bipartite.

Lemma 3. *Let* $(v_1, \ldots, v_L, v_{L+1} = v_1)$ *be a cycle of length* L *in* G. *For* $l = 1, \ldots, L$, *let* (f^l, g^l) *be the label of* (v_l, v_{l+1}). *Then*

$$\sum_{l=1}^{L} (-1)^l d(f^l, g^l) = 0 \bmod rs \ .$$

Proof. By definition, we have $(a(v_{l+1}) - a(v_l)) d(f^l, g^l) = b(v_l) - b(v_{l+1}) \bmod rs$ for $l = 1, \ldots, L$. W.l.o.g. we may assume that $a(v_1) = 1$. Then summation over l yields the claim. $\square$

Definition 4. *The* tensor product $f \otimes g$ *of two vectors* $f, g \in \{0, 1\}^m$ *is defined as the matrix* $(f_i g_j)_{ij}$.

Lemma 4. *Let* $f^1, g^1, \ldots, f^8, g^8 \in \{0,1\}^m$ *with*

$$\sum_{l=1}^{8} (-1)^l f^l \otimes g^l \neq 0 \ ,$$

and let $d_1, \ldots, d_m$ *be independently randomly chosen from* $\mathbf{Z}_{\phi(n)}$. *Then with probability at most* $4/rs$

$$\sum_{l=1}^{8} (-1)^l d(f^l, g^l) = 0 \bmod rs \ . \tag{5}$$

Proof. Equality in (5) is equivalent to equality mod r and mod s. We show that equality mod r holds only with probability $2/r$. Analogously, one can see that the probability of equality mod s is $2/s$.

We set

$$\bar{c}_{i,j} = \sum_{l=1}^{8} (-1)^l f_i^l g_j^l \ .$$

and, for $1 \leq i < j \leq m$,

$$c_{i,j} = \bar{c}_{i,j} (j + 3m) + \bar{c}_{j,i}(i + 3m) \bmod r$$
$$c_{i,i} = \bar{c}_{i,i}(i + 3m) \bmod r.$$

If $\sum_{l=1}^{8} (-1)^l f^l \otimes g^l \neq 0$, then there is a $\bar{c}_{i,j} \neq 0$. We show that there is a $c_{i',j'} \neq 0 \bmod r$ as well.

This is obvious for $i = j$. If $i \neq j$ we set $i' = \min(i, j)$ and $j' = \max(i, j)$. Assume $c_{i',j'} = \bar{c}_{i',j'} (j' + 3m) + \bar{c}_{j',i'} (i' + 3m) = 0 \bmod r$. Since $r \gg 32m$ this equation holds in $\mathbf{Z}$ as well and we get

$$\frac{i' + 3m}{j' + 3m} = \frac{\bar{c}_{i',j'}}{-\bar{c}_{j',i'}} \ .$$

Since the right hand side of the last equation is either equal to 1 or no closer to 1 than 3/4 or 4/3 this equation cannot hold. This shows that $c_{i',j'} \neq 0$.

On the other hand, modulo r (5) can be written as $\sum_{i<j} c_{i,j} d_i d_j = 0 \bmod r$. Since $\mathbf{Z}_r$ is a field and $c_{i',j'} \neq 0$ this equation can only hold with probability $2/r$. $\square$

Definition 5. *For an edge* (v, w) *labeled by* (f, g), *we write* $f^{v,w} = f$ *and* $g^{v,w} = g$. *We call* $f^{v,w}$ *the F-color and* $g^{v,w}$ *the G-color of* (v, w).

Lemma 5. *With probability at least* $(1 - 4N^6/rs)$ *(over a randomly chosen* d) *the graph* G *has the following property:*

For all $v, w \in V$ *there is only one path* (v, a, b, w) *with* $f^{v,a} \neq f^{a,b} \neq f^{b,w}$ *and* $g^{v,a} \neq g^{a,b} \neq g^{b,w}$.

Proof. Assume that two paths (v, a, b, w) and (v, a', b', w) labeled by $(\boldsymbol{f}^1, \boldsymbol{g}^1), \ldots,$ $(\boldsymbol{f}^3, \boldsymbol{g}^3)$ and $(\boldsymbol{f}^4, \boldsymbol{g}^4), \ldots, (\boldsymbol{f}^6, \boldsymbol{g}^6)$, respectively, have this property. Using Lemma 3, we obtain

$$\sum_{l=1}^{6} (-1)^l d(\boldsymbol{f}^l, \boldsymbol{g}^l) = 0 \bmod rs \ .$$

By Lemma 4, with probability $1 - 4N^6/rs$ for all $(\boldsymbol{f}^1, \boldsymbol{g}^1), \ldots, (\boldsymbol{f}^6, \boldsymbol{g}^6)$, this equation implies

$$\sum_{l=1}^{3} (-1)^l \boldsymbol{f}^l \otimes \boldsymbol{g}^l = \sum_{l=4}^{6} (-1)^l \boldsymbol{f}^l \otimes \boldsymbol{g}^l \ .$$

In this case, the sum $\sum_{l=1}^{3} (-1)^l \boldsymbol{f}^l \otimes \boldsymbol{g}^l$ only depends on v and w. The following fact shows that $\boldsymbol{g}^2$ is uniquely determined by this sum, i.e. $\boldsymbol{g}^2 = \boldsymbol{g}^5$. Analogously, one can see $\boldsymbol{f}^2 = \boldsymbol{f}^5$. Since each pair $(\boldsymbol{f}, \boldsymbol{g})$ labels at most one edge this implies $a = a'$ and $b = b'$, and the lemma follows.

Fact 1. *If $\boldsymbol{f}^1 \neq \boldsymbol{f}^2 \neq \boldsymbol{f}^3$, then $\boldsymbol{g}^2$ is uniquely determined by the matrix $\mathbf{A} := \sum_{l=1}^{3} (-1)^l \boldsymbol{f}^l \otimes \boldsymbol{g}^l$.*

Proof. If there is an i_0 with $\sum_{j=1}^{m} A_{i_0 j} = k$ (which is equivalent to $f_{i_0}^1 = f_{i_0}^3 = 0$ and $f_{i_0}^2 = 1$), then $\boldsymbol{g}^2$ equals A_{i_0} (the i_0-th row of $\mathbf{A}$).

Now let $\sum_{j=1}^{m} A_{ij} \neq k$ hold for all i. Since $\boldsymbol{f}^2 \neq \boldsymbol{f}^3$, there is an i_1 with $f_{i_1}^2 = 1$ and $f_{i_1}^3 = 0$. From $\sum_{j=1}^{m} A_{i_1 j} \neq k$ we get $f_{i_1}^1 = 0$. Analogously, we can conclude that there is an i_2 with $f_{i_2}^2 = 1$, $f_{i_2}^3 = 1$ and $f_{i_2}^1 = 0$. The rows A_{i_1} and A_{i_2} are (as vectors) uniquely determined up to permutation by the condition $\sum_{j=1}^{m} A_{i_l j} = 0$ for $l = 1, 2$. Now we distinguish two cases.

If there is an i_3 with $\sum_{j=1}^{m} A_{i_3 j} = -2k$ (which is equivalent to $f_{i_l}^1 = f_{i_l}^3 = 1$ and $f_{i_l}^2 = 0$,) then $\boldsymbol{g}^2$ is determined by $2\boldsymbol{g}^2 = A_{i_2} - A_{i_3} + A_{i_1}$.

On the other hand, if $\sum_{j=1}^{m} A_{ij} \neq -2k$ holds for all i, then since $\boldsymbol{f}^1 \neq \boldsymbol{f}^2$, there is an i_3 with $f_{i_3}^1 = 1$ and $f_{i_3}^2 = 0$. From $\sum_{j=1}^{m} A_{i_3 j} \neq -2k$ we get $f_{i_3}^3 = 0$. Analogously, we see that there is an i_4 with $f_{i_4}^1 = f_{i_4}^2 = 0$ and $f_{i_4}^3 = 1$. The rows A_{i_3} and A_{i_4} are (as vectors) uniquely determined up to permutation by the condition $\sum_{j=1}^{m} A_{i_l j} = -k$ for $l = 3, 4$. Now $\boldsymbol{g}^2$ is determined by $2\boldsymbol{g}^2 = A_{i_1} + A_{i_2} - A_{i_3} - A_{i_4}$.

$\square$

Definition 6. *We call $v \in V$ F-monochromic, if all edges incident to v have the same F-color f. Then we say f is the F-color of v. We call $\tilde{V} \subseteq V$ F-monochromic, if all $v \in \tilde{V}$ are F-monochromic. For any F-color f, we define $V^F(f)$ as the set of vertices in V with F-color f. Analogously, we define G-monochromic, the G-color of a vertex and $V^G(g)$ for a G-color g.*

Lemma 6. *With probability at least $1 - 4N^6/rs$ (over a randomly chosen $\mathbf{d}$) the graph G has the following property:*

For any F-monochromic $v, w \in V_1$, the number of 4-paths (v, a, b, c, w) with $a \neq c$ and $f^{v,a} \neq f^{a,b} = f^{b,c} \neq f^{c,w}$ is bounded by

- $\mathrm{dg}(v)M$ if the F-colors of v and w are equal,
- $2M$ if the F-colors of v and w are distinct,

where $M := \max_f(|V_1^F(f)|)$ and $\mathrm{dg}(v)$ denotes the degree of v.

Proof. By Lemma 3, for any two such 4-paths (v, a, b, c, w) and (v, a', b', c', w), we obtain an equation

$$\sum_{l=1}^{4}(-1)^l d(f^l, g^l) = \sum_{l=5}^{8}(-1)^l d(f^l, g^l) \bmod rs$$

in the labels of the edges with $f^1 \neq f^2 = f^3 \neq f^4$ and $f^5 \neq f^6 = f^7 \neq f^8$. Furthermore, since v and w are F-monochromic it holds that $f^1 = f^5$ and $f^4 = f^8$ (see Fig.1).

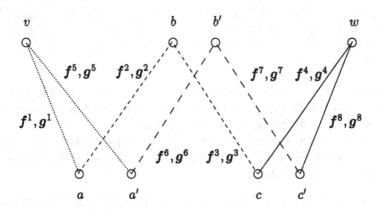

Fig. 1. Two 4-paths from v to w. (*the line style refers to the F-colors.*) The resulting cycle keeps its F-color when it passes a vertex in V_1 (*at the top*) and changes it, when passing a vertex in V_2 (*at the bottom*)

Since the number of tuples $(f^1, g^1, \ldots, f^8, g^8)$ fulfilling these conditions is bounded by N^6, by Lemma 4, with probability at least $1 - 4N^6/rs$ for each two such paths we obtain

$$\sum_{l=1}^{4}(-1)^l f^l \otimes g^l = \sum_{l=5}^{8}(-1)^l f^l \otimes g^l . \tag{6}$$

We will first show that for fixed a there are at most M such paths (v, a, b, c, w). The first bound immediately follows from that. Then we show that there are at most two possible choices for a, if the F-colors of v and w are distinct. This proves the second bound.

Assume that $a = a'$ and therefore $g^1 = g^5$. Equation (6) now simplifies to

$$-f^3 \otimes g^3 + f^4 \otimes g^4 - f^6 \otimes g^6 = -f^7 \otimes g^7 + f^8 \otimes g^8 - f^2 \otimes g^2 \ .$$

If $f^3 \neq f^6$ the vectors f^3, f^4, f^6 are all distinct. Fact 1 yields $g^8 = g^4$. Together with $f^8 = f^4$ this yields $f^2 \otimes g^2 + f^3 \otimes g^3 = f^6 \otimes g^6 + f^7 \otimes g^7$. Since $a \neq c$ this is nonzero. Using $f^2 = f^3$ and $f^6 = f^7$, we see that this can obviously not hold for $f^2 \neq f^6$. Hence, $f^2 = f^6$, i.e. f^2 is uniquely determined by a. This shows that there are at most $|V_1^F(f^3)| \leq M$ many possibilities for b.

On the other hand, if $b = b'$, (6) simplifies to $f^4 \otimes g^4 - f^8 \otimes g^8 = f^3 \otimes g^3 - f^7 \otimes g^7$. Since $f^4 = f^8 \neq f^3 = f^7$ this can not hold unless $g^3 = g^7$ and $g^4 = g^8$, i.e. $c = c'$. Thus, a and b already uniquely determine the path, and, for fixed a, there are at most M paths.

We complete our proof by showing that if the F-colors of v and w are distinct (i.e. $f^1 \neq f^4$), then there are only two possibilities for g^1. Since a is uniquely determined by g^1 (f^1 is fixed by v), there are only two possibilities for a as well.

Let $f^1 \neq f^4$. Set $A := \sum_{l=1}^4 (-1)^l f^l \otimes g^l$. For all i with $f_i^1 = 1$ and $f_i^4 = 0$, it holds that $\sum_j A_{ij} = -k$. On the other hand, since $f^2 = f^3$ there are at most two (as vectors) distinct rows A_{i_1} and A_{i_2} with $\sum_j A_{i_l j} = -k$ for $l = 1, 2$. Hence, $g^1 = A_{i_1}$ or $g^1 = A_{i_2}$ holds. $\qquad \square$

Definition 7. *For a vertex v, let $\mathcal{N}(v)$ denote the set of vertices w adjacent to v. For an F-color f, let $\mathrm{dg}_f(v)$ be the number of edges incident to v with F-color f. Analogously, we define $\mathrm{dg}_g(v)$ for a G-color g.*

We call a vertex v F-dominated, if $\mathrm{dg}_f(v) \geq \frac{3}{4} \mathrm{dg}(v)$ holds for an F-color f. Analogously, we define v to be G-dominated. If v is neither F-dominated nor G-dominated we call it colorful.

Lemma 7. *Let $G = (V_1, V_2, E)$ be a graph with $|V_1|, |V_2| \leq K$. Then G contains a subgraph $\tilde{G} = (\tilde{V}_1, \tilde{V}_2, \tilde{E})$ with $|\tilde{E}| > |E| - 3K \log_2 K$ so that, for all $v \in \tilde{V}_1$,*

$$\max_{v \in \mathcal{M}(v)} (\mathrm{dg}(w) - \mathrm{dg}_{f^v,w}(w)) \leq \frac{1}{2} \sum_{w \in \mathcal{M}(v)} \mathrm{dg}(w) - \mathrm{dg}_{f^v,w}(w) \ , \qquad (7)$$

where $\mathcal{M}(v)$ is the set of vertices adjacent to v which are not F-dominated.

Proof. We consider the function $D(G) := \sum_{v \in V_1} \sum_{w \in \mathcal{M}(v)} \mathrm{dg}(w) - \mathrm{dg}_{f^v,w}(w)$. For every $v \in V_1$ for which (7) does not hold, we remove the edge (w_v, v) with $w_v \in \mathcal{M}(v)$ for which $\mathrm{dg}(w) - \mathrm{dg}_{f^v,w}(w)$ is maximal. By that procedure, we decrease $D(G)$ at least by a factor of 2. Since

$$D(G) \leq \sum_{v \in V_1} \sum_{w \in \mathcal{N}(v)} \mathrm{dg}(w) = \sum_{w \in V_2} \mathrm{dg}(w)^2 \leq K^3 \ ,$$

we can perform this procedure at most $3 \log_2 K$ many times. $\qquad \square$

Definition 8. *For $G = (V, E)$ and $U_1, U_2 \subset V$, we set $E(U_1, U_2) := \{(v, w) \in E \mid v \in U_1 \land w \in U_2\}$.*

Lemma 8. *Let $v \in V$ be colorful and for $w \in \mathcal{N}(v)$ let $A_v(w)$ be the set of edges $(v, z) \neq (v, w)$ with $f^{v,z} = f^{v,w}$ or $g^{v,z} = g^{v,w}$. Then there is at most one $w \in \mathcal{N}(v)$ with $|A_v(w)| > \frac{7}{8} \operatorname{dg}(v)$.*

Proof. We show that $|A_v(w) \cap A_v(w')| \leq \frac{3}{4} \operatorname{dg}(v)$ holds for distinct $w, w' \in \mathcal{N}(v)$. The lemma follows from this immediately.

Let $w \neq w' \in \mathcal{N}(v)$. Then either $f^{v,w} \neq f^{v,w'}$ or $g^{v,w} \neq g^{v,w'}$. We may assume that $f^{v,w} \neq f^{v,w'}$. Then we have $|A_v(w) \cap A_v(w')| = \operatorname{dg}_{g^{v,w}}(v)$ if $g^{v,w} = g^{v,w'}$ and $A_v(w) \cap A_v(w') = \emptyset$ otherwise. Since v is colorful we obtain $|A_v(w) \cap A_v(w')| \leq \frac{3}{4} \operatorname{dg}(v)$. $\qquad\square$

We can now prove Lemma 2.

Proof of Lemma 2. Assume, to the contrary, $|V| < 2^{-4.75} |E| N^{-1/4}$. Furthermore, assume that (x, d) is a good pair and G has the properties described in Lemma 5 and Lemma 6. This holds with probability at least $1 - 9N^6/rs$. Set $V_c := \{v \in V \mid v \text{ is colorful}\}$, $V_F := \{v \in V \mid v \text{ is F-dominated}\}$ and $V_G := \{v \in V \mid v \text{ is G-dominated}\}$.

In our estimations, we use constants ϵ_i which will be determined at the end of the proof.

If $|E(V_F, V_2)| > \epsilon_1 |E|$ then G contains a subgraph $G' = (V_1', V_2', E')$ so that V_1' is F-monochromic and $|E'| > \frac{3}{4} \epsilon_1 |E|$. If the number of F-colors f satisfying $|V_1'^F(f)| > N^{1/4}$ is greater than $\epsilon_2 |E'| N^{-1/2}$ we have $|V| > \frac{3}{4} \epsilon_1 \epsilon_2 |E| N^{-1/4}$.

On the other hand, if the number of those colors is at most $\epsilon_2 |E'| N^{-1/2}$, using Lemma 7, we see that G' contains a subgraph $\hat{G} = (\hat{V}_1, \hat{V}_2, \hat{E})$ so that (7) holds for $w \in \hat{V}_2$, $|\hat{V}_1^F(f)| \leq N^{1/4}$ holds for all F-colors f, and $|\hat{E}| > (1 - \epsilon_2)|E'| - 3|V| \log_2 |V| = \alpha_1 |E|$. Let $U_2 := \{w \in \hat{V}_2 \mid w \text{ is F-dominated}\}$. There are only two possibilities:

1. If $\hat{E}(\hat{V}_1, U_2) > \epsilon_3 |\hat{E}|$ then $\hat{G}$ contains a subgraph $\tilde{G} = (\tilde{V}_1, \tilde{V}_2, \tilde{E})$ so that $\tilde{V}_1$ and $\tilde{V}_2$ are both F-monochromic and $|\tilde{E}| > \frac{3}{4} \epsilon_3 |E|$. Using $|x| + |y| \geq \sqrt{xy}$ for all $x, y \in \mathbf{R}$, we can estimate $|\tilde{V}_1| + |\tilde{V}_2| \geq 2 \sum_f \sqrt{|\tilde{V}_1^F(f)| \cdot |\tilde{V}_2^F(f)|}$. Since $|\tilde{V}_1^F(f)| \leq N^{1/4}$ holds for all F-colors f, this is lower bounded by $2N^{-1/4} \sum_f |\tilde{V}_1^F(f)| \cdot |\tilde{V}_2^F(f)|$. On the other hand $|\tilde{E}| \leq \sum_f |\tilde{V}_1^F(f)| \cdot |\tilde{V}_2^F(f)|$ and we obtain $|V| > \frac{3}{4} \epsilon_3 \alpha_1 |E| N^{-1/4}$.

2. If $|\hat{E}(\hat{V}_1, \hat{V}_2 \setminus U_2)| > (1 - \epsilon_3)|\hat{E}|$ we consider the graph $\tilde{G} = (\hat{V}_1, \hat{V}_2 \setminus U_2, \hat{E}(\hat{V}_1, \hat{V}_2 \setminus U_2))$. Since $\hat{V}_1$ is F-monochromic and $|\hat{V}_1^F(f)| \leq N^{1/4}$ holds for all F-colors f, using Lemma 6, we see that the number of 4-paths (v, a, b, c, w) in $\tilde{G}$ with $v, w \in \tilde{V}_1$, $f^{v,a} \neq f^{a,b}$ and $f^{b,c} \neq f^{c,w}$ is bounded by

$$\sum_{w \in \tilde{V}_1} \left(2N^{1/4}|V| + \operatorname{dg}(w) N^{1/4} \right) \leq 4|V|^2 N^{1/4} \; .$$

On the other hand, since $\tilde{V}_1$ is F-monochromic the number of those 4-paths is at least

$$\sum_{\substack{(v,a)\in\tilde{E}}} \sum_{\substack{b\in\mathcal{N}(a)\\ f^{v,a}\neq f^{a,b}}} \sum_{c\in\mathcal{N}(b)\setminus\{a\}} dg(c) - dg_{f^{b,c}}(c) .$$

Using (7), we can estimate this by

$$1/2 \sum_{\substack{(v,a)\in\tilde{E}}} \sum_{\substack{b\in\mathcal{N}(a)\\ f^{v,a}\neq f^{a,b}}} \sum_{c\in\mathcal{N}(b)} dg(c) - dg_{f^{b,c}}(c)$$

$$= 1/2 \sum_{b\in\tilde{V}_1} \left(\sum_{c\in\mathcal{N}(b)} dg(c) - dg_{f^{b,c}}(c) \right)^2 .$$

Since all $c\in\tilde{V}_2$ are not F-dominated, i.e. $dg_{f^{b,c}}(c) \leq \frac{1}{4}dg(c)$ holds for all $b\in\tilde{V}_1$ and $c\in\mathcal{N}(b)$, using the Cauchy-Schwarz inequality, we can bound this by

$$2^{-5}|\tilde{V}|^{-1}\left(\sum_{(b,c)\in\tilde{E}} dg(c) \right)^2 = 2^{-5}|\tilde{V}|^{-1}\left(\sum_{c\in\tilde{V}_2} dg(c)^2 \right)^2 .$$

Applying the Cauchy-Schwarz inequality to $\sum_{c\in\tilde{V}_2} dg(c)^2$, we obtain the lower bound $2^{-5}|\tilde{V}|^{-3}|\tilde{E}|^4$ for the number of those paths. Together with the upper bound $4|V|^2N^{1/4}$ we finally obtain $|V| > 2^{-7/5}(1-\epsilon_3)^{4/5}\alpha_1^{4/5}|E|N^{-1/4}$.

If $|E(V_G, V_2)| \geq \epsilon_1|E|$, $|E(V_1, V_F)| \geq \epsilon_1|E|$ or $|E(V_1, V_G)| \geq \epsilon_1|E|$ we get the same estimations analogously.

If $|E(V_c, V_c)| \geq (1-4\epsilon_1)|E|$ let E' denote the set of colorful edges (v, w) with $|A_v(w)| \leq 7/8\,dg(v)$ and $|A_w(v)| \leq 7/8\,dg(w)$. By Lemma 8, we get $|E'| > (1-4\epsilon_1)|E| - 2|V|$.

From Lemma 5, we see that the number of 3-paths (v, a, b, w) in G' with $v\in V_2'$, $f^{v,a}\neq f^{a,b}\neq f^{b,c}$ and $g^{v,a}\neq g^{a,b}\neq g^{b,c}$ is bounded by $|V|^2$.

On the other hand, it is at least

$$\sum_{(a,b)\in E'} \Big(dg(a) - |A_a(b)|\Big)\Big(dg(b) - |A_b(a)|\Big)$$

which is greater than $2^{-6}\sum_{(a,b)\in E'} dg(a)dg(b)$. Using $|V| = \sum_{(a,b)} dg(a)^{-1} = \sum_{(a,b)} dg(b)^{-1}$, we can estimate this by $2^{-6}\min\left(\sum x_iy_i \mid \sum x_i^{-1} + y_i^{-1} \leq 2|V|\right)$, where the minimum is taken over all $x, y \in \mathbf{R}^{|E'|} - \{0\}$. The minimum occurs, when all x_i and y_i are equal. Setting $|E'| \geq (1-4\epsilon_1)|E| - 2|V| = \alpha_2|E|$, we get the bound $2^{-6}\alpha_2^3|E|^3|V|^{-2}$ which yields $|V| > 2^{-3/2}\alpha_2^{3/4}|E|N^{-1/4}$.

We now fix the constants as $\epsilon_1 = 0.2$, $\epsilon_2 = 0.3$, $\epsilon_3 = 0.5$. Using $|V| < 2^{-4.75}|E|N^{-1/4}$, $N \geq 2^{92}$ and $|V| \leq |E| \leq N$, we find $\alpha_1 \geq 0.11$, $\alpha_2 \geq 0.2$ and finally $|V| > 2^{-4.75}|E|N^{-1/4}$. This contradicts our assumption. $\square$

References

[BL96]   D. Boneh and R. Lipton. Algorithms for black-box fields and their applica-
           tion to cryptography. In *Advances in Cryptology - Proceedings of Crypto'96*,
           volume 1109 of *Lecture Notes in Computer Science*, pages 283–297. Springer
           Verlag, 1996.

[Bol78]   B. Bollobas. *Extremal graph theory*, volume 11 of *L. M. S. Monographs*,
           page 158. Academic Press. XX, London, 1978.

[BQ95]   P. Béguin and J. J. Quisquater. Fast server-aided rsa signatures secure
           against active attacks. In *Advances in Cryptology - Proceedings of Crypto'95*,
           volume 963 of *Lecture Notes in Computer Science*, pages 57–69. Springer
           Verlag, 1995.

[BS84]   L. Babai and E. Szemerédi. On the complexity of matrix group problems I.
           In *25th Annual Symposium on Foundations of Computer Science - FOCS'84*,
           pages 229–240, 1984.

[LL95]   C. H. Lim and P. J. Lee. Security and performance of server-aided RSA com-
           putation protocolls. In *Advances in Cryptology - Proceedings of Crypto'95*,
           volume 963 of *Lecture Notes in Computer Science*, pages 70–83. Springer
           Verlag, 1995.

[LLMP90]   A. K. Lenstra, H. W. Lenstra, M. Manasse, and J. M. Pollard. The number
           field sieve. In *Proceedings 22nd Ann. ACM Symp. on Theory of Computing
           (STOC)*, pages 564–572, 1990.

[MILY93]   T. Matsumoto, H. Imai, C. S. Laih, and S. M. Yen. On verifiable implicit
           asking protocols for RSA computation. In *Advances in Cryptology - Pro-
           ceedings of Auscrypt'92*, volume 718 of *Lecture Notes in Computer Science*,
           pages 296–307. Springer Verlag, 1993.

[MKI89]   T. Matsumoto, K. Kato, and H. Imai. Speeding up computation with inse-
           cure auxiliary devices. In *Advances in Cryptology - Proceedings of Crypto'88*,
           volume 403 of *Lecture Notes in Computer Science*, pages 497–506. Springer
           Verlag, 1989.

[MS]   J. Merkle and C. P. Schnorr. Perfect, generic pseudo-randomness for cyclic
           groups. Unpublished.

[MW]   U. Maurer and S. Wolf. Lower bounds on generic algorithms in groups. To
           appear in Proceedings of Eurocrypt'98.

[Nec94]   V. I. Nechaev. Complexity of a determinate algorithm for the discrete log-
           arithm. *Mathematical Notes*, 55(2):165–172, 1994.

[PW93]   B. Pfitzmann and M. Waidner. Attacks on protocols for server-aided RSA
           computation. In *Advances in Cryptology - Proceedings of Eurocrypt'92*, vol-
           ume 658 of *Lecture Notes in Computer Science*, pages 153–162. Springer
           Verlag, 1993.

[Sch]   C. P. Schnorr. Security of arbitrary RSA and of all discrete log bits. Un-
           published.

[Sho97]   V. Shoup. Lower bounds for discrete logarithms and related problems. In
           Advances in Cryptology - Proceedings of Eurocrypt'97, volume 1233 of *Lec-
           ture Notes in Computer Science*, pages 256–266. Springer Verlag, 1997.

[Sti95]   D. R. Stinson. *Cryptography: Theory and practice*. CRC Press, 1995.

[vOW96]   P. van Oorschot and M. Wiener. Improving implementable meet-in-the-
           middle attacks by orders of magnitude. In *Advances in Cryptology - Pro-
           ceedings of Crypto'96*, volume 1109 of *Lecture Notes in Computer Science*,
           pages 229–236. Springer Verlag, 1996.

On the Security of ElGamal Based Encryption

Yiannis Tsiounis[1] and Moti Yung[2]

[1] GTE Laboratories Inc., Waltham MA. e-mail: ytsiounis@gte.com
[2] CertCo, NY, NY. e-mail: moti@certco.com

Abstract. The ElGamal encryption scheme has been proposed several years ago and is one of the few probabilistic encryption schemes. However, its security has never been concretely proven based on clearly understood and accepted primitives. Here we show directly that the decision Diffie-Hellman assumption implies the security of the original ElGamal encryption scheme (with messages from a subgroup) without modification. In addition, we show that the opposite direction holds, i.e., the semantic security of the ElGamal encryption is actually *equivalent* to the decision Diffie-Hellman problem. We also present an exact analysis of the efficiency of the reduction.

Next we present additions on ElGamal encryption which result in non-malleability under adaptive chosen plaintext attacks. Non-malleability is equivalent to the decision Diffie-Hellman assumption, the existence of a random oracle (in practice a secure hash function) or a trusted beacon (as needed for the Fiat-Shamir argument), and one assumption about the unforgeability of Schnorr signatures. Our proof employs the tool of message awareness.

1   Introduction

Discrete-log based building blocks are heavily used in protocols. For example in ElGamal encryption and signatures, Schnorr signatures or discrete-log based bit commitments. However, most of these sub-protocols have not been shown equivalent to some natural discrete-log or Diffie-Hellman variant, thus several practical systems are forced to rely on a multitude of arbitrary security assumptions. In this work we prove security which is a step towards reducing some of these sub-protocols to more natural and widely used assumptions by showing that the semantic security of the ElGamal encryption [ElG85] is equivalent to the decision Diffie-Hellman assumption. Note that obtaining the full plaintext of an ElGamal encrypted ciphertext is equivalent to the Diffie-Hellman assumption [ElG85,SS98]; thus the fact that the *semantic security* [GM84] of ElGamal encryption is equivalent to the decision Diffie-Hellman problem provides a natural analogy. In fact, ElGamal has stated this result as a conjecture in his earlier work [ElG98].

We also discuss efficiency (security degradation) of our reduction. As a result of the proof, one can deduce the availability (under a proper assumption) of having a very efficient semantically secure scheme which is ElGamal-based (unlike the typically more theoretical constructions). The scheme can be very efficient since encryption can be done with preprocessing of the exponentiation operations, and decryption involves one exponentiation which can be accelerated using preprocessing (e.g., as in [BGM93]).

This result can also be seen as a "shortcut" to the provability of the ElGamal encryption, bypassing the need to first prove security under the random oracle model [BR94,BR97] and then construct "practical random oracles" under, e.g., variants of the decision Diffie-Hellman assumption as was advocated and done in [Can97].

Recently, some results have utilized the decision Diffie-Hellman assumption or some of its variants (see [FTY96,Bea97,Bea96,NR97,Can97,CS98]). The last three works also claim the correctness of the first result we report here, but as a side issue (since they mainly deal with other interesting problems) and without a proof. We believe that the exact proof of security together with related results presented here is a central issue which deserves publicity (indeed, we first reported our work in [TY97]).

We then proceed in the second part of the paper to show extensions of the ElGamal encryption; in particular, an instatiation of a non-malleable [DDN91] under adaptive chosen plaintext attacks [RS92] variant of ElGamal which is provably secure under the random oracle model, the decision Diffie-Hellman assumption, and one assumption about the security of Schnorr signatures. Other instatiations (for semantic security under chosen ciphertext attacks or message awareness) have been proposed earlier [ZS93,BR94,BR97] (our constructions have some similarity to those in [ZS93]) but their security proofs rely on random-oracle like hash functions which hide all partial information and (for [ZS93]) some other assumptions. Our results use the random oracle in a different way than [ZS93,BR94,BR97]; the only use of the oracle is for the Fiat-Shamir argument, i.e., as an unpredictable beacon. Thus, the common practice of substituting random oracles with collision-resistant hash functions is more suited to our assumptions. Recently, [CS98] presented another variation of ElGamal encryption which remarkably is semantically secure under adaptive chosen plaintext attacks (thus also non-malleable), based on the decision Diffie-Hellman assumption and Collision Intractable Hash Functions, i.e., in the standard model (without the use of random oracles).

Organization: We begin with the basic definitions in section 2, and proceed with the proofs in both directions in sections 3 and 4. Then we discuss the efficiency of our reductions in section 5, and we show security extensions, in particular a provably non-malleable and message aware scheme under the random oracle model, in section 6.

2 Preliminaries

In this section we provide a consistent background for the proofs in the sequel.

2.1 The Diffie-Hellman problem and ElGamal encryption

First we formally define the decision Diffie-Hellman problem and the ElGamal encryption scheme.

The following setup is common for all definitions.

Setup: For security parameter n, primes P and Q are chosen such that $|P-1| = \delta + n$ for a specified constant δ, and $P = \gamma Q + 1$, for a specified integer γ. Then a unique subgroup G_Q of prime order Q of the multiplicative group Z_P^* and generator g of G_Q are defined.

> **(Decision Diffie-Hellman problem)** For security parameter n, P a prime with $|P - 1| = \delta + n$ for a specified constant δ, for $g \in Z_P^*$ a generator of prime order $Q = (P-1)/\gamma$ for a specified integer γ and for $a, b \in_R Z_Q$ random, given $[g^a, g^b, y]$ output 0 if $y \equiv g^{ab} \pmod{P}$ and 1 otherwise, with probability better than $1/2 + 1/n^c$ for any constant c for large enough n.

For example if P is a strong prime $P = 2Q + 1$, then g can be a generator which generates all the quadratic residues.

The *decision Diffie-Hellman assumption* (decision D-H) states that it is infeasible for a p.p.t. adversary to solve the decision Diffie-Hellman problem.

Next we define the ElGamal public-key encryption scheme (modified to have messages from a subgroup). The ElGamal encryption scheme [ElG85] is based on the Diffie-Hellman assumption and it is a probabilistic encryption scheme, i.e., a specific message has many—exponential in the security parameter—possible encryptions. Formally,

Definition 1. (ElGamal public-key encryption scheme) *The* ElGamal public key encryption *scheme is defined by a triplet* (G, E, D) *of probabilistic polynomial time algorithms, with the following properties:*

- *The system setup algorithm, S, on input 1^n, where n is the security parameter, outputs the system parameters (P, Q, g), where (P, Q, g) is an instance of the DLP collection, i.e., P is a uniformly chosen prime of length $|P| = n + \delta$ for a specified constant δ, and g is a uniformly chosen generator of the subgroup G_Q of prime order Q of Z_P^*, where $Q = (P - 1)/\gamma$ is prime and γ is a specified small integer.*
- *The key generating algorithm, G, on input (P, Q, g), outputs a public key, $e = (P, Q, g, y)$, and a private key, $d = (P, Q, g, x)$, where*
  - *x is a uniformly chosen element of Z_Q, and*
  - *$y \equiv g^x \bmod P$.*

(Note: In the proofs below we abuse the notation and assume that the input on G is simply 1^n.)

- *The encryption algorithm, E, on input (P, Q, g, y) and a message $m \in G_Q$, uniformly selects an element k in Z_Q and outputs*

$$E((P, Q, g, y), m) = (g^k \pmod{P}, my^k \pmod{P}) .$$

- *The* decryption algorithm, *D, on input* (P, Q, g, x) *and a ciphertext* (y_1, y_2), *outputs*

$$D((P, g, x), (y_1, y_2)) = y_2(y_1^x)^{-1} \pmod{P} .$$

For example for P a strong prime $P = 2Q + 1$ and where g is a generator which generates all the quadratic residues, the above system may be useful to send messages which are quadratic residues mod P; one can have a message with added random field which is chosen so as to make the entire sent message a residue. (Other modifications are easily obtainable to use the variant of ElGamal over a subgroup).

2.2 Semantic security

Here we reiterate the definition of semantic security.

Semantic security for an encryption scheme [GM84,Gol93] is defined as follows:

Definition 2. (semantically secure encryption) *An encryption scheme* (G, E, D) *is said to be* semantically secure *if, for every ensemble* $X = \{X_n\}_{n \in N}$ *of polynomial random variables, for every polynomial function* h, *for every function* f, *and for every probabilistic polynomial time algorithm* A, *there exists a probabilistic polynomial time algorithm* A' *such that for every constant* $c > 0$ *and for every sufficiently large* n,

$$Pr\left[A(E_{G(1^n)}(X_n), h(X_n), 1^n) = f(X_n)\right] \leq Pr[A'(h(X_n), 1^n) = f(X_n)] + \frac{1}{n^c} ,$$

where the probability is taken over the coin tosses of A *(resp.* A'*),* E *and* G, *and the distribution of* X.

Intuitively, given any a-priori information, $h(X_n)$, no algorithm A can obtain some information, $f(X_n)$, from the ciphertext that could not have been efficiently computed by A' without the ciphertext.

There is an alternative way to define secure encryption, which sometimes proves more useful in practice. The definition is based on indistinguishability; intuitively, if it is infeasible for an adversarial algorithm to distinguish between the encryptions of *any* two messages, even if these messages are given, then the encryption should not reveal any information about the messages (in the uniform case it suffices that two such messages cannot be efficiently found). Here we include, for completeness, the definition of security in the sense of indistinguishability (from [Gol89]).

Definition 3. (encryption secure in the sense of indistinguishability) *An encryption scheme* (G, E, D) *is said to be* secure in the sense of indistinguishability *if, for every probabilistic polynomial time algorithm* F *(for "Find"), for every probabilistic polynomial time algorithm* A, *for every constant* $c > 0$ *and for every sufficiently large* n,

$$Pr\left[F(1^n) = (\alpha, \beta, \gamma) \text{ s.t. } \Omega(\alpha, \beta, \gamma) > \frac{1}{n^c}\right] < \frac{1}{n^c} ,$$

with

$$\Omega(\alpha, \beta, \gamma) = \left| Pr\left\{ A((\gamma), E_{G(1^n)}(\alpha)) = 1 \right\} - Pr\left\{ A(\gamma, E_{G(1^n)}(\beta)) = 1 \right\} \right| ,$$

where the probability is taken over the coin tosses of F, A, E and G.

It has been proven that *an encryption scheme secure in the sense of indistinguishability is semantically secure* [GM84]. The opposite direction was shown in [MRS88].[1] In the sequel we show the equivalence of the decision Diffie-Hellman with the security in the sense of indistinguishability of ElGamal encryption. In the non-uniform model this is equivalent to semantic security.

3   ElGamal is at least as hard as the decision D-H

Theorem 1. *If the ElGamal encryption scheme is not secure in the sense of indistinguishability, then there exists a p.p.t. TM that solves the decision Diffie-Hellman problem with overwhelming probability.*

Proof. We show the uniform case. If the ElGamal encryption is not secure in the sense of indistinguishability then there exists a p.p.t. adversarial algorithm A (which can be seen as the "oracle" that "breaks" the ElGamal scheme), a (polynomial) random variable Z_n and two independent (polynomial) random variables (X_n, Y_n) that have the same distribution, such that:

$$\exists\, c > 0, \exists\, N, \text{s.t. for infinitely many } n > N ,\, \Pr[(X_n Y_n Z_n) \in B_n^c] > \frac{1}{n^c} ,\text{where}$$

$$B_n^c = \left\{ (\alpha, \beta, \gamma) : \left| \Pr\left[A(\gamma, E_{G(1^n)}(\alpha)) = 1 \right] - \Pr\left[A(\gamma, E_{G(1^n)}(\beta)) = 1 \right] \right| > \frac{1}{n^c} \right\} ,$$

where the probabilities are taken over the coin tosses of the key generating algorithm G, the encryption algorithm $E_{G(1^n)}$, the adversarial algorithm A, and the selection of (α, β, γ).

We now show how this adversarial algorithm can be used by a translator T to solve an instance of the decision D-H problem.

Translation:
The translator is given a triplet

$$[g^a \pmod{P}, g^b \pmod{P}, y] ,$$

for g a generator of G_Q, $y \stackrel{\text{def}}{=} g^x \pmod{P}$, and $a, b \not\equiv 0 \pmod{Q}$. Its purpose is to decide (non-negligibly better than random guessing) whether it is a correct Diffie-Hellman triplet (i.e., whether $x \equiv ab \pmod{Q}$) or not.

The translator then performs the following steps, for the above P, Q, g.

---

[1] These results were generalized for the uniform case in [Gol89,Gol93], but the proof of the reverse direction (i.e., semantic security implying distinguishable encryptions) requires the additional assumption of *decomposability* (given $E(\alpha)$ one should be able to find $E(\beta)$ for any suffix β of α with $|\beta| = 1/3|\alpha|$).

1. **Preparation stage:** The translator first tries to find a pair of messages (m_1, m_2) that can be distinguished by the adversarial algorithm ("oracle"). Intuitively, the translator chooses random message pairs and evaluates the oracle's effectiveness on distinguishing them. It is shown that this step is guaranteed to succeed in polynomial steps, based on the contradiction of indistinguishability of encryptions.

   Specifically, the translator chooses a triplet (m_1, m_2, γ) from the distribution (X_n, Y_n, Z_n) and tries to estimate the difference

   $$\Delta(m_1, m_2, \gamma) = \left| \Pr[A(\gamma, E_{G(1^n)}(m_1)) = 1] - \Pr[A(\gamma, E_{G(1^n)}(m_2)) = 1] \right| ,$$

   with accuracy better than $\frac{1}{4n^c}$. This accuracy can be achieved with over-whelming probability $(1 - 2^{-n})$ with $s_1 = 64 \ln 2(n+1)n^{2c}$ experiments (us-ing the Hoefding inequality, with each experiment allowing new coin tosses for A, E and G). (We refer to section 5 for more details). If the difference is greater than $\frac{3}{4n^c}$ then the pair is accepted. In this case the translator also records the calculated probability for $[A(\gamma, E_{G(1^n)}(m_1)) = 1]$, as this is to be used in the next phase. It is then guaranteed (with overwhelming prob-ability) that the actual difference $\Delta(m_1, m_2, \gamma)$ for this pair is at least $\frac{1}{2n^c}$. In other words, for this particular pair (m_1, m_2) the oracle finds a difference whose expected (mean) value is at least $\frac{1}{2n^c}$.

   If the estimate for the difference is smaller or equal than $\frac{3}{4n^c}$ then the pair is rejected and a new one is tried. From the properties of the oracle (A) it is guaranteed that the probability of finding such a pair with the required difference is at least $\frac{1}{n^c}$, thus an average of at most $\frac{n^c}{2}$ experiments will be performed.

2. **Testing phase:** In this stage the translator tries to see if the oracle is successful in distinguishing between m_1 and uniformly chosen messages.

   Specifically, the translator uniformly chooses messages $m \in G_Q$ and esti-mates the value

   $$\Pr[A(\gamma, E_{G(1^n)}(m)) = 1] ,$$

   with accuracy better than $\frac{1}{32n^c}$. For an error that is negligible in n (i.e., probability of success $(1 - 2^{-n})$) we need $s_2 = 512 \ln 2(n+1)n^{2c}$ experiments, where a different m is used in each experiment (and of course $E_{G(1^n)}(m)$ is created using new coin tosses for E). Then it calculates the difference

   $$\Delta(m_1, m, \gamma) = \left| \Pr[A(\gamma, E_{G(1^n)}(m_1)) = 1] - \Pr[A(\gamma, E_{G(1^n)}(m)) = 1] \right| ,$$

   again with accuracy $\frac{1}{32n^c}$; some of the calculations of the first phase can be reused here (see section 5). If the difference is greater than $\frac{3}{16n^c}$ then the actual difference is at least $\frac{1}{8n^c}$, and the oracle can distinguish between m_1 and random messages (i.e., in comparing m_1 with random messages the oracle finds a difference whose expected (mean) value is at least $\frac{1}{8n^c}$). Otherwise the actual difference is less than $\frac{1}{4n^c}$.

   Now we show that if the oracle does not distinguish between m_1 and random messages it must be the case that it can distinguish between m_2 and random messages. To see this, consider that for any message m we have

$$\frac{1}{2n^c} < \Delta(m_1, m_2, \gamma)$$

$$= \left| \Pr[A(\gamma, E_{G(1^n)}(m_1)) = 1] - \Pr[A(\gamma, E_{G(1^n)}(m_2)) = 1] \right|$$

$$= \left| \Pr[A(\gamma, E_{G(1^n)}(m_1)) = 1] - \Pr[A(\gamma, E_{G(1^n)}(m)) = 1] + \right.$$
$$\left. \Pr[A(\gamma, E_{G(1^n)}(m)) = 1] - \Pr[A(\gamma, E_{G(1^n)}(m_2)) = 1] \right|$$

$$\leq \left| \Pr[A(\gamma, E_{G(1^n)}(m_1)) = 1] - \Pr[A(\gamma, E_{G(1^n)}(m)) = 1] \right| +$$
$$\left| \Pr[A(\gamma, E_{G(1^n)}(m)) = 1] - \Pr[A(\gamma, E_{G(1^n)}(m_2)) = 1] \right|$$

$$= \Delta(m_1, m, \gamma) - \Delta(m, m_2, \gamma) \ .$$

Thus, for m_i uniformly chosen (i.e., $\Pr[m_i] = \frac{1}{|G_Q|}$), we have

$$\Sigma_i \left[\Delta(m_1, m_i, \gamma) - \Delta(m_i, m_2, \gamma) \right] > \Sigma_i \frac{1}{2n^c} \iff$$

$$\Sigma_i \Delta(m_1, m_i, \gamma) - \Sigma_i \Delta(m_i, m_2, \gamma) > |G_Q| \frac{1}{2n^c} \iff$$

$$\Sigma_i \frac{\Pr[m_i]}{\Pr[m_i]} \Delta(m_1, m_i, \gamma) - \Sigma_i \frac{\Pr[m_i]}{\Pr[m_i]} \Delta(m_i, m_2, \gamma) > |G_Q| \frac{1}{2n^c} \iff$$

$$|G_Q| \Sigma_i \Pr[m_i] \Delta(m_1, m_i, \gamma) - |G_Q| \Sigma_i \Pr[m_i] \Delta(m_i, m_2, \gamma) > |G_Q| \frac{1}{2n^c} \iff$$

$$\text{Exp}[\Delta(m_1, m_i, \gamma)] - \text{Exp}[\Delta(m_i, m_2, \gamma)] > \frac{1}{2n^c} \ ,$$

where the expected value is taken over the choice of messages m_i (and the last step holds based on the uniform choice of m_i's).

Therefore if $\text{Exp}\Delta(m_1, m, \gamma) < \frac{1}{4n^c}$ then it must be that $\text{Exp}\Delta(m, m_2, \gamma) > \frac{1}{4n^c}$.

This step requires $P_2 = 992 \ln 2(n+1)n^{2c}$ executions of the oracle (see section 5 for details).

3. **Decision phase:** Here the translator proceeds according to the result of the testing phase.

   - If the oracle can distinguish between m_1 and a random message then the translator "randomizes" m_1 to m_1' and runs the oracle on (m_1, m_1'). This randomization is based on the given triplet, such that $m_1' = m_1$ if the triplet is a correct D-H triplet, or m_1' is a uniformly chosen message otherwise. The randomization also has to guarantee that $E(m_1)$ is independent of $E(m_1')$ (i.e., the coin tosses of E are not affected by the selection of m_1').

   - If the oracle cannot distinguish between m_1 and random messages then (as we saw in the testing phase) it can distinguish between m_2 and random messages. Thus the translator randomizes m_2 and runs the oracle on (m_2', m_2).

If the oracle manages to distinguish between the values then the D-H triplet is incorrect (i.e., $x \not\equiv ab \pmod{Q}$); and it is a correct triplet otherwise.

For this step we first show how the randomization is performed and then how the translator tries to distinguish between m and m' (where m is either m_1 or m_2, based on the result of the testing phase).

(a) **Randomization:** Given a message $m \in G_Q$ (and the candidate triplet $[g^a, g^b, y]$), the translator uniformly selects exponents $u, v, t \in_R Z_Q^*$, and outputs the ElGamal ciphertexts

$$E(m) = [m(g^b)^{wu}, g^u], \quad E(m') = [my^{wt}(g^b)^{wv}, (g^a)^t g^v = g^{(at+v)}] ,$$

based on public key g^{bw} and generator g, for $w \in_R Z_Q^*$. This transformation results in a random and independently selected (from m) message m' when the D-H triplet is incorrect, while it produces the same message $m' = m$ when the given triplet is a correct D-H triplet. To see this, observe the following:

- The random coin tosses of the key generating algorithm G are simulated by the selection of w: g^{bw} is now a uniformly chosen public key, since $g^b \not\equiv 1 \pmod{P}$ is a generator of G_Q.
- The plaintext m' is equal to m when $y \equiv g^{ab} \pmod{P}$, but if $x \not\equiv ab \pmod{Q}$ the message is $m' \equiv mg^{(x-ab)tw} \pmod{P}$ because the oracle sees the ciphertext as

$$c \stackrel{\text{def}}{=} [(g^{bw})^{(at+v)} m', g^{(at+v)}] .$$

It is also easy to verify that $m \equiv m' \pmod{P} \iff g^{tw(x-ab)} \equiv 1 \pmod{P} \iff tw(x - ab) \equiv 0 \pmod{Q}$, that is $x \equiv ab \pmod{Q}$.
- If $x - ab \not\equiv 0 \pmod{Q}$, i.e., $m \not\equiv m' \pmod{P}$, we have that $g^{w(x-ab)} \not\equiv 1 \pmod{P}$ is a generator of G_Q; thus by changing t the "message" $m' \stackrel{\text{def}}{=} mg^{tw(x-ab)}$ can get any value in G_Q, i.e., $m' \in_R G_Q$, and furthermore it is independent of m (due to the random choice of t).
- Finally, $E(m')$ is independent of $E(m)$, due to the additional choice of v.

(b) **Distinguishing:** Here the difference between m and m' is estimated

$$\Delta(m, m', \gamma) = \left| \Pr[A(\gamma, E_{G(1^n)}(m)) = 1] - \Pr[A(\gamma, E_{G(1^n)}(m')) = 1] \right| ,$$

with accuracy better than $\frac{1}{16n^c}$ if $m = m_2$ or $\frac{1}{32n^c}$ if $m = m_1$. The number of experiments required for obtaining such accuracy with error probability less than 2^{-n} is $s_3 = 992 \ln 2(n + 1)n^{2c}$ or $s_3 = 3584 \ln 2(n + 1)n^{2c}$. (Each experiment requires a different randomized m', so that the approximation of $\text{Exp}[\Delta(m, m', \gamma)]$ is found).

Now since the real difference is either at least $\frac{1}{4n^c}$, if $m \not\equiv m' \pmod{P}$ (resp. $\frac{1}{8n^c}$ for $m = m_1$), or 0 if $m = m'$, the estimate can either be greater than $\frac{3}{16n^c}$ (resp. $\frac{3}{32n^c}$) or lower than $\frac{1}{16n^c}$ (resp. $\frac{1}{32n^c}$). In the first case the triplet given is an incorrect D-H triplet and in the second it is a correct triplet.

Finally, the expected number of oracle calls for this step is on the average $P_3 = 2288 \ln 2(n + 1)n^2 c$. $\qquad\qquad\qquad\square$

4 Decision D-H is at least as hard as ElGamal

For this proof we show that if there exists an oracle solving the decision Diffie-Hellman problem then the ElGamal encryption is not secure in the sense of indistinguishability, and therefore it is not semantically secure. This part completes section 3, to show that the semantic security of the ElGamal encryption and the decision Diffie-Hellman assumption are equivalent.

Note that this direction is much easier and intuitive than the previous one. Also notice that the decision D-H oracle allows us to build a very strong El-Gamal oracle that distinguishes between any two messages; that is, there are no restrictions in terms of the probability distribution of the messages to be distinguished (i.e., the messages *need not* be constructed in any particular way).

Theorem 2. *If there exists an oracle $\mathcal{O}$ which solves the decision Diffie-Hellman problem with probability non-negligibly better than random guessing then the El-Gamal encryption scheme is not secure in the sense of indistinguishability.*

Proof. In order to show that an encryption algorithm is not secure in the sense of indistinguishability it suffices to show that we can find, with non-negligible probability, a pair of plaintext messages such that their encryptions can be distinguished with non-negligible probability of success.

Let $y \equiv g^x \pmod{P}$ be the public key of a party in an ElGamal encryption scheme. Our adversarial algorithm selects random $m_0, m_1 \in_R G_Q$.

Then given the ElGamal encryptions of these messages, i.e.,

$$((P, Q, g, y), [y^{r_0} m_i, g^{r_0}]) , i \in_R \{0, 1\} \text{ and}$$

$$((P, Q, g, y_1), [y^{r_1} m_{1-i}, g^{r_1}]) ,$$

where $r_0, r_1 \in_R Z_Q$, we only need to show that given the decision D-H oracle we can distinguish non-negligibly better than random guessing which ciphertext encrypts which message, i.e., find i.

To this effect we employ a translator which constructs an instance of the decision D-H problem in such a way that solving this instance allows us to distinguish the ciphertext for messages m_0 and m_1.

Translation:

Given the above ciphertexts and the messages m_0, m_1 the translator selects random $v \in_R Z_Q^*$ and outputs:

$$g^{r_0} \pmod{P} , \quad yg^v \equiv g^{x+v} \pmod{P} \text{ and}$$

$$g^{r_0 v} y^{r_0} m_i / m_0 \pmod{P} .$$

It is now easy to see that if $m_i \equiv m_0 \pmod{P}$ we have $i = 0$ except with negligible probability (namely, i can be 1 when $m_1 = m_0$), and the first ciphertext encrypts the first message; then the decision D-H oracle would output 0 (i.e., "correct triple") with probability non-negligibly better than random guessing, since the input would be a (uniformly distributed, since r_0 and v are randomly chosen) correct D-H triplet. Otherwise, if $m_i \not\equiv m_0 \pmod{P}$, we have that $i = 1$, and the input to the oracle would still be valid and uniformly distributed, but the output would be 1, again with probability non-negligibly better than random guessing. Therefore the oracle can be used to determine i with probability non-negligibly better than random guessing. □

5 Efficiency of reductions

For an exact treatment of our reductions we analyze here the amount of computation that the translator has to perform in order to solve the decision Diffie-Hellman problem given an ElGamal oracle.[2]

We concentrate on the number of calls to the ElGamal oracle, as well as the number of exponentiations that need to be performed. For concreteness we assume that we have an oracle for which $\Pr[(X_n Y_n Z_n) \in B_n^c] > \epsilon$. The analysis proceeds with the steps of the reduction.

1. **Preparation stage.** The difference $\Delta(m_1; m_2, \gamma)$ is estimated using the Hoefding inequality. For completeness we repeat the definition of the latter:

   Hoefding inequality: Let $X_1, X_2, \ldots, X_n$ be n independent random variables with identical probability distribution, each ranging over the (real) interval $[a, b]$, and let μ denote the expected value of each of these variables. Then,

   $$\Pr\left(\left|\frac{\sum_{i=1}^n X_i}{n} - \mu\right| > \delta\right) < 2 \cdot e^{-\frac{2\delta^2}{b-a} \cdot n} .$$

   The estimation proceeds as follows. First we define

   $$W_i = \Pr[A^i(\gamma, E^i_{G^i(1^n)}(m_1)) = 1] ,$$

   for $i = 1 \ldots k$ where A^i, E^i, G^i denote the i-th call of algorithms A, E, G, such that in each call the algorithms are allowed a new, independent set of coin tosses.
   Then, the above $W_1, W_2, \ldots, W_k$ are independent random variables with identical probability distribution, each ranging over the interval $[0, 1]$. If $\text{Exp}(W_i)$ is the expected value of each of those variables then, from the Hoefding inequality, substituting for $\delta = \frac{1}{d \cdot n^c}$, we have

   $$\Pr\left(\left|\frac{\sum_{i=1}^k W_i}{k} - \text{Exp}(W_i)\right| > \frac{1}{d \cdot n^c}\right) < 2 \cdot e^{-\frac{2}{d^2 \cdot n^{2c}} \cdot k} = P_k .$$

   Thus, with probability $1 - P_k$, the average value of k experiments is an estimate of the expected value of each W_i with accuracy $\frac{1}{dn^c}$. Since we want

---

[2] The other direction is easier and the efficiency of the reduction apparent.

$1 - P_k$ to be at least $1 - 2^{-n}$ we can find the number of required experiments by solving the following inequality:

$$P_k = 2 \cdot e^{-\frac{2}{d^2 \cdot n^{2c}} \cdot k} \leq 2^{-n} ,$$

which results in $k \geq \frac{\ln 2 \cdot (n+1) \cdot d^2 \cdot n^{2c}}{2}$.

For the estimation we compute the estimate of $\mathrm{Exp}(W_i)$ and $\mathrm{Exp}(V_i)$ with accuracy $\frac{1}{8n^c}$, where

$$V_i = \Pr[A^i(\gamma, E^i_{G^i(1^n)}(m_2)) = 1] ,$$

and we subtract the two estimates to find $\mathrm{Exp}\Delta(m_1, m_2, \gamma)$ with accuracy $\frac{1}{4n^c}$.

For each estimate we need $\frac{\ln 2 \cdot (n+1) \cdot 8^2 \cdot n^{2c}}{2} = 32 \cdot \ln 2 \cdot (n+1) \cdot n^{2c}$ experiments and each experiment requires two modular exponentiations (i.e., computing one ElGamal encryption).

Since we need $\frac{1}{\epsilon}$ experiments on the average to find two messages that can be distinguished, we have that in average this step requires $P_1 = 64 \cdot \ln 2 \cdot (n+1) \cdot n^{2c} \cdot \epsilon^{-1}$ oracle calls, and $D_1 = 2P_1 = 128 \cdot \ln 2 \cdot (n+1) \cdot n^{2c} \cdot \epsilon^{-1}$ modular exponentiations.

2. **Testing phase.** Here the estimates for $\Pr[A(\gamma, E_{G(1^n)}(m)) = 1]$ and $\Pr[A(\gamma, E_{G(1^n)}(m_1)) = 1]$ are computed, with accuracy $\frac{1}{32 \cdot n^c}$. The estimate for m_1 is stored for the next phase. Some number of experiments for m_1 have already been conducted in the preparation phase, so this step requires $P_2 = (2 \cdot 512 - 32) \cdot \ln 2 \cdot (n+1) \cdot n^{2c} = 992 \cdot \ln 2 \cdot (n+1) \cdot n^{2c}$ oracle calls and $D_2 = 1984 \ln 2 (n+1) n^{2c}$ modular exponentiations.

3. **Decision phase.** (*Distinguishing* step.) Here the oracle calls for estimating $\Pr[A(\gamma, E_{G(1^n)}(m')) = 1]$ with accuracy $\frac{1}{32 \cdot n^c}$ or $\frac{1}{64 \cdot n^c}$ are either $512 \cdot \ln 2 \cdot (n+1) \cdot n^{2c}$ or $2048 \cdot \ln 2 \cdot (n+1) \cdot n^{2c}$. In the first case some experiments for m_2 can be reused from the preparation phase, so $(512 - 32) \cdot \ln 2 \cdot (n+1) \cdot n^{2c} = 480 \cdot \ln 2 \cdot (n+1) \cdot n^{2c}$ calls are needed; similarly, if $m = m_1$, $(2048 - 512) = 1536 \cdot \ln 2 \cdot (n+1) \cdot n^{2c}$ calls are needed. Each new experiment requires 2 modular exponentiations for each of m, m'. In total, and considering that the oracle can distinguish with the same probability between m_1 and random m' or m_2 and random m', we have that the (average) total number of oracle calls is $P_3 = \frac{1}{2}(512 + 2048 + 480 + 1536) \cdot \ln 2 \cdot (n+1) \cdot n^{2c} = 2288 \cdot \ln 2 \cdot (n+1) \cdot n^{2c}$ while the (average) total number of exponentiations is $D_3 = 4576 \cdot \ln 2 \cdot (n+1) \cdot n^{2c}$.

Thus the reduction requires, on the average, a total of $P_0 = P_1 + P_2 + P_3 = (5568 + \epsilon^{-1}) \cdot \ln 2 \cdot (n+1) \cdot n^{2c} \approx (3859 + \epsilon^{-1}) \cdot (n+1) \cdot n^{2c}$ oracle calls and $D_0 = 2 \cdot P_0$ exponentiations for solving the decision Diffie-Hellman problem, given an ElGamal oracle. We note that the reductions can be made more efficient (e.g., by requiring that the error of an estimate is $\frac{1}{8 \cdot n^c} - \frac{1}{128 \cdot n^c}$ instead of $\frac{1}{16 n^c}$), but the above numbers are meant to simplify calculations. In general we would have $P_0 = (C + \epsilon^{-1}) \cdot (n+1) \cdot n^{2c}$ oracle calls, for $C \leq 3859$, and $D_0 = 2 \cdot P_0$ modular exponentiations.

6 Security extensions

We now extend the basic scheme to provide enhanced security. Our goal is non-malleability under chosen ciphertext attacks; this is achieved using non-malleable non-interactive zero knowledge proofs of knowledge of the plaintext under the random oracle model (namely, message-awareness is employed). The notion of *chosen ciphertext security* was first defined and implemented for public keys in [NY90]; a more generalized (adaptive) attack was formalized in [RS92]. Informally, it states that an active adversary does not obtain any advantage in breaking the system by asking for decryptions of arbitrarily chosen ciphertexts.

Non-malleability, first defined in [DDN91], is a security notion stronger than semantic security. Informally, it requires that it is infeasible, given a ciphertext, to create a *different* ciphertext such that their plaintexts are related. The difference may be simply the claim that the ciphertext came from party B instead of party A (and indeed self-protecting of a party by the "use of its unique name" is the basic motivation for non-malleability). Thus, for non-malleability to hold, the least requirement is that of unique names. In practice, each party should be allowed to choose a unique (although not necessarily certified) name.

Non-malleability is an extension of semantic security in that it considers security and self-protection of senders in the context of a network of users, and not simply between one sender and one receiver. For example, consider a chosen-ciphertext secure scheme for which it has been proven that the party which constructed the encryption is "aware" of what he is encrypting ("message awareness"). But this does not imply that a *third* party is also aware of the plaintext. Thus, in a network setting, it may be the case that a man-in-the-middle (i.e., an adversary other than the original sender) is not aware of the plaintext. For a concrete example consider the scheme of [Dam91], where the encryption of m is $E(m) = g^u, y^u \cdot m, Y^u$, where Y is a public value. Under some assumptions this scheme is (semantically) secure against ("lunch-time," [NY90]) chosen ciphertext attacks [Dam91], but it is easy to see that a man-in-the-middle can, given $E(m) = [A, B, C]$, produce $E(m') = [A \cdot g^v, B \cdot y^v/t, C \cdot Y^v]$, a randomized encryption of a related message $m' = m/t$. Thus the scheme is not non-malleable; furthermore, if the man-in-the-middle is not the party that constructed the original encryption $E(m)$ then s/he does not know the plaintext of $E(m')$ and therefore the scheme is not message-aware. Again, the reason is that in a network setting it is not only important to show a proof of knowledge, but a proof of knowledge with respect to some identity (i.e., a *non-malleable* proof of knowledge [DDN91]).

We now proceed to show the non-malleable scheme. The tool we use is message-awareness with respect to the sender's identity (i.e., the party which included the identity is also aware of the plaintext).

Finally, as we also note in the next section, proof of origin of messages is typically given by a digital signature (i.e., by a step additional to non-malleable encryption). Our scheme can also easily integrate a signature scheme together with non-malleable encryption, to provide a proof of message origin (i.e., "non-malleable signcryption").

7 Non-malleable encryption

Setup:
As discussed above (and in more detail in [DDN91]) for non-malleability it is necessary for each party to have a unique name (or some unique information that can be traced back to that party). We denote the name of party S (the sender of the encryption) with ID_S.

In what follows we show how to achieve non-malleability concisely, by resorting to proofs of knowledge of discrete logarithms. For concreteness we demonstrate the scheme using Schnorr proofs of knowledge [Sch91] but other protocols may be used instead; for example Fiat-Shamir proofs [FS87]. We present Schnorr proofs here simply for their efficiency advantages. For security we require an assumption about the unforgeability of Schnorr signatures which will be formalized in the body of the proof.

We will get the following:

Theorem 3. *Based on the decision Diffie-Hellman and assumption 1, the scheme presented below is non-malleable, in the random oracle model.*

Encryption:
The idea here is that the sender sends a zero-knowledge (ZK) proof of knowledge of the randomness used, but the ZK proof is non-malleable, i.e., it includes her/his chosen name. Using random oracles this can be done concisely by including the name in the input of the random oracle:

$$A = g^u , \quad B = y^u \cdot m , \quad F = g^{u'} ,$$
$$ID_S = \text{Name, other information} ,$$
$$C = u \cdot H(g, A, B, F, ID_S) + u' ,$$
$$E^n(m) = [A, B, F, C, ID_S] ,$$

where $u' \in_R Z_Q$ is randomly chosen and H is a random oracle.

Note: It is important to note that the oracle above is not used to hide information (a property investigated in [Can97] and utilized in [BR94,BR97]) but rather only as an unpredictable challenge generator (the Fiat-Shamir construction which is used for the proofs in [PS96]). Thus the properties required of the oracle are unpredictability rather than secrecy; which means that also a "trusted beacon" can be employed.

Decryption:
The receiver obtains the ciphertext $[A, B, F, C, ID_S]$ and decrypts as in the original ElGamal scheme:

$$m = B/A^x ,$$

(we remind that $y = g^x$ is the receiver's public key). The receiver only accepts this encryption if the following equation is satisfied:

$$g^C = A^{H(g,A,B,F,ID_S)} \cdot F ,$$

otherwise it rejects and outputs *reject*.

7.1 Proof of non-malleability

Here we sketch the proof of non-malleability under adaptive chosen ciphertext attacks. The proof proceeds in two steps: (1) first we show that the semantic security is equivalent to the decision D-H assumption, i.e., the addition of the proof of knowledge does not affect semantic security; (2) then we assume that the scheme is not non-malleable and, using an assumption about Schnorr signatures, proceed to get a contradiction on its (proven) semantic security.

The semantic security of E^n is equivalent to the decision D-H :

We do not yet consider chosen ciphertext attacks; thus we can refer directly to the proofs of section 3. In the first direction (E^n is as hard as the decision D-H) the proof follows the same steps as the proof of section 3; we omit repetition for conciseness. It is straightforward to verify that the proof carries over in all parts, with the only exception being the randomization part of the decision phase (step 3(a)). Here we have to show that this step can be repeated and still results in a randomly generated encryption, while the message m' is randomly chosen if $y \not\equiv g^{ab}$ and equal to the original message m otherwise.

To this effect, the translator computes, for each ciphertext to be generated, the identity of the sender ID_S. Now we can see how the translator can generate the appropriate encryptions:

$$E^n(m) = [A = g^u, \ B = m \cdot (g^b)^{w \cdot u}, \ F = g^{u'},$$
$$C = u \cdot H(g, A, B, F, ID_S) + u', \ ID_S] ,$$

and

$$E^n(m') = [A' = (g^a)^t g^v = g^{(a \cdot t + v)}, \ B' = m \cdot y^{w \cdot t}(g^b)^{w \cdot v}, \ F' = g^{u''},$$
$$C' = (a \cdot t + u) \cdot H(g, A', B', F', ID_S) + u'', \ ID_S] ,$$

where w, u, v, t, u' are random numbers, and the choice of F', u'' is discussed below.

The main issue we have to guarantee here is that the translator can actually produce $C' = (at + u) \cdot H(g, A', B', F', ID_S) + u''$, since it does not know a (meanwhile it is easy to verify that the rest of the values can be produced and are of the required form). To this effect, the translator computes $F' = (g^a)^s \cdot g^{s'}$, effectively setting $u'' = as + s'$, where s, s' are chosen at random. If we substitute this value in C' we have

$$C' = a \cdot t \cdot H(g, A', B', F', ID_S) + a \cdot s + s' = a \cdot [t \cdot H(g, A', B', F', ID_S) + s] + s' .$$

Now we force the output of the function H above such that the part that is multiplied by a becomes zero, and thus the translator can simply output s' (which it knows); i.e.,

$$t \cdot H(g, A', B', F', ID_S) + s \equiv 0 \pmod{Q} \iff$$

$$H(g, A', B', F', ID_S) \equiv \frac{-s}{t} \pmod{Q} .$$

This manipulation of H is possible due to the properties of random oracles. Specifically, when the translator calls the ElGamal oracle on the above entries it also supplies the oracle with a random oracle that has the desired output; this "tweaking" of the oracle cannot be detected since (1) the output supplied is random ($-s/t$ where both s, t are random numbers), so it still resembles the output of a random oracle, while (2) any random oracle is as good as any other random oracle, i.e., the ElGamal oracle cannot detect the difference and "change" its response. Notice that the main trick here is that the translator gets to "pick" its own oracle, since it is only performing a simulation, i.e., it does not need to "share" this oracle with another party in advance, but can generate the oracle outputs "on-the-fly" as needed (much in the way a "non-random oracle" ZK simulation proceeds for the Fiat-Shamir argument).

Now it is easy to verify that, as required, the randomization properties of both m' and $E^n(m')$ with respect to $m, E^n(m)$ are satisfied.

On the second direction the translator can simply ignore the values F, C, ID_S.

Non-malleability :

Now assume that the scheme is not non-malleable. That is, there exists an adversary A which (1) firsts adaptively queries the deciphering algorithm on ciphertexts of her choice; (2) then selects a distribution $\mathcal{M}$ of messages and is given a challenge ciphertext $c = E^n(m)$ for a message $m \in_R \mathcal{M}$; (3) and finally adaptively queries the deciphering algorithm on ciphertexts of her choice (other than c) and tries to produce a ciphertext $c' = E^n(m')$ such that a polynomial-time computable relation $R(m, m')$ holds. We will show that, under assumption 1, this contradicts the semantic security of $E^n(m)$ which was shown above.

First, observe that the triplet (which is a subset of the encryption $E^n(m)$)

$$[A = g^u, F = g^{u'}, C = u \cdot H(g, A, B, F, ID_S) + u'] ,$$

in combination with the verification of the receiver (deciphering oracle)

$$g^C = A^{H(g, A, B, F, ID_S)} \cdot F ,$$

forms a Schnorr signature on the message (g, A, B, F, ID_S), with public key $A = g^u$. This signature is existentially unforgeable against adaptive chosen plaintext attacks [PS96] under the discrete logarithm assumption *(DLA)*, which is of course a weaker assumption than the decision D-H assumption. However, the proof of this unforgeability depends on the external queries of the adversarial algorithm (in our case, queries to the decryption oracle), which have to be answered by a simulator that does not possess the decryption (private) key. We capture this difference in the following assumption.

Assumption 1. Let $\mathcal{A}$ be a p.p.t. adversary that succeeds with non-negligible probability in an existential forgery of Schnorr signatures under a public key P of its choice, when it is given some adaptively obtained information $\mathcal{I}$. Then there exists a p.p.t. adversary $\mathcal{A}'$ having access to the same information $\mathcal{I}$ that succeeds with non-negligible probability in extracting the private key corresponding to public key P.

In fact this assumption is stronger from what our proof requires, but it is phrased more generally to cover all applications of Schnorr signatures. The intuition is that if the adversary can forge a signature, then there is a modified adversarial algorithm which: (1) constructs a random oracle H and runs the adversary until she produces a forged signature (A, F, C) on "message" $M = (g, A, B, F, ID_S)$; (2) fabricates a second random oracle H' which is identical to H except for its output on M (i.e., $H(M) \neq H'(M)$) and re-runs the adversary on the same inputs; (3) outputs the private key u corresponding to the Schnorr signature, and from this computes the plaintext $m = B/y^u$. In other words, if the adversary can produce a signature, then it is within her computational power (via the modification above) to compute the private key corresponding to this signature. However, this is not a complete argument as the assumption must be proven depending on the "adaptively obtained information $\mathcal{I}$". In particular if $\mathcal{I}$ is obtained from adaptive plaintext attacks against a signing oracle then the assumption holds [PS96]. For our case we need assumption 1 to hold when $\mathcal{I}$ is the information returned from the decryption oracle.

Now, under assumption 1 the encryption is *message (plaintext) aware* with respect to the name ID_S, since the party which included that name in the encryption (i.e., the party who produced the Schnorr signature) can compute the "private key" u corresponding to the signature, and from this compute the plaintext $m = B/y^u$. Therefore the adaptive chosen ciphertext attack in step (1) above ("lunch-time attack" [NY90]) provides no information to the adversary, if she has produced the ciphertexts by herself. If she has not produced the ciphertexts herself but has instead asked for decryptions of previously seen/captured ciphertexts, then this is equivalent as having some a-priori information; this is handled by the semantic security proof (see definitions of semantic security and indistinguishability of encryptions in section 2.2).

Now also note that if the adversary changes any part of the ciphertext $c = E^n(m)$ then she needs to obtain a signature on the "message" $(g, A', B', F', ID_{S'}) \neq (g, A, B, F, ID_S)$ which she has not seen before; therefore, again from assumption 1, she is required to know (or be able to efficiently compute) v (where $A' = g^v$). Thus for any *modified* ciphertexts submitted by the adversary to the deciphering oracle the adversary already knows v and therefore the plaintext; thus the adaptive ciphertext attack in step (3) above provides no additional information to the adversary, since she is not allowed to submit the same ciphertext that she has been challenged with in step (2). Therefore we can relax the attack model to a no-message attack, under which (as proven above) the scheme is semantically secure.

To complete the proof observe that if the adversary manages to create a ciphertext $c' = E^n(m') = [A', B', F', C', ID_{S'}] \neq [A, B, F, C, ID_S] = E^n(m) = c$ such that a poly-time computable relation $R(m, m')$ holds, then the adversary has effectively produced a Schnorr signature on the message $(g, A', B', F', ID_{S'}) \neq (g, A, B, F, ID_S)$ and, again from assumption 1 (and since she has not seen this signature before, as is required in step (3) of the attack model above), she must know the discrete logarithm of A' base g (i.e., the v for which $A' = g^v$), and therefore she must be able to obtain m'. But this means that the adversary knows some information about m, since she knows m' and the polynomial time computable relation $R(m, m')$; this contradicts the semantic security of the scheme. QED

Note: In practical encryption applications we would like a transmitted message to be both authenticated and secret. In such a setting non-malleability is not by itself sufficient, since it does not incorporate a signature of the sender: in effect the sender only states a name and binds the encryption to that name, but any other party could bind an encryption to the same name (i.e., impersonate the sender); therefore the transmission is not authenticated.[3] A digital signature is thus still required for authentication of a sent message for strong origin authentication; alternatively a combination of encryption and signature can be used, to create a "signcryption" scheme [Zhe97] in which the encryption part is non-malleable (in our scheme a Schnorr signature can be added smoothly).

Acknowledgements

We would like to thank Victor Shoup for pointing out the need for assumption 1; Berry Schoenmakers for pointing out an inconsistency in an earlier version; and Yair Frankel for helpful discussions.

References

[Bea96] D. Beaver.   Plausible deniability.   In *Advances in Cryptology — PraguoCrypt '96 Proceedings*, Prague, Czech Republic, 1996.

[Bea97] D. Beaver. Plug and play cryptography. In *Advances in Cryptology — CRYPTO '97 Proceedings, LLNCS 1294*, Santa Barbara, CA, August 17–21 1997. Springer-Verlag.

[BGM93] E. F. Brickell, D. Gordon, and K. S. McCurley. Fast exponentiation with precomputation. In *Advances in Cryptology — Eurocrypt '92, Proceedings (Lecture Notes in Computer Science 658)*. Springer-Verlag, 1993.

[BR94] M. Bellare and P. Rogaway. Optimal assymetric encryption— how to encrypt with RSA. In A. De Santis, editor, *Advances in Cryptology, Proc. of Eurocrypt '94, (Lecture notes in Computer Science Volume 950)*, Perugia, Italy, May 9–12 1994. Springer-Verlag.

[BR97] M. Bellare and P. Rogaway. Minimizing the use of random oracles in authenticated encryption schemes. In *ISICS '97*, 1997.

[Can97] R. Canetti. Towards realizing random oracles: Hash functions that hide all partial information. In B. Kaliski, editor, *Advances in Cryptology — CRYPTO '97 Proceedings, LLNCS 1294*, pages 455–469, Santa Barbara, CA, August 17–21 1997. Springer-Verlag.

[CS98] R. Cramer and V. Shoup. A practical public key cryptosystem provably secure against adaptive chosen ciphertext attack, 1998. Preprint. Available at http://www.cs.wisc.edu/ shoup/papers/.

---

[3] We divert from [BR97] who define "authenticated encryption" as "plaintext awareness + semantic security," or intuitively knowledge of the plaintext; here we consider authentication of both the sender and the message, as required in a network setting.

[Dam91] I. B. Damgård. Towards practical public key systems against chosen ciphertext attacks. In J. Feigenbaum, editor, *Advances in Cryptology, Proc. of Crypto '91 (Lecture Notes in Computer Science 576)*, pages 445–456. Springer-Verlag, 1991.

[DDN91] O. Dolev, C. Dwork, and M. Naor. Non-malleable cryptography. In *Proceedings of the 23rd Symposium on Theory of Computing, ACM STOC*, 1991.

[ElG85] T. ElGamal. A public key cryptosystem and a signature scheme based on discrete logarithms. *IEEE Trans. Inform. Theory*, 31:469–472, 1985.

[ElG98] T. ElGamal, January 1998. Personal communication.

[FS87] A. Fiat and A. Shamir. How to prove yourself: Practical solutions to identification and signature problems. In A. Odlyzko, editor, *Advances in Cryptology, Proc. of Crypto '86 (Lecture Notes in Computer Science 263)*, pages 186–194. Springer-Verlag, 1987. Santa Barbara, CA, August 11–15.

[FTY96] Y. Frankel, Y. Tsiounis, and M. Yung. Indirect discourse proofs: achieving fair off-line e-cash. In *Advances in Cryptology, Proc. of Asiacrypt '96 (Lecture Notes in Computer Science 1163)*, pages 286–300, Kyongju, South Korea, November 3–7 1996. Springer-Verlag. http://yiannis.home.ml.org/pubs.html

[GM84] S. Goldwasser and S. Micali. Probabilistic encryption. *Journal of Computer and System Sciences*, 28(2):270–299, April 1984.

[Gol89] O. Goldreich. Foundations of cryptography, 1989. Class notes. Available at http://www.wisdom.weizmann.ac.il/people/homepages/oded/ln89.html.

[Gol93] O. Goldreich. A uniform-complexity treatment of encryption and zero-knowledge. *Journal of Cryptology*, 6(1):21–53, 1993.

[MRS88] S. Micali, C. Rackoff, and B. Sloan. The notion of security for probabilistic cryptosystems. *SIAM Journal of Computing*, 17:412–426, 1988.

[NR97] M. Naor and O. Reingold. On the construction of pseudo-random permutations: Luby-Rackoff revisited. In *38th Annual Symp. on Foundations of Computer Science (FOCS)*, 1997.

[NY90] M. Naor and M. Yung. Public-key cryptosytems provably secure against chosen ciphertext attack. In *Proceedings of the twenty second annual ACM Symp. Theory of Computing, STOC*, pages 427–437, May 14–16, 1990.

[PS96] D. Pointcheval and J. Stern. Security proofs for signature schemes. In U. Maurer, editor, *Advances in Cryptology– Eurocrypt '96*, pages 387–398, Zaragoza, Spain, May 11–16, 1996. Springer-Verlag.

[RS92] C. Rackoff and D. Simon. Non-interactive zero-knowledge proof of knowledge and chosen ciphertext attack. In *Advances in Cryptology–Crypto '91 (LLNCS 576)*, pages 433–444, Santa Barbara, CA, 1992. Springer-Verlag.

[Sch91] C. P. Schnorr. Efficient signature generation by smart cards. *Journal of Cryptology*, 4(3):161–174, 1991.

[SS98] K. Sakurai and H. Shizuya. Relationships among the computational powers of breaking discrete log cryptosystems. *Journal of Cryptology*, 1998. To appear.

[TY97] Y. Tsiounis and M. Yung. The semantic security of El Gamal encryption is equivalent to the decision Diffie-Hellman. Technical Report, GTE Laboratories Inc., May 1997.

[Zhe97] Y. Zheng. Digital signcryption or how to achieve cost(signature & encryption) << cost(signature) + cost(encryption). In B. Kaliski, editor, *Advances in Cryptology-Crypto '97 (Lecture Notes in Computer Science 1294)*, pages 165–179, Santa Barbara, CA, August 17–21 1997. Springer-Verlag.

[ZS93] Y. Zheng and J. Seberry. Immunizing public key cryptosystems against chosen ciphertext attacks. *IEEE Journal on Selected Areas in Communications*, 11(5):715–724, June 1993.

An Authenticated Diffie-Hellman Key Agreement Protocol Secure Against Active Attacks

Shouichi Hirose and Susumu Yoshida

Department of Electronics and Communication, Graduate School of Engineering,
Kyoto University
Yoshidahonmachi, Sakyo-ku, Kyoto, 606–8501 Japan

Abstract. A two-party authenticated Diffie-Hellman key agreement protocol is proposed. The protocol is practical and provably secure against passive eavesdropping, impersonation, interference, active eavesdropping and pretense in the random oracle model on the assumptions that the Diffie-Hellman problem is intractable and that the secret pieces of information of users are selected at random and independently of each other. All of these attacks are assumed to be known-key attacks. The security against passive eavesdropping is proved on the assumption that the attacker knows the secret pieces of information of the participants. As an application of the proposed protocol, a star-based conference key distribution protocol is also designed.

1 Introduction

In using private key encryption for secure communication, it is necessary for the participants to share a common key securely with some key agreement scheme. Key agreement schemes can be classified into two types: non-interactive schemes and interactive schemes. In this manuscript, we discuss the interactive schemes, which are called the key agreement protocols.

Many of the previously proposed key agreement protocols do not provide key confirmation, that is, they do not guarantee that the participants share a common key [8, 11, 12, 14, 15]. For any of these protocols, an attacker is able to prevent the participants from sharing a common key by altering the messages exchanged during the execution of the protocol. Moreover, Burmester [3] presented the insider known key attack and applied it to some of the protocols without key confirmation. Thus, key confirmation is indispensable for secure key agreement.

Key agreement protocols with key confirmation [6, 10] have been proposed based on the Diffie-Hellman key agreement protocol [5]. In these protocols, the participants compute the shared key and use it explicitly for key confirmation. In the station-to-station protocol [6], the participants encrypt the signatures for the values used for key generation with the shared key and exchange the ciphertexts. In the protocol of Just and Vaudenay [10], the participants compute the authenticators of the values used for key generation with keyed hashing using the shared key and exchange them.

In this manuscript, a new two-party authenticated key agreement protocol is presented based on the Diffie-Hellman key agreement protocol. This protocol also guarantees that the participants share a common key, though the participants confirm it without computing the shared key. In the proposed protocol, each of the participants shows the other participant that he knows the discrete logarithm of his value used for key generation by using a redundant signature scheme, which is an extended version of Schnorr's signature scheme [13].

The proposed protocol is practical and provably secure against passive eavesdropping, impersonation, interference, active eavesdropping and pretense in the random oracle model [2] on the assumptions that the Diffie-Hellman problem is intractable and that the secret pieces of information of the users are selected randomly and independently of each other. All of these attacks are assumed to be known-key attacks. The security against passive eavesdropping is proved on the assumption that the attacker knows the secret pieces of information of the participants. In [12], key agreement protocols with provable security have been proposed based on the Fiat-Shamir identification protocol [7] and the Diffie-Hellman key agreement. These protocols have an interesting feature that they compute a shared key utilizing the random values of the Fiat-Shamir identification protocol. However, these protocols are not secure against interference, and the protocols secure against known key attacks are not practical.

As an application of the proposed two-party protocol, a star-based conference key distribution protocol is also designed.

In Section 2, the two-party authenticated key agreement protocol is proposed. In Section 3, it is shown that the proposed protocol is provably secure against passive eavesdropping, impersonation, interference, active eavesdropping and pretense. Section 4 includes the star-based protocol for conference key distribution based on the proposed two-party protocol. Section 5 is a conclusion.

2 Authenticated Diffie-Hellman key agreement protocol

2.1 Design principle and redundant signature scheme

Let p and q be large primes and q divide $p - 1$. Let g be an element of $GF(p)$ whose order is qD

Fig. 1 presents the Diffie-Hellman key agreement protocol. I_A and I_B represents the ID's of participants A and B, respectively. $\in_R$ represents a random selection of an element of the set on its right side. $\mathbf{Z}_q = \{0, 1, \ldots, q-1\}$. For the Diffie-Hellman key agreement protocol, if, for example, A gets the information which guarantees the following three points, then A makes sure that B is really able to compute $K_B(= K_A)$.

- B received u_A.
- B sent u_B to A in response to the receipt of u_A.
- B knows k_B, the discrete logarithm of u_B.

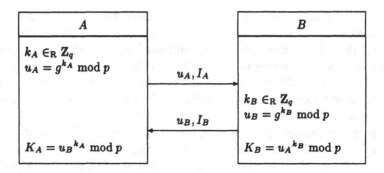

Fig. 1. Diffie-Hellman key agreement protocol

In order to guarantee the above three points, we present a new signature scheme. This scheme, which we call a redundant signature scheme, is an extended version of Schnorr's signature scheme [13].

Redundant signature scheme. Let $s_i \in Z_q$ be a secret piece of information of the user i and $v_i = g^{-s_i} \bmod p$ be a public piece of information of the user i. Let $h : \{0,1\}^* \to Z_q$ be a public collision free hash function.

Let $k_B \in Z_q$ and $u_B = g^{-k_B} \bmod p$. Suppose that B knows k_B. B's signature (u_B, e_B, w_B) for u_A is computed with the following procedure.

1. B selects $r_B \in Z_q$ at random and computes $x_B = g^{r_B} \bmod p$.
2. B computes $e_B = h(x_B, u_B, u_A)$ and $w_B = r_B + e_B k_B + e_B^2 s_B \bmod q$.

The procedure for checking the validity of the signature (u_B, e_B, w_B) for u_A is as follows:

1. Let $z_B = g^{w_B}(u_B v_B^{e_B})^{e_B} \bmod p$.
2. The signature is valid if and only if $e_B = h(z_B, u_B, u_A)$.

2.2 Protocol

The same notations as in the last section are used. p, q, g, h are public and shared among all of the users.

The proposed protocol is shown below. This is called KAP in this manuscript. It is assumed that each of the participants knows the public piece of information of the other participant or that the public piece of information of each participant is contained in his ID.

KAP.

S1. A randomly selects $k_A \in Z_q$ and computes $u_A = g^{-k_A} \bmod p$. A sends u_A, I_A to B.

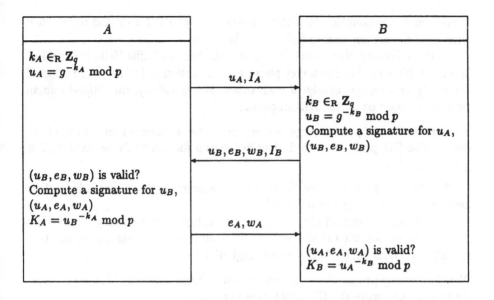

Fig. 2. The proposed key agreement protocol KAP

S2. B randomly selects $k_B \in \mathbf{Z}_q$ and computes $u_B = g^{-k_B} \bmod p$. Then, B computes a signature (u_B, e_B, w_B) for u_A using the redundant signature scheme. B sends u_B, e_B, w_B, I_B to A.

S3. A checks the validity of the signature (u_B, e_B, w_B). If it is not valid, then A terminates the execution of the protocol. Otherwise, A computes a signature (u_A, e_A, w_A) for u_B using the redundant signature scheme and sends e_A, w_A to B. A also computes $K_A = u_B^{-k_A} \bmod p$.

S4. B checks the validity of the signature (u_A, e_A, w_A). If it is not valid, then B terminates the execution of the protocol. Otherwise, B computes $K_B = u_A^{-k_B} \bmod p$.

KAP is also shown in Fig. 2.

It is clear that A and B can compute K_A, K_B such that $K_A = K_B$ if they behave honestly. For example, by checking the validity of the signature (u_B, e_B, w_B) for u_A, A makes sure that B is able to compute K_B which is equal to K_A, that is, that B received u_A, sent u_B in response to the receipt of u_A and knows k_B.

3 Security

In this section, it is proved that KAP is secure against passive eavesdropping, impersonation, interference, active eavesdropping and pretense in the random oracle model [2]. All of the above attacks are known-key ones and the security is proved on the assumption that the discrete logarithms of u_A's and u_B's which were used for key generation before are disclosed.

In the following discussions, it is assumed that the Diffie-Hellman problem is intractable and that the secret pieces of information of the users are selected randomly and independently of each other. For simplicity, the Diffie-Hellman problem is denoted by the DH problem.

Definition 1. Let p, q be large primes and g be an element in GF(p) of order q. The DH problem is to find $\alpha^{\log_g \beta} \bmod p$ for randomly selected $\alpha, \beta \in \{g^0, \ldots, g^{q-1}\}$.

The length of q is used for the security parameter and is denoted by n. It is assumed that the length of p is $O(n)$.

A real-valued function $\varepsilon(n)$ is said to be negligible, if, for every $c > 0$, there exists some $n_c > 0$ such that $\varepsilon(n) < n^{-c}$ for all $n > n_c$. A real-valued function is said to be non-negligible if it is not negligible.

Note 2. For any probabilistic polynomial time Turing machine M, the probability that M can solve the DH problem is negligible.

Note 3. The secret pieces of information of the users are selected randomly and independently of each other.

Suppose that there exist three users, A, B and C, which are probabilistic polynomial time Turing machines. Let A and B be honest users and C be an attacker. An execution of KAP by the users X, Y is denoted by (X, Y), where X is the initiator of the execution.

An attack consists of an observation phase and an attack phase. First, C obtains the histories of (A, B)'s, (B, A)'s, (A, C)'s and (B, C)'s during the observation phase. Then, C makes an attack on A, B or both during the attack phase. During the observation phase, C need not obtain the histories of (C, A)'s and (C, B)'s, because it is more advantageous that C first receives messages from his partner. The history of (X, Y) obtained by C during the observation phase is $(u_X, I_X; u_Y, e_Y, w_Y, I_Y; e_X, w_X; k_X, k_Y)$. C is able to obtain both k_X and k_Y, because the attacks are assumed to be known-key ones.

A probabilistic polynomial time Turing machine M with an oracle C is denoted by M^C. It is assumed that M^C can rewind C by any number of steps and replay it.

3.1 Passive attack

In this section, it is proved that KAP is secure against passive eavesdropping.

In the following theorem, it is assumed that C knows the secret pieces of information of A and B, s_A and s_B. Thus, C can omit the observation phase.

Theorem 4. *If the probability that C succeeds in computing $K_A(= K_B)$ by passive eavesdropping on (A, B) is non-negligible, then there exists some probabilistic polynomial time Turing machine M^C that is able to solve the DH problem with non-negligible probability.*

Proof. For a given instance of the DH problem, a, b, M^C first simulates (A, B) in the following way:

1. M^C determines $u_A = a$ and $u_B = b$.
2. M^C randomly selects $e_B, w_B \in \mathbf{Z}_q$, computes $x_B = g^{w_B}(u_B v_B{}^{e_B})^{e_B} \bmod p$, and determines $e_B = h(x_B, u_B, u_A)$.
3. M^C randomly selects $e_A, w_A \in \mathbf{Z}_q$, computes $x_A = g^{w_A}(u_A v_A{}^{e_A})^{e_A} \bmod p$, and determines $e_A = h(x_A, u_A, u_B)$.

In the above procedure, x_B and x_A are randomly selected, because e_B, w_B and e_A, w_A are randomly selected, respectively.

Then, M^C feeds $(u_A, I_A; u_B, e_B, w_B, I_B; e_A, w_A)$ to C and outputs the value that C outputs to this input. The output of C is $a^{\log_g b} \bmod p$ when C succeeds in passive eavesdropping.

During the simulation of (A, B), if it happens that $(x_B, u_B, u_A) = (x_A, u_A, u_B)$ and that $e_B \neq e_A$, then M^C fails in the simulation. The probability is, however, negligible.

Hence, M^C is able to solve the DH problem with non-negligible probability if C succeeds in passive eavesdropping on (A, B) with non-negligible probability. $\square$

From Theorem 4 and Note 2, it follows that KAP is secure against passive eavesdropping. It also follows that KAP provides forward secrecy, that is, the keys shared before cannot be compromised even if the secret pieces of information of the users are leaked.

3.2   Active attacks

In this section, it is shown that KAP is provably secure against impersonation, interference, active eavesdropping and pretense.

Let $Msg((X, Y), X)$ denote the messages sent and received by X during (X, Y). $Msg((X, Y), Y)$ is defined in the same way.

The attacks except impersonation are intruder-in-the-middle attacks, which is shown in Fig. 3. $(A, B)^C$ denotes (A, B) with an intruder C. For $(A, B)^C$,

$$Msg((A, B)^C, A) = (u_A, I_A; \tilde{u}_B, \tilde{e}_B, \tilde{w}_B, \tilde{I}_B; e_A, w_A),$$
$$Msg((A, B)^C, B) = (\tilde{u}_A, \tilde{I}_A; u_B, e_B, w_B, I_B; \tilde{e}_A, \tilde{w}_A).$$

Let $Valid$ be a function such that, for example, $Valid(Msg((A, B)^C, A), v_B) = 1$ if and only if $\tilde{I}_B = I_B$ and $\tilde{e}_B = h(\tilde{x}_B, \tilde{u}_B, u_A)$, where $\tilde{x}_B = g^{\tilde{w}_B}(\tilde{u}_B v_B{}^{\tilde{e}_B})^{\tilde{e}_B} \bmod p$.

First, it is shown that the redundant signature scheme is provably secure against adaptive existential forgery.

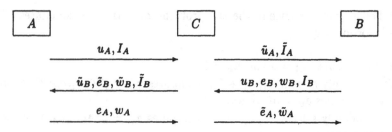

Fig. 3. Intruder-in-the-middle attack

Security of redundant signature scheme. A well-known lemma is shown first without a proof.

Lemma 5. *Let S, R be discrete random variables and let $S \in \{0, 1\}$ and $\Pr[S = 1] = \alpha$. Then, for every constant c such that $0 < c < 1$,*

$$\sum_{\{a \mid \Pr[S=1 \mid R=a] \geq c\alpha\}} \Pr[R = a] \geq (1 - c)\alpha.$$

The procedure for adaptive existential forgery by C is as follows:

1. Query phase: First C selects and sends to an honest signer A a message m_i after receiving $u_i = g^{-k_i} \bmod p$ from A, and then, receives a signature (u_i, e_i, w_i) for m_i and k_i from A. C repeats the procedure some adequate t times.
2. Forgery phase: C tries to forge A's signature for some m using $u \in \{g^j \mid 0 \leq j \leq q - 1\}$ such that $(m, u) \notin \{(m_i, u_i) \mid 1 \leq i \leq t\}$.

It is said that C succeeds in forgery of a signature if C succeeds in making a signature (u, e, w) for m such that (m, u) does not appear during the query phase. This definition is somewhat different from the previous ones. The definition is adopted since it is suitable for the reductions of the security against some of the active attacks to the security of the redundant signature.

Theorem 6. *If the probability of C's success in adaptive existential forgery of A's signature is non-negligible, then there exists some probabilistic polynomial time Turing machine M^C that is able to compute the secret piece of information of A with non-negligible probability.*

Proof. First, during the query phase of C, M^C simulates A and computes a signature (u_i, e_i, w_i) for m_i for $i = 1, \ldots, t$. The procedure is as follows:

1. M^C computes $u_i = g^{-k_i} \bmod p$ for random $k_i \in \mathbf{Z}_q$ and sends u_i to C. After receiving u_i, C selects m_i and sends it to M^C.
2. M^C randomly selects $e_i, w_i \in \mathbf{Z}_q$, computes $x_i = g^{w_i}(u_i v_A^{e_i})^{e_i} \bmod p$ and determines $e_i = h(x_i, u_i, m_i)$. M^C sends $(u_i, e_i, w_i), k_i$ to C.

If $(x_i, u_i, m_i) = (x_j, u_j, m_j)$ and $e_i \neq e_j$ for i, j such that $i \neq j$, then M^C fails in the simulation. The probability of this failure is negligible.

Let α be the probability of C's success in forgery. Then, from Lemma 5, the probability that the probability of C's success in forgery with the pairs of the messages and the signatures obtained during the query phase is at least $\alpha/2$ is at least $\alpha/2$.

Next, C tries to forge a signature during the forgery phase. C selects m, u, x and sends them to M^C, where $(m, u) \notin \{(m_i, u_i) \mid 1 \leq i \leq t\}$. The probability is at least $\alpha/4$ that the probability of C's success in forgery of a signature for m, u, x is at least $\alpha/4$.

M^C randomly selects e and sends it back to C in response to m, u, x, where $e = h(x, u, m)$. If M^C repeats this procedure $8/\alpha$ times, then C can compute correct w, w', w'' for different e, e', e'' with non-negligible probability.

$$
\begin{pmatrix} w \\ w' \\ w'' \end{pmatrix} = \begin{pmatrix} 1 & e & e^2 \\ 1 & e' & (e')^2 \\ 1 & e'' & (e'')^2 \end{pmatrix} \begin{pmatrix} r \\ k \\ s_A \end{pmatrix} \bmod q,
$$

where $x = g^r \bmod p$ and $u = g^{-k} \bmod p$, and the coefficient matrix is regular. Thus, the probability that M^C can compute s_A is non-negligible. $\square$

From Theorem 6 and Notes 2 and 3, it is clear that the redundant signature scheme is secure against adaptive existential forgery.

Impersonation. It is assumed that impersonation is not an intruder-in-the-middle attack. This is because we would like to exclude the middleperson attack against identification schemes [1], which has no effect on KAP.

The procedure of C for impersonating A on (C, B) is as follows:

1. Observation phase: C obtains some adequate number of the histories of (A, B)'s, (B, A)'s, (A, C)'s and (B, C)'s.
2. Attack phase: C tries to impersonate A on (C, B).

Definition 7. It is said that C succeeds in impersonating A on (C, B), if $Valid(Msg((C, B), B), v_A) = 1$ for (C, B) during the attack phase.

Theorem 8. *If the probability of C's success in impersonation of A on (C, B) is non-negligible, then there exists some probabilistic polynomial time Turing machine M^C that succeeds in forgery of A's signature with non-negligible probability.*

Proof. In order to succeed in impersonation, C has to forge A's signature for randomly selected u_B during the attack phase. $\square$

The same kind of theorem can be established for C's impersonation of B on (A, C). Hence, KAP is secure against impersonation.

143

Interference. Interference is defined as an active attack that alters the messages exchanged by participants in order that they fail to share a common key.

Definition 9. It is said that C succeeds in interference on (A, B) if the following two conditions hold for $(A, B)^C$ during the attack phase.

- $Valid(Msg((A, B)^C, A), v_B) = 1$ or $Valid(Msg((A, B)^C, B), v_A) = 1$.
- $\tilde{u}_B^{-k_A} \not\equiv \tilde{u}_A^{-k_B}$ (mod p).

Theorem 10. *If the probability that C succeeds in interference on (A, B) is non-negligible, then there exists some probabilistic polynomial time Turing machine M^C that succeeds in forging a signature of A or B with non-negligible probability.*

Proof. First, during the observation phase of C, M^C generates an adequate number of the histories of (A, B)'s, (B, A)'s, (A, C)'s and (B, C)'s. The following is the procedure for (A, C). The histories of the other executions are able to be generated in the same way.

1. M^C receives $u_A = g^{-k_A} \bmod p$ from A and sends u_A, I_A to C. Then, M^C receives u_C, e_C, w_C, I_C from C.
2. M^C sends u_C to A and receives from A a signature (u_A, e_A, w_A) for u_C and k_A. Then, M^C sends e_A, w_A and k_A to C.

The procedure of M^C during the attack phase of C is as follows:

1. M^C receives $u_A = g^{-k_A} \bmod p$ from A.
2. M^C sends u_A, I_A to C and receives $\tilde{u}_A, \tilde{I}_A$ from C.
3. M^C receives $u_B = g^{-k_B} \bmod p$ from B and sends $\tilde{u}_A$ to B. Then, M^C receives a signature (u_B, e_B, w_B) for $\tilde{u}_A$ from B.
4. M^C sends u_B, e_B, w_B, I_B to C and receives $\tilde{u}_B, \tilde{e}_B, \tilde{w}_B, \tilde{I}_B$ from C.
5. M^C sends $\tilde{u}_B$ to A and receives a signature (u_A, e_A, w_A) for $\tilde{u}_B$ from A.
6. M^C sends e_A, w_A to C and receives $\tilde{e}_A, \tilde{w}_A$ from C.
7. M^C outputs $(\tilde{u}_A, \tilde{e}_A, \tilde{w}_A)$ as a forged signature of A for u_B and $(\tilde{u}_B, \tilde{e}_B, \tilde{w}_B)$ as a forged signature of B for u_A.

From the definition of interference, if C succeeds in interference on (A, B), then $\tilde{u}_A \neq u_A$ or $\tilde{u}_B \neq u_B$ and $Valid(Msg((A, B)^C, A), v_B) = 1$ or $Valid(Msg((A, B)^C, B), v_A) = 1$. Thus, the probability that at least one of the following four conditions holds is non-negligible since the probability of success in interference is non-negligible.

- $\tilde{u}_A \neq u_A$ and $Valid(Msg((A, B)^C, B), v_A) = 1$.
- $\tilde{u}_A \neq u_A$ and $Valid(Msg((A, B)^C, A), v_B) = 1$.
- $\tilde{u}_B \neq u_B$ and $Valid(Msg((A, B)^C, B), v_A) = 1$.
- $\tilde{u}_B \neq u_B$ and $Valid(Msg((A, B)^C, A), v_B) = 1$.

Suppose that $\tilde{u}_A \neq u_A$ and $Valid(Msg((A, B)^C, B), v_A) = 1$. During the attack phase, C receives A's signature (u_A, e_A, w_A) for $\tilde{u}_B$, and forges A's signature $(\tilde{u}_A, \tilde{e}_A, \tilde{w}_A)$ for randomly selected u_B. Thus, in this case, C succeeds in forgery of A's signature since $(u_A, \tilde{u}_B) \neq (\tilde{u}_A, u_B)$.

It can be proved that C succeeds in forgery of a signature of A or B if any one of the other three conditions holds. □

From this theorem and Theorem 6, it follows that KAP is secure against interference.

Active eavesdropping. Active eavesdropping is defined as an active attack by which an attacker alters the messages exchanged between participants and tries to establish at least a key with one of them.

Definition 11. It is said that C succeeds in active eavesdropping on (A, B) if at least one of the following conditions holds for $(A, B)^C$ during the attack phase.

- $Valid(Msg((A, B)^C, B), v_A) = 1$ and C can compute $K_c = u_B^{-\tilde{k}_A} \bmod p$.
- $Valid(Msg((A, B)^C, A), v_B) = 1$ and C can compute $K_c = u_A^{-\tilde{k}_B} \bmod p$.

Theorem 12. *If the probability of C's success in active eavesdropping on (A, B) is non-negligible, then there exists some probabilistic polynomial time Turing machine M^C that succeeds in forging a signature of A or B with non-negligible probability.*

Proof. The same procedures as in the proof of Theorem 10 is used by M^C.

Since the probability that C succeeds in active eavesdropping is non-negligible, the probability that at least one of the conditions in Definition 11 holds is also non-negligible. Suppose that $Valid(Msg((A, B)^C, B), v_A) = 1$ and that C can compute $K_c = u_B^{-\tilde{k}_A} \bmod p$. Since KAP is secure against passive eavesdropping and C can compute $K_c = u_B^{-\tilde{k}_A} \bmod p$, it can be assumed that $\tilde{u}_A \neq u_A$. During the attack phase, C receives A's signature (u_A, e_A, w_A) for $\tilde{u}_B$ and sends to B a forged signature of A, $(\tilde{u}_A, \tilde{e}_A, \tilde{w}_A)$, for randomly selected u_B. Thus, C succeeds in forging A's signature since $\tilde{u}_A \neq u_A$.

It can also be proved that C succeeds in forging B's signature if $Valid(Msg((A, B)^C, A), v_B) = 1$ and C can compute $K_c = u_A^{-\tilde{k}_B} \bmod p$. □

From Theorems 12 and 6, it follows that KAP is secure against active eavesdropping.

Pretense. In this section, the attack on the key agreement protocol in [4] presented in [10] is considered. We call this kind of attack pretense. Fig. 4 shows pretense of (C, B) on (A, B). By pretense of (C, B) on (A, B), C tries to make B believe that the key is shared between B and C. Thus, pretense does not involve any alterations of u_A, u_B and C does not know the value of $K_A (= K_B)$.

Definition 13. It is said that C succeeds in pretense of (C, B) on (A, B) if the following conditions hold for $(A, B)^C$ during the attack phase.

- $Msg((A, B)^C, A) = (u_A, I_A; u_B, e_B, w_B, I_B; e_A, w_A)$ and
  $Valid(Msg((A, B)^C, A), v_B) = 1$.

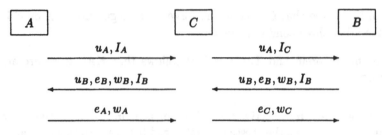

Fig. 4. Pretense of (C, B) on (A, B)

- $Msg((A, B)^C, B) = (u_A, I_C; u_B, e_B, w_B, I_B; e_C, w_C)$ and
  $Valid(Msg((A, B)^C, B), v_C) = 1$.

Theorem 14. *If the probability of C's success in pretense of (C, B) on (A, B) is non-negligible, then there exists some probabilistic polynomial time Turing machine M^C that is able to compute the discrete logarithm of v_A/v_C with non-negligible probability. It is assumed that C always uses x_A during the attack phase.*

Proof. M^C first generates some adequate number of the histories of (A, B)'s, (B, A)'s, (A, C)'s and (B, C)'s during the observation phase of C. The following is the procedure for (A, C).

1. M^C computes $u_A = g^{-k_A} \bmod p$ and sends u_A, I_A to C.
2. M^C receives u_C, e_C, w_C, I_C from C.
3. M^C randomly selects $e_A, w_A \in \mathbf{Z}_q$, computes $x_A = g^{w_A}(u_A v_A{}^{e_A})^{e_A} \bmod p$ and determines $e_A = h(x_A, u_A, u_C)$. Then, M^C sends e_A, w_A and k_A to C.

Next, M^C computes the discrete logarithm of v_A/v_C utilizing the attack phase of C. The procedure is as follows:

1. M^C computes u_A and sends u_A, I_A to C.
2. M^C receives u_A, I_C from C and sends u_B, e_B, w_B, I_B to C.
3. M^C receives u_B, e_B, w_B, I_B from C and sends e_A, w_A to C.
4. M^C receives e_C, w_C from C.

If C succeeds in computing the correct e_C, w_C, then $e_C = e_A = h(x_A, u_A, u_B)$ and

$$\begin{cases} w_A = r_A + e_A k_A + e_A{}^2 s_A \bmod q \\ w_C = r_A + e_C k_A + e_C{}^2 s_C \bmod q. \end{cases}$$

From these equations, M^C can compute

$$s_A - s_C = e_A{}^{-2}(w_A - w_C) \bmod q,$$

which is the discrete logarithm of v_A/v_C.

Since the probability that M^C fails in the simulation of A, B and the random oracle is negligible, M^C can compute the discrete logarithm of v_A/v_C with non-negligible probability. $\square$

Theorem 15. *If the probability of C's success in pretense of (C, B) on (A, B) is non-negligible, then there exists some probabilistic polynomial time Turing machine M^C that is able to solve the discrete logarithm problem with non-negligible probability. It is assumed that C does not use x_A during the attack phase.*

Proof. Let α be the probability of C's success in pretense. Let a be the instance of the discrete logarithm problem given to M^C. M^C's procedure during the observation phase of C is the same as in Theorem 14. The probability that C succeeds in pretense with probability at least $\alpha/2$ using the histories obtained during the observation phase is at least $\alpha/2$.

The procedure of M^C during the attack phase of C is as follows:

1. M^C sends u_A, I_A to C, where $u_A = a$.
2. M^C receives u_A, I_C from C and sends u_B, e_B, w_B, I_B to C.
3. M^C receives u_B, e_B, w_B, I_B from C and sends e_A, w_A to C.
4. M^C repeats the following procedure $8/\alpha$ times.
   - M^C receives x_C, u_A, u_B from C and sends randomly selected e_C to C, where $e_C = h(x_C, u_A, u_B)$. Then, M^C receives e_C, w_C from C.

In the step 4 of the procedure, for different $e_{C,1}, e_{C,2}, e_{C,3}$, if C can compute correct $w_{C,1}, w_{C,2}, w_{C,3}$, then

$$
\begin{pmatrix} w_{C,1} \\ w_{C,2} \\ w_{C,3} \end{pmatrix} = \begin{pmatrix} 1 & e_{C,1} & (e_{C,1})^2 \\ 1 & e_{C,2} & (e_{C,2})^2 \\ 1 & e_{C,3} & (e_{C,3})^2 \end{pmatrix} \begin{pmatrix} r_C \\ k_A \\ s_C \end{pmatrix} \bmod q
$$

and M^C can obtain k_A, the discrete logarithm of a, from the equation.

For x_C, u_A, u_B in the step 4, the probability that C succeeds in computing correct w_C with probability at least $\alpha/4$ is at least $\alpha/4$. Thus, the probability that C can compute correct $w_{C,1}, w_{C,2}, w_{C,3}$ for different $e_{C,1}, e_{C,2}, e_{C,3}$, respectively, with constant probability is at least $\alpha/4$.

The probability that M^C can solve the discrete logarithm problem is non-negligible since the probability that M^C fails in executing the procedure is negligible. □

The same kind of theorem can be established for the pretense of (A, C) on (A, B). Thus, KAP is secure against pretense.

4 Star-based protocol for conference key distribution

As an application of KAP, a star-based protocol for conference key distribution is designed based on KAP. The conference key distribution protocol presented in this section is called CKDP.

Let $U_0, \ldots, U_m$ be participants. In CKDP, messages are exchanged only between U_0 and each one of $U_1, \ldots, U_m$. The shared key is generated by U_0 and distributed to the other participants with the protocol based on KAP. CKDP is shown in Fig. 5. After U_0 receives e_i, w_i from U_i, he checks the validity of

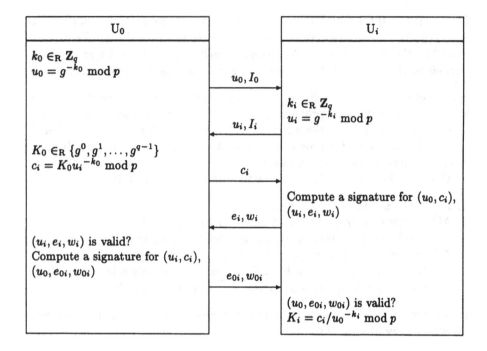

Fig. 5. The proposed conference key distribution protocol CKDP

U_i's signature (u_i, e_i, w_i) for (u_0, c_i) by checking if $e_i = h(z_i, u_i, u_0, c_0)$, where $z_i = g^{w_i}(u_i v_i^{e_i})^{e_i} \mod p$. U_0 continues the execution of CKDP only if all the signatures of the other participants are valid.

By checking the validity of (u_i, e_i, w_i), U_0 makes sure that U_i is able to compute $K_i = c_i/u_0^{-k_i} \mod p$ such that $K_i = K_0$, that is, that U_i received u_0 and c_i, sent u_i in response to u_0 and c_i and knows k_i, the discrete logarithm of u_i. On the other hand, U_i makes sure that U_0 is able to compute $K_0 = c_i/u_i^{-k_0} \mod p$, which is equal to K_i by checking the validity of (u_0, e_{0i}, w_{0i}).

If U_0 is assumed to be honest during the execution of CKDP, then U_0 sends a common K_0 to all U_i's and continues the execution of CKDP only if all (u_i, e_i, w_i)'s are valid. Thus, in this case, U_i can make sure that all the participants share a common key if (u_0, e_{0i}, w_{0i}) is valid.

On the other hand, if U_0 is not necessarily honest during the execution of the protocol, then some kind of check is needed to guarantee each U_i that the participants share a common key. For example, the protocol in [9] specifies that the participants make a multi-signature for the shared key and check its validity.

In an execution of CKDP, U_0 has to generate three random sequences and compute $5m + 2$ modular exponentiations, where m is the number of the participants other than U_0. Each one of $U_i(i = 1, 2, \ldots, m)$ has to generate two random sequences and compute six modular exponentiations. The number of the moves of the protocol is five.

5 Conclusion

In this manuscript, a two-party authenticated key agreement protocol based on the Diffie-Hellman key agreement protocol was presented and its security was discussed. The proposed protocol is practical and provably secure against passive eavesdropping, impersonation, interference, active eavesdropping and pretense in the random oracle model if the Diffie-Hellman problem is intractable and the secret pieces of information of the users are selected randomly and independently of each other. All of the above attacks are known-key attacks. The proposed protocol is also provably secure against passive eavesdropping even if the eavesdropper knows the secret pieces of information of the participants. As an application of the proposed two-party key agreement protocol, a star-based conference key distribution protocol was designed.

References

1. Bengio, S., Brassard, G, Desmedt, Y. G., Goutier, C. and Quisquater, J.-J., "Secure implementation of identification systems," J. Cryptology, vol. 4, pp. 175–183, 1991.
2. Bellare, M. and Rogaway, P., "Random oracles are practical: A paradigm for designing efficient protocols," Proc. the 1st ACM Conference on Computer and Communications Security, pp. 62–73, 1993.
3. Burmester, M., "On the risk of opening distributed keys," Proc. CRYPTO'94, LNCS 839, pp. 308–317, 1994.
4. Burmester, M. and Desmedt, Y., "A secure and efficient conference key distribution system," Proc. EUROCRYPT'94, LNCS 950, pp. 275–286, 1995.
5. Diffie, W. and Hellman, M. E., "New directions in cryptography," IEEE Trans. Infor. Theory, vol. IT-22, pp. 644–654, 1976.
6. Diffie, W., van Oorschot, P. and Wiener, M. J., "Authentication and authenticated key exchanges," Designs, Codes and Cryptography, vol. 2, pp. 107–125, 1992.
7. Fiat, A. and Shamir, A., "How to prove yourself: practical solutions to identification and signature problems," Proc. CRYPTO'86, LNCS 263, pp. 186–194, 1987.
8. Günther, C. G., "An identity-based key exchange protocol," Proc. EUROCRYPT'89, LNCS 434, pp. 29–37, 1990.
9. Hirose, S. and Ikeda, K., "A conference key distribution system for the star configuration based on the discrete logarithm problem," Information Processing Letters, vol. 62, no. 4, pp. 189–192, 1997.
10. Just, M. and Vaudenay, S., "Authenticated multi-party key agreement," Proc. ASIACRYPT'96, LNCS 1163, pp. 36–49, 1996.
11. Matsumoto, T., Takashima, Y. and Imai, H., "On seeking smart public-key distribution systems," Trans. of IECE of Japan, vol. E69, no. 2, pp. 99–106, 1986.
12. Okamoto, T. and Ohta, K., "How to utilize the randomness of zero-knowledge proofs," Proc. CRYPTO'90, LNCS 537, pp. 456–475, 1991.
13. Schnorr, C. P., "Efficient identification and signatures for smart cards," Proc. CRYPTO'89, LNCS 435, pp. 239–252, 1990.
14. Yacobi, Y., "A key distribution paradox," Proc. CRYPTO'90, LNCS 537, pp. 268–273, 1991.
15. Yacobi, Y. and Shmuely, Z., "On key distribution systems," Proc. CRYPTO'89, LNCS 435, pp. 344–355, 1990.

On the Security of Girault's Identification Scheme

Shahrokh Saeednia[1] and Rei Safavi-Naini[2]

[1] Université Libre de Bruxelles
Département d'Informatique
CP 212, Boulevard du Triomphe
1050 Bruxelles, Belgium
email: saeednia@ulb.ac.be

[2] University of Wollongong
Department of Computer Science
Northfields Ave., Wollongong 2522, Australia
email: rei@uow.edu.au

Abstract. In this paper, we describe two serious weaknesses of an identity-based identification scheme proposed by Girault (presented at Eurocrypt '90) that enables adversaries to forge identity, key pairs for a large group of users. We also show how to modify the scheme to make the attacks ineffective.

1 Introduction

In [2] Girault proposed an interesting modification of Schnorr's identification scheme [4] in which prime modulus is replaced by a composite modulus resulting in a more secure scheme. The modification has some similarity with Brickell-McCurley's scheme [1], but has the advantage that it is identity-based - or more accurately, self-certified as later discussed in [3].

Girault's proposal has the particularity that unlike the usual identity-based schemes, each user chooses his own secret key and only gives a shadow of this secret key to the authority. The shadow is calculated by applying a one-way function to the secret key which makes it infeasible for the authority to determine the secret key from the knowledge of the shadow. The authority computes the users's public key using the shadow of the secret key, user's identity and some secret trapdoor known only to it. The trapdoor is used to prevent adversaries from forging identity, key pairs. That is, the system is secure if it is difficult to create a public key and its corresponding identity for a user without the knowledge of the authority's secret, even if the identity, public key pair for all the users are known. We will show that Girault's scheme does not meet this requirement.

In this paper, we show that it is possible to generate public keys for some identities without knowing authority's secrets. We will give a modification of the key generation phase of Giraults's scheme to remove this weakness without reducing the performance of the system. In section 2 we review Girault's scheme as it is described in [2] and in section 3 and 4 present the attacks and the proposed repair, respectively.

2   Girault's identification Scheme

Girault's scheme assumes the existence of a trusted authority who computes users' public keys linked to their identities.

In the *setup phase* of the scheme, the authority chooses,

- an integer n as the product of two primes p and q such that $p = 2fp' + 1$ and $q = 2fq' + 1$, where f, p' and q' are also distinct primes;
- an integer b of order f both modulo p and q (thus $b^f \pmod{n} = 1$); and
- an integer e which is coprime with both $p - 1$ and $q - 1$.

It then computes $h = b^e \pmod{n}$, as well as d such that $e \cdot d \equiv 1 \pmod{\lambda(n)}$.

Finally, the authority makes n, f, b, e and h public, keeps d secret and discards p and q.

In the basic version of the system f is suggested to be 200 bits long and p' and q' are of 300 bits, each.

In the *key generation phase*, Alice applies for a certified public key. She chooses her secret key s, computes $v = b^{-s} \pmod{n}$ and sends v to the authority. The authority forms an integer I based on Alice's identity and computes her public key as $P = I^{-d} \cdot v \pmod{n}$.

In the *identification phase*:

1. Alice chooses a random integer $r \in \{0, \ldots, f-1\}$, computes $x = h^r \pmod{n}$ and sends x to Bob together with the pair (P, I).
2. Bob checks whether I reflects Alice's identity, if so, chooses a random number $c \in \{0, \ldots, e-1\}$ and sends it to Alice.
3. Alice computes $y = r + sc \pmod{f}$ and sends it to Bob.
4. Bob checks whether $h^y (P^e I)^c \pmod{n} = x$.

If this holds Bob accepts Alice, otherwise rejects and halts.

3   How to forge identity, public key pairs

In this section, we describe two attacks on the setup phase of the above scheme which allow adversaries to forge identity, public key pairs without the knowledge of the authority's secret. The first attack succeeds if there is an identity I with the property that $I^{2f} = 1 \pmod{n}$. That is the attack works for all identities I that are of order 2, f and $2f$. we will show that if a given identity I is of one of these orders then it is possible to compute a public key linked to it without knowing the authority's secret. The second attack is successful if one can find identities, I_1, I_2 such that $I_3 = I_1 I_2$ corresponds to a valid identity. The attack may be performed by any subset of users who have valid public and secret keys related to their identities.

3.1 Attack 1

In Girault's scheme, $\lambda(n) = 2fp'q'$. So there are integers in Z_n that are of the order $t \in \{2, f, 2f\}$ modulo n. Let $\mathcal{F}$ denote the set of all such integers. Obviously, for all $k \in \mathcal{F}$, we have $k^{2f} = 1 \pmod{n}$.

Since, e is coprime with $p - 1$ and $q - 1$, it is also coprime with $2f$. So, as $2f$ is publicly known, one can compute d' such that $e \cdot d' \equiv 1 \pmod{2f}$. This implies that for all $k \in \mathcal{F}$, $k^{ed'} \pmod{n} = k$.

Now, it is easy to see that if an identity I belongs to $\mathcal{F}$, then it is possible to generate a forged public key connected to it. In fact, for any $I \in \mathcal{F}$ one can compute the related public key as $P' = I^{-d'}b^{-s} \pmod{n}$, where s is any arbitrarily chosen secret key.

Using these keys, Alice can prove her identity to Bob without deviating from the identification protocol. Indeed, in the last step of the protocol Bob verifies if $h^y(P'^e I)^c \pmod{n} = x$. If $I \in \mathcal{F}$, this always holds because

$$\begin{aligned}
h^y(P'^e I)^c \pmod{n} &= h^y((I^{-d'}b^{-s})^e I)^c \pmod{n} \\
&= h^y(I^{-d'e}b^{-se}I)^c \pmod{n} \\
&= h^y(I^{-1}b^{-se}I)^c \pmod{n} \\
&= h^y b^{-sec} \pmod{n} \\
&= h^y h^{-sc} \pmod{n} \\
&= x.
\end{aligned}$$

In general the number of integers in Z_n that correspond to acceptable identities, and the number of acceptable identities belonging to $\mathcal{F}$, depends on the way that the authority determines an identity. However, if we assume that I's are uniformly distributed over Z_n, then there are $(4f^2 - 1)|\mathcal{I}|/n$ I's belonging to $\mathcal{F}$, where $\mathcal{I}$ denotes the set of valid identities[1]. This is the number of identities that may potentially be forged. We know that there is no efficient algorithm to find elements of $\mathcal{F}$ (and in particular those corresponding to valid identities) without knowing prime factors of n. Moreover, considering the size of f, p' and q', a given identity has a small chance of being an element of $\mathcal{F}$. However, in our case the knowledge of $b \in \mathcal{F}$ allows an intruder to efficiently generate other elements of $\mathcal{F}$. In fact, as b is of order f, all integers of the form $b^k \pmod{n}$; $k = 1, \ldots, f-1$; are also of order f and are all distinct. So, b generates a subset $\mathcal{B}$ of $\mathcal{F}$, of (nonnegligible) size $f-1$, in which there would be integers corresponding to acceptable identities. This is clearly a serious weakness of the scheme that must be removed, as we will see in the next section.

---

[1] $|\mathcal{F}| = 4f^2 - 1$, since there are exactly 3 elements of order 2 modulo n, $f^2 - 1$ elements of order f modulo n and $3(f^2 - 1)$ elements of order $2f$ modulo n in Z_n. Thus, considering the suggested size for f, there are more than 2^{400} elements in $\mathcal{F}$.

3.2 Attack 2

A second attack on Girault's scheme is by noting that combining public keys might result in other valid public keys if the combination of the identities gives a valid identity.

More precisely, if there are two identity, public key pairs (I_1, P_1) and (I_2, P_2), not necessarily distinct, such that $I_3 = I_1 I_2$ is a valid identity, then (I_3, P_3) is a valid identity, public key pair where $P_3 = P_1 P_2$.

In general, m users ($m \geq 1$) with identity $I_1, \ldots, I_m$, who have $(s_1, P_1), \ldots, (s_m, P_m)$ as their secret and public keys, can calculate

$$\prod_{j=1}^{m} P_j^{k_j} \equiv (\prod_{j=1}^{m} I_j^{k_j})^{-d} \cdot b^{-(\sum_{j=1}^{m} k_j s_j)} \pmod{n}$$

where k_j, $j = 1, \ldots, m$, are arbitrary chosen integers. Now if $\prod_{j=1}^{m} I_j^{k_j} \pmod{n}$ corresponds to an acceptable identity then they know a pair of valid public and secret keys for that identity; namely,

$$P = \prod_{j=1}^{m} P_j^{k_j} \pmod{n} \quad \text{and} \quad s = \sum_{j=1}^{m} k_j s_j \pmod{f}$$

which may easily be computed.

Here again, we do not know the probability that a given $\prod_{j=1}^{m} I_j^{k_j} \pmod{n}$ corresponds to an acceptable identity. As noted before this depends on the way identities are determined but this is again a weakness of the system which must be removed.

4 How to avoid forged identity, key generation

We propose a simple modification to Girault's scheme that makes it secure against the above two attacks. The modification is independent of the way identities are defined by the authority and what constitutes an acceptable identity.

Firstly, note that to avoid the second attack, it is sufficient for the authority to compute users' public keys using $g(I)$, instead of I itself, where g is a one-way hash function. With this modification, in step 1 of the identification phase Alice sends her identity string I to Bob, who checks in step 2 whether I reflects Alice's identity. If the check is successful, then Bob continues with the protocol as before, except that in step 4, he performs his check using $g(I)$ instead of I.

Now, a set of users who want to forge an identity and its corresponding public key are required to invert g to determine the identity. That is, although they can still combine their keys, as shown in 3.2, to find the corresponding identity they must be able to find $g^{-1}(\prod_{j=1}^{m} g(I_j)^{k_j} \pmod{n})$ which, if exists, is computationally infeasible by the assumption on g.

Next, we note that the above modification provides security against the first attack too. In fact, attack 1 consists of searching for an acceptable identity in the known subset $\mathcal{B}$. By introducing g in the scheme one has to search in $\mathcal{B}$ for integers that correspond to $g(I)$, where I is an acceptable identity. However, this requires the ability of inverting g to verify the validity of I.

A second approach is to fix I and compute $g(I)$ afterward. Now, if $g(I)$ belongs to $\mathcal{F}$ (that may easily be verified), then one can compute a forged key for that identity. However, assuming that the elements of $\mathcal{F}$ are uniformly distributed over Z_n, the probability of $g(I) \in \mathcal{F}$ is exactly the same as the probability that a randomly chosen integer in Z_n belongs to $\mathcal{F}$. This probability is $|\mathcal{F}|/n = (4f^2 - 1)/n$, which is negligible for the suggested values for f and n.

If we want completely avoid the risk due to attack 1, we may extend the above solution as follows.

After forming I (of a prescribed length k), the authority chooses an arbitrary k-bit integer J such that $ID = g(J \,\|\, I)$ is an integer not belonging to $\mathcal{F}$ (this means that ID is not of order 2, f nor $2f$). Now, the authority computes user's public key using ID, as $P = ID^{-d} \cdot v \pmod{n}$. In that case, in step 1 of the protocol Alice sends the $2k$-bit integer $(J \,\|\, I)$, whose correctness (with respect to both Alice and the authority) will be verified by Bob in step 2. More precisely, Bob checks firstly whether the k low order bits of the received integer reflects Alice's identity and if the check is successful, constructs ID and checks whether $ID^{2f} \pmod{n} \neq 1$. This suffices to guarantee the authenticity of the public key. The rest of the protocol remains unchanged, except that in step 4, Bob performs his check using ID (instead of I).

References

1. E. Brickell and K. McCurley, "An interactive identification scheme based on discrete logarithms", *Advances in Cryptology* (Proceedings of *EuroCrypt* '90), Lecture Notes in Computer Science, vol. 473, Springer-Verlag, 1991, pp. 63-71
2. M. Girault, "An identity-based identification scheme based on discrete logarithms modulo a composite number", *Advances in Cryptology* (Proceedings of *EuroCrypt* '90), Lecture Notes in Computer Science, vol. 473, Springer-Verlag, 1991, pp. 481-486
3. M. Girault, "Self-certified public keys", *Advances in Cryptology* (Proceedings of *EuroCrypt* '91), Lecture Notes in Computer Science, vol. 547, Springer-Verlag, 1991, pp. 490-497
4. C. Schnorr, "Efficient signature generation by smart cards", *Journal of Cryptology*, vol. 4, no. 3, 1991, pp. 161-174

A Scheme for Obtaining a Message from the Digital Multisignature

Chin-Chen Chang, Jyh-Jong Leu, Pai-Cheng Huang, and Wei-Bin Lee

Institute of Computer Science and
Information Engineering
National Chung Cheng University,
Chiayi, Taiwan 621, R.O.C

Abstract

A new digital multisignature scheme shall be proposed in this paper to allow some members of a group signing the same document and sending it to the receiver, who in turn shall verify and authenticate the signature consequently. When the receiver acquires the signature, he can verify it and obtain the message by computing the signature with some public keys. With this method, the signers do not need to send the original message to the receiver, and this reduces half the communication routine for the signer and the receiver. By the way, because the receiver can get the message from the digital signature itself, we call this signature a message recovery signature.

Key word: message recovery, digital signature, multisignature

1. Introduction

As far as we know, the digital signature is a very popular scheme that can sign a document and send it to a receiver. Naturally, the signature is designed to be unforgeable, authentic, not reusable, and repudiation-free. However, it still cannot satisfy some special needs, e.g. some cases when the receiver is to get the signature from a group. For this reason, Boyd [1] proposed the first multisignature scheme to enable multiple signers to sign the same document and send it to the receiver. Up to the present, many people have been devoted to the revision of the multisignature systems, and many great schemes have been proposed, such as [4, 8], as well as [5]. Unfortunately, in their schemes, there are still some weaknesses; for example, the hierarchical relationship in Itakura's scheme[4] should be determined in advance. Aside from those mentioned above, there is still other scheme proposed by Nyberg and Ruppel[7], that focuses on the possibility of message recovery from digital signatures. The key idea of their scheme is that the message can be recovered by the sent digital signature so that only half of the communication, stored space, and time cost can be saved. More than this, it also raises the security level of the message sending process.

In this paper, we shall propose a scheme which reaches both desired validity and authenticity. With the help of a clerk, the digital multisignature will be sent to the receiver. In Section 2, we shall propose a new scheme for obtaining a message from the digital multisignature. Section 3 gives the security analysis of our scheme. Finally, we come to our conclusions in Section 4.

2. A New Digital Multisignature Scheme with Message Recovery

In this section, we shall propose a new digital multisignature scheme with message recovery. This scheme allows multiple signers to sign some official document and send the digital signature to a receiver who can verify the signature by a verification process. In this scheme, with the assistance of an appointed clerk who is one of the signers, the partial signatures signed by the signers of the group can be combined to obtain the whole multisignature, which is then sent to the receiver. Assume that there are n signers u_1, u_2, ... , u_n who would like to sign the message jointly. Firstly, let's define a list of parameters to be used in the following.

p: a large prime number,

α: a primitive element of GF(p),

y_i: a public key of the signer u_i,

x_i: a secret key of the signer u_i,

where x_i is coprime to p-1 and $y_i \equiv \alpha^{x_i} \pmod{p}$.

Someone should be selected to decide the public parameters p and α, so that the clerk among all the signers can be randomly assigned, whom we call u_c, where $1 \leq c \leq n$. Now we shall show what the scheme can do. Let's divide the whole process into three parts: 2.1 Individual Signature Generation, 2.2 Multisignature Generation, 2.3 Verification and Message Recovery, 2.4 The Signer's part, and 2.5 The Receiver's part.

2.1 Individual Signature Generation:

In this part, each signer of the group should produce his/her partial digital signature, which will later be combined by the clerk so that the whole digital multisignature can be obtained.

Step 1: Signer u_i randomly chooses a number k_i, where $1 \leq k_i \leq p-1$, and then computes his share of partial signature r_i as follows.

$r_i \equiv \alpha^{-k_i} \pmod{p}$, where i=1,2,¡K,n.

Then the signer u_i broadcasts r_i to the other.

Step 2: After receiving all partial signatures r_i's of the group, where $1 \leq i \leq n$, each member of the group can compute the common parameter

$$r \equiv m \prod_{i=1}^{n} r_i \pmod{p}.$$

Here r is a component of the whole multisignature, and the next step is to compute the other component.

Step 3: Each signer u_i signs the message m with his secret parameters x_i and k_i as follows

s_i ¡Ý $k_i - x_i r \pmod{p-1}$, where i=1, 2, ..., n.

After calculating, each signer transmits his/her s_i to the clerk.

2.2 Multisignature Generation:

In this part, the clerk needs to generate the whole digital multisignature pair (r, s). The task is done as follows:

Step 1: After receiving the individual digital signature pairs (r_i, s_i) from the signers of the group, the clerk has to verify the validity of the signature pairs with the following equation

$$\alpha^{s_i} y_i^r r_i \equiv 1 \pmod p .$$

If the equation holds for the pair (r_i, s_i), then it is really signed by the signer u_i.

Step 2: After all signature pairs are through with Step1, the clerk can finally generate another whole multisignature $s = s_1 + s_2 + {}_iK + s_n \pmod{p-1}$.

Step 3: The clerk transmits the multisignature (r, s) to the receiver.

2.3 Verification and Message Recovery:

Step 1: The receiver first modules the public keys of all the signers to get the public key of the group by computing the following equation

$$y \equiv \prod_{i=1}^{n} y_i \pmod p .$$

Step 2: Then the receiver can recover the message m by his/her known parameters (α, y, s, r) by computing the following equation

$$\begin{aligned}
\alpha^s y^r r &\equiv (\alpha^{s_1} \alpha^{s_2} ... \alpha^{s_n})(y_1^r y_2^r ... y_n^r) r \\
&\equiv (\alpha^{s_1} \alpha^{s_2} ... \alpha^{s_n})(\alpha^{x_1 r} \alpha^{x_2 r} ... \alpha^{x_n r}) r \\
&\equiv (\alpha^{k_1} \alpha^{k_2} ... \alpha^{k_n})(m\alpha^{-k_1} \alpha^{-k_2} ... \alpha^{-k_n}) \\
&\equiv m \pmod p ,
\end{aligned}$$

where m is the message signed by n signers $u_1, u_2, {}_iK, u_n$ of the group.

Here, we shall give some comments on the above procedures. We shall point out that there have some weaknesses in the above procedure. In 1996, Michels and Patrick[6] reminded us the risk of disruption in several multiparty signature schemes; they proposed some possible attacker models and divided them into an insider-attack, an outsider-attack, and a clerk attack. Because the clerk is one of the signers in the above method, what we have to say is that the insider- attack or the clerk attack can let the above method get some unexpected forgery. Assume that some signer 1, say Tom, who is an insider attacker wishing his victim partners 2,3,$_1$K,n to sign any message m' chosen by him, and suppose he is also a chosen clerk. His partners abnegate it, but they approve to sign the eligible message m with him. Thus, every signer u_i , where $2 \le i$ $\le n$, selects a random number $k_i \in Z^*_{p-1}$ and calculates his/her own partial signature $r_i \equiv \alpha^{-k_i}$ (mod p) and then sends it to all the other signers, including the clerk of course. Tom, who is the clerk, receives r_2, r_3, $_1$K,r_n, chooses his random number $k_1 \in Z^*_{p-1}$, and computes $r_1 \equiv \alpha^{-k_1}$ (mod p). We let $r' \equiv mr_1' \prod_{i=2}^{n} r_i$ (mod p). Next, he computes $r_1' \equiv r'm^{-1} \prod_{i=2}^{n} r_i^{-1}$ (mod p). Then Tom sends r'_1 to all the other signers u_2, u_3, $_1$K, u_n instead of r_1. Therefore, each signer computes $r' \equiv mr_1' \prod_{i=1}^{2} r_i$ (mod p) $\equiv m' \prod_{i=1}^{n} r_i$ (mod p), then calculates another individual signature $s_i \equiv k_i - x_i r'$ (mod p-1), where $2 \le i \le n$, and then sends s_i to Tom. When Tom receives all the other s_i, firstly he computes his own $s_1 \equiv k_1 - x_1 r'$ (mod p-1), and secondly he computes $s \equiv \sum_{i=1}^{n} s_i$ (mod p-1). After the computation above, Tom obtains a valid multisignature (r', s), and sends the pair(r', s) to the receiver.

When the receiver obtains the multisignature pair (r', s), she/he has to make the verification and do the message recovery for this pair. She/He firstly moduloes the result of multiplying the public key y_i's of all signers to get $y \equiv \prod_{i=1}^{n} y_i$ (mod p), where 1 $\le i \le n$,. Secondly, she/he verifies the message and gets the message m' by computing the following equation

$$\alpha^s y^{r'} r' \equiv (\alpha^{s_1} \alpha^{s_2} ... \alpha^{s_n})(y_1^{r'} y_2^{r'} ... y_n^{r'}) r'$$

$$\equiv (\alpha^{s_1} \alpha^{s_2} ... \alpha^{s_n})(\alpha^{x_1 r'} \alpha^{x_2 1 r'} ... \alpha^{x_n r'}) m' \prod_{i=1}^{n} r_i$$

$$\equiv (\alpha^{k_1} \alpha^{k_2} ... \alpha^{k_n}) m' (\alpha^{-k_1} \alpha^{-k_2} ... \alpha^{-k_n})$$

$$\equiv m' \pmod{p}.$$

Successfully, Tom achieves his goal: Every one of the group signs the message m but the receiver obtains the message m' that Tom wants to sign.

Based on the method and our comments above, we propose a modified scheme that can solve the above observed problem and can also achieve the goal of the digital multisignature with message recovery. Assume that there are n signers u_1, u_2,..., u_n and they want to sign the message m. Let h() be a public collision-free one way hashing function. Note that we add a collision-free one way hashing function into the scheme. Surely, we need a clerk to help us to collect the partial multisignatures (r_i, s_i), and the clerk is randomly chosen among all the signers of the group. For the sake of accuracy and convenience, we divide our main method into the signer's part and the receiver's part, and we make detailed delineation as follows:

2.4 The Signer's Part

Each signer u_i selects his/her random number $k_i \in Z_{p-1}^*$, where $1 \le i \le n$, and calculates one of his/her own partial digital multisignature r_i as follows

$$r_i \equiv \alpha^{-k_i} \pmod{p}, \text{ where } i=1,2,...,n$$

,and then sends r_i to all the other signers.

If all the r_i's are available, the signer computes one of the whole digital multisignature by the follow two equations.

$$R \equiv \prod_{i=1}^{n} r_i \pmod{p},$$

and $r_i \acute{Y} m*h(R) \pmod{p}$.

After calculating this whole digital multisignature r, each signer goes on computing the other partial multisignature s_i by the next equation

$s_i = k_i - x_i r \pmod{p-1}$.

And each signer u_i transmits s_i to the clerk.

Once the clerk obtains the partial digital multisignature pair (r_i, s_i) sent from the signers, she/he must validate each signer by calculating the follow equation

$\alpha^{s_i} y_i^r r_i \equiv 1 \pmod{p}$.

If the condition is matched, then it is a true partial digital multisignature pair, and the clerk can adjacently make another whole digital multisignature s with the follow equation

$$s \equiv \sum_{i=1}^{n} s_i \pmod{p-1}.$$

After all these are done, the clerk has the whole digital multisignature (r, s), and she/he can send this pair to the receiver.

2.5 The Receiver's Part

The receiver firstly calculates the whole public key y of the group by moduling each signer's public key y_i by the following equation

$$y \equiv \sum_{i=1}^{n} y_i \pmod{p}.$$

Upon computing, the receiver can get R right away by the equation below

$$(y^r \alpha^s)^{-1} \equiv ((y_1^r y_2^r ... y_n^r)(\alpha^{s_1} \alpha^{s_2} ... \alpha^{s_n}))^{-1} \pmod{p}$$

$$\equiv ((\alpha^{rx_1} \alpha^{rx_2} ... \alpha^{rx_n})(\alpha^{s_1} \alpha^{s_2} ... \alpha^{s_n}))^{-1} \pmod{p}$$

$$\equiv (\alpha^{s_1 + rx_1} \alpha^{s_2 + rx_2} ... \alpha^{s_n + rx_n})^{-1} \pmod{p}$$

$$\equiv (\alpha^{k_1} \alpha^{k_2} ... \alpha^{k_n})^{-1} \pmod{p}$$

$$\equiv (\alpha^{-k_1} \alpha^{-k_2} ... \alpha^{-k_n}) \pmod{p}$$

$$\equiv (\prod_{i=1}^{n} r_i) \pmod{p}$$

$$\equiv R \pmod{p}.$$

As we know, h is a public collision-free one way hashing function. Now we use it to recover the message m.

$$m \equiv r \times (h(R))^{-1} \pmod{p}.$$

Using this method, the receiver can affirm that she/he really gets the true signature of the message m, and it is truly signed by all the signers $u_1, u_2, \ldots, u_n$.

3. Security Analysis

In this section, we shall do some security analysis on our scheme. Certainly, we have to satisfy two demands, validity and authenticity, which must be as strict as possible. For validity, if there is an outside attacker who wants to forge the digital multisignature of the message m', the attacker must find the eligible pair (r, s) to satisfy the following equation,

$$\alpha^s y^r r \equiv m \pmod{p}, \text{ where } y \equiv \sum_{i=1}^{n} y_i \pmod{p},$$

It is known that y_i is the public key of the signer u_i. Suppose that the outside attacker wants to sign the message m' and she/he can compute the result of y and α from the public channel, she/he still cannot obtain the corresponding pair (r', s') because there in front of her/him is a discrete logarithm problem. However, if the outside attacker chooses another way to attack our scheme finding a random digital multisignature pair (r, s) and getting the corresponding value m, then is our scheme still secure? In fact, the message recovered from the digital signature must satisfy some redundancy schemes. Thus, it is very difficult to find a random pair(r, s) that satisfies them. Another demand we must pay attention to is about authenticating the identities of the signers. We must be able to detect if there is another group signing some faked message and sending it to us. Checking the following equation is true or false may tell us something

$$\alpha^s (y_1 y_2 \ldots y_n)^r r \equiv \alpha^s (y_{a+1} y_{a+2} \ldots y_{a+m})^r r, \text{ where a and m are chosen numbers.}$$

According to our assumption, p is a very large number, and the probability of satisfying this equation is rather small. Finally, we must fight against our own comments on the first method stated in Section 2. Assume that the clerk, an inside attacker, wants the group to sign the false message m', can she/he achieve this evil goal? Now, because we use a public one-way hashing function, it is very difficult for the clerk to compute her/his r so that r can eliminate the message m and replace it with m'. Check the following equation which lets the receiver get her/his message.

$$m \equiv r \times (h(R))^{-1} \pmod{p}, \text{ where } R \equiv \prod_{i=1}^{n} r_i \pmod{p}.$$

The clerk cannot do any abominable thing with his partial r_c because she/he cannot predict what $(h(R))^{-1}$ will be. The reason is that we use a collision-free one way hashing function where the probability of finding two numbers with the same hash value is very small. Based on the analysis above, we can say that our scheme is a valid and authenticated method.

4. Conclusions

In this paper, we have proposed a new digital multisignature scheme, which provides a simple way with message recovery. Our scheme takes precautions against the cheating of the clerk and an inside attacker, which even some well known multisignature schemes cannot do. Certainly, our scheme has also satisfied the two basic requirements: validity and authenticity.

References

1. Boyd, C., [1988]: "Some Applications of Multiple Key Ciphers", Lecture Notes in Computer Science: Advances in Cryptology-EUROCRYPT'88, 1988, pp. 455-467

2. Harn, L., [1994]: "New Digital Signature Scheme Based on Discrete Logarithm", Electronics Letters, 3rd, March 1994, Vol. 30, No. 5, pp. 396-397

3. Harn, L. and Kiesler, T., [1989]: "New Scheme for Digital Multisignature", Electronics Letters, Vol.25, No. 15, 1989, pp. 1002-1003.

4. Itakura, K. and Nakamura, K., [1983]: "A Public-Key Cryptosystem Suitable for Digital Multisignature", Advances in Cryptology-ASIACRYPT'91, 1991, pp. 75-79.

5. Kiesler, T. and Harn, L., [1990]: "RSA Blocking and Multisignature Schemes with No Bit Expansion", Electronics Letters, Vol. 16, No. 18, 1990, pp. 1490-1491.

6.Michels, M. and Horster, P. [1996]: "On the Risk of Disruption in Sereval Multiparty Signature Schemes", Advances in Cryptology-Proceedings of Asiacrypto'96, Berlin: Springer-Verlag, Nov. 1996, pp. 334-345.

7.Nyberg, K. and Rueppel, R. A. [1993]: "A New Signature Scheme Based on the DSA, Giving Message Recovery", Fairfax 93, pp. 58-61.

8.Okamoto, T. [1988]: "A Digital Multisignature Scheme Using Bijective Public-key Cryptosystem", ACM Trans. on Computer Sciences, Vol. 6, No. 8, 1988, pp. 432-441.

9.Piveteau, J. M. [1993]: "New Signature Scheme with Message Recovery", Electronics Letters, 9th December 1993, Vol. 29, No. 25, pp. 2185.

Secure Hyperelliptic Cryptosystems and Their Performance

Yasuyuki Sakai[1], Kouichi Sakurai[2]* and Hirokazu Ishizuka[1]

[1] Mitsubishi Electric Corporation,
5-1-1 Ofuna, Kamakura, Kanagawa 247, Japan
e-mail: {ysakai,ishizuka}@iss.isl.melco.co.jp
[2] Kyushu University,
6-10-1 Hakozaki, Higashi-ku, Fukuoka 812-81, Japan
e-mail: sakurai@csce.kyushu-u.ac.jp

Abstract. We investigate the discrete logarithm problem over jacobian varieties of hyperelliptic curves suitable for public-key cryptosystems, and clarify practical advantages of hyperelliptic cryptosystems compared to the elliptic cryptosystems and to RSA. We focus on the curves defined over the ground field of characteristic 2, and we present hyperelliptic cryptosystems from the jacobian associated with curves $C : v^2 + v = u^{2g+1}$ of genus $g = 3$ and 11, which are secure against the known attacks. We further discuss the efficiency in implementation of such secure hyperelliptic cryptosystems.

Keywords. Public key, Hyperelliptic curve, Discrete logarithm, Jacobian

1 Introduction

A recent attention in public-key cryptosystems has focused on the use of elliptic curves for obtaining intractable discrete logarithm problems, which was proposed by Koblitz [Ko87] and Miller [Mil85]. A practical advantage of elliptic curve cryptosystems is that they can be constructed over a smaller definition field compared to the conventional discrete-log based cryptosystems or RSA cryptosystems. This is because there is no known sub-exponential time algorithm for solving the discrete logarithm problem based on a general elliptic curve.

Koblitz [Ko88, Ko89] has further investigated jacobians of hyperelliptic curves defined over finite fields as a source of finite abelian groups suitable for cryptographic discrete logarithm problems. Koblitz's approach on designing hyperelliptic cryptosystems is indeed interesting. However, Koblitz's obtained results in [Ko88, Ko89] are still incomplete in the following aspects:

- No practical advantage of hyperelliptic cryptosystems compared to elliptic cryptosystems or RSA is known, whereas a practical advantage of elliptic curve cryptosystems is that they can be constructed over a smaller definition

---

* A part of this work was done while visiting in Columbia Univ. Computer Science Dept. from September 1997 for one year.

field compared to the conventional discrete-log based cryptosystems and to RSA cryptosystems.

- Though Koblitz considered the security of hyperelliptic cryptosystems against Shanks' baby-step giant-step method [OD85] and Pohlig-Hellman method [PH78], no other attacks are discussed in designing hyperelliptic cryptosystems. In fact, Frey's generalization [FR94] of MOV-attack [MOV93] solves in subexponential-time some of the discrete-logarithm problems over Koblitz's hyperelliptic cryptosystems.

Thus, the aim of this work is to clarify a practical advantage of hyperelliptic cryptosystems compared to other cryptosystems like elliptic curve cryptosystems or RSA, then to design hyperelliptic cryptosystems secure against known attacks including FR-method [FR94]. This paper investigates jacobians of the curves $v^2 + v = u^{2g+1}$, which was initially studied by Koblitz [KO88], over characteristic 2 finite fields to find the induced hyperelliptic cryptosystems secure against three known attacks[3]: (1) Shanks' baby-step giant-step method [OD85] and Pohlig-Hellman method [PH78] (2) Frey's generalization [FR94] of MOV-attack [MOV93]. (3) Adleman-DeMarrais-Huang method [ADH94] of a subexponential-time algorithm for discrete logarithm over the rational subgroup of the jacobians of *large* genus hyperelliptic curves over finite fields.

Firstly, we examine jacobians of curves $C : v^2 + v = f(u)$, where $deg(f(u)) = 5$ (genus 2), defined over $\mathbf{F}_{2^n}$. These were investigated by Koblitz [KO88, KO89] and the discrete logarithm over some of which are broken by Frey [FR94]. As a negative result, we have failed to find secure curves of genus 2 over finite field with characteristic 2. [4]

Secondary, we examine jacobians of $C : v^2 + v = u^{2g+1}$. As positive results of our experiments, we have found secure jacobian varieties $J(C; \mathbf{F}_{2^{113}})$ and $J(C; \mathbf{F}_{2^{47}})$ in case of genus 3 and 11 respectively. The case of genus 1 is investigated by Agnew et al. [AMV93]. The case of genus 2 is investigated by Koblitz [KO89], though the described examples are no longer secure against Frey's attack [FR94]. Thus, our discovered curves induces the first concrete examples of secure hyperelliptic cryptosystems.

Thirdly, we discuss the efficiency of an addition in jacobians compared to an addition in points on elliptic curves. Then we discuss practicality of hyperelliptic cryptosystems. Explicit formulas for addition in the jacobian variety of a hyperelliptic curve have been introduced by Cantor [CA87] and Koblitz [KO88, KO89]. Although the formulas for addition are more complex compared to formulas for addition in the points of an elliptic curve, in the case that the order of a jacobian variety has the same size as the order of elliptic curve points, the size of ground

---

[3] Our designed cryptosystems are secure also against another recent attack by Rück [RU97], which is a generalization of Semaev's idea [SEM98].

[4] The coefficients of our examined curves are only in $\mathbf{F}_2$ because our construction is based on the order-counting method based on the Weil-conjecture. However, we should remark that secure genus 2 curves over (larger) prime fields have been constructed by other methods [Fre97, KO97, MCT97].

field of a jacobian is smaller than the that of an elliptic curve, because the order of an abelian variety of genus g over a finite field $\mathbf{F}_q$ is about q^g [LN87].

In resent years, IC cards play an important part in information security systems. Unfortunately, however, IC cards have poor hardware resources that can be implemented on. Only small size of RAM, ROM and co-processor can be implemented. Therefore, as Koblitz suggested [Ko88], hyperelliptic cryptosystems which have small ground field might be efficient in practical. The results of our evaluation on encryption/decryption speed that hyperelliptic cryptosystems are indeed practical. Even in the software implementation, our theoretical estimation suggests that the designed hyperelliptic cryptosystem is faster than RSA cryptosystem with the same level of security.

2 Preliminaries

This section gives a brief description of jacobian varieties and reviews Weil-conjecture for counting the order of jacobian varieties.

2.1 Jacobian varieties

Let $\mathbf{K}$ be an arbitrary field and let $\bar{\mathbf{K}}$ denotes its algebraic closure. We define a hyperelliptic curve C of genus g over $\mathbf{K}$ to be an equation of the form $v^2 + h(u)v = f(u)$, where $h(u)$ is a polynomial of degree at most g and $f(u)$ is a monic polynomial of degree $2g+1$. A divisor D is a finite formal sum of $\bar{\mathbf{K}}$-points $D = \sum_i m_i P_i, m_i \in \mathbf{Z}, P_i \in C$. We define the degree of D to be $\deg(D) = \sum m_i$. The divisors form an additive group $\mathbf{D}$, in which the divisors of degree 0 form a subgroup $\mathbf{D}^0$. The principal divisors form a subgroup $\mathbf{P}$ of $\mathbf{D}^0$. The jacobian variety is defined as $\mathbf{J}(C; \mathbf{K}) = \mathbf{D}^0 / \mathbf{P}$.

2.2 Discrete logarithm problem for jacobian varieties

Let $\mathbf{F}_q$ be a finite field with q elements. The discrete logarithm problem on $\mathbf{J}(C; \mathbf{F}_{q^n})$ is the problem, given two divisors D_1 and D_2 defined over $\mathbf{F}_{q^n}$, of determining an integer $m \in \mathbf{Z}$ such that $D_2 = mD_1$ if such m exists [Ko89]. We should recall that explicit formulas for addition in the jacobian group of a hyperelliptic curve proposed by Cantor [CA87].

2.3 Order counting method using Weil's conjecture

We must count the order of jacobian varieties to construct secure hyperelliptic cryptosystems. Beth and Schaefer [BeSc91] used Weil's conjecture for their constructing elliptic cryptosystems and Koblitz [Ko88, Ko89] uses Weil's conjecture to construct jacobian varieties of hyperelliptic curves defined over finite fields, which we also adopt in this paper.

We now give a brief description of the method. Firstly, we define a hyperelliptic curve C over a small finite field $\mathbf{F}_q$. Then we count the number of solutions

$u, v \in \mathbf{F}_q$ of the equation $v^2 + h(u)v = f(u)$. Note that this is easy to count because $\mathbf{F}_q$ is small. Secondary, we count the order of jacobian varieties over finite extension field $\mathbf{F}_{q^n}$ using Weil's conjecture in the following way.

Let $M_n = \sharp C(\mathbf{F}_{q^n}) - q^n$, where $\sharp C(\mathbf{F}_{q^n})$ is the number of solutions $u, v \in \mathbf{F}_{q^n}$ of the equation $C : v^2 + h(u)v = f(u)$. Associated with the curve C is a polynomial $Z(T)$ of degree $2g$ with integer coefficients having the form

$$Z(T) = T^{2g} + a_1 T^{2g-1} + \cdots + a_{g-1}T^{g+1} + a_g T^g$$
$$+ qa_{g-1}T^{g-1} + q^2 a_{g-2}T^{g-2} + \cdots + q^{g-1}a_1 T + q^g$$
$$= \prod_{j=1}^{g} ((T - \alpha_j)(T - \bar{\alpha}_j))$$

where $a_1, \cdots, a_g \in \mathbf{Z}$ and $\bar{\alpha}_j = q/\alpha_j$. The relationship between $Z(T)$ and $\{M_n\}$ is the following power series identity: $\log(\tilde{Z}(T)) = \sum_{n=1}^{\infty} \frac{M_n}{n} T^n$,where $\tilde{Z}(T)$ denotes the reciprocal polynomial $T^{2g} Z(1/T)$. Once $Z(T)$ has been found, $\sharp J(C; \mathbf{F}_{q^n})$ can be determined from the following formula.

$$\sharp J(C; \mathbf{F}_{q^n}) = \prod_{j=1}^{g} |1 - \alpha_j^n|^2 \tag{1}$$

3 Security against known attacks

We consider three conditions to resist all known attacks. We should choose jacobian varieties to satisfy the following:

C1 : $\sharp J(C; \mathbf{F}_{q^n})$ is divisible by a large prime.
C2 : $J(C; \mathbf{F}_{q^n})$ can not be imbedded into a small finite field $\mathbf{F}_{(q^n)^k}$
C3 : $2g + 1 \leq \log q^n$

We give here a brief description of the conditions.

3.1 C1 : General algorithms

The condition C1 is for against Shanks' baby-step giant-step method [OD85] and Pohlig-Hellman method [PH78]. The algorithms have a running time that is proportional to the square root of the largest prime factor of $\sharp J$. Therefore, we need to choose curves such that $\sharp J$ has a large prime factor.

3.2 C2 : Imbedding into a small finite field

The condition C2 is for against Frey's generalization [FR94] of MOV-attack [MOV93] using Tate pairing. Until 1990, the discrete logarithm algorithms known for an elliptic curve were exponential time algorithms, provided that the order of the group is divisible by a large prime. However, Menezes, Okamoto and Vanstone [MOV93] found a novel approach to the discrete logarithm problem on an elliptic curve E defined over $\mathbf{F}_q$. They used the Weil pairing to imbed the group $E(\mathbf{F}_q)$ into a field $\mathbf{F}_{q^k}$. Note that the extension degree k can be small for the *supersingular* elliptic curves (in precise $k \leq 6$). Frey [FR94] has generalized MOV-reduction to hyperelliptic curves by using the Tate pairing to imbed the group J into a field, and remarked that some of hyperelliptic cryptosystems (with genus two) proposed by Koblitz [Ko89] are not so secure as previously believed. Methods of avoiding MOV-attack are discussed in [BESc91, CTT94, MIY92]. We take the similar approach: choose curves such that the induced jacobian J cannot be imbedded via Tate pairing into $\mathbf{F}_{(q^n)^k}$ with small extension degree k. Therefore, we can replace **C2** by the following sufficient condition:

C2' : The largest prime factor of $\sharp J(C; \mathbf{F}_{q^n})$ does not divide $(q^n)^k - 1$, $k < (\log q^n)^2$

3.3 C3 : Large genus hyperelliptic curves

The condition **C3** is for against Adleman-DeMarrais-Huang method [ADH94]. In 1994, Adleman, DeMarrais and Huang found a subexponential algorithm for discrete logarithm over the rational subgroup of the jacobians of large genus hyperelliptic curves over finite fields. It is a heuristic algorithm under certain assumptions. Therefore, we need to choose curves such that the genus of curves are not so large.

On a new attack on Elliptic cryptosystems with Frobenius-trace one

Satoh-Araki [SA97] and Smart [SMA97] have independently found an $O((\log p)^3)$ algorithm for discrete logarithm problem for elliptic curves over a prime field $\mathbf{F}_p$ with order exactly equal to prime p. The elliptic curves defined over a prime field $\mathbf{F}_p$ with order exactly equal to the prime p was discussed by Miyaji [MIY92, MIY93] as an induced cryptosystem has provable immunity against MOV-attack. The method by Satoh-Araki [SA97] and Smart [SMA97] is not known to be applicable to hyperelliptic cryptosystems. So this paper does not consider the security against this attack [5].

4 On Curves with genus two

Koblitz [Ko88, Ko89] considered the security of the discrete logarithm problem for jacobian varieties of genus 2 curves when the ground field has characteristic 2. However, Frey [FR94] generalized MOV-reduction to hyperelliptic curves. He has

---

[5] The attack on elliptic cryptosystems with Frobenius-trace one is independently proposed by Semaev [SEM98] by using a different technique. Furthermore, Rück [RU97] generalizes Semaev's idea to hyperelliptic curves. Rück's algorithm works for jacobians over a field of characteristic p that have a cyclic group structure of order p^n and solves the discrete logarithm over the jacobian in time $O(n^2 \log p)$. Thus, this attack is not directly applicable to our designed hyperelliptic cryptosystems

found that some of hyperelliptic cryptosystems presented by Koblitz [Ko89] are breakable in sub-exponential time. This section discusses the security of genus 2 curves, which has the form $v^2 + v = f(u)$ and has characteristic 2 field, some of which has not been studied in the article [FR94].

4.1 $C : v^2 + v = u^5$

The order $\sharp J(C; F_{2^n})$ is given by:

$$Z(T) = T^4 + 4$$
$$\sharp J(C; F_{2^n}) = (2^n + 2^{(n+1)/2} + 1)(2^n - 2^{(n+1)/2} + 1)$$

We give examples of $\sharp J(C; F_{2^n})$ for prime $n, 50 \leq n < 100$. Throughout this subsection, we will give the case prime $n, 50 \leq n < 100$. We have made an experiment as if the largest prime factor of $\sharp J$ divide $(2^n)^k - 1$ or not. As the negative results, the largest prime factor of $\sharp J$ divide $(2^n)^k - 1$ with $k = 4$, which implies that the condition **C2'** does not hold. In fact, Frey [FR94] remarked that $J(C; F_{2^n})$ can be imbedded into the small group $F_{(2^n)^4}$ by Tate-pairing. Therefore, this curve does not satisfy the security condition **C2**.

Remark. Even the first security condition **C1** does not hold for the curve $v^2 + v = u^5$. This is because $Z(T)$ is not irreducible [Ko89], i.e., $\sharp J(C; F_{2^n})$ has two factors $(2^n + 2^{(n+1)/2} + 1)$ and $(2^n - 2^{(n+1)/2} + 1)$.

extension degree n	$\sharp J(C; F_{2^n})$	the largest prime factor of $\sharp J(C; F_{2^n})$
53	107-bit	51-bit
59	119-bit	37-bit
61	123-bit	40-bit
67	135-bit	44-bit
71	143-bit	39-bit
73	147-bit	73-bit
79	159-bit	79-bit
83	167-bit	58-bit
89	179-bit	87-bit
97	195-bit	45-bit

Table 1. $\sharp J(C; F_{2^n})$ for $C; v^2 + v = u^5$

4.2 $C : v^2 + v = u^5 + u^3$

The order $\sharp J(C; F_{2^n})$ is given by [Ko88]:

$$Z(T) = T^4 + 2T^3 + 2T^2 + 4T + 4$$
$$\sharp J(C; F_{2^n}) = 2^{2n} + 2^n + 1$$

We have made an experiment as if the largest prime factor of $\sharp J$ divide $(2^n)^k - 1$ or not. As the negative results, the largest prime factor of $\sharp J$ divide $(2^n)^k - 1$

with $k = 12$. Therefore, this curve does not satisfy the security condition **C2'**. In fact, Frey remarked that $\mathbf{J}(C; \mathbf{F}_{2^n})$ can be imbedded into the group $\mathbf{F}_{(2^n)^{12}}$ by Tate-pairing [FR94]. Therefore, this curve does not satisfy the condition **C2**.

extension degree n	$\sharp\mathbf{J}(C; \mathbf{F}_{2^n})$	the largest prime factor of $\sharp\mathbf{J}(C; \mathbf{F}_{2^n})$
53	106-bit	85-bit
59	118-bit	92-bit
61	122-bit	38-bit
67	134-bit	38-bit
71	143-bit	112-bit
73	147-bit	104-bit
79	159-bit	91-bit
83	166-bit	83-bit
89	179-bit	134-bit
97	195-bit	82-bit

Table 2. $\sharp\mathbf{J}(C; \mathbf{F}_{2^n})$ for $C : v^2 + v = u^5 + u^3$

4.3 $C : v^2 + v = u^5 + u^3 + u$

The order $\sharp\mathbf{J}(C; \mathbf{F}_{2^n})$ is given by [Ko88]:

$$Z(T) = T^4 + 2T^2 + 4$$
$$\sharp\mathbf{J}(C; \mathbf{F}_{2^n}) = 2^{2n} - 2^n + 1$$

We have made an experiment as if the largest prime factor of $\sharp\mathbf{J}$ divide $(2^n)^k - 1$ or not. As the negative results, the largest prime factor of $\sharp\mathbf{J}$ divide $(2^n)^k - 1$ with $k = 6$. Therefore, this curve does not satisfy the security condition **C2'**. In fact, Frey remarked that $\mathbf{J}(C; \mathbf{F}_{2^n})$ can be imbedded into the small group $\mathbf{F}_{(2^n)^6}$ by Tate-pairing [FR94]. Therefore, this curve does not satisfy the condition **C2**.

extension degree n	$\sharp\mathbf{J}(C; \mathbf{F}_{2^n})$	the largest prime factor of $\sharp\mathbf{J}(C; \mathbf{F}_{2^n})$
53	106-bit	92-bit
59	118-bit	61-bit
61	122-bit	121-bit
67	134-bit	86 bit
71	142-bit	98-bit
73	146-bit	92-bit
79	158-bit	114-bit
83	166-bit	122-bit
89	178-bit	153-bit
97	194-bit	67-bit

Table 3. $\sharp\mathbf{J}(C; \mathbf{F}_{2^n})$ for $C : v^2 + v = u^5 + u^3 + u$

4.4 $C : v^2 + v = u^5 + u^3 + 1$

The order $\sharp J(C; \mathbf{F}_{2^n})$ is given by [Ko88]:

$$Z(T) = T^4 - 2T^3 + 2T^2 - 4T + 4$$
$$\sharp J(C; \mathbf{F}_{2^n}) = 2^{2n} + 2^n + 1 - (-1)^{[(n+1)/4]} 2^{(n+1)/2} (2^n + 1)$$

We should note that this curve was not mentioned in the article [FR94]. Then, we have made an experiment as if the largest prime factor of $\sharp J$ divide $(2^n)^k - 1$ or not. As the negative results, the largest prime factor of $\sharp J$ divide $(2^n)^k - 1$ with $k = 12$. Therefore, this curve does not satisfy the security condition **C2'**.

extension degree n	$\sharp J(C; \mathbf{F}_{2^n})$	the largest prime factor of $\sharp J(C; \mathbf{F}_{2^n})$
53	107-bit	93-bit
59	119-bit	55-bit
61	123-bit	79-bit
67	135-bit	104-bit
71	142-bit	45-bit
73	146-bit	77-bit
79	158-bit	141-bit
83	167-bit	89-bit
89	178-bit	113-bit
97	194-bit	146-bit

Table 4. $\sharp J(C; \mathbf{F}_{2^n})$ for $C : v^2 + v = u^5 + u^3 + 1$

4.5 $C : v^2 + v = u^5 + u$

We should note that this curve was not studied in the previous papers [Ko88, Ko89, FR94]. The order $\sharp J(C; \mathbf{F}_{2^n})$ is given by:

$$Z(T) = T^4 + 2T^3 + 4T^2 + 4T + 4$$
$$\sharp J(C; \mathbf{F}_{2^n}) = (1 + 2^n)(1 + 2^n + (-1)^{[(n+1)/4]} 2^{(n+1)/2}$$

The largest prime factor of $\sharp J$ divide $(2^n)^k - 1$ with $k = 2$. Therefore, this curve does not satisfy the security condition **C2'**.

extension degree n	$\sharp J(C; \mathbf{F}_{2^n})$	the largest prime factor of $\sharp J(C; \mathbf{F}_{2^n})$
53	106-bit	51-bit
59	118-bit	31-bit
61	122-bit	60-bit
67	134-bit	43-bit
71	143-bit	44-bit
73	147-bit	61-bit
79	159-bit	78-bit
83	166-bit	58-bit
89	179-bit	87-bit
97	195-bit	60-bit

Table 5. $\sharp J(C; \mathbf{F}_{2^n})$ for $C : v^2 + v = u^5 + u$

On the existence of secure hyperelliptic cryptosystems with genus 2

Our experimental study has failed to find secure curves of genus 2 defined over $\mathbf{F}_{2^n}$. We should remark that the coefficients of the equation of our examined curves are only in $\{0, 1\}$ because our construction is based on the order-counting method of the Weil-conjecture, in which the initial jacobian is defined over $\mathbf{F}_2$.

However, secure genus 2 curves over (larger) prime fields have been constructed by other methods [Ko97, MCT97, Fre97]. For example, the article [MCT97] discusses how to construct secure jacobian varieties with Complex-Multiplication, and a genus 2 curve, $v^2 = c - u^5$, where $c \in \mathbf{F}_{11^{37}}$ and a jacobian variety $J(C; \mathbf{F}_{11^{37}})$ has been given as an example of secure jacobian varieties which satisfy the conditions **C1** and **C3**. Though the security against condition **C2** has not been discussed in the article [MCT97], we have made experiments on the condition **C2'** for $k = 10000 \ (> (\log 11^{37})^2)$. As the results, we have confirmed that it satisfy the condition **C2'**.

Further note that our failure of constructing secure genus 2 curves and jacobians over $\mathbf{F}_{2^n}$ using Weil-conjecture does never imply the non-existence of such a curve. Secure genus 2 curves and jacobians over $\mathbf{F}_{2^n}$ could exist among the general family of curves with these coefficient are not restricted to belong to $\{0, 1\}$ but in $\mathbf{F}_{2^n}$. A method of finding such a curve would use Pila's generalization [PIL90] of Schoof's algorithm [SCH85], though no report are published yet on the implementation Pila's algorithm.

5 On curves with genus larger than two

Koblitz [Ko88] considered the hyperelliptic curve C of the form:

$$C : v^2 + v = u^{2g+1} \tag{2}$$

defined over $\mathbf{F}_2$, and discussed the jacobian of which has a large prime factor. In such curves, there are two necessary conditions for the condition **C1** [Ko88]. **C1** is satisfied only if n is prime to f, where f denotes the multiplicative order of q modulo $(2g + 1)$. A second necessary condition is that $Z(T)$ is not factored over the rational numbers [Ko88]. Koblitz [Ko88] has given the following theorem.

Theorem 1 [Ko88]. *Let $g > 1$ be an integer. Then:*
(1) $Z(T)$ *factors over the rationales* (a) *if* $d = 2g + 1$ *is composite; or* (b) *if* $d = 2g + 1$ *is prime and either* (i) q *is a quadratic non residue modulo* d, *or else* (ii) q *has order* g *modulo* d *and* g *is even.*
(2) $Z(T)$ *is irreducible over the rationales if* $d = 2g + 1$ *is a prime,* g *is add, and* q *has order* g *modulo* d.

This implies that, for $q = 2$ and $g < 100$, the polynomial $Z(T)$ is irreducible over **Q** for $g = 1, 3, 11, 15, 23, 35, 39, 51, 83, 95, 99$ [Ko88], and reducible over **Q** for all other values except possibility for $g = 36, 44, 56, 63, 75$ Therefore, we investigate the curves with genus 3 and 11.

5.1 Curves with genus three

Koblitz have given $\mathbf{J}(C; \mathbf{F}_{2^n})$ which satisfy the condition **C1** in case of genus 3 curves $C : v^2 + v = u^7$ over $\mathbf{F}_2$. However, the security against the condition **C2** has not been discussed and the security of other genus curves have not been discussed. Note that genus 2 curves which has the form have been confirmed to be imbedded into small finite field [FR94]. Now we discuss the jacobian of curves with genus 3, which defined the equation (2). Moreover, we give secure jacobian varieties which satisfy the three conditions **C1**, **C2** and **C3**. We make experiments to find secure jacobian varieties as follows:

- Compute $\sharp\mathbf{J}$ and factorize $\sharp\mathbf{J}$, then find the largest prime factor of $\sharp\mathbf{J}$.
- Confirm if the largest prime factor of $\sharp\mathbf{J}$ divide $(2^n)^k - 1$, where $2 \leq k \leq (\log 2^n)^2$ or not.

We will factorize $\sharp\mathbf{J}(C; \mathbf{F}_{2^n})$ using elliptic curve method of factoring to find the factorization of $\sharp\mathbf{J}(C; \mathbf{F}_{2^n})$. In this experiment, we set parameters of elliptic curve method to be able to find factors which have the size smaller than 50 bits. Although this setting would not be able to factor perfectly, it is sufficient to find $\mathbf{J}(C; \mathbf{F}_{2^n})$ such that $\sharp\mathbf{J}(C; \mathbf{F}_{2^n})$ is divisible by a large prime. Extension degree n is examined up to 500.

In case of genus 3 curve, equation (2) be $v^2 + v = u^7$, then, $Z(T) = T^6 - 2T^3 + 8$ [Ko88]. Therefore, $\sharp\mathbf{J}(C; \mathbf{F}_{2^n})$ can be determined from the formula: [6]

$$\sharp\mathbf{J}(C; \mathbf{F}_{2^n}) = |1 - (1 - i\sqrt{7})^n|^2$$

Table 6 shows examples for $40 < n < 500$. [7]

---

[6] We can compute the formula by a numerical calculation method. Note that the results are to be integers.
[7] In case of $90 < n < 500$, we have succeeded to factor only when $n = 113, 179, 277$ and 431, because we used the setting for factoring described above.

extension degree n	$\sharp J(C; \mathbf{F}_{2^n})$	the largest prime factor of $\sharp J(C; \mathbf{F}_{2^n})$
41	123-bit	48-bit
43	130-bit	109-bit
47	141-bit	139-bit
53	159-biy	117-bit
59	178-bit	165-bit
61	184-bit	149-bit
71	214-bit	137-bit
73	219-bit	173-bit
89	267-bit	246-bit
113	339-bit	310-bit
179	538-bit	510-bit
277	832-bit	788-bit
431	1293-bit	1148-bit

Table 6. $\sharp J(C; \mathbf{F}_{2^n})$ for $C : v^2 + v = u^7$

There exist jacobian varieties which satisfy the conditions **C1**, **C2'** and **C3**. For example:

$\sharp J(C; \mathbf{F}_{2^{59}})$

$= 19156194260823610729479337893770727594502371684227481 7$

$= 7 \cdot 827 \cdot 3309067932427640478403755034335934979185070251205 3$

$\sharp J(C; \mathbf{F}_{2^{89}})$

$= 23714219875802356822747337729779283528347603092989610828799156060526 45$
45285406721

$= 7 \cdot 179 \cdot 2671 \cdot 70857183122325533127823325792054243244435303883153993362 53$
9134263544967267

$\sharp J(C; \mathbf{F}_{2^{113}})$

$= 11198723710889021052787211402842221390608227486173247542866394118454 21$
$760799788034183646686079373803521$

$= 7 \cdot 1583 \cdot 75937 \cdot 133087154459125850390435059436398888423626351517540604 20$
$763267396674295645712955192381380 50393$

These three examples, $J(C; \mathbf{F}_{2^{59}})$, $J(C; \mathbf{F}_{2^{89}})$ and $J(C; \mathbf{F}_{2^{113}})$, approximately have the same level of security as RSA with 1024-bit, 2048-bit and 5000-bit moduli, respectively. The next section discusses the efficiency of these jacobian. $\sharp J(C; \mathbf{F}_{2^{113}})$ has the size of 339 bits, and its largest prime factor has the size of 310 bits. We have confirmed the largest prime factor does not divide $(2^{113})^k - 1$, $k < (\log 2^{113})^2$. Therefore, it satisfies the condition **C2'**. $J(C; \mathbf{F}_{2^{59}})$ and $J(C; \mathbf{F}_{2^{89}})$ also satisfy **C2'**.

5.2 Curves with genus 11

In case of genus 11 curves, equation (2) be $v^2 + v = u^{23}$, then, $Z(T) = T^{22} - 48T^{11} + 2048$ [Ko88]. Therefore, $\sharp J(C; \mathbf{F}_{2^n})$ can be determined from the formula:

$$\sharp \mathbf{J}(C; \mathbf{F}_{2^n}) = |1 - (24 - i8\sqrt{23})^n|^2$$

There exist jacobian varieties which satisfy the conditions **C1**, **C2'** and **C3** such as: [8]

$\sharp \mathbf{J}(C; \mathbf{F}_{2^{47}})$

$= 429049853758163107186368799942587076079339706258965658808715396619909644$
$ 489623546934829884915833670630615633469225307037593006945993234360057$
$ 1492407610966017$

$= 3 \cdot 23 \cdot 29 \cdot 34687 \cdot 254741 \cdot 381077 \cdot 836413 \cdot 4370719 \cdot 122803256446193$
$ \cdot 1015784056219160029 \cdot 1396360023741601228722804905934361404439480177105$
$ 9094600961201080138678351892941240936676874577$

$\sharp \mathbf{J}(C; \mathbf{F}_{2^{47}})$ has the size of 518 bits, and its largest prime factor has the size 310 bits. We have confirmed the largest prime factor does not divide $(2^{47})^k - 1$, $k < (\log 2^{47})^2$. Therefore, it satisfies the condition **C2'**.

6   Computing in groups

As the results of experiments in the last section, We have obtained secure jacobian varieties in case of genus 3 and 11 curves. In practical point of view, it is important factor that how many operations are needed for computing in jacobian varieties. In the previous studies on computing in jacobian varieties, only the order of operations has been discussed [FR94, Ko88], however, no one has estimated how many operations would be needed in computing using concrete ground fields in the open literature, and no one has confirmed the difference between computing in points of elliptic curves and in jacobian varieties. The order of an abelian variety $\mathbf{A}(\mathbf{F}_q)$ of genus g lies in the range: $(q^{\frac{1}{2}} - 1)^{2g} \le \sharp \mathbf{A}(\mathbf{F}_q) \le (q^{\frac{1}{2}} + 1)^{2g}$ [LN87]. Therefore, if we compare how many operations are needed in computing between elliptic curves and hyperelliptic curves which have same level of security, namely, of which the order of groups constructing discrete logarithm problem have same size of the largest prime factor, the difference would be not so much because the size of ground field of hyperelliptic curves is smaller compared to that of elliptic curves.

In the article [CA87, Ko89], the order of field operations for jacobian varieties $\mathbf{J}(C; \mathbf{F}_{q^n})$ have been estimated. In this section, we estimate the number of bit operations in addition of divisors obtained in the last section for practical purpose. Then we compare the efficiency of hyperelliptic cryptosystem with that of elliptic curve cryptosystems and of RSA. Although some methods of fast implementation for elliptic curve cryptosystems have been developed, we estimate the efficiency based on basic formulas.

[8] In case of $n < 20$, we have not found **J** which is divisible by a large prime. In case of $20 < n < 500$, we have succeeded to factor only when $n = 47$, because we used the setting for factoring described above.

6.1 Computing in elliptic curves

In case of $g = 1$ (elliptic curve), divisors D are in one-to-one correspondence with the points $P \in C$. Therefore, in case of $g = 1$, formulas for addition of points be more simple compared to formulas for addition of divisors in case of $g \geq 2$.

Let (x_1, y_1), (x_2, y_2) and (x_3, y_3) denote the coordinates of P, Q, and $P+Q$, respectively. x_3 and y_3 are expressed as follows:

$$x_3 = \left(\frac{y_2 - y_1}{x_2 - x_1} \right)^2 - x_1 - x_2 \tag{3}$$

$$y_3 = -y_1 + \left(\frac{y_2 - y_1}{x_2 - x_1} \right) (x_1 - x_3) \tag{4}$$

The addition of points takes 3 multiplications and 1 inversion in the ground field. In [AMV93, ITT86], an efficient implementation of an arithmetic in $F_{2^{155}}$ has been discussed. An inversion in $F_{2^{155}}$ takes 10 multiplications. So in the later discussions in this paper, we will make assumption that an inversion in a field takes 10 multiplications. Therefore, addition takes 13 multiplications and also doubling takes 13 multiplications.

6.2 Computing in jacobian varieties

A divisor D is regarded simply as a pair of polynomials $D = \text{div}(a(u), b(u))$ such that $\deg b < \deg a$ and $\deg a < g$. We give here a brief description of the algorithm for addition: $D_3 = D_1 + D_2$, where $D_3 = \text{div}(a_3, b_3)$, $D_1 = \text{div}(a_1, b_1)$, $D_2 = \text{div}(a_2, b_2)$ (see [CA87, KO89] for more details). In case of $v^2 + v = u^{2g+1}$ and $\mathbf{J}(C; F_{2^n})$, the algorithm is given bellow.

Algorithm1 Addition in $\mathbf{J}$
Input: two divisors $D_1 = \text{div}(a_1, b_1)$, $D_2 = \text{div}(a_2, b_2) \in \mathbf{J}$
Output: $D_3 = \text{div}(a_3, b_3) = D_1 + D_2$
Step A1 Compute d_1, s_1 and s_2 which satisfy
$\quad\quad\quad d_1 = \gcd(a_1, a_2)$ and $d_1 = s_1 a_1 + s_2 a_2$
Step A2 If $d_1 = 1$ then
$\quad\quad\quad a := a_1 a_2$, $b := s_1 a_1 b_2 + s_2 a_2 b_1 \pmod{a}$
$\quad\quad$ else
$\quad\quad\quad$ Compute d_2, s_1', s_2' and s_3 which satisfy
$\quad\quad\quad d_2 = \gcd(d_1, b_1 + b_2 + 1)$ and $d_2 = s_1' a_1 + s_2' a_2 + s_3(b_1 + b_2 + 1)$
$\quad\quad\quad a := a_1 a_2 / d_2^2$, $b := (s_1' a_1 b_2 + s_2' a_2 b_1 + s_3(b_1 b_2 + u^{2g+1})) / d_2 \pmod{a}$
Step A3 While $\deg(a_3) \geq g$ do the following:
$\quad\quad\quad a_3 := (u^{2g+1} - b - b^2)/a$, $b_3 := -1 - b \pmod{a_3}, a := a_3, b := b_3$
Step A4 Return $D_3 = \text{div}(a_3, b_3)$

If a_1 and a_2 have no common factor, **Step A2** to be simpler. Note that the case $\gcd(a_1, a_2) = 1$ is extremely likely if the ground field is large and a_1 and a_2 are the coordinates of two randomly chosen elements of the jacobian. Therefore, we will estimate the number of multiplications and bit operations in an addition of divisors based on the case.

We here make an estimation of computation cost of the addition. In general cases, when polynomial a has degree n and polynomial b has degree m, multiplication of polynomial takes nm field multiplications. Division of polynomial takes also nm field multiplications. Note that we don't need field inversions to compute division of polynomial. In case of $n = m$, the number of iteration-steps in the extended euclidean algorithm is approximately $1.9405n + (lower\ term)$ in average [KN81]. We make assumption here that the number of iterations equals to $2n$. In each steps of the iteration, it takes 3 multiplications of polynomial and 1 division of polynomial. Therefore, when 2 polynomials have degree n, the extended euclidean takes $4n^3$ field multiplications.

The computation cost of the addition can be estimated in the following: Attention should be taken into degree of polynomials and the number of iterations in Step A3.

- **Step A1**: We need to compute GCD which can be done by the extended euclidean method. It takes $4g^3$ field multiplications.
- **Step A2**: a_1 and a_2 have degree g. Therefore, it takes g^2 field multiplications in computing a. The polynomials s_1 and s_2 given by Step A1 have small degree: that is, they satisfy $deg(s_1) < deg(a_1)$ and $deg(s_2) < deg(a_2)$. b_1 and b_2 have degree $g - 1$. Therefore, when s_1 and s_2 have degree $g - 1$, it takes $2\{g(g-1)+(2g-1)(g-1)\}$ field multiplications in computing $s_1a_1b_2+s_2a_2b_1$. The product has degree $3g - 2$ and a has degree $2g$. Therefore, it takes $(3g - 2)(2g)$ field multiplications in the division. In Step A2 totally, it takes $13g^2 - 12g + 2$ field multiplications.
- **Step A3**: In the 1st iteration, a has degree $2g$ and b has degree $2g-1$. It takes $(2g - 1)(2g - 1)$ field multiplications in computing b^2. b^2 has degree $4g - 2$ and a has degree $2g$. Therefore, it takes $(4g - 2)(2g) + (2g - 1)(2g - 1)$ field multiplications in computing a_3 for the 1st iteration. b has degree $2g - 1$ and a_3 has degree $2g - 2$. Therefore, it takes $(2g - 1)(2g - 2)$ field multiplications in computing b_3 for the 1st iteration. Step A3 takes $16g^2 - 14g + 3$ field multiplications in total. When 1st iteration has done, a_3 has degree $2g - 2$ and b_3 has degree $2g - 3$. In case of genus 3, the number of iterations is 2, and in case of genus 11, the number of iterations is 6 in most cases.

When $D_1 = D_2$, i.e., doubling an element of J, we can take $s_2 = 0$. Therefore, we can compute a doubling as the following.

Algorithm2 Doubling in J		
Input:	a divisor $D_1 = \mathrm{div}(a_1, b_1) \in J$	
Output:	$D_2 = \mathrm{div}(a_2, b_2) = D_1 + D_1$	
Step D1	$a := a_1^2,\ b := b_1^2 + u^{2g+1}\ (\mathrm{mod}\ a)$	
Step D2	While $\deg(a_2) \geq g$ do the following:	
	$a_2 := (u^{2g+1} - b - b^2)/a,\ b_2 := -1 - b\ (\mathrm{mod}\ a_2),\ a := a_2, b := b_2$	
Step D3	Return $D_2 = \mathrm{div}(a_2, b_2)$	

The number of field multiplications in a doubling is the following:

- **Step D1**: a_1 has degree g and b_1 has degree $g-1$. Therefore, it takes g^2 field multiplications in computing a. It takes $(g-1)(g-1)$ field multiplications in computing $b_1{}^2$. u^{2g+1} has degree $2g+1$ and a has degree $2g$. Therefore, it takes $(2g+1)(2g)$ field multiplications in the division. In Step D1 totally, it takes $6g^2+1$ field multiplications.
- **Step D2**: This step is the same operation as the Step A1 of addition. Therefore, it takes $16g^2 - 14g + 3$ field multiplications. In case of genus 3, the number of iterations is 2, and in case of genus 11, the number of iterations is 6 in most cases.

Then in the case genus 3 and 11, the number of field multiplications can be estimated as the table shown bellow. To compare with genus 1 (elliptic curve), we also show the case genus 1 estimated in the last subsection.

genus	addition		doubling	
	multiplications	inversions	multiplications	inversions
$g = 1$	3	1	3	1
$g = 3$	401	0	265	0
$g = 11$	17,477	0	10,437	0

Table 7. Number of field operations

6.3 Comparison of efficiency between elliptic curves and hyperelliptic curves

Based on the estimation in the last subsection, in this subsection, we compare the efficiency (the number of bit operations) in computation in the secure genus 3 and 11 hyperelliptic curves which have the ground fields obtained in the last section with the efficiency in computation in elliptic curves. Namely, we estimate and compare the efficiency in computation in curves which have the same level of security. Here we use the notation "*same level of security*" in the sense that curves have the same size of the largest prime factor of $\sharp J$. Although the most important factor in encryption/decryption is multiplication of a divisor by an integer, here we estimate the efficiency from the number of bit operations required in an addition and doubling of divisors (or points in an elliptic curve). The number of bit operations can be determined from the number of field multiplications estimated in the last subsection and from the size of a field. Here we make assumption that a multiplication of field F_{2^n} elements takes n^2 bit operations.

The estimation have been made from the two jacobian varieties obtained in the last section: $J(C; F_{2^{113}})$ given by genus 3 curve $C : v^2 + v = u^7$ defined over F_2 and $J(C; F_{2^{47}})$ given by genus 11 curve $C : v^2 + v = u^{23}$ defined over F_2. Both of the $\sharp J$ have the largest prime factor which has the size of 310 bits. Now we have not obtained an elliptic curve which has the *same level of security*, therefore we make an assumption here that there exists such an elliptic curve which has the ground field $F_{2^{310}}$. The results of the estimation are given in the table shown bellow.

genus	ground field	size of the largest prime factor of $\sharp J$	number of bit operations	
			addition	doubling
$g = 1$	$\mathbf{F}_{2^{310}}$	310-bit	$1.25 \cdot 10^6$	$1.25 \cdot 10^6$
$g = 3$	$\mathbf{F}_{2^{113}}$	310-bit	$5.12 \cdot 10^6$	$3.38 \cdot 10^6$
$g = 11$	$\mathbf{F}_{2^{47}}$	310-bit	$3.86 \cdot 10^7$	$2.53 \cdot 10^7$

Table 8. Number of bit operations in $\mathbf{J}(C; \mathbf{F}_{2^n})$

The data given in the table shows that: in case of the genus 3 curve, about 3 times of bit operations are required compared with the elliptic curve.

The most important factor which determine the encryption/decryption speed is a multiplication of a divisor by an integer as described above. By using Frobenius map, this computation could be faster than using traditional repeated doubling method [Ko89]. Therefore, hyperelliptic cryptosystems could be faster in implementation compared to the estimation above.

6.4 Comparison of efficiency between RSA and genus 3 curves

Here we will roughly compare the efficiency between hyperelliptic cryptosystems obtained in the last section and RSA cryptosystem. One of the most efficient algorithm of integer factoring is the number field sieve method. The method takes $exp(c(\ln n)^{1/3}(\ln \ln n)^{2/3})$ time, where $1.5 < c < 1.9$ and n denotes the size of an integer. On the other hand, Pohlig-Hellman method, which is efficient algorithm for discrete log problem for elliptic curve, takes $\sqrt{m}$, where m denotes the size of the largest factor of $\sharp J$. Therefore, $\mathbf{J}(C; \mathbf{F}_{2^{59}})$, $\mathbf{J}(C; \mathbf{F}_{2^{89}})$ and $\mathbf{J}(C; \mathbf{F}_{2^{113}})$ with $C : v^2 + v = u^7$ $(g = 3)$ have the same level of security of RSA with 1024, RSA with 2048 and RSA with 5000-bit moduli respectively.

A modular multiplication of integers which have the size of 2^n takes n^2 bit operations. Therefore, we can evaluate the efficiency in implementation of hyperelliptic cryptosystems obtained in this paper compared to RSA as Table 9. The efficiency of elliptic curve cryptosystems which have the same level of security is also given.

	number of bit operations
$\mathbf{J}(C; \mathbf{F}_{2^{59}})$ (addition)	$1.40 \cdot 10^6$
$\mathbf{J}(C; \mathbf{F}_{2^{59}})$ (doubling)	$9.22 \cdot 10^5$
RSA-1024	$1.05 \cdot 10^6$
$\mathbf{E}(\mathbf{F}_{2^{160}})$	$3.33 \cdot 10^5$
$\mathbf{J}(C; \mathbf{F}_{2^{89}})$ (addition)	$3.18 \cdot 10^6$
$\mathbf{J}(C; \mathbf{F}_{2^{89}})$ (doubling)	$2.10 \cdot 10^6$
RSA-2048	$4.19 \cdot 10^6$
$\mathbf{E}(\mathbf{F}_{2^{210}})$	$5.73 \cdot 10^5$
$\mathbf{J}(C; \mathbf{F}_{2^{113}})$ (addition)	$5.12 \cdot 10^6$
$\mathbf{J}(C; \mathbf{F}_{2^{113}})$ (doubling)	$3.38 \cdot 10^6$
RSA-5000	$2.50 \cdot 10^7$
$\mathbf{E}(\mathbf{F}_{2^{310}})$	$1.25 \cdot 10^6$

Table 9. Number of bit operations in RSA, $\mathbf{E}(\mathbf{F}_{2^n})$ and $\mathbf{J}(C; \mathbf{F}_{2^n})$, $C : v^2 + v = u^7$

7 Concluding remarks

There are no algorithms which can work in sub-exponential time to solve the discrete logarithm problem defined over elliptic curves, if elliptic curves are chosen carefully. On the other hand, more study and analysis may be needed before it is mature [RSA97], because the elliptic curve discrete logarithm problem has been around for a relatively short amount of time. Therefore, in practical point of view, we should study on hyperelliptic cryptosystems. The arithmetic in F_{2^n} can be efficiently accomplished if we can find *"optimal normal bases"*. In case of $F_{2^{89}}$ and $F_{2^{113}}$, there exist such a special base (see [MOVW88]). Therefore, the hyperelliptic cryptosystem using $J(C; F_{2^{89}})$ and $J(C; F_{2^{113}})$, $C : v^2 + v = u^7$ discussed in this paper could be more efficient.

Acknowledgments

The second author would like to thank Andrew Odlyzko and Iwan Duursma for giving him a chance to present the preliminary work at AT & T Lab. Stimulus discussion with the attendee at the talk improves the quality of this paper, in particular, the performance analysis of the cryptosystems. The second author wish to thank Zvi Galil and Moti Yung for their hospitality while his visiting Columbia Univ. Computer Science Dept.

References

[ADH94] L.M. ADLEMAN, J. DEMARRAIS and M. HUANG, "A Subexponential Algorithm for Discrete Logarithm over the Rational Subgroup of the Jacobians of Large Genus Hyperelliptic Curves over Finite Fields", *Proc. of ANTS1, LNCS*, vol. 877, Springer-Verlag, (1994), 28-40

[AMV93] G.B. AGNEW, R.C. MULLIN and S.A. VANSTONE, "An Implementation of Elliptic Curve Cryptosystems Over $F_{2^{155}}$", *IEEE J. Selected Areas in Communications* 11, No.5 (1993), 804-813

[BeSc91] T. BETH and F. SCAEFER, "Non supersingular elliptic curves for public key cryptosystems", *Advances in Cryptology - EUROCRYPT '91, Lecture Notes in Computer Science*, 547, pp.316-327 (1991).

[Ca87] D.G. CANTOR, "Computing in the Jacobian of a Hyperelliptic Curve", *Math. Comp*, 48, No.177 (1987), 95-101

[CTT94] J. CHAO, K. TANAKA, and S. TSUJII, "Design of elliptic curves with controllable lower boundary of extension degree for reduction attacks", *Advances in Cryptology - Crypto'94*, Springer-Verlag, (1994), 50-55.

[Fre97] G. FREY, "Aspects of DL-systems based on hyperelliptic curves", *Keynote Lecture in Waterloo-Workshop on Elliptic Curve Discrete Logarithm Problem*, 4th of Nov. (1997).

[FR94] G. FREY and H.G. RÜCK, "A Remark Concerning m-Divisibility and the Discrete Logarithm in the Divisor Class Group of Curves", *Math. Comp*, 62, No.206 (1994), 865-874

[ITT86] T. ITOH, O. TEECHAI and S. TSUJII, "A fast algorithm for computing multiplicative inverse in $GF(2^t)$ using normal bases" (in Japanese), *J. Society for Electronic Communications (Japan)*, 44, (1986), 31-36.

[Kn81] D.E. KNUTH, "The Art of Computer Programing, Vol.2, Seminumerical Algorithm", Addison-Wesley, Reading MA, 2nd edition (1981)

[Ko87] N. KOBLITZ, "Elliptic curve cryptosystems", *Mathematics of Computation*, **48** (1987), 203–209.

[Ko88] N. KOBLITZ, "A Family of Jacobians Suitable for Discrete Log Cryptosystems", *Advances in Cryptology - Crypto'88*, Springer-Verlag, (1990), 94-99

[Ko89] N. KOBLITZ, "Hyperelliptic Cryptosystems", *J.Cryptology*, **1** (1989), 139-150

[Ko97] N. KOBLITZ, "A Very Easy Way to Generate Curves over Prime Fields for Hyperelliptic Cryptosystems", *Crypto'97* Rump Talk (1997)

[Mil85] V. MILLER, "Uses of elliptic curves in cryptography", *Lecture Notes in Computer Science*, **218** (1986), 417–426. (Advances in Cryptology – CRYPTO '85.)

[MCT97] K. MATSUO, J. CHAO and S.TSUJII, "Design of Cryptosystems Based on Abelian Varieties over Extension Fields", *IEICE ISEC*, **97-30** (1997), 9-18

[Miy92] A. MIYAJI, "Elliptic curve over F_p suitable for cryptosystems", *Advances in Cryptology - Asiacrypt'92*, Springer-Verlag, (1993), 479-491.

[Miy93] A. MIYAJI, "Elliptic curve cryptosystems immune to any reduction into the discrete logarithm problem", *IEICE Trans.*, Fundamentals, **E76-A** (1993), pp. 50–54.

[MOV93] A.J. MENEZES, T. OKAMOTO and S.A. VANSTONE, "Reducing elliptic curve logarithm to logarithm in a finite field", *IEEE Trans. on IT*, **39**, (1993), 1639-1646

[MOVW88] R.C. MULLIN, I.M. ONYSZCHUK, S.A. VANSTONE and R.M. WILSON, "Optimal Normal Bases in GF(p^n)", *Discrete Applied Mathematics*, **22**, (1988/89), 149-161

[Od85] A. ODLYZKO, "Discrete logarithm and their cryptographic significance", *Advances in Cryptology - Eurocrypto'84*, Springer-Verlag, (1985), 224-314

[Pil90] J. PILA, "Frobenius maps of abelian varieties and finding roots of unity in finite fields", *Math. Comp*, **55**, No.206 (1990), 745-763.

[PH78] S.C. POHLIG and M.E. HELLMAN, "An improved algorithm for computing logarithms over $GF(p)$ and its cryptographic significance", *IEEE Trans. on IT*, **24**, (1978), 106-110

[LN87] R. LIDL and H. NIEDERREITER, "Finite Fields", Encyclopedia of Mathematics and Its Application, (1987)

[RSA97] http://www.rsa.com

[Ru97] H.G. RÜCK, "On the discrete logarithms in the divisor class group of curves", To appear in *Math. Comp.* (1997)

[SA97] T. SATOH and K. ARAKI, "Fermat Quotients and the Polynomial Time Discrete Log Algorithm for Anomalous Elliptic Curves", *preprint*, (1997)

[Sem98] I.A. SEMAEV, "Evaluation of discrete logarithms in a group of p-torsion points of an elliptic curve in characteristic p", *Math. Comp.*, Vol.76 (1998),pp.353-356.

[Sch85] R. SCHOOF, "Elliptic curves over finite fields and the computation of square root mod p", *Math. Comp*, **44**, (1985), 483-494.

[Sma97] N.P. SMART, "The Discrete Logarithm Problem on Elliptic Curves of Trace One", *preprint*, (1997)

A Practical Implementation of Elliptic Curve Cryptosystems over $GF(p)$ on a 16-bit Microcomputer

Toshio HASEGAWA, Junko NAKAJIMA and Mitsuru MATSUI

Information Technology R&D Center
Mitsubishi Electric Corporation
5-1-1, Ofuna, Kamakura, Kanagawa, 247, Japan
{toshio, june15, matsui}@iss.isl.melco.co.jp

Abstract. Recently the study and implementation of elliptic curve cryptosystems (ECC) have developed rapidly and its achievements have become a center of attraction. ECC has the advantage of high-speed processing in software even on restricted environments such as smart cards. In this paper, we concentrate on implementation of ECC over a field of prime characteristic on a 16-bit microcomputer M16C (10MHz). We report a practical software implementation of a cryptographic library which supports 160-bit elliptic curve DSA (ECDSA) signature generation, verification and SHA-1 on the processor. This library also includes general integer arithmetic routines for applicability to other cryptographic algorithms. We successfully implemented the library in 4Kbyte code/data size including SHA-1, and confirmed a speed of 150msec for generating an ECDSA signature and 630msec for verifying an ECDSA signature on M16C.

1 Introduction

When we use a software public key cryptosystem on high speed hardware platforms such as modern PCs, its computation time or program size is now rarely a serious problem. However in restricted hardware environments with limited computational power and small ROM/RAM size such as smart cards, it is still a heavy load to process public key cryptographic algorithms such as digital signature. We need a public key cryptosystem with small code/data size and less computational complexity to enjoy benefits of digital signature in these circumstances.

Recently the study and implementation of elliptic curve cryptosystems (ECC) [1, 2, 3, 8, 9, 10, 11] have developed rapidly and its achievements have become a center of attraction because of its many advantages in comparison to conventional public key systems. ECC has the highest strength-per-key-bit of any known public-key system. For example, ECC with a 160-bit modulus offers the same level of cryptographic security as RSA with 1024-bit moduli. The smaller key sizes result in smaller system parameters, bandwidth savings, faster implementations and lower power consumptions. These advantages lead to the possibility to achieve public key schemes more easily in software.

For a software implementation of ECC over a field of characteristic 2, a smart card system with an 8-bit microprocessor is known [4]. It contains an elliptic curve digital signature function, which generates a signature in 600msec, but does not have a signature verification function, which generally requires much heavier computation than signature generation. As for ECC over a field of prime characteristic, many papers have been presented about high performance implementation on powerful software computational environments [11] or on a special public key co-processor hardware, and however, as far as the authors know, a serious example of software implementation on restricted hardware resources has not been reported yet.

ECC over a field of prime characteristic has two advantages: one is a potential use of an existent co-processor (for instance, a modular-multiplier for RSA), and the other is a possibility for efficiently using a multiplier/divider embedded in a target processor. Hence we tried to implement a practical ECC over a field of prime characteristic only in software. As a target processor, we have chosen a 16-bit microcomputer M16C (10MHz) [12, 13], which has been widely used for engineering applications such as mobile telecommunication systems.

One of our purposes is to design a practical cryptographic library which supports SHA-1 [15], ECDSA signature generation and verification [7], which is currently being standardized in the ANSI X9F1 and IEEE P1363 standards committees. We also regarded applicability to other cryptographic algorithms, not only ECC but also RSA, for example, as important. To achieve this, we designed two independent integer arithmetic modules, where one is a group of routines that execute modular arithmetic modulo a fixed prime characteristic p for high speed computation, and the other is a collection of general integer routines that accept any positive integers with arbitrary length for wider applicability.

For arithmetic algorithms of an elliptic curve, in order to realize 4Kbyte code/data size, which we regard as a reasonable size for most applications on M16C, we mainly adopted standard methods described in [6]. We also show improved elliptic doubling and addition formulas on projective coordinates, which reduce the code size and the number of temporary variables.

As a result, we successfully implemented the library in 4Kbyte code and data size including SHA-1, and confirmed a speed of 150msec for generating a 160-bit ECDSA signature and 630msec for verifying an ECDSA signature on M16C. There are many trade-offs between speed and code/data size. We can further reduce code/data size at the cost of processing speed, or it is also possible to get higher performance with more code/data size.

This paper is organized as follows. In section 2, we give a brief explanation of arithmetic and DSA algorithm on an elliptic curve. In section 3, we introduce a 16-bit engineering microcomputer M16C. In section 4, we discuss the curve parameters and algorithms used in this paper for a small and fast implementation. In section 5, we show our software architecture and programming style. Results and possible enhancements are given in detail in section 6.

2 Arithmetic on Elliptic Curve

In this section, we briefly explain arithmetic and DSA algorithm on an elliptic curve over a field of prime characteristic.

2.1 Elliptic Curve

An elliptic curve over K is given as follows:

$$E : y^2 = x^3 + ax + b \quad (a, b \in K, 4a^3 + 27b^2 \neq 0), \tag{1}$$

where K is a finite field of characteristic $\neq 2, 3$. Then the set of K-rational points on E (with a special element O at infinity), denoted $E(K)$, is a finite abelian group, where $E(K) = \{(x, y) \in K^2 | y^2 = x^3 + ax + b\} \cup \{O\}$.

2.2 Addition Formula in the Affine Coordinates

We show the addition formulas in the affine coordinates. Let $P = (x_1, y_1)$, $Q = (x_2, y_2)$ and $P + Q = (x_3, y_3)$ be points on $E(K)$.

Curve addition formula in the affine coordinates ($P \neq \pm Q$):

$$x_3 = \lambda^2 - x_1 - x_2, \tag{2}$$
$$y_3 = \lambda(x_1 - x_3) - y_1, \tag{3}$$
$$\lambda = \frac{y_2 - y_1}{x_2 - x_1}. \tag{4}$$

Curve addition formula in the affine coordinates ($P = Q$):

$$x_3 = \lambda^2 - 2x_1, \tag{5}$$
$$y_3 = \lambda(x_1 - x_3) - y_1, \tag{6}$$
$$\lambda = \frac{3x_1^2 + a}{2y_1}. \tag{7}$$

2.3 Addition Formula in the Projective Coordinates

Because the addition formula in the affine coordinates requires a modular inversion which is expensive, we often use the projective coordinates to reduce the number of modular inversions. The conversion from affine to projective is as follows:

$$X = x, Y = y, Z = 1. \tag{8}$$

After this conversion, the elliptic addition and doubling can be done on this projective coordinates without any inversion. And then we convert from projective to affine as follows.

$$x = \frac{X}{Z^2}, y = \frac{Y}{Z^3}. \tag{9}$$

In this procedure, we need a modular inverse operation only once.

Next we give a brief explanation of the addition formula on projective coordinates. Let $P = (X_1, Y_1, Z_1), Q = (X_2, Y_2, Z_2)$ and $P + Q = (X_3, Y_3, Z_3)$.

Doubling formula in the projective coordinates $(P = Q)$ is as follows.

$$2(X_1, Y_1, Z_1) = (X_2, Y_2, Z_2), \tag{10}$$

where

$$X_2 = (3X_1{}^2 + aZ_1{}^4)^2 - 8X_1Y_1^2, \tag{11}$$
$$Y_2 = (3X_1{}^2 + aZ_1{}^4)(4X_1Y_1{}^2 - X_2) - 8Y_1^4, \tag{12}$$
$$Z_2 = 2Y_1Z_1. \tag{13}$$

Addition formula in the projective coordinates $(P \neq \pm Q)$ is as follows.

$$(X_0, Y_0, Z_0) + (X_1, Y_1, Z_1) = (X_2, Y_2, Z_2), \tag{14}$$

where

$$V = (X_0Z_1{}^2 + X_1Z_0{}^2)(X_0Z_1{}^2 - X_1Z_0{}^2)^2 - 2X_2, \tag{15}$$
$$X_2 = (Y_0Z_1{}^3 - Y_1Z_0{}^3)^2 - (X_0Z_1{}^2 + X_1Z_0{}^2)(X_0Z_1{}^2 - X_1Z_0{}^2)^2, \tag{16}$$
$$2Y_2 = V(Y_0Z_1{}^3 - Y_1Z_0{}^3) - (Y_0Z_1{}^3 + Y_1Z_0{}^3)(X_0Z_1{}^2 - X_1Z_0{}^2)^3, \tag{17}$$
$$Z_2 = Z_0Z_1(X_0Z_1{}^2 - X_1Z_0{}^2). \tag{18}$$

2.4 DSA Signature Generation and Verification on Elliptic Curve

We define P as the base point whose order is a large prime number n. The private key d and the public key Q have the relation that $Q = dP$. The DSA signature $sig = (r, s)$ generation scheme is as follows:

1. Generate a random number k.
2. Calculate elliptic scalar multiplication $R = kP$.
3. Calculate $r = (R)_x \mod n$. If $r = 0$, then go to step 1.
4. Calculate $s = \frac{e + dr}{k} \mod n$. If $s = 0$, then go to step 1.
5. Output $sig = (r, s)$.

The DSA verification scheme is as follows:

1. If r is not in $[1, n-1]$ or s is not in $[1, n-1]$, then output 'false'.
2. Calculate modular inverse $\frac{1}{s} \mod n$
3. Calculate elliptic scalar multiplication $(\frac{e}{s} \mod n)P$
4. Calculate elliptic scalar multiplication $(\frac{r}{s} \mod n) Q$
5. Calculate elliptic addition $r' = ((\frac{e}{s} \mod n)P + (\frac{r}{s} \mod n)Q)_x$
6. If $r = r'$ then output 'true', else output 'false'.

This elliptic curve DSA is currently being standardized within the ANSI X9F1 and IEEE P1363 standards committees.

3   16-bit Microcomputer M16C

We have implemented an elliptic curve cryptosystem on a 16-bit single-chip microcomputer M16C designed by Mitsubishi Electric Corporation. M16C series were developed for embedded applications and have been widely used in practice such as mobile telecommunications, industrial applications, audio-visual systems, etc. M16C family currently has the following characteristics:

- **Memory:**
  - ROM: romless, 32KB, 64KB, 96KB
  - RAM: 2KB, 3KB, 4KB, 10KB

- **Shortest instruction execution time:**
  - 100ns (at f (Xin) = 10MHz)

- **Registers:**
  - Data register: 16-bit × 4 (two of them are usable as two 8-bit registers)
  - Address register: 16-bit × 2
  - Base register: 16-bit × 2

- **Instruction Sets:** 91 instructions
  - multiplication (hardwired) and division (microcode) operations
  - stack frame generation/release instructions
  - register-to-register, register-to-memory and memory-to-memory modes.
  - single-bit operations and four-bit operations.

M16C is a typical CISC processor; memory-to-memory operations can reduce code size significantly, and stack frame generation/release instructions make a simple and small subroutine calling sequence possible. M16C is designed to assign instructions of high frequency to short opcode, and has some complex instructions and various addressing modes. Moreover because it includes multiplier and DMAC, it carries out many instructions in the shortest execution time (about 70% of the instructions are executed in less than 3 cycles).

However, because of the unequal registers and complex instructions, optimizing size and performance of the code is not an easy task; for instance, a C language-like subroutine interface often results in a large code due to redundancy of parameter passing. A module interface design plays an important role for code optimization.

Therefore we wrote programs in assembly language carefully to extract maximum performance of M16C, analyzing the architecture in detail. To improve performance, we utilized special operations of M16C which can condense several instructions, and took priority over choosing short instructions. For the code/data size, we aimed at a total of 4KB so that our program can be applicable to a future M16C family with a smaller ROM/RAM size.

4 Elliptic Curve Parameters and Algorithms

4.1 Elliptic Curve Parameters

Base Field

In this paper we propose a prime characteristic of the base field with the following form:

$$p = e2^a \pm 1. \tag{19}$$

where e is an integer whose size is within machine word size (16 in our case), and a is an integer whose size is a multiple of machine word size. Use of this form enables us to execute a galios field multiplication in a small code. In our implementation on M16C, we have adopted the following 160-bit prime number:

$$p = 65112 \times 2^{144} - 1. \tag{20}$$

Curve Parameters

We generated an elliptic curve over the prime field using complex multiplication, and for speeding up an elliptic doubling, we adjusted the constant term a of the curve equation to $p - 3$. The base point (P_x, P_y) was selected randomly:

$$a = 1452046121366725933991673688168680114377396846588 = p - 3, \tag{21}$$
$$b = 621468235513391651506736229084534968416800501622, \tag{22}$$
$$n = 1452046121366725933991671292371452349213344743009, \tag{23}$$
$$d = -6259 \; (discriminant), \tag{24}$$
$$P_x = 915905815259634185505956735251349426573212034266, \tag{25}$$
$$P_y = 1431589911282020630356314725439635170402984418778. \tag{26}$$
$$\tag{27}$$

4.2 Elliptic Addition/Doubling

The IEEE-P1363 document [6] describes a detailed implementation algorithm that realizes elliptic addition and doubling, where the addition formula requires four temporary variables (excluding three output variables). We however used the following improved addition algorithm which requires only two temporary variables even when $z_1 \neq 1$. This algorithm can be implemented using galois field addition, subtraction, multiplication, and halving routines only. If we accept one more temporary variable, the six steps from step 09 to step 14 can be four. Note that the case $z_1 \neq 1$ appears only once in the ECDSA signature verification procedure.

Our elliptic doubling algorithm can be applied to the case $a = p - 3$ and it reduces the program size. Another advantage of our addition/doubling implementation is that the third variable of the subtraction (the subtracting variable) is always different from the first variable (the output variable). This often enables a small implementation of the subtraction function.

Elliptic Addition Formula $(X, Y, Z) = (X, Y, Z) + (X', Y', Z')$	Elliptic Doubling Formula $(X, Y, Z) = 2(X, Y, Z)$

if $(Z' \neq 1)$
 01: $\qquad T_1 = Z' * Z'$
 02: $\qquad X = X * T_1$
 03: $\qquad T_1 = Z' * T_1$
 04: $\qquad Y = Y * T_1$
 endif
 	
 05: $T_1 = Z * Z$
 06: $T_2 = X' * T_1$
 07: $T_1 = Z * T_1$
 08: $T_1 = Y' * T_1$
 	
 09: $Y = Y - T_1$
 10: $T_1 = 2T_1$
 11: $T_1 = Y + T_1$
 12: $X = X - T_2$
 13: $T_2 = 2T_2$
 14: $T_2 = X + T_2$
 	
 if $(Z' \neq 1)$
 15: $\qquad Z = Z * Z'$
 endif
 16: $Z = Z * X$
 	
 17: $T_1 = T_1 * X$
 18: $X = X * X$
 19: $T_2 = T_2 * X$
 20: $T_1 = T_1 * X$
 	
 21: $X = Y * Y$
 22: $X = X - T_2$
 	
 23: $T_2 = T_2 - X$
 24: $T_2 = T_2 - X$
 25: $T_2 = T_2 * Y$
 26: $Y = T_2 - T_1$
 27: $Y = Y/2$
	01: $T_1 = Z * Z$
	 02: $Z = Y * Z$
	 03: $Z = 2Z$
	
	 if $(a = p - 3)$
	 04: $T_2 = X - T_1$
	 05: $T_1 = X + T_1$
	 06: $T_2 = T_1 * T_2$
	 07: $T_1 = 2T_2$
	 08: $T_1 = T_1 + T_2$
	 else
	 09: $T_1 = T_1 * T_1$
	 10: $T_1 = a * T_1$
	 11: $T_2 = X * X$
	 12: $T_1 = T_1 + T_2$
	 13: $T_2 = 2T_2$
	 14: $T_1 = T_1 + T_2$
	 endif
	
	 15: $Y = 2Y$
	 16: $Y = Y * Y$
	 17: $T_2 = Y * Y$
	 18: $T_2 = T_2/2$
	 19: $Y = Y * X$
	
	 20: $X = T_1 * T_1$
	 21: $X = X - Y$
	 22: $X = X - Y$
	
	 23: $Y = Y - X$
	 24: $Y = Y * T_1$
	 25: $Y = Y - T_2$

Table 1: Elliptic Addition/Doubling Formula.

4.3 Scalar Multiplication of a Random Point

In ECDSA, a scalar multiplication of a given random point is used in signature verification and is the most time-consuming part of the total signature computation. Although there are various works for speeding up this calculation, we here adopted a standard binary method for minimizing temporary memory, which occupies RAM area that is expensive in our environments.

Algorithm [Random Point]

- Input : a positive integer k and a random point P on an elliptic curve.
- Output: the elliptic curve point $Q = kP$.

1. Let $(0 \cdots 01 k_{l-2} k_{l-3} \cdots k_1 k_0)$ be the binary representation of k.
2. Set $Q \leftarrow P$.
3. For i from $l - 2$ down to 0 do
    (a) Set $Q \leftarrow 2Q$.
    (b) If $k_i = 1$, then set $Q \leftarrow Q + P$.
4. Output Q.

4.4 Scalar Multiplication of a Fixed Point

In ECDSA, this procedure is used for a scalar multiplication of the base point, which is a fixed system parameter. We can hence reduce the calculation time by having a precomputed loop-up table in ROM area, which is less expensive than RAM area. Again to reduce the code and temporary buffer size, we adopted the following standard window method for the scalar multiplication.

Algorithm [Fixed Point]

Precomputed Table Generation (31 entries):

$$table[n] = \sum_{j=0}^{4} n_j 2^{32j} P \quad (1 \leq n \leq 31), \text{ where } n_j \text{ is the } j\text{-th bit of } n.$$

Online Scalar Multiplication:

- Input : a positive integer k.
- Output: the elliptic curve point $Q = kP$.

1. Let $(k_{159} k_{158} \cdots k_1 k_0)$ be the binary representation of k.
2. For $i = 31$ down to 0 do
    (a) Set $n_i = \sum_{j=0}^{4} k_{32j+i} 2^j$.
    (b) If $n_i \neq 0$, set $Q = table[n_i]$ and go to Step 3.
3. For $i = i - 1$ down to 0 do
    (a) Set $n_i = \sum_{j=0}^{4} k_{32j+i} 2^j$.
    (b) Set $Q \leftarrow 2Q$.
    (c) If $n_i \neq 0$, set $Q \leftarrow Q + table[n_i]$.
4. Output Q.

The above algorithm requires a total of at most 31 elliptic additions and 31 elliptic doublings with a 1240-byte precomputed table. This leads to 589 field multiplications. On the other hand, the binary method on a random point requires 2400 field multiplications in average.

5 Software Architecture and Programming

To balance the signature generation/verification speed with the total program size, we designed the ECDSA software on M16C on the basis of the following hierarchical module architecture. We also regarded independence of modules as important so that we could easily change elliptic curve parameters or even change cryptographic algorithms when necessary.

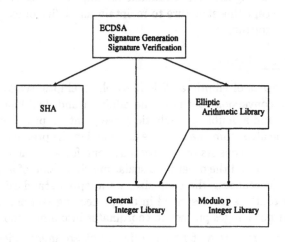

Figure 1: Library Architecture

Modulo p Integer Library

This module consists of modular addition, subtraction, multiplication, and halving routines for the embedded modulus p, which is the characteristic of the base field. The first three routines have two interfaces; one has two arguments, one of which is an input/output parameter; and the other has three independent arguments, one of which is used for an output parameter only. The speed of these routines dominates the overall performance of the signature. Hence for maximizing the performance rather than reducing the code size, we adopted a 160-bit fixed I/O interface and introduced an extensive use of loop unrolling technique. We also designed this module so that no other modules could depend on elliptic parameters.

For reducing the code size, we have not included an optimized modular square routine, which is generally 20 – 30 % faster than a modular multiplication routine.

General Integer Library

This module is intended to be a collection of general purpose routines for treating integers with arbitrary length. It covers move, addition, subtraction, multiplication, division and inversion (modulo an integer) routines, accepting any length as input. In ECDSA, this module is mainly used for deriving an inverse element both in modulus n, the order of the curve, and in modulus p, the order of the field, where the latter is necessary for transforming a projective coordinate into an affine coordinate.

This module is slightly size-redundant for implementing ECDSA only, but we decided to accept this structure to maintain an ability of extension to other cryptographic algorithms.

Elliptic Arithmetic Library

This library consists of elliptic addition/doubling, elliptic scalar multiplication and coordinate conversion routines. The addition and doubling routines carry out an addition and a doubling of elliptic curve points in projective coordinates, respectively. The algorithms we used are described in the preceeding section. The scalar multiplication consists of two routines: one for a scalar multiplication of the fixed base point and the other for a scalar multiplication of a randomly given point. Mainly for reducing the code size, we adopted standard algorithms for realizing these routines, as described in the preceeding section. The coordinate conversion routine changes projective coordinates into affine coordinates.

These routines require a 160-bit interface, but are independent of the value of the prime characteristic p or the base point (P_x, P_y). While the conversion routine requires both of the modulo p library and the general integer library because of necessity for an inversion operation in modulus p, the other routines use the modulo p library only.

It could be possible to design a special (modulo p) inversion routine which would slightly speed up the coordinate conversion procedure. But we did not adopt this strategy because the improvement of the total performance of signature generation/verification would be small, while the increase in the code size would not be negligible.

ECDSA Signature Generation/Verification

This top level module makes procedure calls for SHA-1, the elliptic scalar multiplication, the elliptic coordinate conversion and the general integer operations. The general integer library is needed for modulo n arithmetic operations, particularly an inversion modulo n.

6 Implementation Results

In this section, we summarize our results of implementation, including the code size of each module and performance of some major functions. We also discuss possible size/speed enhancements of this library at the end of this section.

6.1 Code/Data Size

We have successfully designed the program in a total size of 4Kbyte code/data, which was one of our goals in the implementation. The size of each module is as follows:

Module	Size
ECDSA Signature Generation/Verification	220 bytes
Elliptic Arithmetic Library	690 bytes
Modulo p Integer Library	600 bytes
General Integer Library	780 bytes
SHA-1	430 bytes
DATA Table	1280 bytes
Total Size	4000 bytes

Table 2: Code size of our library

The fixed data table consists of the 1240byte precomputed table, the 20byte base prime p and the 20byte curve order n.

6.2 Processing Time

The following table shows the processing time of a scalar multiplication of a randomly given point and the fixed point (the base point), a modulo inversion of a given 160-bit data, and SHA-1.

This result clearly shows that although the inversion routine and the hash function take much less time than the elliptic scalar multiplication, their computational time can not be ignored.

Module	Elapsed Time
Elliptic Scalar Multiplication (Random Point)	480msec
Elliptic Scalar Multiplication (Fixed Point)	130msec
Inversion Modulo 160-bit Integer	8msec
SHA-1 (time for processing one block)	2msec

Table 3: Performance of our library

Table 4 shows a total computational time of ECDSA signature generation and verification. In both signature generation and verification, we have included time for one-block processing of SHA-1 for hashing a message.

Function	Elapsed Time
ECDSA signature generation	150msec
ECDSA signature verification	630msec

Table 4: Performance of 160-bit ECDSA on M16C

6.3 Estimation of 1024-bit RSA

Since our program includes the general integer library, it is easy to implement RSA cryptosystem using the library. Table 5 shows our estimation of 1024-bit RSA signature generation/verification operations. Because the library is not speed-optimized, the signature generation is slow, but the verification is still faster than that of ECDSA.

Function	Elapsed Time
RSA signature generation (Chinese remainder theorem)	10sec
RSA signature verification ($e = 2^{16} + 1$)	400msec

Table 5: Performance of 1024-bit RSA on M16C

6.4 Possible Enhancements

In this paper, to realize 4KB code/data, we adopted standard computation algorithms and coding methods. In the following, we give a list for possible enhancements for further speeding up and/or reducing code size.

Since the modulo p integer library has been coded with a loop unrolling for fast computation, the code size is expected to be reduced by up to 200-300 bytes by introducing a usual loop rolling. It is also possible to reduce the precomputed table or even ignore scalar multiplication of the base point, but this will lead to a heavy penalty of time for the signature generation. Another possibility is to reduce the code size of the general integer library at the cost of applicability to other algorithms. We estimate that it is possible to reduce another 300–400 bytes with 50% loss of the overall performance.

On the other hand, adding an optimized modulo square routine is expected to speed up the signature generation/verification by 10 to 20 %. Optimizing the speed of the general integer routine will make RSA faster. We estimate that RSA can be up to twice faster with another 500 bytes.

7 Conclusions

In this paper, we dealt with a practical implementation of ECC over prime characteristic on limited resources. As a result, we successfully implemented 4KB software cryptographic library for 160-bit ECDSA signature generation, verification and SHA-1 on M16C (10MHz) and confirmed a speed of 150msec for generating an ECDSA signature and 630msec for verifying an ECDSA signature. We conclude that it is possible to provide a practical cryptographic library of elliptic curve cryptosystems over a field of prime characteristic on restricted resources. We can also apply this library to other cryptographic algorithms using the general integer library, such as RSA.

References

1. N.Koblitz, "Elliptic curve cryptosystems", Mathematics of Computation, 48(1987),203-209.
2. V.S.Miller, "Use of elliptic curves in cryptography", Advances in Cryptology-Proceedings of Crypto'85, Lecture Notes in Computer Science, 218(1986), Springer-Verlag, 417-426.
3. G.Agnew, R.Mullin and S.Vanston, "An Implementation of elliptic curve cryptosystems over $F_{2^{155}}$", IEEE Journal on Selected Areas in Communications, 11(1993),804-813.
4. Certicom SigGen Smart Card, http://205.150.149.57/ce2/embed.htm.
5. T.ElGamal, "A public key cryptosystem and a signature scheme based on discrete logarithm", IEEE Trans. Inform. Theory, Vol.IT-31(1985),469-472.
6. IEEE P1363 Working Draft Appendices, February 6, 1997.
7. IEEE P1363 Draft Version 1, December 19, 1997.
8. G. Harper, A.Menezes and S.Vanstone, "Public-key cryptosystems with very small key lengths", Advances in Cryptology-Proceedings of Eurocrypt'92, Lecture Notes in Computer Science, 658(1993), Springer-Verlag, 163-173.
9. R.Schroeppel, H.Orman, S.O'Malley and O.Spatscheck, "Fast key exchange with elliptic curve systems", Advances in Cryptology-Proceedings of Crypt'95, Lecture Notes in Computer Science, 963(1995), Springer-Verlag, 43-56.
10. E.D.Win, A.Bosselaers and S.Vandenberghe, "A fast software implementation for arithmetic operations in $GF(2^n)$ ", Advances in Cryptology-Proceedings of Asiacrypt'95, Lecture Notes in Computer Science, 1163(1996), Springer-Verlag, 65-76.
11. A.Miyaji, T.Ono and H.Cohen, "Efficient Elliptic Curve Exponentiation", Information and Communications Security ICICS'97, Lecture Notes in Computer Science, 1334(1997), Springer-Verlag, 282-291.
12. "User Manual of M16C/60 Series", Mitsubishi Electric Corporation, 1996.
13. "Software Manual of M16C/60 Series", Mitsubishi Electric Corporation, 1996.
14. National Institute of Standards and Technology, NIST FIPS PUB 186, "Digital Signature Standard", U.S. Department of Commerce, 1994.
15. National Institute of Standards and Technology, NIST FIPS PUB 180, "Secure Hash Standard", U.S. Department of Commerce, 1995.

Two Efficient Algorithms for Arithmetic of Elliptic Curves Using Frobenius Map

Jung Hee Cheon, Sungmo Park, Sangwoo Park, and Daeho Kim

Electronics and Telecommunications Research Institute,
161 Kajong-Dong,Yusong-Gu, Taejon, 305-350, ROK
{cheon, smp, psw, dhkim}@dingo.etri.re.kr

Abstract. In this paper, we present two efficient algorithms computing scalar multiplications of a point in an elliptic curve defined over a small finite field, the Frobenius map of which has small trace. Both methods use the identity which expresses multiplication-by-m maps by polynomials of Frobenius maps. Both are applicable for a large family of elliptic curves and more efficient than any other methods applicable for the family. More precisely, by Algorithm 1(Frobenius k-ary method), we can compute mP in at most $2l/5 + 28$ elliptic additions for arbitrary l bit integer m and a point P on some elliptic curves. For other curves, the number of elliptic additions required is less than l. Algorithm 2(window method) requires at average $2l/3$ elliptic additions to compute mP for l bit integer m and a point P on a family of elliptic curves. For some 'good' elliptic curves, it requires $5l/12 + 11$ elliptic additions at average.

1 Introduction

To implement elliptic curve cryptosystems, it is important to compute efficiently scalar multiplications of a point in a given elliptic curve. The problem of multiplying a point P of an elliptic curve by an integer m is analogous to exponentiation of an element in a multiplicative group to the m-th power. The standard algorithm for this problem on elliptic curves is the binary method which repeats 'doublings' and 'additions' of points. This method requires at average $3l/2$ elliptic operations to compute mP for l bit integer m and a point P in an elliptic curve. A generalization of the binary method is the signed binary method (or the addition-subtraction method) [8]. This method use the fact that subtraction of points on an elliptic curve is just as efficient as addition. It performs the same procedure with the binary method except that it allows subtractions of points. This method requires at average $4l/3$ elliptic operations to compute mP for l bit integer m and a point P in an elliptic curve.

One can use also complex multiplications to speed up scalar multiplications. Every elliptic curve over a finite field is equipped with a set of operations (One of them is called the Frobenius map.) which can be viewed as multiplication by complex algebraic integers. These operations can be carried out efficiently for certain families of elliptic curves if we take normal basis for base field representation. This method is first suggested by Koblitz in [5] and [4] and improved by

Meier and Staffelbach in [6]. The method in [6] requires at average $l/2$ elliptic operations to compute mP for l bit integer m and a point P in an elliptic curve. Further improvements were made by Solinas in [11], which requires at average $l/2$ elliptic operations. But these methods in [4], [6] and [11] can be applied just for two special elliptic curves, the anomalous binary curve(or ABC) defined over $\mathbf{F}_2$ and its twist.

In this paper, we present two methods using complex multiplications. Both methods use the identity which expresses multiplication-by-m maps by polymomials of the Frobenius map and are applicable for a larger family of elliptic curves than the methods in [4], [6] and [11]. These methods are efficient for elliptic curves defined over a small finite field, the Frobenius map of which has small trace. For some elliptic curves, the first methods requires at maximum $2l/5 + 28$ elliptic operations to compute mP for arbitrary l bit integer m and arbitrary point P in the elliptic curves.

We assume throughout this paper that elliptic curves are defined over a finite field $\mathbf{F}_q$ for $q = 2^r$ and the elements of finite fields are represented by normal basis, where the Frobenius map is just a bit rotate.

2 Frobenius Map

Consider an elliptic curve E defined over $\mathbf{F}_q$ with q elements. We define the q-th power Frobenius map ϕ_q on $E(\mathbf{F}_q)$ as follows [7] :

$$\phi_q : (x, y) \mapsto (x^q, y^q)$$

Then the followings are equivalent :

1. $\#E(\mathbf{F}_q) = q + 1 - t$
2. The trace of ϕ_q is t
3. $\phi_q^2 - t\phi_q + q = 0$

In particular, we call E to be supersingular if $t = 0$ and to be anomalous binary curve(or ABC) if $t = 1$.

For any poitive integer k, put $N_k = \#E(\mathbf{F}_{q^k})$. By the Weil theorem on elliptic curves [7] [10],

$$N_k = q^k + 1 - t_k,$$

where t_k is the sequence satisfying

$$t_0 = 2, t_1 = t \text{ and } t_{k+1} = t_k^2 - q^k t_{k-1} \quad (k \geq 1). \tag{1}$$

Since $\phi_{q^k} = \phi_q^k$, ϕ_q satisfies the equation as a map :

$$\phi_q^{2k} - t_k \phi_q^k + q^k = 0. \tag{2}$$

Hence when t_k is small, we can calculate efficiently $q^k M$ for $M \in E(\mathbf{F}_{q^k})$ using the above equation.

Note that following Waterhouse theorem [7], we know that if q is the power of 2, for any odd number t with $|t| \leq 2\sqrt{q}$, there exist elliptic curves E such that $\#E(\mathbf{F}_q) = q + 1 - t$, i.e. the Frobenius map of E has the trace t. Furthermore, all of them are not supersingular since the characteristic 2 of q does not divide t.

3 Frobenius k-ary Method

For an elliptic curve E defined over $\mathbf{F}_q$ where $q = 2^r$, let E_n be the curve regarded over the extension field $\mathbf{F}_{2^{nr}}$. Assume that the Frobenius map ϕ_{2^r} of E has small trace t so that we have an identity $2^r = t\phi_{2^r} - \phi_{2^r}^2$ from (2). Then we can calculate qP efficiently using this identity so that we can reduce the number of elliptic additions to compute mP for an integer m and $P \in E_n$. Now, using the Frobenius map, we present an algorithm which improves the usual k-ary method [1].

Theorem 1 (Frobenius k-ary Method). *Assume that an elliptic curve E is defined over $\mathbf{F}_{q^n}$. Let $P \in E(\mathbf{F}_{q^n})$ and $m = (e_{n-1}e_{n-2}\cdots e_1 e_0)_q$ be the radix representation of the multiplier m with base q and $0 \leq e_i < q$. Then $Q = mP$ can be computed using the following algorithm.*

Algorithm 1 (Input: $P = (x,y)$; Output $Q = mP$)

1. *Precomputation*
    (a) $P_0 \leftarrow O$, $P_1 \leftarrow P$
    (b) *For $i = 2$ to $q - 1$, $P_i = P_{i-1} + P$ (i.e. $P_i = iP$)*
2. $Q \leftarrow P_{e_{n-1}}$
3. *For $i = n - 2$ to 0*
    (a) $Q \leftarrow t\phi_q(Q) - \phi_q^2(Q)$ *(i.e. $Q \leftarrow qQ$)*
    (b) $Q \leftarrow Q + P_{e_i}$
4. *Return(Q)*

Let $\epsilon(t)$ be the number of additions required to compute the multiplication-by-t map. Notice that Step 1(b) requires $q - 2$ additions, Step 3(a) requires $(n-1)(\epsilon(t)+1)$ additions and Step 3(b) requires $n-1$ additions. Since ϕ_q is just bit rotate for the normal base representation, the maximal complexity C of this method is thus $(n-1)(\epsilon(t)+2) + q - 2$ additions. That is, for any l-bit integer m, we can compute mP in C elliptic additions. If we let $l = nr$ for convenience, we have

$$C = (\frac{l}{r} - 1)(\epsilon(t) + 2) + q - 2. \tag{3}$$

For example, if $q = 2^4$ and $t = 1$, then the maximal complexity becomes $C = l/2 + 14$, which is very efficient compared with the average complexity $4l/3$ of the addition-subtraction method [8]. When both of q and r varies, the maximal complexities of Frobenius k-ary method are shown in Table 1.

q	$t = \pm 1$	$t = \pm 3$	$t = \pm 5$	$t = \pm 7$	Memory($\times l$ bits)
2^2	l	$2l - 2$	$-$	$-$	2
2^3	$2l/3 + 4$	$4l/3 + 2$	$5l/3 + 1$	$-$	6
2^4	$l/2 + 12$	$l + 10$	$5l/4 + 9$	$3l/2 + 8$	14
2^5	$2l/5 + 28$	$4l/5 + 26$	$l + 25$	$6l/5 + 24$	30
2^6	$l/3 + 60$	$2l/3 + 58$	$5l/6 + 57$	$l + 56$	62

Table 1. The maximal complexities of Frobenius k-ary method

The maximal complexities for most of all elliptic curves in Table 1 are less than the average complexity $4l/3$ of the addition-subtraction method. The best cases for $l \approx 160$ are the elliptic curves with $t = \pm 1$ defined over $\mathbf{F}_{2^5}$. In this case, the maximal complexity is $2l/5 + 28$. That is, we can compute mP in $2l/5 + 28$ elliptic additions for arbitrary l bit integer m.

4 Window Method

We start this section with an example.

Example 1. Let E be an elliptic curve defined over $\mathbf{F}_{2^{12}}$ with the trace 3 of the Frobenius map $\phi_{2^{12}}$ and E_n be the curve regarded over the extension field $\mathbf{F}_{2^{12n}}$. Then we have $2^{12}P = 3\phi_{2^{12}}(P) - \phi_{2^{12}}^2(P)$ for any $P \in E_n$ from (2). For any $12n$-bit integer m, write m as a Non-Adjacent Form(NAF) as follows[8] :

$$m = \sum_{j=0}^{12n} c_j 2^j \quad \text{with } c_j = 0, \pm 1$$

where $c_j = 0$ with the probability $2/3$. Then for any $P \in E_n$, we can write mP as follows :

$$mP = \sum_{j=0}^{12n-1} c_j 2^j P = \sum_{i=0}^{n-1} (\sum_{j=0}^{11} c_{12i+j} 2^j) 2^{12i} P \tag{4}$$

$$= \sum_{j=0}^{11} 2^j (\sum_{i=0}^{n-1} c_{12i+j} 2^{12i} P) \tag{5}$$

$$= \sum_{j=0}^{11} 2^j (\sum_{i=0}^{n-1} c_{12i+j} P_i) \quad \text{for } P_i = 2^{12i} P, \quad 0 \le i \le n-1 \tag{6}$$

We need 3 additions to compute $2^{12}P$ and at average $12n/3 + 11$ additions to compute mP when we know $P_i's$ for $1 \le i \le n - 1$, because $c_j = 0$ with the probability $2/3$. Hence we totally need at average $(4n + 11) + 3(n - 1) = 7n + 8$ additions, which is less than $12n \times 4/3 = 16n$ of the addition-subtraction method. In this case, we improved the addition-subtraction method efficiently more than two times.

More generally, for an elliptic curve E defined over $\mathbf{F}_{2^r}$, let E_n be the curve regarded over the extension field $\mathbf{F}_{2^{nr}}$. Assume that the Frobenius map ϕ_{2^r} of E has the small trace t so that we have an identity $2^r = t\phi_{2^r} - \phi_{2^r}^2$ from (2). For a nr-bit integer m, we can write m as a Non-Adjacent Form as follows :

$$m = \sum_{j=0}^{nr-1} c_j 2^j \quad \text{with } c_j = 0, \pm 1$$

where $c_j = 0$ with the probability $2/3$. Then for any $P \in E_n$, we can write mP as follows :

$$mP = \sum_{j=0}^{nr-1} c_j 2^j P = \sum_{i=0}^{n-1}(\sum_{j=0}^{r-1} c_{ri+j}2^j)2^{ri}P \tag{7}$$

$$= \sum_{j=0}^{r-1} 2^j (\sum_{i=0}^{n-1} c_{ri+j}2^{ri}P) \tag{8}$$

$$= \sum_{j=0}^{r-1} 2^j (\sum_{i=0}^{n-1} c_{ri+j}P_i) \quad \text{for } P_i = 2^{ri}P, \quad 0 \le i \le n-1 \tag{9}$$

Hence we have the following algorithm :

Theorem 2 (Window Method). *Assume that an elliptic curve E is defined over $\mathbf{F}_{2^r}$. Let $P \in E(\mathbf{F}_{2^{nr}})$, $t = 2^r + 1 - \#E(\mathbf{F}_{2^r})$ and $m = \sum_{j=0}^{nr} c_j 2^j$ be the Non-Adjacent Form of m with $c_j = 0, \pm 1$. Then $Q = mP$ can be computed using the following algorithm.*

Algorithm 2 (Input: $P = (x, y)$; Output $Q = mP$)

1. *Precomputation*
   (a) $P_0 \leftarrow P$
   (b) For $i = 1$ to $n-1$, $P_i = t\phi_{2^r}(P_{i-1}) - \phi_{2^r}^2(P_{i-1})$ (i.e. $P_i = 2^r P_{i-1} = 2^{ri}P$)
2. *$Q \leftarrow O$*
3. *For $j = r - 1$ to 0*
   (a) $R \leftarrow O$
   (b) For $i = 0$ to $n - 1$, $R \leftarrow R + c_{ri+j}P_i$
   (c) $Q \leftarrow R + 2Q$
4. *Return(Q)*

Step 1(b) requires $\epsilon(t) + 1$ additions. Also Step 3 requires at average $nr/3 + r$ additions because $c_j = 0$ with the probability $2/3$. Hence the average complexity C is $C = nr/3 + r + (\epsilon(t) + 1)(n - 1)$. If we let $l = nr$, then we have

$$C = l/3 + r + (\epsilon(t) + 1)(l/r - 1), \tag{10}$$

which is less than the average complexity $4l/3$ of the addition-subtraction method if $\epsilon(t) + 1 < r$.

Note that the order of an elliptic curve must be prime or a product of a large prime and a small integer in order that the discrete logarithms on the elliptic curve are intractable. Since $\#E(\mathbf{F}_q)$ divides $\#E_n = E(\mathbf{F}_{q^n})$ and $\#E(\mathbf{F}_q) \approx q$, an elliptic curve E defined over $\mathbf{F}_q$ for large q is not good for elliptic curve cryptosystems.

We present in Table 2 the average numbers of elliptic additions required to compute to mP for nr-bit m and $P \in E_n$ where E is defined over $\mathbf{F}_{2^r}$ for small r. For convenience, we put $l = nr$.

q	$t = \pm 1$	$t = \pm 3$	$t = \pm 5$	$t = \pm 7$
2^2	$4l/3$	$7l/3 - 2$		
2^3	$l + 2$	$5l/3 - 1$	$2l - 2$	
2^4	$7l/12 + 3$	$13l/12 + 1$	$4l/3$	$19l/12 - 1$
2^5	$8l/15 + 4$	$14l/15 + 2$	$17l/15 + 1$	$4l/3$
2^6	$l/2 + 5$	$5l/6 + 3$	$l + 2$	$7l/6 + 1$
2^7	$10l/21 + 6$	$16l/21 + 4$	$19l/21 + 3$	$22l/21 + 2$
2^8	$11l/24 + 7$	$17l/24 + 5$	$5l/6 + 4$	$23l/24 + 3$
2^9	$4l/9 + 8$	$2l/3 + 6$	$7l/9 + 5$	$8l/9 + 4$
2^{10}	$13l/30 + 9$	$19l/30 + 7$	$22l/30 + 6$	$5l/6 + 5$
2^{12}	$5l/12 + 11$	$7l/12 + 9$	$2l/3 + 8$	$3l/4 + 7$

Table 2. The average complexities of window method using $q = t\phi_q - \phi_q^2$

In Table 2, we see that when $q \geq 2^8$, the average numbers of elliptic additions for $l \approx 160$ are less than $l/2$ for $t = \pm 1$. Even for the case of $t = \pm 7$, the number of elliptic additions are less than l, which is more efficient result, compared with the average complexity $4l/3$ of addition-subtraction method. For the best case, it requires at average $5l/12 + 11$ elliptic additions to compute mP for l bit integer m.

We can also make use of t_2 and t_3 instead of $t = t_1$. We also explain this method by an example.

Example 2. Let E be an elliptic curve defined over $\mathbf{F}_{2^2}$ with the trace $t = 1$ of the Frobenius map ϕ_{2^2}. Consider $E_n = E(\mathbf{F}_{2^{2n}})$. Since $t_6 = -7$ in (1), we have $4^6 = 2^{12} = -7\phi_4^6 - \phi_4^{12}$ from (2) so that we need just 5 elliptic additions to multiply 2^{12} to a point in E_n. Apply Algorithm 2 for $r = 12$ and $t = t_6$. Then $3l/4 + 7$ elliptic additions are required for computing mP for l-bit integer m and $P \in E_n$. In this case, since $\#E(\mathbf{F}_{2^2}) = 4$, it is probable that E_n is 4 times a prime when we take n to be prime.

More generally, we can take an elliptic curve E defined over $\mathbf{F}_q$ for small q, the Frobenius map of which has the trace t satisfying $t_s \approx 0$ for some s. But it is not frequent case that t_s is small for $s \geq 4$. The previous example is just one case we found for $q = 2^r$ and $r \leq 20$.

For $s = 3$, there are two cases. One example is the case of $t_3 = \pm 5$ for the elliptic curves with $t = \pm 5$ defined over $\mathbf{F}_{2^3}$. In this case, we have the identity $2^9 = 5\phi_{2^3}^3 - \phi_{2^3}^6$ from (2) so that the average complexity becomes $7l/9 + 5$ by (10). Another example is the case of $t_3 = \pm 7$ for the elliptic curves with $t = \pm 7$ defined over $\mathbf{F}_{2^4}$. In this case, we have the identity $2^{12} = 7\phi_{2^4}^3 - \phi_{2^4}^6$ so that the average complexity becomes $3l/4 + 7$ by (10).

For $q = 2$, there are lots of examples. For an elliptic curve E defined over $\mathbf{F}_q$ for $q = 2^r$, consider $E_n = E(\mathbf{F}_{q^n})$. If we take t near $\sqrt{2q}$, we have $t_2 \approx 0$ since $t_2 = t^2 - 2q$. Then use the identity $q^2 = t_2\phi_q - \phi_q^2$ from (2) to compute $q^2 P$ for $P \in E_n$. For the elliptic curve with small t_2, Table 3 presents the number of elliptic additions required to compute mP for l-bit integer m and $P \in E_n$.

q	t	t_2	Possible Multiple	$\epsilon(t_2) + 1$	# of E.Addition
2^2	3	1	2^4	1	$7l/12 + 3$
2^3	5	9	2^9	4	$7l/9 + 5$
2^4	5	-7	2^8	5	$23l/24 + 3$
2^5	7	-15	2^{10}	6	$14l/15 + 4$
2^5	9	17	2^{10}	6	$14l/15 + 4$
2^6	11	-7	2^{12}	5	$3l/4 + 7$
2^7	15	-31	2^{14}	7	$5l/6 + 7$
2^7	17	33	2^{14}	7	$5l/6 + 7$
2^8	23	17	2^{16}	6	$17l/24 + 10$
2^9	31	-63	2^{18}	8	$7l/9 + 10$
2^9	33	65	2^{18}	8	$7l/9 + 10$
2^{10}	45	-23	2^{22}	7	$43l/66 + 15$
2^{12}	90	-92	2^{24}	9	$17l/24 + 15$
2^{12}	91	89	2^{24}	9	$17l/24 + 15$
2^{14}	181	-7	2^{28}	5	$43l/84 + 23$
2^{16}	362	-28	2^{32}	7	$53l/96 + 25$
2^{18}	724	-112	2^{36}	9	$7l/12 + 27$
2^{20}	1448	-448	2^{40}	11	$73l/120 + 29$

Table 3. The average complexities of window method using $q^2 = t_2\phi_q^2 - \phi_q^4$

In all cases, the average complexities are far less than l, which are improved results. The best case is the elliptic curve with $t = 181$ defined over $\mathbf{F}_{2^{14}}$. In this case, the average complexity becomes $43l/84 + 23$, which is 109 less than $2l/3$ for $l = 168 (= 14 \cdot 12)$.

5 Conclusion

In this paper, we have presented two efficient methods to compute scalar multiplications of a point of elliptic curves. Both methods use the identity expressing multiplication-by-m maps to some polynomials of the Frobenius map. Both methods can be applicable for a large family of elliptic curves with small defining field and small trace and more efficient than any other methods applicable for the family. By Algorithm 1(Frobenius k-ary method), we can compute mP in $2l/5 + 28$ elliptic additions for any l bit integer m and a point P for some 'good' curves. For other curves, the number of elliptic additions needed is also less than l.

Algorithm 2(window method) requires at average $2l/3$ elliptic additions to compute mP for $P \in E$ and l bit integer m. For some 'good' curves, it requires just $5l/12 + 11$ elliptic additions.

Our methods are useful when one implements elliptic curve cryptosystems in small hardware such as a smart card, because our methods provide high computational speed and require small size of memories.

References

1. J. Guajardo and C. Paar, "Efficient algorithms for elliptic curve cryptosystems", *Proc. Crypto '97*, Springer-Verlag, 1997, pp. 342-356.
2. K. Koyama and Y. Tsuruoka, "Speeding up Elliptic Cryptosystems by using a singed binary window method", *Proc. Crypto '92*, Springer-Verlag, 1993, pp. 43-56.
3. N. Koblitz, *A Course in Number Theory and Cryptography*, Springer-Verlag, 1991.
4. N. Koblitz, "CM curves with good cryptographic properties", *Proc. Crypto '91*, Springer-Verlag, 1992, pp. 279-287.
5. N. Koblitz, "Hyperelliptic Cryptosystems", *Journal of Cryptology* 1(1989), pp. 139-150.
6. W. Meier and O. Staffelbach, "Efficient multiplication on certain non-supersingular elliptic curves", *Proc. Crypto '92*, Springer-Verlag, 1993, pp. 333-344.
7. A. Menezes, *Elliptic Curve Public Key Cryptosystems*, Kluwer Academic Publishers, 1993.
8. F. Morain and J. Olivos, "Speeding up the computations on an elliptic curve using additions-subtraction chains", *Inform. Theory. Appl. 24 (1990)*, pp.531-543.
9. R. Schoof, "Elliptic curves over finite fields and the computation of square roots mod p", *Math. Comp.* 44(1985), pp.483-494.
10. J. Silverman, *The Arithmetic of Elliptic Curves*, Springer-Verlag, 1992.
11. J. Solinas, "An improved algorithm for arithmetic on a family of elliptic curves", *Proc. Crypto '97*, Springer-Verlag, 1997, pp. 357-371.

Public-Key Cryptosystems
Using the Modular Group

Akihiro Yamamura

Telecommunications Advancement Organization of Japan
1-1-32 Shin'urashima, Kanagawa-ku,
Yokohama, 221-0031 Japan
yamamura@yokohama.tao.or.jp

Abstract. We propose a public-key cryptosystem using the amalgamated free product structure of the modular group and the action on the upper half plane. The main purpose of this paper is to examine possibilities of building public-key cryptosystems using technology from combinatorial group theory. As a possible example of such a system, we offer a new public-key cryptosystem not depending on specific number theoretical problems but on difficulties of solving several problems in algebra.

1 Introduction

Many public-key cryptosystems depend on difficulties of solving some number theoretical problems. We propose a public-key cryptosystem based on a different discipline. Our intention is to inspire researches in public-key cryptosystems not depending on the difficulty of solving some specific number theoretical problems. We propose a public-key cryptosystem using the *modular group* $SL(2, Z)$ and consider possible further developments of the research. Our system is based on the amalgamated free product structure of the modular group and its action on the upper half of the Gaussian plane. Combinatorial group theory is a study of presentations of groups by generators and relations, that is, a study of words on an alphabet and rules of their manipulations. Many algorithmic results related to presentations of groups have been obtained and applied to problems in topology and geometry. An amalgamated free product is one of the most important constructions in combinatorial group theory. It seems interesting to investigate applications of techniques in combinatorial group theory to cryptography. First, we recall basics of the modular group as well as group theoretical concepts. We briefly look over the action on the upper half plane, the matrix representation and a group presentation as an amalgamated free product of cyclic groups. Secondly, we provide efficient algorithms that make us possible to find a unique decomposition of an element in the modular group as a product of two well chosen matrices. The expression is called the *normal form* of a matrix in the modular group. Using these ideas we construct a public-key cryptosystem. We explain encryption and decryption methods. Finally, we discuss security issues of the system and then consider further developments of the study.

2 Preliminaries

We recall a few fundamental facts of the modular group. The group of 2×2 matrices over integers with determinant 1 is called the *modular group* and denoted by $SL(2, Z)$, that is,

$$SL(2, Z) = \left\{ \begin{pmatrix} a & b \\ c & d \end{pmatrix} \mid a, b, c, d \in Z \quad ad - bc = 1 \right\}$$

where Z is the set of all integers. This group appears often in the literature of number theory, complex analysis, hyperbolic geometry, discrete group theory, combinatorial group theory and geometric group theory. We refer the reader to [2], [7], [11] and [12] for more details of the results described here. We denote the upper half plane (of Gaussian plane) by $\mathcal{H}$, that is,

$$\mathcal{H} = \{z \in C \mid Im(z) > 0\}$$

where C is the field of all complex numbers. Let M be a matrix in $SL(2, Z)$. A *fractional linear (Möbius) transformation* f_M determined by the matrix M is the mapping of $\mathcal{H}$ into $\mathcal{H}$ given by:
for $z \in C$,

$$f_M(z) = \frac{az + b}{cz + d}$$

where

$$M = \begin{pmatrix} a & b \\ c & d \end{pmatrix}.$$

Since the matrix M is in $SL(2, Z)$, we have $ad - bc = 1$. It is easy to see that for $z \in \mathcal{H}$, we have $f_M(z) \in \mathcal{H}$. A group action of $SL(2, Z)$ on $\mathcal{H}$ is naturally induced as follows:
For M in $SL(2, Z)$ and $z \in \mathcal{H}$ the point obtained from z by acting M is given by:

$$Mz = f_M(z).$$

It is easy to see that this gives a group action of $SL(2, Z)$ on $\mathcal{H}$, that is, for $M, N \in SL(2, Z)$ and $z \in \mathcal{H}$, we have

$$M(Nz) = (MN)z$$

where MN stands for the multiplication of 2×2 matrices M and N in the usual sense and

$$Iz = z$$

where I is the 2×2 identity matrix, that is,

$$I = \begin{pmatrix} 1 & 0 \\ 0 & 1 \end{pmatrix}.$$

The equivalence relation on $\mathcal{H}$ is induced by the group action as follows:
For $z_1, z_2 \in C$, $z_1 \sim z_2$ if there is $M \in SL(2, Z)$ such that $Mz_1 = z_2$. A

fundamental domain S is a simply connected closed subset of $\mathcal{H}$ such that every point in $\mathcal{H}$ is ~equivalent to a point in S but no two distinct points in the interior of S are ~equivalent. We note that two points on the boundary of S may be ~equivalent. The following is an essential result of the action of the modular group.

Proposition 1. *Let $\mathcal{F}$ be the set $\{z \in C \mid |Re(z)| \le 1/2, \, 1 \le |z|\}$ where $Re(z)$ is the real part of z and $|z|$ is the absolute value of z. Then $\mathcal{F}$ is a fundamental domain of the modular group.*

We remark that a proof given in [11] gives us an algorithm to find a matrix that gives ~equivalence between a given point in $\mathcal{H}$ and the corresponding point in the fundamental domain $\mathcal{F}$ as a product of two previously chosen matrices. We give an algorithm to find a sequence of matrices whose product gives the equivalence when looking for the equivalent point in the fundamental domain (algorithm 7.4.2 in [3]).

Algorithm 1

Fisrt of all, let $T = \begin{pmatrix} 1 & 1 \\ 0 & 1 \end{pmatrix}$ and $S = \begin{pmatrix} 0 & -1 \\ 1 & 0 \end{pmatrix}$. We note that for each $z \in \mathcal{H}$, we have

$$Tz = z + 1$$

and

$$Sz = -\frac{1}{z}.$$

Let z be a given point on the upper half plane $\mathcal{H}$. We find a point y in $\mathcal{F}$ and a matrix M in the modular group such that $y = Mz$. Moreover, we find a decomposition of M as a product of a sequence in which powers of T and S appear alternately, that is,

$$M = S^{i_0} T^{j_1} S T^{j_2} \ldots S T^{j_n} S^{i_{n+1}}$$

where i_0 and i_{n+1} may be 0 or 1 and $j_k = \pm 1, \pm 2, \ldots$.

Step 0) Let M be the identity matrix I and let $y = z$. Then go to *Step 1)*.
Step 1) Let r be the integer nearest to $Re(z)$. If there are two possible integers, take one of them. If $|r| > 1$, then let $N = T^{-r}$ and set $M \Leftarrow NM$ and $y \Leftarrow Ny$. Go to *Step 2)*.
Step 2) If $|y| \ge 1$, then return M and y and the algorithm ends. Otherwise we set $M \Leftarrow SM$ and $y \Leftarrow Sy$. Then go to *Step 1)*.

A proof in the literature gurantees that this algorithm stops within finite steps and we eventually obtain a matrix M and the equivalent point y in the fundamental domain such that $M \in \mathrm{SL}(2, Z)$ and $y = Mz$. We record the matrices multiplied in the algorithm and obtain a sequence of matrices T and S so that we can get the point y from the point z by acting the product of the sequence.

We now discuss the modular group from the point of view of combinatorial group theory. In combinatorial group theory one study presentations of groups by generators and relators. Intuitively a group G is *presented by* $Gp(X \mid R)$ if G is the freest group generated by the set X subject to the relators R. We now give a formal definition. Let X be a non-empty set and R a set of words on $X \cup X^{-1}$. A group G is presented by $Gp(X \mid R)$ if G is a quotient of a free group $F(X)$ on the set X by the normal subgroup N generated by the set R, that is, $G = F(X)/N$. For more details of presentations of groups, we refer the reader to the standard text books in combinatorial group theory [2] and [7]. Several constructions of new groups from groups already known are significant in combinatorial group theory. These constructions are often used to solve algorithmic problems in group theory and topology. An amalgamated free product is one of the important constructions. A free product of two groups G_1 and G_2 amalgamating a subgroup H is a group containing both groups G_1 and G_2 such that the intersection of G_1 and G_2 is exactly H in the amalgamated free product. For example, the modular group has an amalgamated free product structure as we see later. We now introduce the formal definition of an amalgamated free product of groups. Let G_1, G_2 be groups. Suppose that H_1, H_2 are subgroups of G_1, G_2, respectively. We also assume that $\phi : H_1 \to H_2$ is an isomorphism. Then the *free product of G_1 and G_2 amalgamating H_1 and H_2* is a group presented by

$$Gp(G_1, G_2 \mid \phi(H_1) = H_2)$$

where this presentation is an abbreviated form of the following presentation

$$Gp(X_1, X_2 \mid R_1, R_2, h^{-1}\phi(h) \; \forall h \in H_1')$$

provided that the groups G_1 and G_2 have the presentations as follows

$$G_1 = Gp(X_1 \mid R_1)$$

and

$$G_2 = Gp(X_2 \mid R_2)$$

where X_1 and X_2 are disjoint and H_1' is a set of generators for H_1. The amalgamated free product is usually denoted by $G_1 *_{H_1=H_2} G_2$.

It is known that $SL(2, Z)$ is generated by matrices

$$S = \begin{pmatrix} 0 & -1 \\ 1 & 0 \end{pmatrix}$$

and

$$T = \begin{pmatrix} 1 & 1 \\ 0 & 1 \end{pmatrix}.$$

We should note that $(ST)^6 = 1 = S^4$ and $(ST)^3 = S^2$ hold in $SL(2, Z)$. As a matter of fact, $SL(2, Z)$ has a presentation

$$Gp(S, T \mid (ST)^6 = 1 = S^4, (ST)^3 = S^2)$$

(see [11] [6]). We should note that there are many other generators satisfying the relations $(ST)^6 = 1 = S^4$ and $(ST)^3 = S^2$. By rewriting ST by A and

S by B, respectively, we can easily check that the modular group has a group presentation

$$Gp(A, B \mid A^6 = B^4 = 1, \ A^3 = B^2).$$

Therefore, $SL(2, Z)$ is generated by an element A of order 6 and an element B of order 4 subject to the relation $A^3 = B^2$. In fact the matrices

$$A_1 = \begin{pmatrix} 0 & -1 \\ 1 & 1 \end{pmatrix}$$

and

$$B_1 = \begin{pmatrix} 0 & -1 \\ 1 & 0 \end{pmatrix}$$

generates $SL(2, Z)$ and satisfy the relations $A_1^6 = B_1^4 = 1$ and $A_1^3 = B_1^2$. This implies that $SL(2, Z)$ is the freest group generated by two matrices A and B subject to the relations $A^6 = B^4 = 1$ and $A^3 = B^2$. We state this fact as a proposition and refer the interested reader to [12] in which the modular group is shown to be an amalgamated free product using the action of the modular group on a tree on the upper half plane.

Proposition 2. *The modular group $SL(2, Z)$ is the free product of Z_6 and Z_4 amalgamating Z_2 where Z_6, Z_4 and Z_2 are cyclic groups of order 6, 4, 2, respectively.*

We show how we can find matrices A and B that generate $SL(2, Z)$ subject to the relations $A^6 = B^4 = 1$ and $A^3 = B^2$

Proposition 3. *For a matrix $M \in SL(2, Z)$, the matrices $A = M^{-1}A_1 M$ and $B = M^{-1}B_1 M$ generate $SL(2, Z)$ and satisfy the relations $A^6 = B^4 = 1$, $A^3 = B^2$*

Proof. It is enough to show that A and B generate the matrices A_1 and B_1. Since A and B generate $SL(2, Z)$, M can be written as a product of A and B. Suppose that $M = C_1 C_2 \ldots C_n$ where C_i is either A or B or their inverses for $i = 1, 2, \ldots n$. Then we have

$$M = M^{-1}MM = M^{-1}C_1 C_2 \ldots C_n M$$

$$= M^{-1}C_1 M M^{-1} C_2 M \ldots M^{-1} C_n M$$

$$= D_1 D_2 \ldots D_n$$

where $D_i = M^{-1}C_i M$ is either A_1 or B_1. Therefore M is written as a product of A_1 and B_1. Then $A = M A_1 M^{-1}$ and $B = M B_1 M^{-1}$ are written as products of A and B and their inverses. It follows that $SL(2, Z)$ is generated by A_1 and B_1.

Proposition 4. *There are infinitely many distinct conjugates of A and B, respectively.*

Proof. Using the action of the modular group on the upper half plane, we can easily see that elements $(AB)^{-i}A(AB)^i$ $(i = 1, 2, \ldots)$ are all distinct. Similarly, we can find infinitely many different conjugates of B.

By the previous two propositions, there are infinitely many choices for the matrices A and B generating $SL(2, Z)$ and subject to the relation $A^6 = B^4 = 1$ and $A^3 = B^2$.

The most important aspect of an amalgamated free product is that every element in the amalgamated free product is expressed uniquely in some way. Let G be the free product of groups G_1 and G_2 amalgamating H_1 and H_2, that is,

$$G = Gp(G_1, G_2 \mid H_1 = H_2).$$

We consider coset decomposition of G_1 by H_1 and G_2 by H_2, respectively. Choose a set of coset representatives for each coset decomposition. Suppose that $\{a_i \mid i \in I\}$ is the set of coset representatives of G_1 by H_1 and that $\{b_j \mid j \in J\}$ is the set of coset representatives of G_2 by H_2. We may assume that the representative of H_1 (resp. H_2) is the identity element of G_1 (resp. G_2). Then we have

$$G_1 = \bigcup_{i \in I} a_i H_1$$

and

$$G_2 = \bigcup_{j \in J} b_j H_2.$$

A non-trivial element g of the group G can be uniquely written as

$$s_{j_1} r_{i_1} s_{j_2} r_{i_2} s_{j_2} \ldots r_{i_n} s_{j_{n+1}}$$

where r_{i_k} is a coset representative of G_1 (for $k = 1, 2, \ldots, n$), s_{j_k} is a coset representatives of G_2 (for $k = 1, 2, \ldots, n$), respectively, or vice versa and $s_{j_{n+1}}$ is in H_1 or H_2 and is not necessarily a coset representative. Then the expression is called the *normal form* of the element g if $s_{j_k} \neq 1$ $(k \leq n)$ and $r_{i_l} \neq 1$ $(l \leq n)$. The basic result on normal forms in amalgamated free products is the following:

Proposition 5. *Every nontrivial element of the free product of G_1 and G_2 amalgamating H_1 and H_2 can be written uniquely as a normal form, that is, if a nontrivial element g in the amalgamated free product of G_1 and G_2 have two normal forms*

$$s_{j_1} r_{i_1} s_{j_2} r_{i_2} s_{j_3} \ldots r_{i_n} s_{j_{n+1}}$$

and

$$s_{p_1} r_{q_1} s_{p_2} r_{q_2} s_{p_3} \ldots r_{p_m} s_{q_{m+1}},$$

then we have

$$n = m,$$

$$s_{j_k} = s_{p_k}$$

and

$$r_{i_l} = r_{p_l}.$$

For the proof we refer the reader to [2] or [7]. An easy consequence of Proposition 5 is that both G_1 and G_2 are embedded into the amalgamated free product $G_1 *_{H_1=H_2} G_2$, and hence, G_1 and G_2 can be identified as subgroups of $G_1 *_{H_1=H_2} G_2$. Now suppose that a group G is a free product of finite groups G_1 and G_2 amalgamating a subgroup H. We note that the modular group is an amalgamated free group of finite groups. We may regard H as a common subgroup of G_1 and G_2. We choose sets of coset representatives of G_1 and G_2 by H, respectively. Then there is an algorithm that finds the normal form of an element of G once it is written as a product of elements of G_1 and G_2. First of all, we choose the sets of coset representatives of H in G_1 and H in G_2. Then we can find a unique expression of each element of G_1 (resp. G_2) as a product of a representative and an element of H since G_1 is finite (resp. G_2). An input of the algorithm is a product of elements from the groups G_1 and G_2 and an output is the normal form of the input.

Let X be a non-trivial element of G. Suppose that $X = U_1 U_2 \dots U_n$ is a product of alternate elements from G_1 and G_2, that is, if $U_i \in G_1$ then $U_{i+1} \in G_2$ and vice versa. Then we give an algorithm that finds the normal form

$$Q_1 Q_2 \dots Q_m$$

of X.

Algorithm 2

Step 0) We note that $U_1 \in G_1$ or G_2. We may assume that $U_1 \in G_1$ without loss of generality. Then we have $U_1 = Q_1 V_1$ where Q_1 is a representative of H in G_1 and $V_1 \in H$. Hence we have

$$X = Q_1 V_1 U_2 U_3 \dots U_n.$$

Step 1) We suppose that

$$X = Q_1 Q_2 \dots Q_s V_s U_t U_{t+1} \dots U_n$$

where $V_s \in H$ and Q_i is an representative of G_1 or G_2 for $i = 1, 2, \dots s$ such that if $Q_i \in G_1$ then $Q_{i+1} \in G_2$ and vice versa. It is also satisfied that if $Q_s \in G_1$ (or G_2) then $U_t \in G_2$ (or G_1). If there is no U_j in the sequence, then we get a normal form

$$X = Q_1 Q_2 \dots Q_s V_s$$

and so the procedure ends. Now we may assume that Q_s is a representative of G_1. Then U_t is in G_2 and we can write $V_s U_t = Q_{s+1} V_{s+1}$ where Q_{s+1} is a representative of G_2 and $V_{s+1} \in H$. We replace $v_s U_t$ by $Q_{s+1} V_{s+1}$ in the sequence. Then go to *Step 2)*.

Step 2)

Case 1) If $Q_{s+1} \neq 1$, then we have

$$X = Q_1 Q_2 \dots Q_s Q_{s+1} V_{s+1} U_{t+1} \dots U_n.$$

Then continue to *Step 1)*.
Case 2) If $Q_{s+1} = 1$, then we have $Q_s V_{s+1} U_{t+1} \in G_1$ since $Q_s, U_{t+1} \in G_1$ and $V_{s+1} \in H \subset G_1$. Then we have

$$Q_s V_{s+1} U_{t+1} = Q_s' V_s'$$

where Q_s' is a representative of G_1 and $V_s' \in H$. Then set $Q_s \Leftarrow Q_s'$ and $V_s \Leftarrow V_s'$. Then we have

$$X = Q_1 Q_2 \ldots Q_s V_s U_{t+2} \ldots U_n.$$

Then continue to *Step 1)*.
Since the given element is written as a product of length m, the procedure ends within $2m$ steps and we obtain the normal form for the given element.

3 A public-key cryptosystem using the modular group

Let A and B be generators of $SL(2, Z)$ subject to $A^6 = B^4 = 1$ and $A^3 = B^2$. We have seen that there are infinitely many choices for A and B. We choose words V_1 and V_2 on letters A and B such that V_1 and V_2 generates a free subsemigroup of $SL(2, Z)$, that is, if two words X_1 and X_2 on letters V_1 and V_2 are equal as elements of $SL(2, Z)$, then X_1 and X_2 are identical as words on letters V_1 and V_2. We also require that V_1 and V_2 have the property that any concatenation of words V_1 and V_2 is a normal form for relative to the generators A and B. In particular, V_1 and V_2 are in the normal form. It is easy to find such a pair of matrices in general using the combinatorics on words. For example, suppose that A and B are matrices generating $SL(2, Z)$ and satisfying the relations $A^6 = B^4 = 1$ and $A^3 = B^2$. Then the matrices $(BA)^i$ and $(BA^2)^j$ form a free subsemigroup of $SL(2, Z)$ for all positive integers i and j and satisfy the requirement. Let $C[x]$ be the polynomial ring over the field C of complex numbers and $M_2(C[x])$ be the ring of all 2×2 matrices over $C[x]$. We now choose a pair of matrices $F_1(x)$ and $F_2(x)$ from $M_2(C[x])$ such that $F_1(a) = V_1$ and $F_2(a) = V_2$ for some $a \in C$ where $F(a)$ is obtained from $F(x)$ by substituting a in x. It is clear that a substitution is a homomorphism of $M_2(C[x])$ to $M_2(C)$. The restriction of the homomorphism to the subsemigroup generated by $F_1(x)$ and $F_2(x)$ is a semigroup isomorphism since the subsemigroup generated by V_1 and V_2 in $SL(2, Z)$ is free. Now we choose a matrix M arbitrarily from $GL(2, C)$. Let $W_1(x) = M^{-1} F_1(x) M$ and $W_2(x) = M^{-1} F_2(x) M$. It is clear that a subsemigroup S of $M_2(C[x])$ generated by $W_1(x)$ and $W_2(x)$ is free and $W_1(x)$ and $W_2(x)$ form a set of free generators of S. The mapping Φ of S into $SL(2, Z)$ defined by

$$\Phi(G_1(x)) = M G_1(a) M^{-1}$$

is an injective homomorphism. We now describe our public-key cryptosystem.

Public keys:

The public keys are the matrices $W_1(x)$ and $W_2(x)$.

Secret keys:

The secret key is the homomorphism Φ, or equivalently, the pair of (M, a) of the matrix M and the complex number a.

Encryption method:

Suppose that the plaintext is the sequence

$$i_1 i_2 \ldots i_n$$

where $i_j \in \{1, 2\}$. Then the sequence is encrypted as follows:

Compute the matrix

$$W_2(x) W_1^{i_1}(x) W_2(x) W_1^{i_2}(x) W_2(x) \ldots W_2(x) W_1^{i_n}(x) W_2(x)$$

and then call this matrix $E(x)$. The matrix $E(x)$ over $C[x]$ is the encrypted text.

Decryption method:

Since
$$E(x) =$$
$$M^{-1} F_2(x) M (M^{-1} F_1(x) M)^{i_1} M^{-1} F_2(x) M \ldots (M^{-1} F_1(x) M)^{i_n} M^{-1} F_2(x) M$$
$$= M^{-1} F_2(x) F_1^{i_1}(x) F_2(x) F_1^{i_2}(x) F_2(x) \ldots F_2(x) F_1^{i_n}(x) F_2(x) M,$$

we have
$$\Phi(E(x)) = M E(a) M^{-1} =$$
$$M M^{-1} F_2(a) F_1^{i_1}(a) F_2(a) F_1^{i_2}(a) F_2(a) \ldots F_2(a) F_1^{i_n}(a) F_2(a) M M^{-1} =$$
$$F_2(a) F_1^{i_1}(a) F_2(a) F_1^{i_2}(a) F_2(a) \ldots F_2(a) F_1^{i_n}(a) F_2(a) =$$
$$V_2 V_1^{i_1} V_2 V_1^{i_2} V_2 \ldots V_2 V_1^{i_n} V_2.$$

We note that V_1 and V_2 are free generators for a free subsemigroup of $SL(2, Z)$. We also note that the sequence $V_2 V_1^{i_1} V_2 V_1^{i_2} V_2 \ldots V_2 V_1^{i_n} V_2$ is of the normal form by our requirement. Using Algorithm 1 and Algorithm 2 the legal receiver can obtain the original message $i_1 i_2 \ldots i_n$ as follows. Let $N = \Phi(E(x))$. Let p be the point $2i$ on the upper half plane $\mathcal{H}$ (or any other point in the interior of $\mathcal{F}$). Let $q = Np$. Using Algorithm 1 we can find effectively the matrix decomposition of N as a product of the matrices S and T since $M_1 p = M_2 p$ for $M_1, M_2 \in SL(2, Z)$ implies $M_1 = M_2$ up to $\pm I$ (as an element M of the modular group such that $M \neq \pm I$ does not fix a point in the interior of $\mathcal{F}$). Since A and B are generators of the modular group and that $A^{-1} = A^5$, $B^{-1} = B^3$, S and T can be written as a product of A's and B's. Then using Algorithm 2 we can find a normal form of the matrix N relative to A and B. On the other hand, by our requirement on V_1 and V_2, the normall form must be of the form $V_2 V_1^{i_1} V_2 V_1^{i_2} V_2 \ldots V_2 V_1^{i_n} V_2$. Therefore, the encrypted text $E(x)$ can be decrypted within linear time.

4 Security issues

To break the system using Algorithm 1 and Algorithm2 it seems necessary to find an injective homomorphism of the subsemigroup of $M_2(C[x])$ generated by $W_1(x)$ and $W_2(x)$ into the modular group. The trapdoor Φ is one of such homomorphisms. To find Φ it is necessary to find a complex number a' and a matrix $M' \in GL(2,C)$ such that the matrices

$$M'W_1(a')M'^{-1}$$

and

$$M'W_2(a')M'^{-1}$$

are free generators for a free subsemigroup of $SL(2,Z)$. A complex number a' and a matrix M' may be found so that $M'W_1(a')M'^{-1}$ and $M'W_2(a')M'^{-1}$ are in $SL(2,Z)$, however it is not always guaranteed that these matrices are free generators for a free subsemigroup of $SL(2,Z)$. Moreover, these may not satisfy the condition that all products of $M'W_1(a')M'^{-1}$ and $M'W_2(a')M'^{-1}$ are of the normal form of some generators of the modular group. For instance, let us see the following example. Let

$$V_1 = \begin{pmatrix} -1 & 0 \\ 1 & -1 \end{pmatrix}$$

and

$$V_2 = \begin{pmatrix} -1 & 1 \\ 0 & -1 \end{pmatrix}.$$

Then it is clear that V_1 and V_2 are free generators for a free subsemigroup for $SL(2,Z)$ since $V_1 = A_1 B_1$ and $V_2 = A_1^2 B_1$ where

$$A_1 = \begin{pmatrix} 0 & -1 \\ 1 & 1 \end{pmatrix}$$

and

$$B_1 = \begin{pmatrix} 0 & -1 \\ 1 & 0 \end{pmatrix}$$

that are generators for $SL(2,Z)$ satisfying the relations $A_1^6 = B_1^4 = 1$ and $A_1^3 = B_1^2$. Now we define matrices $F_1(x)$ and $F_2(x)$ over $C[x]$ by

$$F_1(x) = \begin{pmatrix} -1 & (x-\sqrt{3})(x-2\sqrt{3}) \\ \frac{1}{3}(x-\sqrt{3})^2 & -1 \end{pmatrix}$$

and

$$F_2(x) = \begin{pmatrix} -1 & \frac{1}{3}(x-\sqrt{3})^2 \\ (x-\sqrt{3})(x-2\sqrt{3}) & -1 \end{pmatrix}.$$

Then we have

$$F_1(\sqrt{3}) = \begin{pmatrix} -1 & 0 \\ 0 & -1 \end{pmatrix}$$

and

$$F_2(\sqrt{3}) = \begin{pmatrix} -1 & 0 \\ 0 & -1 \end{pmatrix}$$

and so we have $F_1(\sqrt{3}) = F_2(\sqrt{3})$. On the other hand, we have

$$F_1(2\sqrt{3}) = \begin{pmatrix} -1 & 0 \\ 1 & -1 \end{pmatrix} = V_1$$

and

$$F_2(2\sqrt{3}) = \begin{pmatrix} -1 & 1 \\ 0 & -1 \end{pmatrix} = V_2.$$

Therefore, for $a = 2\sqrt{3}$ we get a set of free generators satisfying our requirement, however, for $a' = \sqrt{3}$ we do not get a set of free generators. It is clear that there are many ways to choose such a pair of matrices in $M_2(C[x])$. We even do not know an efficient algorithm that decides for a given pair of matrices U and V in $\mathrm{SL}(2, Z)$ whether U and V are free semigroup generators or not. Therefore, it does not seem easy to verify that the two obtained matrices are free generators.

To break the system, we may want to find a solution a for the system of equations

$$|W_1(x)| = 1$$

and

$$|W_2(x)| = 1$$

and then find a matrix M such that $M^{-1}W_1(a)M$, $M^{-1}W_2(a)M \in \mathrm{SL}(2, Z)$. We note that these two equations may have different solutions. Let

$$F_1(x) = \begin{pmatrix} (x+\sqrt{3})(x-\sqrt{3})(x-2\sqrt{3}) - 1 & (x+\sqrt{3})(x-\sqrt{3})(x-2\sqrt{3}) \\ \frac{1}{3}(x-\sqrt{3})^2 & -1 \end{pmatrix}$$

and

$$F_2(x) = \begin{pmatrix} (x+2\sqrt{3})(x-\sqrt{3})(x-2\sqrt{3}) - 1 & \frac{1}{3}(x+2\sqrt{3})(x-\sqrt{3})^2 \\ (x-\sqrt{3})(x-2\sqrt{3}) & -1 \end{pmatrix}.$$

Let

$$M = \begin{pmatrix} 1 & 0 \\ 0 & 1 \end{pmatrix}.$$

Then the first equation $|W_1(x)| = 1$ has real solutions $\pm\sqrt{3}, 2\sqrt{3}$ with the other two non-real solutions. The second equation $|W_2(x)| = 1$ has solutions $\sqrt{3}, \pm2\sqrt{3}$ with other two non-real solutions. We note that $F_1(2\sqrt{3}) = V_1$ and $F_2(2\sqrt{3}) = V_2$. Therefore, solutions of the first equation does not necessarily coincide with the ones of the second.

We then need to verify that these two matrices generate freely a free sub-semigroup of $\mathrm{SL}(2, Z)$ satisfying the condition we require. Hence, we also need an algorithm that decides whether or not given two matrices generate freely a free subsemigroup of $\mathrm{SL}(2, Z)$. Therefore, to break the system we must solve three problems, that is, solving a system of equations of possibly high degree, the conjugacy problem and the problem of deciding whether or no two given matrices in $SL(2, Z)$ freely generate a free subsemigroup. The degrees of the equations can be large and so there may be many solutions for the system of equations. It is impossible to give a general formula for an equation of degree 5 using field operations and radicals (Galois theory), although there is a formula using the theta function. Solving an equation of higher degree is harder and there is no theoretical or algorithmical solution as far as the author knows. Numerical methods are not taken into consideration here. The conjugacy problem and the decision problem concerning free generators do not seem easy although the author does not know how hard (or easy) the problems are. It seems inevitable to investigate algorithms and its complexity of these specific problems in algebra to develop cryptosystems using combinatorial group theory. Actually the study of such algorithms is interesting in its own right. We may use $M_2(C[x_1, x_2, \ldots, x_n])$ instead of $M_2(C[x])$ to make eavesdroppers difficult to find the trapdoor or its alternative, that is, the injective homomorphism Φ of a free subsemigroup of $M_2(C[x_1, x_2, \ldots, x_n])$ into $SL(2, Z)$.

There is another issue on security. We need to be concerned about the possibility of decomposing the matrix $E(x)$ by the matrices $W_1(x)$ and $W_2(x)$. We note that $W_1(x)$ and $W_2(x)$ form a set of free subsemigroup generators in $M_2(C[x])$ because the images of these two matrices under the isomorphism Φ form a set of free semigroup generators in $SL(2, Z)$. The legal receiver use the homomorphism Φ of S into $SL(2, Z)$ to decrypt the message. On the other hand, the author does not know any efficient algorithm that decomposes a matrix in $M_2(C[x])$ by given two matrices $W_1(x)$ and $W_2(x)$, although there always exist a non-deterministic polynomial time algorithm, that is, we first guesse a possible product of matrices $W_1(x)$ and $W_2(x)$ and then check that it is actually equal to the given matrix. We must not deny the possibility of an effective algorithm. Algorithm 1 is very efficient because it depends on $SL(2, Z)$ action on the upper half plane and employ a geometrical method. On the other hand, we do not have enough geometrical interpretation of the group $M_2(C[x_1, x_2, \ldots, x_n])$ and its action on a certain geometrical space that gives us an effective matrix decomposition algorithm.

5 Remarks

The main purpose of this stusy is to examine possible applications of combinatorial group theory to cryptography. Therefore, we focus on theoretical scheme of a cryptosystem and pay no attention to issues of practicality or implementability of the system. We consider the ring $M_2(C[x])$ of 2×2 matrices over the ring $C[x]$ of polynomials over the complex numbers. This makes difficult to implement the system on real computers, because the field of the complex numbers can not be realized on computers. Hence, the system proposed in this paper is not practical. However, if we consider a subfield of the field C which is s finite dimensional extenstion of the field Q of the rational numbers, it is possible to realize the system on computers to some extent. Another way to overcome this defect is to employ numerical analysis methods. We do not go further into this issue here.

There are researches on hash functions using $SL(2, F_q)$ ([1], [13], [15]). In their study they used the Cayley graph of $SL(2, F_q)$. The groups $SL(2, F_q)$ are finite and so their Cayley graphs are necessarily finite while $SL(2, Z)$ is an infinite group. It might be interesting to investigate the relationship between these two approaches using group theory. Graphical methods in group theory give us tremendous information of structures of groups. It is well known that an amalgamated free product of groups acts on a tree which is graph isomorphic to the universal cover of the graph of groups associated to the amalgamated free product structure of the group. In the case of $SL(2, Z)$ which is an amalgamated free product of finite cyclic groups, the corresponding tree consists of the points on the upper half plane $\mathcal{H}$ whose function images under the modular j-function are in the interval $[0, 1728]$. Using the action of the modular group on this tree we can unify Algorithm 1 and Algorithm 2 to an efficient algorithm that gives a normal form of an element giving equivalence for a given point on the upper half plane. The study of groups acting on trees was initiated by Serre in collaboration with Bass ([2], [12]). It has been giving strong impacts on combinatorial and geometrical group theory. We would like to consider applications of such a powerful tool in mathematics to cryptography and like to expect further research using ideas in combinatorial and geometrical group theory toward building cryptosystems as we propose a cryptosystem using the modular group.

Salomaa and several other authors investigated functional cryptosystems using grammar theoretical notions ([4], [5], [8], [9], [10]). It may be plausible to construct a functional cryptosystem using techniques from combinatorial group theory. We also note that there is a research on a possible application of word problem of a group ([14]). The word problem is one of the most important decision problems in combinatorial group theory and studied by many researchers with fruitful outcomes. It is also interesting to consider applications of algorithmic problems like the word problem of groups to cryptography.

6 Acknowledgements

The author would like to express his deep gratitude to Professor S.Tsujii for valuable advice, guidance and support and to Professor K.Kurosawa for inviting him to research of cryptography. He also wants to thank the members of the information security project at Telecommunications Advancement Organizations of Japan for their helpful comments on this research.

References

1. C.Charpes and J Pieprzyk, Attacking the SL2 hashing scheme, Proc. Asiacrypt'94 LNCS 917 (1995) 322-330
2. D.E.Cohen, *Combinatorial Group Theory: A Topological Approach*, (Cambridge University Press, Cambridge) (1989)

3. H.Cohen, *A Course in Computational Algebraic Number Theory*, Springer, New York, (1996)
4. J.Kari, A cryptoanalytic observation concerning systems based on language theory, Discr. Appl. Math. 21 (1988) 265-268
5. J.Kari, Observations concerning a public-key cryptosysytem based on iterated morphisms, Theor. Compt. Sci. 66 (1989) 45-53
6. N.Koblitz, *Introduction to Elliptic Curves and Modular Forms*, Springer, New York (1991)
7. R.C.Lyndon and P.E.Schupp, *Combinatorial Group Theory*, Springer, New York, (1976)
8. A.Salomaa, A public-key cryrptosystem based on language theory, Computers and Security, 7 (1988) 83-87
9. A.Salomaa, *Public-Key Cryptography*, Springer, Berlin, (1990)
10. A.Salomaa and S.Yu, On a public-key cryptosystem based on iterated morphisms and substitutions, Theor. Compt. Sci. 48 (1986) 283-296
11. J-P.Serre, *A Course in Arithmetic*, Springer, New York (1973)
12. J-P.Serre, *Trees*, Springer, New York (1980)
13. J-P.Tillich and G.Zémor, Hashing with SL2, Proc. Crypto'94, LNCS 839 (1994) 40-49
14. N.R.Wagner and M.R.Magyarik, A public-key cryptosystems based on the word problem, In Lecture Notes in Computer Science, 196 (1985) 19-37
15. G.Zémor, Hash functions and Cayley graphs, Designs, Codes and Cryptography 4 (1994) 381-394

A Cellular Automaton Based Fast One-Way Hash Function Suitable for Hardware Implementation

Miodrag Mihaljević[1,3], Yuliang Zheng[2] and Hideki Imai[3]

[1] Academy of Science and Arts, Kneza Mihaila 35, Belgrade Yugoslavia
Email: emihalje@ubbg.etf.bg.ac.yu
[2] Monash University, McMahons Road, Frankston, Melburne, VIC 3199, Australia
Email: yzheng@fcit.monash.edu.au
[3] The University of Tokyo, 7-22-1 Roppongi, Minato-ku, Tokyo 106, Japan,
Email: imai@iis.u-tokyo.ac.jp

Abstract. One-way hash functions are an important tool in achieving authentication and data integrity. The aim of this paper is to propose a novel one-way hash function based on cellular automata whose cryptographic properties have been extensively studied over the past decade or so. Furthermore, security of the proposed one-way hash function is analyzed by the use of very recently published results on applications of cellular automata in cryptography. The analysis indicates that the one-way hash function is secure against all known attacks. An important feature of the proposed one-way hash function is that it is especially suitable for compact and fast implementation in hardware, which is particularly attractive to emerging security applications that employ smart cards, such as digital identification cards and electronic cash payment protocols,

1 Introduction

Cryptographic hash functions play an important role in modern cryptography. The basic idea of cryptographic hash functions is that a hash-value serves as a compact representative image (sometimes called an imprint, digital fingerprint, or message digest) of an input string, and can be used as if it were uniquely identifiable with that string.

Following [1], at the highest level, cryptographic hash functions may be classified into two classes: hash functions, whose specification dictates a single input parameter - a message (unkeyed hash functions); and keyed hash functions, whose specification dictates two distinct inputs - a message and a secret key. This paper is concerned with unkeyed hash functions which are also called one-way hash functions.

A typical usage of one-way hash functions for data integrity is as follows. The hash-value corresponding to a particular message M is computed at time t_1. The integrity of this hash-value (but not the message itself) is protected in some manner. At a subsequent time t_2, the following test is carried out to determine whether the message has been altered, i.e., whether a message M' is the same as the original message. The hash-value of M' is computed and compared to the protected hash-value; if they are identical, one accepts that the inputs are also equal, and thus that the message has not been altered. The problem of preserving the integrity of a potentially large message is thus reduced to that of a small fixed-size hash-value. Since the existence of collisions is guaranteed in many-to-one mappings, the unique association between the inputs and hash-values can, at best, be in a computational sense. A hash-value should be uniquely identifiable with a single input in practice, and collisions should be computationally infeasible to find (essentially never occurring in practice).

In this paper, a novel and fast one-way hash function is proposed and analyzed. The proposed one-way hash function is based on a quite different approach than these employed in other one-way hash functions in that it is based on programmable cellular automata. Advantages of one-way hash functions that employ cellular automata include: it is fast and suitable for hardware implementation, and its security can be analyzed by borrowing some of the well-established research results in cellular automaton theory.

In Sections 2 - 4 relevant background about one-way hash functions and cellular automata is summarized. In Section 5 the novel one-way hash function is proposed. Its security together with efficiency is analyzed in Section 6. Some concluding remarks are made in Section 7.

2 One-Way Hash Functions

A hash function (in the unrestricted sense) is a function $hash(\cdot)$ which has, as minimum the following two properties (see [1], for example):

- *compression* - $hash$ maps an input M of arbitrary finite bit-length, to an output $hash(M)$ of a fixed bit-length n.
- *ease of computation* - given $hash(\cdot)$ and an input M, $hash(M)$ is easy to compute.

In addition, for a one-way hash function $hash(\cdot)$ with inputs M, M' and outputs Z, Z', the following three properties are expected to hold (see [1], for example):

1. *preimage resistance* - for essentially all pre-specified outputs, it is computationally infeasible to find any input which hashes to the output, i.e., to find any preimage M' such that $hash(M') = Z$ when given any Z for which a corresponding input is not known.
2. *2nd-preimage resistance* - it is computationally infeasible to find any second input which has the same output as any specified input, i.e., given M, to find a 2nd-preimage $M' \neq M$ such that $hash(M) = hash(M')$.
3. *collision resistance* - it is computationally infeasible to find two distinct inputs M and M' which hash to the same output, i.e., such that $hash(M) = hash(M')$.

Note that the following relationships between the three properties of a one-way hash function hold:

- 2nd-preimage resistance implies preimage resistance.
- Collision resistance implies both 2nd-preimage resistance and preimage resistance.

2.1 General Model for Iterated Hash Functions

Most one-way hash functions $hash(\cdot)$ are designed as iterative processes which hash arbitrary-length inputs by processing successive fixed-size blocks of the input (see [1], for example). A hash input M of arbitrary finite length is divided into fixed-length ℓ-bit blocks M_i. This preprocessing typically involves appending extra bits (padding) as necessary to attain an overall bit-length which is a multiple m of the block-length ℓ and often includes (for security reasons, see [3] and [4]) a block indicating the bit-length of the unpadded input. Each block M_i then serves as input to an internal fixed-size function h, the *compression function* of $hash$, which computes a new intermediate result of bit-length n for some fixed n, as a function of the previous n-bit intermediate results and the next input block M_i. Let H_i denote the partial result after Stage i Then the general process for an iterated one-way hash function with inputs $M = (M_1, M_2, ..., M_m)$ can be modeled as follows:

$$H_0 = IV \ ,$$
$$H_i = h(H_{i-1}, M_i) \ , \quad 1 \leq i \leq m \ ,$$
$$hash(M) = g(H_m) \ . \tag{1}$$

H_{i-1} serves as the n-bit *chaining variable* between Stage $i-1$ and Stage i, and H_0 is a pre-defined starting value or initial value IV. An optional transformation g is used in a final step to map the n-bit chaining variable to an n'-bit result $g(H_m)$; g is often the identity mapping $g(H_m) = H_m$.

Specific one-way hash functions proposed in the literature differ from one another in preprocessing, compression function, and output transformation.

2.2 Dedicated One-Way Hash Functions

¿From a structural viewpoint, one-way hash functions may be categorized based on the nature of the operations comprising their internal compression functions. From this viewpoint, the three broadest categories of iterated one-way hash functions studied to date are:
- one-way hash functions based on block ciphers,
- one-way hash functions based on modular arithmetic, and
- dedicated one-way hash functions.

Dedicated one-way hash functions are those designed specifically for hashing, with speed in mind and independent of other system subcomponents (e.g., block cipher or modular multiplication subcomponents which may already be present for non-hashing purposes).

The following one-way hash functions, all based on the so called MD4 initially proposed in [11] have received the greatest attention:
- MD5, [12],
- SHA-1, [13],
- RIPEMD-160, [14],
- HAVAL, [15] .

A quite different class of dedicated hash functions based on a particular linear finite state machines - cellular automata have been reported in [4], [16] and [17].

The one-way hash function to be proposed below belongs to the class of dedicated one-way hash functions, it is a development of the cellular automata approach, and it is suitable for hardware implementation.

2.3 Security of the One-Way Hash Function

Given a specific one-way hash function, it is desirable to be able to prove a lower bound on the complexity of attacking it under specified scenarios, with as few and weak assumptions as possible. However, such results are scarce. Typically, the best guidance available regarding the security of a particular one-way hash function is the complexity of the (most efficient) applicable known attack, which gives an upper bound on security. An attack of complexity 2^n is one which requires approximately 2^n operations, each being an appropriate unit of work. The storage complexity of an attack should also be considered.

Assuming that the hash-code approximates a uniform random variable it is well known that the following holds:

- For an n-bit hash function h, one may expect a guessing attack to find a preimage or second preimage within 2^n hashing operations.
- For an adversary able to choose messages, a birthday attack, [2], allows colliding pairs of messages M, M' with $hash(M) = hash(M')$ to be found in about $2^{n/2}$ operations and a reasonable amount of memory.

An n-bit one-way hash function $hash(\cdot)$ has *ideal security* if both: (a) given a hash output, producing each of a preimage and a 2nd-preimage requires approximately 2^n operations; and (b) producing a collision requires approximately $2^{n/2}$ operations.

Following [3] and [4] denote by *MD-strengthening* appending an additional block at the end of of the input string containing its length.

Based on [3], [4], [5], [6], [7], [8], in a number of models, it is possible to relate the security of $hash(\cdot)$ to the security of h and g according to the following result:

Theorem 1. (cf. [8]) Let $hash(\cdot)$ be an iterated hash function with MD-strengthening. Then preimage and collision attacks on $hash(\cdot)$ (where an attacker can choose IV freely) have roughly the same complexity as the corresponding attacks on h and g.

Theorem 1 gives a lower bound on the security of $hash(\cdot)$.

According to [10] and [8] the iterated hash functions based on the Davis-Mayer compression function given by the following

$$h(M_i, H_{i-1}) = E_{M_i}(H_{i-1}) \oplus H_{i-1} , \tag{2}$$

where $E_K(\cdot)$ is a block cipher controlled by the key K, are believed to be as secure as the underlying cipher $E_K(\cdot)$ is.

As a direct extension of the results of security related to cipher block chaining [9], and the assumption 1 from [8] (which is a standard one in cryptography today), we assume the following.

Assumption 1. Let the compression function h be the Davis-Meyer function (2) and the employed cryptographic transformation is a secure one. Then finding collisions for h requires about $2^{n/2}$ encryption (of an n-bit block), and finding a preimage for h requires about 2^n encryption.

The above discussions imply that the main problem in the design of a secure one-way hash function can be reduced to the design of a secure compression function and a good output function.

3 Cellular Automata

A one-dimensional binary cellular automaton (CA) consists of a linearly connected array of L cells, each of which takes the value 0 or 1, and a Boolean function $f(\mathbf{x})$ with q variables. The value of the cell x_i is updated in parallel (synchronously) using this function in discrete time steps as $x_i' = f(\mathbf{x})$ for $i = 1, 2, ..., L$. The boundary conditions are usually handled by taking the index value modulo L. The parameter q is usually an odd integer, i.e., $q = 2r + 1$, where r is often named the radius of the function $f(\mathbf{x})$; the new value of the ith cell is calculated using the value of the ith cell and the values of r neighboring cells to the right and left of the ith cell.

Since there are L cells, each of which takes the values of 0 or 1, there are 2^L possible state vectors. Let $\mathbf{S}_k$ denote the state vector at the time step k. Starting from an initial state vector $\mathbf{S}_0$, the cellular automaton moves to the states $\mathbf{S}_1$, $\mathbf{S}_2$, $\mathbf{S}_3$ etc., at time steps $k = 1, 2, 3, ...$ etc. The state vector $\mathbf{S}_k$ takes values from the set of L-bit binary vectors as k advances, and the state machine will eventually cycle, i.e., it will reach a state $\mathbf{S}_{k+P}$ which was visited earlier $\mathbf{S}_k = \mathbf{S}_{k+P}$. The period P is a function of the initial state, the updating function, and the number of cells.

For a CA with $q = 3$, the evolution of of the ith cell in each discrete time step t (clock cycle) can be represented as a function of the present state of the $(i - 1)$th, (i)th, and $(i + 1)$th cells as

$$x_i(t + 1) = f\{x_{i-1}(t), x_i(t), x_{i+1}(t)\} . \tag{3}$$

f is also called the combinatorial logic associated with the CA. Each combinatorial logic represents an updating rule for evolving to the next state.

If the next state function of a cell is expressed in the form of a truth table, then the decimal equivalent of the output column in the truth table is conventionally called a CA rule number. A nonlinear rule, called Rule 30, proposed and considered by Wolfram in [18], realizes updating according to the following:

$$x_i(t+1) = x_{i-1}(t) \ XOR \ [x_i(t) \ OR \ x_{i+1}(t)] \ . \tag{4}$$

Of particular interest are two linear rules in GF(2). These are known as Rule 90 and Rule 150 respectively. Rule 90 specifies an evolution (updating) from current to the next state according the following combinatorial logic:

$$x_i(t+1) = x_{i-1}(t) \oplus x_{i+1}(t) \tag{5}$$

where $\oplus$ denotes XOR operation. Note that when Rule 90 is applied the next state of the ith cell depends on the present state of its left and right neighbors. Similarly, the combinational logic for Rule 150 is given by

$$x_i(t+1) = x_{i-1}(t) \oplus x_i(t) \oplus x_{i+1}(t) \ , \tag{6}$$

that is, the next state of the ith cell depends on the present states of its left and right neighbors and also on its own present state.

If in a CA the same rule applies to all cells, then the CA is called a uniform CA; otherwise it is called a hybrid CA. There can be various boundary conditions; namely, null (where extreme cells are connected to logic "0"), periodic (extreme cells are adjacent), etc.

3.1 Additive Cellular Automata

A very important class of CA are linear CA in GF(2) or additive CA. If the next-state generating logic employs only XOR or $XNOR$ operations, then the CA is said to be an *additive* CA. Linear CA is a special form of *Linear Finite State Machines* (LFSM's). Every LFSM is uniquely represented by a transition matrix over GF(2), and every transition matrix has a characteristic polynomial.

For an L-cell one-dimensional additive CA with XOR operations only, it has been shown in [19] that the CA can be characterized by a linear operator denoted by $\mathbf{T}$ which is an $L \times L$ Boolean matrix and whose ith row specifies the neighborhood dependency of the ith cell. The next state of CA is generated by applying this linear operator on the present CA state represented as a column vector. The operation is the normal matrix multiplication, but the addition involved is modulo-2 sum. If $\mathbf{x}(t)$ is a column vector representing the state of the automaton at the tth instant of time, then the next state of the automaton is given by:

$$\mathbf{x}(t+1) = \mathbf{T} \times \mathbf{x}(t) \ . \tag{7}$$

If the characteristic polynomial of a CA is primitive, then it is referred to as a maximal length CA. Such an L cell CA generates all $2^L - 1$ states in successive cycles excluding the all zero state.

Since, for a fixed order L, there are 2^{L^2} transition matrices (and hence 2^{L^2} LFSM's) but only 2^L degree L polynomials, we have the following situation: There is a one-to-one correspondence between L-cell LFSM and $L \times L$ matrices, and at the same time a many-to-one correspondence between the transition matrices and the polynomials of degree L.

The characteristic polynomial of an LFSM is never difficult to obtain, as it can be calculated by evaluating a determinant. On the other hand, finding a particular type of LFSM (such as a CA) with a specific characteristic polynomial is a problem solved in [20] where a method is presented for obtaining a CA that has a given characteristic polynomial. The same method can also be used to solve the problem as to whether a CA exists for each irreducible polynomial.

A systematic treatment of the additive CA theory and applications is presented in a recent book [22], as well as in [21].

3.2 Programmable Cellular Automata

Positional representations of Rule 90 and Rule 150 show that their neighborhood dependence differ in only one position, viz., on the cell itself. Therefore, by allowing a single control line per cell, one can apply both Rule 90 and Rule 150 on the same cell at different time steps. Thereby, an L cell CA structure can be used for implementing 2^L CA configurations. Realizing different CA configurations (cell updating rules) on the same structure can be achieved using a control logic to control the appropriate switches and a control program, stored in ROM, can be employed to activate the control. The 1(0) state of the ith bit of a ROM word closes (opens) the switch that controls the ith cell. Such a structure is referred as to as a *programmable cellular automaton* (PCA).

Accordingly, allowing one control input per cell that configures the updating rule, we can apply to that cell, either Rule 90 or Rule 150. The n-bits control word for an n cells PCA has 0(1) on the ith cell if Rule 90(150) is applied to the ith cell.

4 Cryptographic Applications of Cellular Automata

Cellular automata have been considered as a building block for the design of both block and stream ciphers, as well as for design of certain hash functions. The first cryptographic application of a cellular automaton was given in [18]. A block and a stream cipher based on cellular automata were proposed in [23]. Two PCA based key stream generators, called PCA with ROM (Read Only Memory) and Two Stage PCA respectively, together with results on theirs security analysis, were proposed in [23]. Some cryptographic CA / PCA applications are summarized in [22].

Also, additional cryptanalysis of certain CA /PCA based key stream generators have been published. A method for reconstructing of a CA initial state based on the sequence of bits generated by a central CA cell is given in [24]. In [26] the inversion algorithm which computes the predecessor of a given state vector, assuming a nonlinear CA configuration rule, is proposed. Cryptographic security examination of the Two Stage PCA and the PCA with ROM have been reported in [27] and [28], respectively, assuming ciphertext only attacks. Some vulnerabilities of these schemes on certain cryptanalytic attacks were demonstrated, and it is shown that the effective secret key size is significantly smaller than its formal length. The same weaknesses are pointed out in [25] assuming known plaintext attacks.

Recently, an improved key stream generator based on programmable cellular automata was proposed and analyzed in [29].

4.1 Hash Functions Based on Cellular Automata

The first proposal of the CA application for one-way hash function design has been reported in [4].

The vulnerability of the scheme from [4] is presented in [16] together with a proposal for new CA based hash function called *Cellhash*. *Callhash* assumes preparation of a message so that it is a concatenation of N 32-bit words M_i, $i = 0, 1, ..., N - 1$, and application of the following procedure:

$H^0 = IV$,
$H^j = F_c(H^{j-1}, M_{j-1}M_{j mod N}...M_{j+\delta mod N})$, $j = 1, 2, ..., N$,
H^N is the hash result,

where $F_c(H, A)$ is a function with argument H a bitstring of length 257, A is a bitstring of length 256, and IV is the all-zero bitstring of length 257; it returns a bitstring of length 257. $F_c(H, A)$ consists of five steps with the following properties [16]:

Step 1 is a nonlinear cellular automation operation where each bitvalue is updated according to the bitvalues in its neighborhood applying a nonlinear updating rule considered in [18]. The nonlinearity of the updating rule has to guarantee the needed confusion.

Step 2 consists merely of complementing 1 bit to eliminate circular symmetry in case bitstring A consists of only $0's$.

Step 3 is a linear CA operation that has to increases the diffusion.

Step 4 realizes the actual messagebits injection in H to be diffused and confused in subsequent rounds.

Step 5 is a bit permutation where bits are placed away from their previous neighbors.

In [17] a one-way function based on two-dimensional CA is proposed and analyzed. The transition function of the two-dimensional CA is the composition of two state transition functions of a one-dimensional CA. The first state transition function is computed by regarding the two-dimensional CA as a one-dimensional one in column order, and the second state transition function is computed by regarding it as a one-dimensional in a row order. For each message block the two-dimensional CA runs certain number of cycles, and the hash result is the CA state after the last cycle.

5 A Novel Cellular Automaton Based Hash Function

In this section, a novel hash function is proposed. The proposed function follows the general model for iterated hash functions (see relation (1)), and employs the Davies-Meyer principle, which according to (2) assumes that the compression function h is defined by the following:

$$h(M_i, H_{i-1}) = F_{M_i}(H_{i-1}) \oplus H_{i-1} , \tag{8}$$

where $F_{M_i}(H_{i-1})$ is a function which maps H_{i-1} according to M_i which consists of $2n$ bits. These would guarantee the approved basis for design and imply secure hash function construction assuming that the compression function and the output function are secure. The novel construction of the compression function h and the output function g is based on cellular automata and recently published results which imply the security of the novel h and g functions.

The proposed hash function provides:

- very fast hashing,
- application of cellular automaton theory for the security examination,
- the preimage and collision resistance due to the employed principles and building blocks.

The novel compression function h^*, the output function g^*, and the whole hash function $hash^*$ are defined by the next three parts of this section.

5.1 Compression Function $h^*(\cdot)$

We assume the following notations:
- ℓ is an integer such that n/ℓ is also an integer (for example $\ell = 8$);
- $\varphi_k(\cdot)$, $k = 1, 2, ..., K$, are functions each of which nonlinearly maps two ℓ-dimensional binary vectors into an ℓ-dimensional binary vector according to the certain ℓ Boolean functions, assuming that the criteria from [15] are satisfied;
- $CA(\cdot)$ is an operator of mapping a current CA state into the next state, assuming CA with primitive characteristic polynomial;
- $PCA_X(\cdot)$ is an operator of mapping a current PCA state into the next state assuming that the applied configuration rule is controlled by a binary vector X according to the following:

(-) if the ith bit of X is 0 then the next state of ith PCA cell is defined by Rule 90,

(-) if the ith bit of X is 1 then the next state of ith PCA cell is defined by Rule 150.

Let M_i be split into $\frac{2n}{\ell}$ successive nonoverlapping equal length blocks of ℓ-bits, $M_{i,1}, M_{i,2}, ..., M_{i,\frac{2n}{\ell}}$, and let H_{i-1} be split into $\frac{n}{\ell}$ blocks of ℓ bits each, $H_{i-1,1}, H_{i-1,2}, ..., H_{i-1,\frac{n}{\ell}}$.

The two vectors X_i and Z_i defined below are certain arguments of the novel compression function.

The novel compression function consists of the following four sets of operations.

- *First Nonlinear Processing*

  X_i is an n-dimensional binary vector obtained by concatenating and interleaving the values V_k of the functions $\varphi_{kmodK}(\cdot)$,

$$V_k = \varphi_{kmodK}(\varphi_{kmodK}(M_{i,k}, H_{i-1,k}), M_{i,\frac{n}{\ell}+k}),$$

$$k = 1, 2, ..., \frac{n}{\ell}, \tag{9}$$

according to the following:
the jth bit of V_k is equal to the $((k-1)\ell+j)$th bit of X_i.

Y_i is an n-dimensional binary vector obtained by concatenating and interleaving the values W_k of the functions $\varphi_{kmodK}(\cdot)$,

$$W_k = \varphi_{kmodK}(V_k, V_{\frac{n}{\ell}+1-k}),$$

$$k = 1, 2, ..., \frac{n}{2\ell}, \tag{10}$$

$$W_k = \varphi_{kmodK}(V_k, V_{k-\frac{n}{2\ell}}),$$

$$k = \frac{n}{2\ell}+1, \frac{n}{2\ell}+2, ..., \frac{n}{\ell}, \tag{11}$$

(where V_k is defined by (9)), according to the following:
the jth bit of W_k is equal to the $((k-1)\ell+j)$th bit of Y_i.

- *CA Processing*

  Y_i' is an n-dimensional binary vector obtained by the following:

$$Y_i' = CA(Y_i). \tag{12}$$

- *Second Nonlinear Processing*

  Let Y_i' be split into $\frac{n}{\ell}$ blocks of ℓ bits each, $Y_{i,1}', Y_{i,2}', ..., Y_{i,\frac{n}{\ell}}'$.
  Z_i is an n-dimensional binary vector obtained by concatenating and interleaving the values Y_k'' of the functions $\varphi_{kmodK}(\cdot)$,

$$Y_k'' = \varphi_{kmodK}(Y_k', Y_{\frac{n}{\ell}+1-k}'),$$

$$k = 1, 2, ..., \frac{n}{2\ell}, \tag{13}$$

$$Y_k'' = \varphi_{kmodK}(Y_k', Y_{k-\frac{n}{2\ell}}'),$$

$$k = \frac{n}{2\ell}+1, \frac{n}{2\ell}+2, ..., \frac{n}{\ell}, \tag{14}$$

(where Y_k' is defined by (12)), according to the following:
the jth bit of Y_k'' is equal to the $((k-1)\ell+j)$th bit of Z_i.

– *PCA Processing*

The compression function $h^*(\cdot)$ is then defined by the following

$$h^*(M_i, H_{i-1}) = PCA_{X_i}(Z_i) \oplus H_{i-1} , \qquad (15)$$

where $\oplus$ denotes bit-by-bit *mod2* addition.

Note that in defining $h^*(\cdot)$, we have assumed that CA and PCA embodied in it run only one transition cycle. Theoretical analysis to be presented below indicates that this arrangement suffices in resisting currently known attacks. In practice, however, one may choose to allow the CA and PCA to run a number of transitions before reaching a state which will be used as an output. Such a variant would provide a higher level of security.

5.2 Output Function $g^*(\cdot)$

The output function $g^*(\cdot)$ is a variant of the cellular automaton based key stream generator proposed and analyzed in [29]. The output function uses the input argument H_m as a secret key and based on it generates n output bits.

The main parts of the key stream generator which realizes the output function g^* are the following: an n-cell PCA, a ROM which contains the configuration rules for the PCA, an n-length binary buffer, and an n-dimensional varying permutation.

Assume that $\eta < n$ maximal length CA's are chosen out of all possible maximal length CA's with Rule 90 and Rule 150. These rules are noted as $\{R_0, R_1, ..., R_\eta\}$. The rule configuration control word corresponding to a rule R_i is stored in a ROM word. The output function operates as following:

– Initially the PCA is configured with the rule $R_{0+\Delta_0}$, where Δ_0 is *mod* η value of H_m decimal representation, and loaded with the output H_m of the compression function from the last iteration. With this configuration the PCA runs one clock cycle. Then it is reconfigured with next rule (i.e., R_i) and runs another cycle. The rule configuration of PCA changes after every run, i.e., in the next run, a rule is $R_{(i+1+\Delta) \bmod \eta}$, where Δ is decimal equivalent of the previous PCA state.

– After each clock cycle, the content of a middle cell of the PCA is taken as an output and stored in the n-length binary buffer.

– After n clock cycles, the buffer content is permuted according the varying permutation controlled by the current PCA state.

5.3 Hash Function $hash^*(\cdot)$ Algorithm

Accordingly, we propose the following fast hash function.

1. INPUT. A bitstring of the message M, and the n-bits initial value IV.

2. PREPROCESSING.
   - MD-strengthening and padding using the approach proposed in [15].

   - Splitting the processed message into m blocks of $2n$-bits each:
     $M = (M_1, M_2, ..., M_m)$.

3. ITERATIVE PROCESSING.
   Assuming that $H_0 = IV$, for each $i = 1, 2, ..., m$, do the following:
   - calculate the compression function $h^*(\cdot)$ value:
     $H_i = h^*(M_i, H_{i-1})$,
   where $h^*(\cdot)$ is defined in the Section 5.1.

4. If H_m is the all zero vector recalculate H_m according to the following:
   $H_m = h^*(M_m, H_0)$, and proceed to the next step.

5. OUTPUT FUNCTION. Calculate $g^*(H_m)$, where $g^*(\cdot)$ is defined in the Section 5.2.

6. OUTPUT. n-bits message digest: $hash^*(M) = g^*(H_m)$.

6 Analysis of the Proposed Hash Function

In this section the security and complexity analysis of the hash function proposed in the previous section are given.

6.1 Security Analysis

Note that according to the Theorem 1, a lower bound on security of the proposed hash function is determined by the characteristics of its compression and output functions. Accordingly, the security will be considered through the security of the proposed functions $g^*(\cdot)$ and $h^*(\cdot)$. Security of both the functions will be examined on the preimage / 2nd preimage and collisions attacks.

The facts and discussions which are given in this section imply that the proposed hash function has ideal security, i.e., given a hash output, producing each of a preimage or 2nd preimage requires approximately 2^n operations and producing a collision requires approximately $2^{n/2}$ operations. Also, due to the structure of the compression function $h^*(\cdot)$, the Assumption 1 implies that we can expect that the proposed hash function is an ideal one.

Security of Compression Function $h^*(\cdot)$

Processing of each message block M_i, $i = 1, 2, ..., m$, by the compression function $h^*(M_i, H_{i-1})$ consists of the following:
- nonlinear mapping of M_i and H_{i-1} into two n-dimensional binary vectors: the CA current state Y_i and the configuration rule vector X_i for the PCA;
- CA mapping of its current state into the next one - an n-bits vector $CA(Y_i)$;
- nonlinear mapping of $CA(Y_i)$ into the vector Z_i.
- PCA mapping of its current state equal to the the vector Z_i into the next one - an n-bits vector $PCA_{X_i}(Z_i)$ assuming that the PCA configuration rule is controlled by the binary vector X according to the following: the next state transition rule for the ith PCA cell is 90 or 150 if the ith bit of X_i is 0 or 1, respectively;
- bit-by-bit $mod2$ addition of the n-bits vectors $PCA_{X_i}(Z_i)$ and H_{i-1} yielding the new intermediate result H_i.

Accordingly, the following facts imply the security of the compression function:

1. The CA has primitive characteristic polynomial so that any nonzero state is mapped into a nonzero state which belongs to the sequence of all possible different $2^n - 1$ nonzero n-dimensional vectors in such manner that the expected Hamming distance between the current state and the next one is $n/2$. The pattern generated by maximal length CA's meet the cryptographic criteria (and the quality of randomness of the patterns generated by CA's is significantly better than that of linear feedback shift register based structures), [23].

2. High nonlinearity of the compression function due to the employed Boolean functions and PCA (with unknown configuration rule, [23]).

3. So far published algorithms for reconstruction of a CA/PCA state employing certain CA/PCA outputs, are the following:
   (a) algorithm from [24] based on noiseless sequence of bits generated by certain CA cell assuming, in general, a nonlinear configuration rule;
   (b) algorithm from [26] based on error-free next CA state assuming a nonlinear configuration rule;
   (c) algorithm from [28] based on the sequence of noisy CA (PCA) states assuming an additive configuration rule;
   (d) algorithm from [29] based on the noisy sequence of bits sampled from CA (PCA) states assuming an additive configuration rule.

   It can be directly shown that all these methods for reconstruction of certain CA (PCA) state can not work in the case of $h^*(\cdot)$.

4. The compression function is a cryptographic transformation.

Facts 1-4 imply that $h^*(\cdot)$ could be considered as a cryptographically secure one-way function, so that according to the Assumption 1 the following hold:
- finding preimage for given $h^*(\cdot)$ output requires about 2^n operations (i.e. testing of 2^n hypothesis);

- finding collision for $h^*(\cdot)$ requires about $2^{n/2}$ operations (testing of $2^{n/2}$ hypothesis).

Security of Output Function $g^*(\cdot)$

Recall that the output function $g^*(\cdot)$ is realized by a variant of the key stream generator proposed and analyzed in [29].

Cryptographic security examination of this generator shows that this generator is resistant on all attacks known so far, assuming that the length of employed PCA is greater than 120, [29].

Accordingly, we can accept that the output function $g^*(\cdot)$ is the secure one, and that finding the input argument of $g^*(\cdot)$ (preimage or 2nd preimage), i.e., the value H_m for given hash value $hash^*(M)$ has complexity 2^n assuming that $n > 120$.

Due to the same reasons, i.e., because $g^*(\cdot)$ is realized by the cryptographically secure key stream generator, we can accept that no better attack than the Yuval's birthday attack, [2], can be expected for finding the collisions for the output function. The previous implies that finding a collision for $g^*(\cdot)$ requires testing about $2^{n/2}$ hypothesis, i.e. employing about $2^{n/2}$ operations.

6.2   Complexity Analysis

As the first, note that the set of functions $\varphi_k(\cdot)$ (see the Section 5.1) can be efficiently realized by the truth tables in ROM.

Based on the structure of the compression function $h^*(\cdot)$ it can be directly shown that processing of each $2n$-bits message block employs no more than $n + 3n + 3n = 7n \; mod2$ additions (recalling that updating of each CA cell employ 2 or 3 $mod2$ additions), and approximately no more than n reading from ROM.

Similarly, it can be directly shown that the processing cost in the output function $g^*(\cdot)$ (for its n-bits input) is approximately equal to $3n^2 \; mod2$ additions $+ \; n \; mod \; \eta$ additions $+$ realization of the permutation.

Accordingly, the overall complexity of processing (hashing) a message consisting of m blocks and each $2n$-bits long, can be estimated as approximately equal to performing $m(8n) + 3n^2 \; mod2$ additions (including the ROM reading costs, $mod \; \eta$ additions, and realization of the permutation). So, the proposed hash function employs the number of operations approximately equal to $4 + \frac{3n}{2m}$ $mod2$ additions for hashing each message bit.

Also, it can be directly shown that, according to the previous result, the proposed hash function is significantly faster than all other dedicated hash functions published so far, assuming hashing of a binary string, i.e. the situations where, due to certain reasons, a word is equal to a bit which appear in hardware implementations. Finally, note that hardware implementation could be realized using 4k ROM (assuming $\ell = 4$ and $K = 3$), two VLSI PCA chips and moderate complexity control logic.

6.3 Comparison with Published CA Based Hash Functions

The novel proposal will be compared with the proposals from [16] and [17], only, because of the reported vulnerabilities of the scheme from [4] (see [16]).

The novel scheme employs a secure and fast PCA based key-stream generator, [29], as the output function. On the other hand, the schemes from [16] and [17] do not employ the output function block.

The compression function from [16] employs a nonlinear CA and a linear CA, and the scheme from [17] could be considered as one which employs two nonlinear CA. But, the employed nonlinear CA's belong to a class of nonlinear CA for which a procedure for inversion of the CA iterations is very recently published in [26].

The compression function, $h^*(\cdot)$, of the hash function proposed in this paper is one of the Davis-Mayer type (which is recognized as a recommended one), and it employs cascade of the nonlinear function and PCA which yields strengthening of security in comparison with employed nonlinear CA in [16] and [17]. Also, it employs an efficient nonlinear and iteration dependent injection of the message blocks into the $h^*(\cdot)$.

Note that employment of the cascade (nonlinear mapping + PCA) for a transformation of the cascade input could be considered as approximately equivalent with processing of the nonlinear CA input through a number of cycles, and that the multiple CA steps are more complex for a factor approximately equal to number of the CA clocks. So, the scheme [17] is significantly more complex than the novel scheme.

Also, it can be directly shown that complexity measured by the average number of elementary operations per bit for a message hashing by the scheme from [16], due to the employed approach of injecting the message bits into the compression function (each message bit is processed 8 times), is nearly eight times greater than the complexity of the here reported scheme.

Accordingly, the proposed hash function preserves all good characteristics of the schemes from [16] and [17], and yields improvement of the security and reduction of the complexity.

7 Conclusions

The paper addresses the problem of designing a fast one-way hash function for bits oriented applications, and it points out a new application of programmable cellular automata.

A novel hash function is proposed and its security and complexity are analyzed. The proposed hash function employs the approved model of iterative hash function with novel compression and output functions.

The proposed compression function is one of the Davis-Meyer type based on cryptographic transformation employing cellular automata, and the output function is a key stream generator, also based on cellular automata. The employment of cellular automata ensures the efficiency of the proposed hash function.

The security of the proposed hash function was analyzed through the security of the compression and output functions. The analysis, based on the so far published results, implies that the proposed hash function has ideal security, i.e., given a hash n-bits output, producing each of a preimage or 2nd preimage requires testing of approximately 2^n hypothesis, and producing of a collision requires testing of approximately $2^{n/2}$ hypothesis, assuming $n > 120$.

Assuming a message of m blocks, each with $2n$ bits, the proposed hash function employs number of operations approximately equal to $4 + \frac{3n}{2m} \, mod2$ additions, for hashing each message bit. Accordingly it can be directly shown that the proposed hash function is significantly faster than all other dedicated hash functions published so far, assuming the bits oriented hashing.

Note that using the linear feedback shift register instead CA / PCA in the proposed hash function yields insecure hash function.

Finally, note that an extension of the proposed hash function for the word oriented applications instead of the here considered bit oriented could be also considered. Future research will be directed toward employment of the CA/PCA over the finite field $GF(q)$ which could be more appropriate for standard word oriented applications.

References

1. A.J. Menezes, P.C. van Oorschot and S.A. Vanstone, *Handbook of Applied Cryptography*. Boca Roton: CRC Press, 1997.
2. G. Yuval, "How to swindle Rabin", *Cryptologia* vol. 3, pp. 187-190, 1979.
3. R. Merkle, "One way hash functions and DES", Advances in cryptology - CRYPTO 89, *Lecture Notes in Computer Science*, vol. 435, pp. 428-446, 1990.
4. I.B. Damgard, "A design principle for hash functions", Advances in Cryptology - CRYPTO 89, *Lecture Notes in Computer Science*, vol. 435, pp. 416-427, 1990.
5. X. Lai, "On the design and security of block ciphers", ETH Series in Information Processing, Vol. 1, J.L. Massey, Ed., Hartung-Gorre Verlag, Konstanz, 1992.
6. M. Naor and M. Yung, "Universal one-way hash functions and their cryptographic applications", Proc. 21st ACM Symp. on the Theory of Computing, ACM, pp. 387-394, 1989.
7. Y. Zheng, T. Matsumoto and H. Imai, "Structural properties of one-way hash functions", Advances in cryptology - CRYPTO 90, *Lecture Notes in Computer Science*, vol. 537, pp. 303-313, 1991.
8. L. Knudsen and B. Preneel, "Fast and secure hashing based on codes", Advances in cryptology - CRYPTO 97, *Lecture Notes in Computer Science*, vol. 1294, pp. 485-498, 1997.
9. M. Bellare, J. Kilian and P. Rogaway, "The security of cipher block chaining", Advances in cryptology - CRYPTO 94, *Lecture Notes in Computer Science*, vol. 839, pp. 341-358, 1994.
10. B. Preneel, R. Govaerts and J. Vandewalle, "Hash functions based on block ciphers: a synthetic approach", Advances in cryptology - CRYPTO 93, *Lecture Notes in Computer Science*, vol. 773, pp. 368-378, 1994.
11. R.L. Rivest, "The MD4 message-digest algorithm", Advances in cryptology - CRYPTO 90, *Lecture Notes in Computer Science*, vol. 537, pp. 303-311, 1991.

12. RFC 1321,"The MD5 message-digest algorithm", Internet request for comments 1321, R.L. Rivest, April 1992.
13. FIPS 180-1, "Secure hash standard", Federal Information Processing Standards Publication 180-1, U.S. Department of Commerce / NIST, 1995.
14. Integrity Primitives for Secure Information Systems: Final Report of RACE Integrity Primitives Evaluation RIPE-RACE 1040. *Lecture Notes in Computer Science*, vol. 1007, 1995.
15. Y. Zheng, J. Pieprzyk and J. Sebery, "HAVAL - a one-way hashing algorithm with variable length of output", Advances in cryptology - AUSCRYPT 92, *Lecture Notes in Computer Science*, vol. 718, pp. 83-104, 1993.
16. J. Daemen, R. Govaerts and J. Vandewalle, "A framework for the design of one-way hash functions including cryptanalysis of Damgard's one-way function based on cellular automaton", Advances in cryptology - ASIACRYPT '91, *Lecture Notes in Computer Science*, vol. 739, 1993.
17. S. Hirose and S. Yoshida, "A one-way hash function based on a two-dimensional cellular automaton", *The 20th Symposium on Information Theory and Its Applications (SITA97)*, Matsuyama, Japan, Dec. 1997, Proc. vol. 1, pp. 213-216.
18. S. Wolfram, "Cryptography with Cellular Automata", Advances in cryptology - CRYPTO 85, *Lecture Notes in Computer Science*, vol. 218, pp. 429-432, 1985.
19. A.K. Das, A. Ganguly, A. Dasgupta, S.Bhawmik, and P. Pal Chaudhuri, "Efficient characterization of cellular automata", *IEE Proc. Pt. E*, vol. 137, pp. 81-87, Jan. 1990.
20. K. Catteell and J.C. Muzio, "Synthesis of one-dimensional linear hybrid cellular automata", *IEEE Trans. Computer-Aided Design*, vol. 15, pp. 325-335, March 1996.
21. S. Wolfram, *Celular Automata and Complexity*. Reading MA: Addison-Wesley, 1994.
22. P.P. Chaudhuri, D.R. Chaudhuri, S. Nandi and S. Chattopadhyay, *Additive Cellular Automata: Theory and Applications*. New York: IEEE Press, 1997.
23. S. Nandi, B.K. Kar and P. Pal Chaudhuri, "Theory and applications of cellular automata in cryptography", *IEEE Trans. Comput.*, vol. 43, pp.1346-1357, 1994.
24. W. Meier and O. Staffelbach, "Analysis of pseudo random sequences generated by cellular automata", Advances in Cryptology - EUROCRYPT 91, *Lecture Notes in Computer Science*, vol. 547, pp. 186-189, 1992.
25. S.R. Blackburn, S. Murphy and K.G. Peterson, "Comments on "Theory and Applications of Cellular Automata in Cryptography"", *IEEE Trans. Comput.*, vol. 46, pp. 637-638, May 1997.
26. C.K. Koc and A.M. Apohan, "Inversion of cellular automata iterations", *IEE Proc. - Comput. Digit. Tech.*, vol. 144, pp. 279-284, 1997.
27. M. Mihaljević, "Security examination of certain cellular automata based key stream generator", *ISITA 96 - 1996 IEEE Int. Symp. Inform. Theory and Appl.*, Canada, Victoria, B.C., Sept. 1996, Proc. pp. 246-249.
28. M. Mihaljević, "Security examination of a cellular automata based pseudorandom bit generator using an algebraic replica approach", Applied Algebra, Algorithms and Error Correcting Codes - AAECC 12, *Lecture Notes in Computer Science*, vol. 1255, pp. 250-262, 1997.
29. M. Mihaljević, "An improved key stream generator based on the programmable cellular automata", Information and Communication Security - ICICS '97, *Lecture Notes in Computer Science*, vol. 1334, pp. 181-191, 1997.

A New Hash Function Based on MDx-family
and Its Application to MAC

Sang Uk Shin[1], Kyung Hyune Rhee[1], Dae Hyun Ryu[2], and Sang Jin Lee[2]

[1] Department of Computer Science, PuKyong National University, 599-1,
Daeyeon-dong, Nam-gu, Pusan, 608-737, Korea,
shinsu@woongbi.pknu.ac.kr , khrhee@dolphin.pknu.ac.kr,
WWW home page: http://unicorn.pknu.ac.kr/~soshin and ~khrhee
[2] Coding Technology Section, Electronics and Telecommunications Research
Institute, 161, Kajong-dong, Yusong-gu,Taejon, 305-350, Korea,
{rdh, sangjin }@etri.re.kr

Abstract. Several fast software hash functions have been proposed since
the hash function MD4 was introduced by R. Rivest in 1990. At the moment, SHA-1, RIPEMD-160, and HAVAL are known as secure dedicated
hash functions in MDx-family hash functions. In this paper, we propose
a new hash function based on advantages of these three hash functions,
which keeps the maximum security of them and is more efficient in performance. The proposed hash function processes an arbitrary finite message by 512-bit block and outputs 160 bits digest. The key feature of the
proposed hash function is *data-dependent rotation*. This feature guarantees the strength against existing known attacks. Moreover, we propose
a new keyed MAC(Message Authentication Code) constructed using the
proposed hash function. The proposed MAC uses a maximum keys of
160 bits and has a bitlength less than equal to the hash result. From the
viewpoint of performance, the proposed MAC is only reduced about 10%
comparing to the underlying hash function.

1 Introduction

Hash functions are used for aims of verification of integrity, construction of
MAC(Message Authentication Code) and increase of efficiency of digital signature. A hash function maps a bitstring of arbitrary finite length into a string
of fixed length. An efficient method to provide the authentication for a large
amount of information is providing the authentication for small-sized hash results computed from that information. Hash functions in digital signature can
be used to make the signature shorter and facilitate the computation of the
signature, and so the efficiency of digital signature can be increased.

Many hash functions are proposed so far, but most of widely used hash functions are iterative processes based on the design rule of Merkle [13] and Damgård
[6]. Since the hash function MD4 [21] was introduced by R. Rivest in 1990, most
of ones were based on design principles of MD4. It is very fast hash function
tuned towards 32-bit processors. Because of unexpected vulnerabilities identified in [4], R. Rivest designed a strengthened version of MD4, called MD5 [22]

in 1991. Although Europe RIPE consortium proposed a strengthened version of MD4 in 1995, which was called RIPEMD [20] based on its independent evaluation of MD4 and MD5, the attack against a shortened version of RIPEMD was found by Dobbertin in 1996 [7]. RIPEMD-128/160 [9], a strengthened version of RIPEMD was proposed by Dobbertin, Bosselaers, and Preneel. Dobbertin showed that there are serious weaknesses in MD4 and MD5 because his attack was able to extend these hash functions [8] [10]. In 1993, NIST (National Institute of Standard and Technology) of United States published SHA(Secure Hash Algorithm) [14] by FIPS PUB 180 and its improved version, SHA-1 [15], which removed weakness found internally and published in 1995. However, no details have been made available. Now SHA-1 is the federal information processing standard for secure hash. Zheng, Pieprzyk and Seberry [26] designed HAVAL hash function in 1992, which would be more flexible and hence more suited for various applications where variable length fingerprints are required. Phil Lee, et al [29] also proposed a variable-length output hash functions, PMD-V and PMD-N, which their strengthened version may be used as Korean digital signature standard.

The MAC(Message Authentication Code) has received widespread use in practice for data integrity and data origin authentication. The first constructions are based on the Cipher Block Chaining (CBC) and Cipher FeedBack(CFB) modes of a block cipher. Most standards and applications use the CBC mode; theoretical supports for this construction was given recently in [2]. Another proposal is the Message Authenticator Algorithm(MAA). MAA is a current ISO standard and is relatively fast in software. However, the disadvantage is that the result, being 32 bits, is considered unacceptable short for many applications. Since 1990, several fast hash functions have been proposed. Because of the factors such as performance, the additional implementation efforts and etc, MAC constructions based on these hash functions were widely used and adopted in Kerberos and SNMP(Simple Network Management Protocol).

In this paper, referring to concrete design principles of MD family hash functions such as MD4, MD5, RIPEMD, RIPEMD-128/160, SHA-1, HAVAL, PMD-N, PMD-V, we propose a new hash function which is secure against known attacks. The proposed hash algorithm processes 512-bit input block, consists of 4 rounds and has 160-bit chaining variables and 160-bit output. It also employs the message expansion of SHA-1 and cryptographically strong boolean functions similar to that of HAVAL. A prominent feature of the proposed hash function is *data-dependent rotations* : rotations are processed by "variable" (input message dependent) amounts [23]. The existing MD family hash functions have fixed values in the rotation of step operation, however, our scheme uses variable rotations. Thus hash results are more strongly dependent on the input message. It is conjectured that finding two collision messages requires the order of 2^{80} operations. Also we propose a new keyed MAC construction using the proposed hash function. The proposed MAC can be constructed by using any MD family hash functions, and is designed to minimize the change of the internal structure of the hash function and keeps the guaranteed security of the underlying hash functions. We conjecture that if the underlying hash function is secure, the best attacks for the new keyed MAC are the exhaustive search with respect to the key, and the following proposition found by Preneel [18] with respect to forgery.

Proposition 1. Let h be an iterated MAC with n-bit chaining variables, m-bit result, a compression function f which behaves like a random function, and output transformation g. An internal collision for h can be found using u known text-MAC pairs, where each text has the same substring of $s \geq 0$ trailing blocks, and v chosen texts. The expected values for u and v are as follows;

$$u = \sqrt{2/(s+1)} \cdot 2^{n/2};$$

if g is a permutation or $s + 1 \geq 2^{n-m+6}$, $v = 0$,
otherwise, $v \approx 2 \cdot (2^{n-m})/(s+1) + 2\lfloor(n - \log_2(s+1))/m\rfloor$

The remainder of this paper is organized as follows. In section 2 we discuss the definition and the general model of the hash function and MAC. In section 3 we give a description of the new scheme and rationale behind the design of the new hash function, and compare the performance of our scheme with existing MD family hash functions. In section 4 we propose a new keyed MAC construction using the proposed hash function. Finally, we have conclusions in section 5.

2 The definition and the general model of the hash functions

Hash functions(more exactly cryptographic hash functions) are functions that map bitstrings of arbitrary finite length into strings of fixed length. This output is commonly called a hash value, a message digest, or a fingerprint. Given h and an input x, computing $h(x)$ must be easy. A one-way hash function must satisfy the following properties [17];

- *preimage resistance* : it is computationally infeasible to find any input which hashes to any pre-specified output. That is, given a y in the image of h, it is computationally infeasible to find an input x such that $h(x) = y$.
- *second preimage resistance* : it is computationally infeasible to find any second input which has the same output as any specified input. That is, given a x in the image of $h(x)$, it is computationally infeasible to find an input $x' \neq x$ such that $h(x) = y$.

A cryptographically useful hash function must satisfy the following additional property :

- *collision resistance* : it is computationally infeasible to find a collision. That is, it is computationally infeasible to find a pair of two distinct inputs x and x' such that $h(x) = h(x')$.

Almost all hash functions are iterative processes which hash inputs of arbitrary length by processing successive fixed-size blocks of input. The input X is padded to a multiple of block length and subsequently divided into t blocks X_1 through X_t. The hash function h can then be described as follows:

$$H_0 = IV, \quad H_i = f(H_{i-1}, X_i), \quad 1 \leq i \leq t, \quad h(X) = H_t$$

Where f is the *compression function* of h, H_i is the *chaining variable* between stage $i - 1$ and stage i, and IV is the initial value. The block diagram of the iterative hash function using the compression function is shown in the Fig. 1.

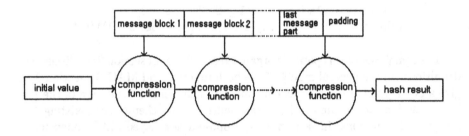

Fig. 1. The use of a compression function in an iterative hash function

The computation of the hash value is dependent on the chaining variable. At the start of hashing, this chaining variable has a fixed initial value which is specified as part of the algorithm. The compression function is then used to update the value of this chaining variable in a suitably complex way under the action and influence of part of the message being hashed. This process continues recursively, with the chaining variable being updated under the action of different part of the message, until all the message has been used. The final value of the chaining variable is then output as the hash value corresponding to that message.

The constructions for hash functions can be classified as ones of using block ciphers and the dedicated hash functions. In the cases of the constructions using block ciphers such as DES and IDEA, some trust has been built on the security of these proposals, but software performance of block ciphers is not very efficient and the performance of hash functions based on them is inferior to the original block ciphers. Therefore, the most popular hash functions, which are currently used in a wide variety of applications, are the dedicated hash functions. The typical examples of the dedicated hash functions are the MD family hash functions such as MD2, MD4, MD5, RIPEMD, RIPEMD-128/160, SHA-1 and HAVAL. MD4 was completely broken by the Dobbertin's attack and also the serious weakness of MD5 was founded [8] [10]. Until now, SHA-1, RIPEMD-160 and HAVAL are considered as secure hash functions. The noticeable feature of SHA-1, which is published in 1995, is the message expansion which additional message words are generated from original input message words [15]. This feature has a strong resistance against existing attacks exploiting the simplicity of applying the message word in the compression function. RIPEMD-160 [9] processes the input message in two parallel lines in order to improve the security. HAVAL [26] has variable length fingerprints and variable number of passes. Also HAVAL makes an elegant use of strong Boolean functions having cryptographically nice properties. Due to this feature, the security is improved. In this paper, we propose a new secure and efficient hash function based on advantages of above three hash algorithms. To remove the simplicity of applying message word in the compression function we may construct as parallel lines same as RIPEMD-160, but it seriously affects the efficiency of speed. Thus we apply the message expansion as that of SHA-1, and use cryptographically strong Boolean functions similar to that of HAVAL. The proposed hash function keeps the sufficient security which the existing hash functions have had, and at the same time, it is more efficient in viewpoint of the performance than other ones [28].

MAC is a hash function with a secondary input, i.e., a secret key K. Given h, an input x, and secret key K, computing $h(x)$ must be easy. The strongest condition one may impose on a MAC is that for someone who does not know the secret key, it may be computationally infeasible to perform an existential forgery, i.e. to find an arbitrary message and its corresponding MAC. This should be contrasted to a selective forgery, where an opponent can determine the MAC for a message of his choice. For a practical attack, one requires that the forgery is verifiable, and for an ideal MAC, any method to find the key is as expensive as an exhaustive search of $O(2^k)$ operations for a k-bit key. Also the number of text-MAC pairs required for verification of such an attack is k/m, and an opponent who has identified the correct key can compute the MAC for any message [18].

General MAC constructions based on cryptographic hash function were proposed by Tsudik [25]. Tsudik proposed the following three constructions for message M and analyzed their security, respectively.(Here, ' $\|$' is a concatenation of strings)

- secret prefix method : $MAC(M) = MD(K \| M)$, K is a 512-bit secret key
- secret suffix method : $MAC(M) = MD(M \| K)$, K is a 512-bit secret key
- envelope method : $MAC(M) = MD(M \| K_2)$, $IV = K_1$ is a 128-bit secret key, K_2 is a 512-bit secret key

Preneel and van Oorshot surveyed the existing MAC constructions and pointed out some of their properties and weaknesses [18] [19]. In particular, they presented a detailed description of the effect of birthday attacks on iterated constructions, and also proposed the MDx-MAC [18]. Kaliski and Robshaw discussed and compared various MAC constructions [11]. Bellare et al proposed NMAC(Nested MAC) and HMAC(Hash based MAC), and analyzed their security and efficiency [1]. In this paper, we propose a new MAC construction similar to MDx-MAC. The key feature of the proposed MAC is that the order of message words applied to each round is randomized by a random permutation generated by the key.

3 Description of the new hash algorithm

In this section we describe details of the proposed hash function. We will first introduce some notation for the algorithm as follows:

- word : 32-bit string
- block : 512-bit string used as input of compression function in the hash function
- + : addition modulo 2^{32} operation between two words
- $X^{<<s}$: left rotation X by s bits
- $X \wedge Y$: bitwise logical AND operation of A and B
- $X \vee Y$: bitwise OR operation of A and B
- $X \oplus Y$: bitwise XOR operation of A and B

The proposed hash function processes all messages by 512-bit, and consists of 4 rounds. Also the proposed algorithm has 160-bit chaining variables and hash result. We may consider a variable length output like HAVAL [26] and PMD-V [29], but it is doubtful yet whether it would have an advantage. Since a 128-bit output can not provide the sufficient security against the brute force attack, it is designed to have a fixed 160-bit output [16]. To use total of 24 message words, additional 8 message variables are generated from 16 input words, and each round performs 24 step operations.

(1) Input block length and padding

The input message is processed by 512-bit block. The proposed hash function pads a message by appending a single bit 1 next to the most significant bit of the message, followed by zero or more bit 0s until the length of the message is 448 modulo 512, and then appends to the message the 64-bit original message length modulo 2^{64}.

(2) Initial Value(IV)

The initial values of 5 chaining variables (A, B, C, D, E) used in processing message are as follows :

A	B	C	D	E
0x67452301	0xefcdab89	0x98badcef	0x10325476	0xc3d2e1f0

(3) Constants

The following numbers are used as constants :

K_1	K_2	K_3	K_4
0	0x5a827999	0x6ed9eba1	0x8f1bbcdc
	$\lfloor 2^{30} \cdot \sqrt{2} \rfloor$	$\lfloor 2^{30} \cdot \sqrt{3} \rfloor$	$\lfloor 2^{30} \cdot \sqrt{5} \rfloor$

(4) Expansion of message variables

8 message variables are additionally generated from original 16 input messages $X_i (i < 16)$ as follows :

$$X_{16+i} = (X_{0+i} \oplus X_{2+i} \oplus X_{7+i} \oplus X_{12+i})^{<<1} \quad (i = 0, 1, \cdots, 7)$$

Because most existing known attacks use the simplicity of the order of message words, we designed so that a message word would affects to steps as many as possible. A total of 24 message words is applied. SHA-1 processes total 80 message variables which is expanded to 64 message variables from 16 input message words. Since a large number of message expansion badly affects the algorithm efficiency, we designed so that each of 16 input words can be applied evenly to total of 24 message words, and the implementation of algorithm can be processed fast.

(5) Ordering of message words

For the order of message words, we referred to the design principle of RIPEMD-160 [9]. We designed so that additionally generated words would be dispersed sufficiently and same word wouldn't be close by in each round. In each step of each round, the same message word cannot be used.

We chose the following permutation ρ :

i	4	1	2	3	4	5	6	7	8	9	10	11
$\rho(i)$	4	21	17	1	23	18	12	10	5	16	8	0

i	12	13	14	15	16	17	18	19	20	21	22	23
$\rho(i)$	20	3	22	6	11	19	15	2	7	14	9	13

The order of the message words is determined by the following permutation table in each round :

Round 1	Round 2	Round 3	Round 4
i	ρ	ρ^2	ρ^3

(6) Operation in one step

The step operation is defined as follows :

$$A = (f(A, B, C, D, E) + X_i + K)^{<<s} \quad , \quad B = B^{<<10}$$

(7) Booelan functions

Boolean functions are based on those of HAVAL. Even though most of the existing MD family hash functions use 3 variable Boolean functions, we use 5 variable Boolean functions which satisfy cryptographically good properties similar to HAVAL [26] [29]. In each round, we use one of the following Boolean functions :

$$f_0(x_1, x_2, x_3, x_4, x_5) = (x_1 \wedge x_2) \oplus (x_3 \wedge x_4) \oplus (x_2 \wedge x_3 \wedge x_4) \oplus x_5$$

$$f_1(x_1, x_2, x_3, x_4, x_5) = x_2 \oplus ((x_4 \wedge x_5) \vee (x_1 \wedge x_3))$$

$$f_2(x_1, x_2, x_3, x_4, x_5) = x_1 \oplus (x_2 \wedge (x_1 \oplus x_4)) \oplus (((x_1 \wedge x_4) \oplus x_3) \vee x_5)$$

Boolean function f_0 is constructed by using the bent function. It is 0-1 balanced and it has a high nonlinearity and satisfies the SAC(Strict Avalanche Criterion) [5] [24]. Boolean function f_1 and f_2 are also 0-1 balanced, highly nonlinear and satisfy the SAC [5] [24] [26]. In each round, the order of Boolean functions is f_0, f_1, f_2, and f_1. We use f_1 once more for the efficiency.

Round 1	Round 2	Round 3	Round 4
f_0	f_1	f_2	f_1

(8) Shifts

A distinguishing feature of the proposed hash function is *data-dependent rotations* [23]. While the existing MD family hash functions have fixed values in the rotation of step operation, our scheme uses variable rotations. Thus, hash results are more strongly dependent on the input messages. Rotation values are dependent on the input messages(5 low-order bits of input message). By using different message word from that used in the step operation(i.e. the word added to result of Boolean function), we made the proposed hash function to be secure against possible attacks. The shift value s used in step operation of each round is dependent on the input message and determined by the following :

$$s = X_i \mod 32$$

The order of applied message X_i is determined by the following permutations in each round(ρ is the permutation used in the order of message words) :

Round 1	Round 2	Round 3	Round 4
ρ^3	ρ^2	ρ	i

We note that the attack by den Boer, Bosselaers [4] and Dobbertin [7] [8] [10] is not directly applicable to our scheme because of its strong data-dependent rotations. Also this feature may help differential cryptanalysis [3] and linear cryptanalysis [12] to be weak, since bit rotations are processed randomly [23]. It is conjectured that the best way to find collision pairs is by using the birthday attack. In such an attack, attacker must prepare two sets of 2^{80} distinct messages, and calculate their fingerprints.

We compared the performance of MD5, SHA-1, RIPEMD-160, HAVAL(5 pass, 160 bits), and our scheme. Implementations were written in C language on the Pentium processor(100MHz). 10Mbytes of data are hashed using an 8K buffer. The program is not optimized and there is a little variation due to the function clock(). Our scheme is about 27% faster than RIPEMD-160, and about 2% faster than SHA-1. Even though MD5 obtained the best result in the performance, it has only 128-bit hash result(which is shorter than other scheme, such as SHA-1, RIPEMD-160, HAVAL and our proposed one) [28].

4 The MAC construction using the proposed hash function

Now we propose a new keyed MAC construction using the proposed hash function in the previous section. With the following design goals, we construct a new MAC algorithm [18]:

(1) The secret key should be involved at the begining and end, and at every iteration of the hash function.

(2) The deviation from the original hash function should be minimal in order to minimize implementation effort and maximize on confidence previously gained.

(3) The performance should be close to that of the hash function.

(4) The additional memory requirements should be minimized.

(5) The approach should be generic, i.e. should apply to any MD-family hash functions.

The new MAC algorithm uses a maximum 160-bit key. Hash function may be any of MD family hash functions. The proposed MAC consists of three steps.

The first step of MAC construction is a key extraction. Concatenate K to itself to a sufficient number of times, and build a 512-blt block size, $\overline{K}$. Then $\overline{K}$ is applied to the hash function, and construct 160-bit key used in MAC as following:

$$k = hash(\overline{K})$$

where *hash* denotes a hash algorithm without both padding and appended length.

The second step is to generate the random permutation of the order of message words applied to each round and to modify the constant used in each round of original hash function. The 160-bit key k is divided into two parts. The first part, $k1$, is used to generate the random permutations and the other part, $k2$, is added to the constants. To generate the random permutation for the order of message words, we use the Knuth algorithm, which bijects an integer between 0 and $(m!-1)$ to any permutation of size m. A pseudo random number is generated by the following simple linear congruential equation,

$$Y = X + Q \bmod m!$$

and then compute a pseudo random permutation corresponding to the pseudo random number. After two consecutive permutations are generated, we combine two resulting permutations by composition rule of two permutations, and use it as the order of message words [27]. Because the proposed hash function uses 24 message words in each round, we use the leftmost 10 bytes of 160-bit key k(actually it is 75 bits). We generate the order of message words, ρ_i, used in each round as the following:

[Round 1]

$$X1 = k1 + Q \bmod 24! \leftrightarrow P1$$

$$X2 = X1 + Q \bmod 24! \leftrightarrow P2$$

$$\rho_1 = P1 \cdot P2$$

[Round 2]

$$X3 = X2 + Q \bmod 24! \leftrightarrow P1$$

$$X4 = X3 + Q \bmod 24! \leftrightarrow P2$$

$$\rho_2 = P1 \cdot P2$$

$$\vdots$$

A similar method can be applied to generate ρ_i in other rounds. Here Q is a constant between 1 and $m! - 1$, and relative prime to $m!$. Now, we take 8 bytes($k2$) followed by $k1$ to modify the constants. It is divided into four 16-bit substrings. Each substring is concatenated to itself repeatedly in order to make 32-bit word, and then each word is added mod 2^{32} to the constants K_i used in each round. The final step is to compute the MAC. After key elements are both prepended and appended to a message M, the hash function is applied.

$$MAC = hash(\overline{k + 0x5c} \parallel \overline{M} \parallel \overline{k + 0x36})$$

where $\overline{M}$ is the message containing the padding and appended length, and $hash()$ is a hash function with randomly permutated order of message words and modified constants. The MAC result is the leftmost m bits of the hash value. From the view of the attack of *Proposition 1*, $m = n/2$ is recommended for the most applications.

The computational overhead of the proposed MAC is one block operation for the key extraction, two blocks prepended and appended to a message M and the generation of random permutations for the order of message words. The generation of the permutation requires a multiprecision operation because of value of 24!. However, in practice, it is required to one division(multiprecision / int) and one modulo operation(multiprecision mod int) for converting 75-bit $k1$ to the factorial number system. Thus only small amount of time is used for the permutation generation. In practice, software implementation indicates that the proposed MAC construction is only 10% slower than that of the original hash function.

In the final step, key elements prepended and appended to a message are similar to K_1 and K_2 of the envelope method. However, a divide-and-conquer attack of envelope method provides no advantage [18]. It is similar to the method of MDx-MAC. The addition of key component to constants provides additional protection over the envelope method where weakness of the hash function become to be known. It is not very strong by itself. In each round, the random permutation of the order of message words is a trapdoor one-way function. That is, computing ρ_i is easy, but its reverse is computationally infeasible. Furthermore, the probability that order of message words is equal or reversed to that of the previous round, is negligible because the period of the random permutation is 24!, about 10^{23} (this is enough long). Since the 160-bit key K is secure against an exhaustive search, and if the underlying hash function is secure, exhaustive search for key k is as difficult as an exhaustive search for K. If, as recommended, the bitsize of the MAC result is equal to half that of the chaining variable(i.e. $m = n/2$), a forgery attack on the proposed MAC requires $O(2^m/(s+1))$ chosen text-MAC pairs and $O(2^m/\sqrt{(s+1)})$ known texts by *Proposition 1*. Also 160-bit key has an advantage when comparing with $672(160 + 512)$ bits previously proposed for the envelope method. Moreover, we believe that the proposed scheme would be strong against attack exploiting the internal structure of the hash function since we keep the order of message words applied to each round securely. We state the following conjecture for the proposed MAC:

Conjecture. If an underlying hash function is secure, the best attack on the proposed MAC is exhaustive one with respect to key search, and that of *Proposition 1* with respect to forgery.

5 Conclusions

We proposed a new hash function based on the design principles of existing MD family hash functions and the analysis of attacks against them. The proposed hash function processes an arbitrary length message by 512-bit block and outputs 160-bit message digest. The structure consists of 4 rounds and each round executes 24 step operations. Also 16 input message words are expanded to 24 words, and in each step operation, we employ cryptographically strong Boolean function. The remarkable feature of our scheme is that the bit rotation of the step function is variable, and dependent on the input message. The data-dependent rotation improves the security because the hash result is more dependent on the input message. In terms of the execution speed, the proposed hash function is about 27% faster than RIPEMD-160, and about 2% faster than SHA-1. Now considering SHA-1 and RIPEMD-160 as secure, the proposed hash function may be used as the alternative to them. We expect that it requires the order of 2^{80} operations to find a pair of collision messages. Hence the proposed hash function is secure against known attacks, and is efficient in terms of the performance.

Moreover, we proposed a new keyed MAC construction based on the proposed hash function. The proposed MAC uses a key up to 160 bits in length and has the MAC result as half of the hash value. We minimized the differences between the hash function and the MAC construction based on it for the convenience of implementation. In the proposed MAC construction, the secret key is involved to all components of the hash function. In particular, by applying the random permutation to the order of message words in each round, the proposed scheme is secure against possible attacks which is using the order of message words. The proposed MAC construction is only 10% slower than the original hash function in software implementation. We conjecture that the proposed MAC construction is secure if the underlying hash function is secure, and the best known attack on the proposed MAC is exhaustive one with respect to key search, and the one of *Proposition 1* with respect to forgery.

For the further research, we are considering the analysis of the security and the optimization of the implementation for the proposed hash function. Furthermore, we need to keep going on more systematic approaches in analysis.

References

1. M. Bellare, R. Canetti, H. Krawczyk, "Keying Hash Functions for Message Authentication", Advances in Cryptology-Crypto'96, Lecture Notes in Computer Science, vol.1109, Springer-Verlag, 1996,

2. M. Bellare, J. Kilian, P. Rogaway, "The security of cipher block chaining", Advances in Cryptology-Crypto'94, Lecture Notes in Computer Science, vol.839, Springer-Verlag, 1994

3. E. Biham, A. Shamir, "Differential cryptanalysis of DES-like cryptosystems", Advances in Cryptology-Crypto'90, Lecture Notes in Computer Science, vol.537, Springer-Verlag, 1991, pp. 2-21

4. B. den Boer, A. Bosselaers, "An attack on the last two rounds of MD4", Advances in Cryptology-Crypto'91, Lecture Notes in Computer Science, vol.576, Springer-Verlag, 1992, pp. 194-203

5. S. Chee, S. Lee, K. Kim, and D. Kim, "Correlation Immune Functions with Controllable Nonlinearity", ETRI J., Vol. 19, No. 4, 389-401, 1997.

6. I.B. Damgård, "A design principle for hash functions", Advances in Cryptology-Crypto'89, Lecture Notes in Computer Science, vol.435, Springer-Verlag, 1990, pp. 416-427

7. H. Dobbertin, "RIPEMD with two-round compress function is not collision-free", Journal of Cryptology, vol.10, no.1, 1997, pp. 51-69

8. H. Dobbertin, "Cryptanalysis of MD4", Fast Software Encryption-Cambridge Workshop, Lecture Notes in Computer Science, vol.1039, Springer-Verlag, 1996, pp. 53-69

9. H. Dobbertin, A. Bosselaers, B. Preneel, "RIPEMD-160: A strengthened version of RIPEMD", Fast Software Encryption-Cambridge Workshop, Lecture Notes in Computer Science, vol.1039, Springer-Verlag, 1996, pp. 71-82

10. H. Dobbertin, "The status of MD5 after recent attack", RSA LABs' CryptoBytes, 2(2), Sep. 1996, pp. 1-6

11. B. Kaliski, M Robshaw, "Message Authentication with MD5", RSA LABs' CryptoBytes, vol.1, no.1, Spring, 1995

12. M. Matsui, "The first experimental cryptanalysis of the Data Encryption Standard", Advances in Cryptology-Crypto'94, Lecture Notes in Computer Science, vol.839, Springer-Verlag, 1994, pp.1-11

13. R. Merkle, "One way hash functions and DES", Advances in Cryptology-Crypto'89, Lecture Notes in Computer Science, vol.435, Springer-Verlag, 1990, pp. 428-446

14. NIST, "Secure hash standard", FIPS 180, US Department of Commerce, Washington D.C., 1993

15. NIST, "Secure hash standard", FIPS 180-1, US Department of Commerce, Washington D.C., April 1995

16. P.C. van Oorshot, M.J. Wiener, "Parallel collision search with applications to hash functions and discrete logarithms", Proc. of the 2nd ACM Conference on Computer and Communications Security, ACM, 1994, pp. 210-218

17. B. Preneel, "Analysis and design of cryptographic hash functions", Doctoral Dissertation, Katholieke Universiteit Leuven, 1993

18. B. Preneel, P. van Oorschot, "MDx-MAC and Building Fast MACs from Hash Functions", Advances in Cryptology-Crypto'95, Lecture Notes in Computer Science, vol.963, Springer-Verlag, 1995

19. B. Preneel, P. van Oorschot, "On the security of two MAC algorithms", Advances in Cryptology-Eurocrypt'96, Lecture Notes in Computer Science, vol.963, Springer-Verlag, 1996

20. RIPE Consortium : RIPE Integrity Primitives-Final report of RACE Integrity Primitives Evaluation (R1040), Lecture Notes in Computer Science, vol.1007, Springer-Verlag, 1995

21. R. Rivest, "The MD4 message-digest algorithm", Request For Comments(RFC) 1320, Internet Activities Board, Internet Privacy Task Force, April 1992

22. R. Rivest, "The MD5 message-digest algorithm", Request For Comments(RFC) 1320, Internet Activities Board, Internet Privacy Task Force, April 1992

23. R. Rivest, "The RC5 Encryption Algorithm", RSA LABs' CryptoBytes, 1(1);9-11, 1995 (Revised 3, 20, 1997, (http://theory.lcs.mit.edu/ rivest/rc5rev.ps)

24. J. Seberry, X. M. Zhang, "Highly nonlinear 0-1 balanced boolean functions satisfying strict avalanche criterion", Advances in Cryptology-Auscrypt'92, Lecture Notes in Computer Science, vol.718, Springer-Verlag, 1993, pp. 145-154

25. G. Tsudik, "Message authentication with one-way hash functions", Proceedings of Infocom 92

26. Y. Zheng, J. Pieprzyk, J. Seberry, "HAVAL - a one-way hashing algorithm with variable length and output", Advances in Cryptology-Auscrypt'92, Lecture Notes in Computer Science, vol.718, Springer-Verlag, 1993, pp. 83-104

27. Seung-Chul Ko, Kyung Hyune Rhee, "Fast generator of random permutation", Proceedings of the 1-st workshop in Applied Mathematics, 1993, pp. 379-384 (Korean)

28. Sang Uk Shin, Dae Hyun Ryu, Sang Jin Lee, Kyung Hyune Rhee, "A new hash function based on MDx-family hash functions", Proceedings of the 8nd KIPS Fall Conference, vol.4, no.2, 1997. pp. 1354-1359 (Korean)

29. Chae Hoon Lim, Nan Kyung Park, Eun Jeong Lee, Pil Joong Lee, "The proposal of the new hash function possible to select the output length", preprint, 1997 (Korean)

Security Issues for Contactless Smart Cards

Michael W. DAVID[1] and Kouichi SAKURAI[2]*

[1] CUBIC Coproration., International Business Development
111 8th Ave., Suite 700, New York, NY, 10011, U.S.A.
email:mike.david@cubic.com
[2] Kyushu University, Compuer Science Dept.
6-10-1 Hakozaki, Higashi-ku, Fukuoka 812-81, Japan
e-mail: sakurai@csce.kyushu-u.ac.jp

Abstract. We review the current technologies of contactless smart cards and compare them with contact cards. We discuss the problems of implementing encryption in contactless cards, and consider how to solve the problems. We also report the state of standardization of contactless smart card.

Keywords. Public key, Smart-card, Contactless-card, Standards, Efficient Implementation

1 Introduction

Smart cards are important tools for the implementation of public key cryptosystems (PKC). There are some pilot systems in electronic cash (e-cash) for banks. The existing cards implementing PKC are for the most part, still contact cards. However, for application to transit systems like railways and highways, the card shall be non-contact: contactless cards are required.

A technical problem for implementing PKC in Contactless Smart Cards (CSC) is the limitation of the card's power of computation and communication: transactions in less than 100 mlliseconds (ms) are desired. Even if we can implement RSA cryptosystem [RSA] over contactless cards, it takes too long to execute the encryption/decryption because RSA requires many arithmetic operations over large modulus. Even the elliptic curve cryptosystems with smaller size keys [Mil,Kob] are still slow, which is 10-times faster than RSA.

So, one direct solution is to develop a new public key algorithm, which is much more efficient than RSA. Another solution is to design a new protocol that reduces the computational tasks of the CSC.

This review reports the current technologies of CSC while comparing them to contact cards. Then we discuss the problem of implementing PKC in the CSC, and discuss how to solve the problem. We also mention the state of standardization of contact/contactless smart-cards.

---

* This work was done while visiting in Columbia Univ., Computer Science Dept. from September 1997 for one year.

2 On Contactless Smart Card (CSC)

2.1 Applications

The applications we have focused on are in public transport. We have considered public transport applications as primarily those found in subway and bus systems, but can include parking lot and taxi revenue collection schemes. These cards are different from those used in toll road collection, since the distance for toll road systems far exceeds the 10 cm transmission distance defined by ISO/IEC 14433343. However, the ISO/IEC 14443 type of card could also be used for access control, ID cards, telephone cards and other areas, depending on the users needs and operating methodology.

2.2 Products (Single frequency)

MIFARE, a registered trademark, was developed by Mikron GmbH. Mikron is now owned by Phillips Semiconductors, and has a major share of the installed contactless smart card base. For example, the Korean firm INTEC, has used the MIFARE card for large scale applications in Korea bus fare collection system. It is also being tested for applications in Korean subways. MIFARE will also be adopted (Single frequency) by the light rail system in Kuala Lumpur and the subway in Shanghai.

Japan's NTT Corporation will be using a CSC for its new telephone card system.

FELICA, a registered trademark, was developed by the Sony Corporation. It is the basis for Hong Kong's "Octopus' card, being used by the Creative Star Limited consortium. Creative Star uses the cards to integrate fare collection on the subway, bus and ferry systems in Hong Kong.

GO CARD, a registered trademark, was developed by the Cubic Corporation. It will be in use in the Chicago and Washington D.C. transit systems. As in Hong Kong, this will apply to multiple modes of transportation to include subway, bus and parking lots.

3 Technical Issues for Cryptographic Applications

3.1 Requirements

Based on experience with the use of existing magnetic fare card systems, and the needs for high passenger throughput, we believe that public transport applications will be a complete transaction speed of less than 100 milliseconds (ms). This includes the need to authenticate, read, write and verify card integrity and values, along with any security related processing. However, transit authorities would like to see these contactless cards migrate in the future to be compatible with the contact cards that will be used by the electronic cash (e-cash) and debit card markets.

3.2 Issues

None of the cards listed in Subsection 2.2 are compatible. Due to variations in modulation, bit coding, protocol, power requirements and approached to security, it is very difficult to configure one reader/writer unit to simultaneously deal with all three products.

Users want to have the ability to combine contact and contactless functions on one card. This is sometimes referred to as a combination or "combi-card". However, the security requirements for an e-cash or debit card are much higher than that of a stored value transit card. In the long term, there may be a move to the expanded use of contactless cards because of the simplicity of the installation of the read/write (r/w) system. However, the fabrication of contactless cards is much more difficult than that of contact cards. The difficulty lies primarily in the placement of the wire leads to the chip contact plates. If this process fails or if the placement of the wires are not secure, the contactless card will not function.

3.3 Market Movements

There are a few approaches that are being taken to deal with the issue in the previous.

The first is to develop a contactless ASIC and a micro-controller to a common memory module, permitting a one chip solution. The shared memory case has the advantage that the value or purse can be loaded through the more secure contact interface. However, this still lacks the ability to permit contactless debits of bank products such as Mondex or Visa Cash due to the inability to exercise the micro-controller based security functions without contact. There are products like this being developed. One uses a Siemens micro-controller and a MIFARE ASIC. Another will use a Motorola microprocessor and a Sony FELICA-based ASIC. Motorola is working on its own contactless micro-controller for integration with the PROTON e-cash system.

The second is to develop a two-chip hybrid card with both a contactless ASIC and a micro-controller, each with its own dedicated memory. This alternative is similar functionally to the one chip solution, but does not enable loading value to the contactless portion from a contact terminal. The advantage is that because the chips are separate, there is no security threat to the contact e-cash / banking side of the card.

Although more difficult from the security perspective, the market may drive a solution based on the one-chip, common memory combi-card.

4 Towards Cryptographic Solutions

How to provide e-cash/debit card level security for the combi-card that permits contactless transactions in less than 100 ms.

4.1 Developing a new very efficient PKC

Even if we can implement RSA cryptosystem over contactless cards, it takes too long to execute the encryption/description because RSA requires many arithmetic operations over large modulus (e.g. 2048 bits). Even the elliptic curve cryptosystems with smaller size keys are still slow, which is 10-times faster than RSA.

So, one direct solution is to develop a new public key algorithm, which is more efficient than RSA. Such an attempt was initiated by Matsumoto and Imai [MI], and modified by Patarian [PG], which use multivariate polynomials and would achieve speeds 100 times faster than RSA.

4.2 Developing a new protocol

Another solution for implementing PKC over contactless cards, instead of developing a new encryption algorithm, is to design a new protocol that decreases the computation tasks of the CSC. In protocols which add a powerful server[MILY], indeed the computation task of cards decreases, however, the number of interactions between the server and cards increases, or the required communication data increases.

A new scheme of signcryption developed by Zheng[ZHE] is a possible solution to this problem. This scheme needs only a few rounds of communication, and less data to be sent based on the current public key algorithms.

5 Standarization

5.1 Contact card

Conventional contact smart cards center around the market for identification (ID) cards, bank cards and telephone cards. The key standards associated with these type of cards are International Standards Organization (ISO) 7810 - 7816. These standards focus on card attributes such as dimension, material quality, magnetic strips placement, embossing standards, integrated circuit (IC) chip placement and interfaces. They are widely accepted throughout the banking and telephone card industries.

There is also a market driven form of standard being adopted by Europay, MasterCard and Visa. This is referred to as the EMV. These uses the physical card standards prescribed by ISO 7810 - 7816. However, the EMV expands the standardization effort to cover smart card initialization, security, operating system utilization and application development and activation issues.

There are also other industry associations working toward commonality within the contact card market.

The Multiple Operating System (MULTOS) [multos] initiative designed to permit multiple stored value e-cash systems on one chip. For example, the use of Mondex, Proton or VisaCash on one card. The OpenCard Framework (OCF) was announced in March 1997, and is an open standard that provides for inter-operability of smart applications across many platforms to include network and personal computers, ATMs, GSM/PCS cellular phones

The Global Chipcard Alliance (GCA) established in November 1997 designed to address interoperability of primarily telephone card systems. However, its goal is to permit multi-functional smart card technology.

5.2 Contactless card

The ISO/IEC 14443 is an initiative underway to define a proposed standard for contactless or proximity cards. It relates to cards that would be used within a read distance of 10 cm or less. The topics under evaluation are:

Part-I : Physical Characteristics
Part-II : RF Power and Signal Interface
Part-III: Initialization and Anti-Collision
Part-IV: Transmission and Protocols

As of the fall of 1997, there was agreement on Part-I. This is true due to the close association with existing ISO 7810 - 7816.

Part-II involves some of the following key elements: (1) Frequency of data transmission, (2) Data rate, (3) Modulation, and (4) Bit coding.

There is basic agreement on the use of the frequency of 13.56 megahertz (mhz) for power, read and write functions. Modulation and bit coding at this point in time differ according to various card applications designers. Some form of standard to provide interoperability between different contactless and reader-writer (r/w) equipment may be necessary to permit users to use multiple suppliers. However, there is as yet no agreement in this area.

Part-III relates to data content for sign-on and sign-off functions. This basically allows the card and its target (r/w) unit to ensure that a transaction has been completed. This is very important in the contactless environment. The contact card is captures and read inside a controlled r/w environment (e.g. inside an ATM or a public telephone). However, the contactless card must operate at the whim of the users hand and arm movements, as well as the surrounding electro-magnetic environment. At this point in time, different methods to deal with these issues.

Part-IV deals with transmission, protocols and security. These are important issues, but are far from being defined within the ISO/IEC 14443 initiative.

6 Concluding Remarks

This paper has reviewed the current technology of contactless cards with a smart chip, and reported the standardization efforts for this technology. Then we considered the difficulty and possibility of public-key crypto's being implemented in Contactless Smart Cards, and discussed future cryptographic topics to be developed for the implementation of PKC over Contactless Smart Card.

Acknowledgments

The authors would like to thank Tohru Inoue of Advanced Mobile Telecomm. Security Tech. Research Lab. for his support on this work. The second author wishes to thank Zvi Galil and Moti Yung for their hospitality while visiting Columbia Univ. Computer Science Dept. Final thanks to Hideki Imai and Yuliang Zheng for giving the first author a chance to present this survey at PKC'98.

References

[Amm] http://www.ammismartcards.com

[Car] http://www.cardshow.com Smart Cards and Systems: Vol 2, Issues 30, 35, 36, 40

[Cer] http://www.certicom.com

[Gem] http://www.gemplus.com

[GUQ] L.C.Guillou, M.Ugon, and J.-J. Quisqater "The smart card: A standardized security device dedicated to public cryptology," in Contemporary Cryptography, edited by G.J.Simmons, IEEE Press.

[Kob] N.Koblitz, "Elliptic Curve Cryptosystems," Math.Comp. Vol.48 (1987).

[Mil] V.S.Miller, "Use of Elliptic CURVES in Cryptography," Proc. CRYPTO'95.

[MI] T.Matsumoto and H.Imai, "Public quadratic polynomial-tuples for efficient signature-verification and message-encryption" Proc. Eurocrypt88.

[MILY] T.Matsumoto, H.Imai, C.S. Laih and S.M.Yen, "On verifiable implicit asking protocols for RSA computation," Proc. ASIACRYPT'92.

[Mul] The Web site at http://www.multos.com

[PG] J.Patarin and L.Goubin, "Trapddor one-way permutations and multivariate polynomials," in Proc. ICICS97.

[Ram] http://www.ramtron.com

[RSA] R.Rivest, A.Shamir, and L.Adleman, "A method for obtaining digital signatures and public key cryptosystems," CACM 21 (1978).

[Slb] http://www.slb.com/ms/et

[Zhe] Y. Zheng, "Signcryption and its applications in efficient public key solutions," in Proc. Information Security Workshop'97.

Parameters for Secure Elliptic Curve Cryptosystem -Improvements on Schoof's Algorithm

Tetsuya Izu[1], Jun Kogure[2], Masayuki Noro[1], and Kazuhiro Yokoyama[1]

[1] Fujitsu Laboratories Ltd., 4-1-1 Kamikodanaka
Nakahara-ku Kawasaki 211-8588, Japan
izu@flab.fujitsu.co.jp, {noro, yokoyama}@para.flab.fujitsu.co.jp
[2] Fujitsu Ltd., Nikko Fudousan Bldg. 2-15-16 Shinyokohama
Kouhoku-ku Yokohama 222-0033, Japan
kogure@rp.open.cs.fujitsu.co.jp

Abstract. The security of elliptic curve cryptosystem depends on the choice of an elliptic curve on which cryptographic operations are performed. Schoof's algorithm is used to define a secure elliptic curve, as it can compute the number of rational points on a randomly selected elliptic curve defined over a finite field. By realizing efficient combination of several improvements, such as Atkin-Elkies's method, isogeny cycles method, and baby-step-giant-step algorithm, we can count the number of rational points on an elliptic curve over $GF(p)$ in a reasonable time, where p is a prime whose size is around 240-bit.

1 Introduction

When we use the Elliptic Curve Cryptosystem(ECC for short), we first have to define an elliptic curve over a finite field. Schoof's method is believed to generate most secure elliptic curves for ECC, as it can compute the cardinality of a randomly selected curve. Though Schoof's algorithm was not efficient in its original form, thanks to the contributions of many people, such as Atkin[1], Elkies[4], Morain[9], Couveignes[3], Lercier[8], and so on, the algorithm became remarkably faster. However, as far as the authors know, there have not been explicit criteria that give an efficient ordering of combining these improvements.

The purpose of this paper is to develop an explicit criterion by introducing several new strategies. Basically our methods can be applied independent of the characteristics of the base field. In section 2, we will briefly look over the improvements of Atkin-Elkies and Couveignes-Morain. In section 3, we will introduce another improvements and show an explicit criterion. In section 4, we will give our experimental results to show our improvements are actually efficient.

2 Overview of Previous Works

Let p be an odd prime. We will consider an elliptic curve E defined over $GF(p)$: $E : y^2 = x^3 + Ax + B$, where $A, B \in GF(p)$ with $4A^3 + 27B^2 \neq 0 \pmod{p}$.

Schoof's algorithm: We will briefly recall the Schoof's algorithm[11]. We denote the subgroup of ℓ-torsion points of E by $E[\ell]$. The Frobenius endomorphism $\phi : (x,y) \to (x^p, y^p)$ is defined on Tate module $T_\ell(E)$ and satisfies the equation: $\phi^2 - t\phi + p = 0$, where t denotes the trace of the Frobenius map and $\#E(GF(p)) = p + 1 - t$. If we find an integer t_ℓ such that $\phi^2(P) + pP = t_\ell\phi(P)$ for any $P \in E[\ell]$, we get $t \equiv t_\ell \pmod{\ell}$. Therefore if we compute $t \bmod \ell$ for various small primes until their product exceeds $4\sqrt{p}$, we can uniquely determine the cardinality of the curve by means of the Chinese Remainder Theorem.

Atkin-Elkies's method: Elkies's idea[4, 12] is to make use of a degree $(\ell-1)/2$ factor g_ℓ of the ℓ-division polynomial f_ℓ when it is possible to compute g_ℓ in $GF(p)[x]$(In this case, ℓ is called an Elkies prime. Otherwise ℓ is called an Atkin prime). g_ℓ represents an eigensubspace of the Frobenius map ϕ, which can be computed as a kernel of an isogeny map. Rather than determining the unique value of $t \bmod \ell$, Atkin [1, 12] obtained certain restrictions on the value. As we have to find the real value of t among a lot of candidates by, for example, the baby-step-giant-step algorithm[6], the Schoof-Elkies-Atkin(SEA) method consists of two phases:
(I) computing $t \bmod \ell$ for various ℓ's
(II) determining the value of t

Isogeny cycles method: According to Morain et al. [2], $t \bmod \ell^2$, $t \bmod \ell^3$, ... can be computed efficiently from $t \bmod \ell$ when ℓ is an Elkies prime. A factor g_{ℓ^k} of the ℓ^k-division polynomial f_{ℓ^k} is computed, and the degree of g_{ℓ^k} is $\ell^{k-1}(\ell-1)/2$.

3 Intelligent Choice System

When we find an Elkies prime ℓ, we have two choices in the next step : (a) compute $t \bmod \ell'$(next prime), and (b) compute $t \bmod \ell^2$. When we find an Atkin prime, we have to decide whether to compute the candidates for the value of t or just abandon it.

In order to reduce the total time needed to compute the cardinality of a curve, we should have an explicit criterion, by which we can make an efficient choice in various situations. For this purpose, we will propose several new strategies.

3.1 Estimation of the Complexity

So far we have three methods to get the information on $t \bmod \ell^k$: (1) Schoof's Algorithm, (2) Atkin-Elkies's method, and (3) isogeny cycles method.

Estimation of the complexity: Before we actually begin computation for each prime ℓ, we will estimate the complexity of each method and choose the most efficient one(and ℓ). For example, we can construct a "complexity function" by estimating the dominating computations. For simplicity, we only deal with $t \bmod \ell^2$ in isogeny cycles case. Here we denote by $M(n)$ the time needed to compute the product of two polynomials of degree n:

(1) In Schoof's (original) algorithm case, we estimate its complexity at $\log p M((\ell^2 - 1)/2)$ for a prime ℓ.

(2) In Atkin-Elkies's method case, we estimate its complexity at $\log p M(\ell + 1)$ for a prime ℓ.

(3) In isogeny cycles method case, we estimate its complexity at $\log p(M(U) + M((\ell - 1)/2))$ for an Elkies prime ℓ, where U is the degree of a factor of g_{ℓ^2} that is used in computing $t \bmod \ell^2$.

3.2 Virtual Atkin Method, Virtual Isogeny Cycles Method

Now we introduce another method: (4) virtual Atkin and virtual isogeny cycles method. If the total number of candidates for the value of $t \bmod \ell$ gets too large, the determination phase will take much time. Therefore we set an upper limit to the total number of candidates, which we denote by `CanMAX`. We define `CanMAX` from experiments according to the size of p.

(4) Let $\mathcal{T}_{\ell^k}$ denote the set of candidates for $t \bmod \ell^k$. If a prime ℓ satisfies the following three conditions, we regard the candidates for $t \bmod \ell^{k+j}$ as

$$\mathcal{T}_{\ell^{k+j}} = \{a + b\ell^k | a \in \mathcal{T}_{\ell^k}, 0 \le b \le \ell^j - 1\}.$$

We estimate its complexity at 0.

(4-a) $t \bmod \ell_i^{k_i}$ are already computed and $4\sqrt{p} > (\prod_{i;\ell_i \ne \ell} \ell_i^{k_i}) \times \ell^k$.

(4-b) $4\sqrt{p} < (\prod_{i;\ell_i \ne \ell} \ell_i^{k_i}) \times \ell^{k+j}$.

(4-c) Total number of candidates for the value t does not exceed `CanMAX`.

We can consider several primes ℓ_m's at the same time. In this case, we can replace the inequality (4-b) with

(4-b)' $4\sqrt{p} < (\prod_i \ell_i^{k_i}) \times (\prod_m \ell_m^{k_m + j_m})$ where $\ell_i \ne \ell_m$.

By this technique, we can reduce the candidates for t as well as the operations in the determination phase.

3.3 Re-ordering Atkin Primes

Even if the total number of candidates for the value t exceeds `CanMAX`, we do not give up using new Atkin primes. "Good" Atkin prime is the one, which itself is fairly large and the number of whose candidates for t is small. We define "Atkin index" of an Atkin prime ℓ as:

(the number of candidates for the value t) / ℓ.

When we find a new Atkin prime and the total number of candidates exceeds `CanMAX`, we look for "worse" Atkin primes and replace them with the new "better" one.

General techniques: In estimating the complexity, we used the dominant term of each method. In order to make the criterion work efficiently, we need to minimize the effect of non-dominant terms.

-We used Karatsuba's method in the multiplication of polynomials so that we can assume $M(n) = n^{1.6}$ instead of n^2. This will be effective when p is around 240-bit long.

-In isogeny cycles case, we made use of a kind of baby-step-giant-step algorithm in calculating an eigenvalue.
-In the determination phase, we made use of projective coordinates and precomputed multiples of a fixed point.
-We used "canonical" modular equations.

4 Experimental Results

We have implemented the Intelligent Choice System using Risa/Asir [3] computer algebra system on Pentium II 300MHz machine. We chose 300 curves over $GF(p)$, where $p = 2^{160} + 7$, $A = 1$, and $1 \leq B \leq 300$. We measured the average time needed to compute the cardinality of one curve. We set the value of CanMAX=10^8. We also put the best and the worst time in the following table. In order to see the effect of our methods we tried several combinations of our methods. We have not yet implemented the Schoof's original algorithm.

(Case I) **Using Intelligent Choice System (seconds):**

No.	isogeny	virtual	re-ordering	best	average	worst
(1)	YES	YES	YES	34.7	66.5	334.7
(2)	NO	YES	YES	56.2	82.8	330.9
(3)	YES	NO	YES	43.7	76.1	339.4
(4)	YES	YES	NO	34.4	68.0	348.2

(Case II) **Not Using Intelligent Choice System (seconds):**

No.	isogeny	virtual	re-ordering	best	average	worst
(5)	YES	NO	NO	43.6	83.4	365.3
(6)	YES	NO	NO	43.6	86.9	374.1

(5) uses isogeny cycles if g_ℓ has a factor of degree ≤ 32.
(6) uses isogeny cycles if g_ℓ has a factor of degree ≤ 64.

Our strategies will be characterized as follows:

(a) The estimation of the complexity strategy has the main effect of speeding up the computation process overall.

(b) The isogeny strategy and the virtual methods strategy have the main effect of speeding up the computation process in good cases. (Case we can proceed to the determination phase early on.)

(c) The re-ordering strategy should have the main effect of speeding up the computation process in bad cases. (Case the number of candidates for t exceeds CanMAX). Currently our implementation of calculation of x^{p^i} has not yet been tuned up. The authors believe that we can see a better effect after tuning up the process.

Remark: When we search an appropriate curve for ECC, we would like to use a curve whose cardinality is a prime. For this purpose, we can use "early

---

[3] developed by Fujitsu Laboratories Ltd. [10]

abort" strategy[7]. We check if the cardinality has a factor in each step of the computation of t mod ℓ. If we find that the cardinality is not a prime, we can abandon the curve and try the next one.

When $p = 2^{240} + 115$, we could try 3569 curves in 52.5 hours, and found 16 curves whose cardinalities are prime numbers.

5 Conclusion

We have introduced an explicit criterion for efficient computation of the cardinality of an elliptic curve over a finite field. The experiment shows that we could speed up the process almost 20%. Therefore we can find elliptic curves whose cardinalities are prime numbers in a reasonable time when the characteristics p of the base field is around 240-bit long.

We are going to tune up the complexity estimation function and CanMAX to get a better result. We will also implement FFT for the case when p is a larger prime. Currently we are preparing another paper[5] for details.

References

1. Atkin, A.O., The number of points on an elliptic curve modulo a prime, preprint, 1988.
2. Couveignes, J.-M., Dewaghe, L., Morain, F., Isogeny cycles and the Schoof-Elkies-Atkin algorithm, LIX/RR/96/03, 1996.
3. Couveignes, J.-M., Morain, F., Schoof's algorithm and isogeny cycles, In *ANT-I*, L.Adleman and M.-D.Huang, Eds., Lecture Notes in Computer Science, **877**, pp.43–58, 1994.
4. Elkies, N.D., Explicit isogenies, preprint, 1991.
5. Izu, T., Kogure, J., Noro, M., Yokoyama, K., Secure Elliptic Curve Cryptosystem: Improvements on Schoof's Algorithm by Intelligent Choice System, in preparation.
6. Lercier, R., Algorithmique des courbes elliptiques dans les corps finis, Doctoral Thesis, L'École Polytechnique, 1997.
7. Lercier, R., Finding good random elliptic curves for cryptosystems definded over F_{2^n}, In *EURO-CRYPTO '97*, W.Fumy, Ed., Lecture Notes in Computer Science, **1233**, pp.379–392, 1997.
8. Lercier, R., Morain, F., Counting the number of points on elliptic curves over finite fields: strategy and performances, In *EURO-CRYPTO '95*, L.C.Guillou and J.-J.Quisquater, Eds., Lecture Notes in Computer Science, **921**, pp.79–94, 1995.
9. Morain, F., Calcul du nombre de points sur une courbe elliptique dans un corps fini: aspects algorithmiques, *J. Théor. Nombres Bordeaux* 7 (1995) 255–282.
10. Noro, M., Takeshima, T., ftp://endeavor.fujitsu.co.jp/pub/isis/asir
11. Schoof, R., Elliptic curves over finite fields and the computation of square roots mod p, *Math. Comp.* **44** (1985) 483–494.
12. Schoof, R., Counting points on elliptic curves over finite fields, *J. Théor. Nombres Bordeaux* 7 (1995) 219–254.

A Note on the Complexity of Breaking Okamoto-Tanaka ID-Based Key Exchange Scheme

Masahiro Mambo   Hiroki Shizuya

ECIP & GSIS, Tohoku University
Kawauchi, Aoba-ku, Sendai, 980-8576 Japan
{mambo, shizuya}@ecip.tohoku.ac.jp

Abstract. The rigorous security of Okamoto-Tanaka identity-based key exchange scheme has been open for a decade. In this paper, we show that (1) breaking the scheme is equivalent to breaking the Diffie-Hellman key exchange scheme over $\mathbf{Z}_n$, and (2) impersonation is easier than breaking. The second result is obtained by proving that breaking the RSA public-key cryptosystem reduces to breaking the Diffie-Hellman scheme over $\mathbf{Z}_n$ with respect to the polynomial-time many-one reducibility.

1 Introduction

The Okamoto-Tanaka scheme proposed in 1989 is an identity-based key exchange scheme described as follows:

A trusted authority picks two primes, p and q, and makes n, g and e public, where $n = pq$, g is a generator of both $\mathbf{Z}_p^*$ and $\mathbf{Z}_q^*$, and $e \in \mathbf{Z}_{\varphi(n)}^*$. Let Alice and Bob be two parties of which identification information is ID_A and ID_B, respectively. Alice keeps s_A as her own secret, where $s_A = ID_A^{-d} \bmod n$ and $ed \equiv 1 \pmod{\varphi(n)}$. Note that s_A is computed by the authority, and Alice has no idea about d. In the same way, Bob keeps s_B secret, where $s_B = ID_B^{-d} \bmod n$.

1. Alice picks k_A at random, computes $c_A = s_A g^{k_A} \bmod n$, and sends c_A to Bob.
2. Bob picks k_B at random, computes $c_B = s_B g^{k_B} \bmod n$, and sends c_B to Alice.
3. Alice computes $C = (ID_B c_B^e)^{k_A} = g^{ek_A k_B} \bmod n$.
4. Bob computes $C = (ID_A c_A^e)^{k_B} = g^{ek_A k_B} \bmod n$.

The scheme is basically the Diffie-Hellman scheme implemented over $\mathbf{Z}_n$. An additional operation for verifying identity is based on the RSA. Thus it is natural to conjecture that the security should be related to the security of the Diffie-Hellman and that of the RSA. In fact, if both the Diffie-Hellman and the RSA were easy to break, so would be the Okamoto-Tanaka. However, it remains open to determine the reductions among these breaking problems.

In this paper, we give a solution for this open question. We show that breaking the Okamoto-Tanaka scheme reduces to breaking the Diffie-Hellman scheme over $\mathbf{Z}_n$, and vice versa, that is, the security of these two schemes is equivalent with respect to the polynomial-time many-one reducibility. We also show that breaking the RSA scheme reduces to breaking the Diffie-Hellman scheme with respect to the polynomial-time many-one reducibility. Since the security against impersonation clearly depends on the security of RSA, this implies that impersonation is easier than breaking.

Related to the second result in this paper, Shmuely [5] showed that breaking the RSA reduces to breaking the Diffie-Hellman scheme over $\mathbf{Z}_n$ in the sense of probabilistic polynomial-time reducibility under some assumption. Since our reduction runs in deterministic polynomial-time without any assumption, the result is regarded as a refinement of Shmuely's one.

2 Definitions

2.1 Functions

We first define a function to break the Okamoto-Tanaka scheme, in a way similar to the definitions for some discrete log cryptosystems shown in [7]. We assume that the base g is just in $\mathbf{Z}_n^*$. This assumption includes the case of g being a primitive root modulo both p and q, defined in the original scheme, and does not affect characterizing the difficulty of breaking the scheme as we will see later.

Definition 1: $\text{OT}(n, e, g, ID_A, ID_B, c_A, c_B)$ is a function that on input $n \in \mathbf{N}_{>1}$, $e \in \mathbf{Z}_{\varphi(n)}^*$, $g \in \mathbf{Z}_n^*$, $ID_A \in \mathbf{Z}_n^*$, $ID_B \in \mathbf{Z}_n^*$, $c_A \in \mathbf{Z}_n^*$, $c_B \in \mathbf{Z}_n^*$, outputs $C \in \mathbf{Z}_n^*$ such that $C = (ID_A c_A^e)^{k_B} = (ID_B c_B^e)^{k_A} = g^{e k_A k_B} \bmod n$, where $c_A = (ID_A)^{-e^{-1}} g^{k_A} \bmod n$, $c_B = (ID_B)^{-e^{-1}} g^{k_B} \bmod n$, and $ee^{-1} = e^{-1}e \equiv 1 \pmod{\varphi(n)}$, if such a C exists.

Any ID belonging to $\mathbf{Z}_n^*$ is employed as input to the function OT in Definition 1.

We also define functions to break the Diffie-Hellman scheme over $\mathbf{Z}_n$ and the RSA scheme, respectively.

Definition 2: $\text{DH}(n, g, A, B)$ is a function that on input $n \in \mathbf{N}_{>1}$, $g \in \mathbf{Z}_n^*$, $A \in \mathbf{Z}_n^*$, $B \in \mathbf{Z}_n^*$, outputs $C \in \mathbf{Z}_n^*$ such that $C = g^{ab} \bmod n$, where $A = g^a$ $\bmod n$ and $B = g^b \bmod n$, if such a C exists.

Definition 3: $\text{RSA}(n, e, y)$ is a function that on input $n \in \mathbf{N}_{>1}$, $e \in \mathbf{Z}_{\varphi(n)}^*$, $y \in \mathbf{Z}_n^*$, outputs $x \in \mathbf{Z}_n^*$ such that $y = x^e \bmod n$, if such an x exists.

Other functions related with those described above are defined as follows:

Definition 4: $\text{DL}(n, g, y)$ is a function that on input $n \in \mathbf{N}_{>1}$, $g \in \mathbf{Z}_n^*$, $y \in \mathbf{Z}_n^*$, outputs x such that $y = g^x \bmod n$ and $0 \le x < n$, if such an x exists.

Definition 5: $\text{Factoring}(n)$ is a function that on input $n \in \mathbf{N}_{>1}$, outputs a such that $1 < a < n$ and $a | n$, if such an a exists.

2.2 Reducibility

We use reductions among functions. These reductions are defined in the same way as the reductions among languages over some finite alphabet.

It is known that DH $\leq_{1\text{-}tt}^{p}$ DL, RSA $\leq_{1\text{-}tt}^{p}$ Factoring, and Factoring $\leq_{T}^{ep}$ DL [1,8], where $\leq_{T}^{ep}$ denotes the expected polynomial-time Turing reducibility.

3 Results

3.1 Difficulty of Breaking

Theorem 1: OT $\equiv_{m}^{p}$ DH.

Proof.

1. OT $\leq_{m}^{p}$ DH:
   $$OT(n, e, g, ID_A, ID_B, c_A, c_B) = DH(n, g^e, ID_A c_A^e, ID_B c_B^e).$$
2. DH $\leq_{m}^{p}$ OT:
   $$DH(n, g, A, B) = OT(n, 1, g, 1, 1, A, B). \qquad \blacksquare$$

Notes

1. Each reduction in Theorem 1 holds whenever g is in $\mathbf{Z}_n^*$. Thus it is not necessary for us to assume that g is a primitive root modulo both p and q. Note that the order of a subgroup generated by a common primitive root is $\text{lcm}(p-1, q-1) \leq \varphi(n)/2$, where φ is the Euler totient function.

2. In the proof of DH $\leq_{m}^{p}$ OT, the input to the oracle OT is set as $e = 1 \in \mathbf{Z}_{\varphi(n)}^*$ and $ID_A = ID_B = 1 \in \mathbf{Z}_n^*$. This is technically allowed, and the reduction works correctly. However, the input is nonsense from a practical viewpoint because $e = 1$ means that the ciphertext is just the plaintext, and $ID_A = ID_B = 1$ implies that "1" is no longer identity information.

   If one wants to obtain a reduction such that e, ID_A, and ID_B remain in their usual values, a different definition for the function to break the scheme is required. The function, denoted by OT*, is basically equal to OT, but it returns $\perp$ if $ID_A = ID_B$ or $e \notin \mathbf{Z}_{\varphi(n)}^* \setminus \{1\}$. Consequently the reduction from DH to OT* becomes different. The following is a probabilistic polynomial-time algorithm that reduces DH to OT*.

   One may pick any odd e from $\mathbf{Z}_n^* \setminus \{1\}$, choose s_A and s_B from $\mathbf{Z}_n^*$, and generate a query to be $(n, e, g, s_A^e A, s_B^e, s_A^{-1} g, s_B^{-1} B)$. If e is in fact in $\mathbf{Z}_{\varphi(n)}^* \setminus \{1\}$, then OT* returns a correct $C = g^{ab+eb}$. This is because $s_A^e A (s_A^{-1} g)^e = A g^e = g^{a+e} = g^{ee^{-1}(a+e)}$, $s_B^e (s_B^{-1} B)^e = B^e = g^{eb}$, and so $C = g^{ee^{-1}(a+e)b} = g^{(ab+eb)}$. Thus,
   $$DH(n, g, A, B) = OT^*(n, e, g, s_A^e A, s_B^e, s_A^{-1} g, s_B^{-1} B)/B^e \bmod n,$$
   if e is in $\mathbf{Z}_{\varphi(n)}^* \setminus \{1\}$. On the other hand, if $e = 1$ or not in $\mathbf{Z}_{\varphi(n)}^*$, OT* returns $\perp$.

The probability ρ that e picked in such a way is in $Z^*_{\varphi(n)}$ is estimated as $\rho > 2\ln(2)/\ln(2n)$. Therefore the reduction algorithm runs in expected polynomial time. Specifically, if the modulus n is chosen such that $n = pq$, $p = 2p' + 1$, $q = 2q' + 1$ with p, q, p', q' prime, the reduction algorithm works in a deterministic manner with overwhelming probability.

3.2 Difficulty of Impersonation

Since the Okamoto-Tanaka scheme uses the RSA scheme for verifying identification, it is natural for us to expect that the security would be related with the RSA. However, Theorem 1 asserts that breaking the Okamoto-Tanaka scheme is equivalent to breaking the Diffie-Hellman scheme over Z_n with respect to the $\leq^p_m$-reducibility, which tells us nothing about the relationship between OT and RSA.

One thing to recall is that the RSA is used only for identification checking. In fact if RSA were a polynomial-time computable function, anyone could *break* identification. That is, one could compute $s_A = ID_A^{-e^{-1}} \bmod n$ by $RSA(n, e, 1/ID_A)$, and impersonate Alice (or Bob in the same way). Therefore computing s_A or s_B from n, e, ID_A, ID_B reduces to computing RSA with respect to the $\leq^p_m$-reducibility. In other words, the security against impersonation depends on the difficulty of computing RSA.

However, we show that even RSA reduces to DH. This implies that impersonation is easier than or equivalent to breaking.

Theorem 2: $RSA \leq^p_m DH$.

Proof.
$$RSA(n, e, y) = DH(n, y^e, y, y).$$
Note that $DH(n, y^e, y, y) = DH(n, y^e, y^{ed}, y^{ed}) = y^{ed^2} = y^d = x \bmod n$, where $ed = de \equiv 1 \pmod{\varphi(n)}$. ∎

The theorem above is a simplified deterministic refinement of [5].

4 Concluding Remarks

We can show that the security of the Okamoto-Tanaka key exchange scheme is stronger than or equivalent to that of the RSA public-key cryptosystem in the sense of polynomial-time reducibility. Since the ElGamal public-key cryptosystem over Z_n is as secure as the Diffie-Hellman scheme (see Appendix), the Okamoto-Tanaka scheme is also as secure as the ElGamal scheme over Z_n. Hence the ElGamal over Z_n is stronger than or equivalent to the RSA.

We finally summarize the reductions related with DL, including the reductions obtained in this paper.

1. $RSA \leq^p_m DH \equiv^p_m OT \leq^p_{1-tt} DL$.

2. $RSA \leq_{1-tt}^{p} Factoring \leq_{T}^{ep} DL$.

It is not known at present to hold that DH reduces to RSA, DL reduces to DH, or Factoring reduces to DH, with respect to some deterministic polynomial-time reducibility. These remain as open questions. Concerning the third question, Shmuely [5] showed that factoring n of the form $n = pq$ reduces to DH with respect to the expected polynomial-time Turing reducibility if the base g of odd order mod n is efficiently generated. McCurley [2] refined this result to implement the Diffie-Hellman scheme over Z_n.

Acknowledgments
The authors are grateful to Eiji Okamoto and Tatsuaki Okamoto for their invaluable comments and encouragement.

References
1. E. Bach, "Discrete logarithms and factoring," Technical Report UCB/CSD 84/186, University of California, Computer Science Division (EECS) (1984).
2. K. S. McCurley, "A key distribution system equivalent to factoring," J. Cryptology, Vol.1, pp.95-105 (1988).
3. E. Okamoto and K. Tanaka, "Key distribution system based on identification information," IEEE J. Selected Areas in Communications, Vol.7, pp.481-485 (1989).
4. P. Ribenboim, "The Book of Prime Number Records," Springer-Verlag (1988).
5. Z. Shmuely, "Composite Diffie-Hellman public-key generating systems are hard to break," Technical Report No.356, Computer Science Department, Technion–Israel Institute of Technology (1985).
6. A. Shamir, "Identity-based cryptosystems and signature schemes," Proc. Crypto'84, LNCS 196, Springer-Verlag, pp.47-53 (1985).
7. K. Sakurai and H. Shizuya, "Relationships among the computational powers of breaking discrete log cryptosystems," Proc. Eurocrypt'95, LNCS 921, Springer-Verlag, pp.341-355 (1995). (J. Cryptology, Vol.11, pp.29-43 (1998).)
8. H. Woll, "Reductions among number theoretic problems," Information and Computation, Vol.72, pp.167-179 (1987).

Appendix

We define a function to break the ElGamal public-key cryptosystem implemented over Z_n. Let $EG(n, g, y, C_1, C_2)$ be a function that on input $n \in N_{>1}$, $g \in Z_n^*$, $y \in Z_n^*$, $C_1 \in Z_n^*$, $C_2 \in Z_n^*$, outputs $m \in Z_n^*$ such that $m = C_2/C_1^x \bmod n$, where $y \equiv g^x \bmod n$, if such an m exists. We claim that $DH \leq_m^p EG$ and $EG \leq_{1-tt}^p DH$.

Proposition: $EG \equiv_{1-tt}^p DH$.

Proof.

$DH \leq_m^p EG$: $DH(n, g, A, B) = EG(n, g, A^{-1}, B, 1)$, where A^{-1} is the inverse of A mod n. Note that $EG(n, g, A^{-1}, B, 1) = EG(n, g, g^{-a}, g^b, g^{ab-ab})$.

$EG \leq_{1-tt}^p DH$: $EG(n, g, y, C_1, C_2) = C_2/DH(n, g, y, C_1) \bmod n$. ∎

Author Index

Springer
and the
environment

At Springer we firmly believe that an international science publisher has a special obligation to the environment, and our corporate policies consistently reflect this conviction.
We also expect our business partners – paper mills, printers, packaging manufacturers, etc. – to commit themselves to using materials and production processes that do not harm the environment. The paper in this book is made from low- or no-chlorine pulp and is acid free, in conformance with international standards for paper permanency.

Springer

Lecture Notes in Computer Science

For information about Vols. 1–1348

please contact your bookseller or Springer-Verlag